Man Against Himself

Dr. Karl Menninger, general director of the educational department and chairman of the board of the Menninger Foundation, was born in Topeka, Kansas, in 1893. After receiving his A.B. and M.S. from the University of Wisconsin, he took a medical degree at the Harvard Medical School. He is clinical professor of psychiatry at the University of Kansas Medical School, former president of the American Psychoanalytic Association, chairman of the committee on reorganization of the American Psychiatric Association, and chief consultant for the Office of Vocational Rehabilitation for the Federal Security Agency. Among his books are *The Human Mind* (1930) and *Love Against Hate* (1942), which is a sequel to *Man Against Himself.*

KARL MENNINGER

MAN AGAINST HIMSELF

HARCOURT BRACE JOVANOVICH
NEW YORK AND LONDON

A HARVEST/HBJ BOOK

BB
ISBN 0-15-656514-5

PRINTED IN THE UNITED STATES OF AMERICA

To those who would use intelligence in the battle against death—to strengthen the will to live against the wish to die, and to replace with love the blind compulsion to give hostages to hatred as the price of living

Preface

It is nothing new that the world is full of hate, that men destroy one another, and that our civilization has arisen from the ashes of despoiled peoples and decimated natural resources. But to relate this destructiveness, this evidence of a spiritual malignancy within us, to an instinct, and to correlate this instinct with the beneficent and fruitful instinct associated with love, this was one of the later flowers of the genius of Freud. We have come to see that just as the child must learn to love wisely, so he must learn to hate expeditiously, to turn destructive tendencies away from himself toward enemies that actually threaten him rather than toward the friendly and the defenseless, the more usual victims of destructive energy.

It is true, nevertheless, that in the end each man kills himself in his own selected way, fast or slow, soon or late. We all feel this, vaguely; there are so many occasions to witness it before our eyes. The methods are legion and it is these which attract our attention. Some of them interest surgeons, some of them interest lawyers and priests, some of them interest heart specialists, some of them interest sociologists. All of them must interest the man who sees the personality as a totality and medicine as the healing of the nations.

I believe that our best defense against self-destructiveness lies in the courageous application of intelligence to human phenomenology. If such is our nature, it were better that we knew it and knew it in all its protean manifestations. To see all forms of self-destruction from the standpoint of their dominant principles would seem to be logical progress toward self-preservation and toward a unified view of medical science.

This book is an attempt to synthesize and to carry forward, in that direction, the work begun by Ferenczi, Groddeck, Jelliffe, White, Alexander, Simmel, and others who have consistently applied these principles to the understanding of human sickness and all those failures and capitulations that we propose to regard as variant forms of suicide. No one is more aware than I of the unevenness of the evidence to follow and of the speculative nature of some of the theory, but in this I beg the indulgence of the reader to whom I submit that to have a theory, even a false one, is better than to attribute events to pure chance. "Chance" explanations leave us in the dark; a theory will lead to confirmation or rejection.

K. A. M.

Acknowledgments

I am indebted to many people for help in the recording and exposition of the views in this book.

I am indebted for an early reading of the manuscript and for valuable suggestions resulting therefrom to my colleague and former teacher, Dr. Franz Alexander of the Chicago Institute for Psychoanalysis, to Dr. Franklin C. McLean of the University of Chicago, to Dr. J. F. Brown of the University of Kansas (also research associate in psychology at our Clinic) and to Nelson Antrim Crawford of Topeka, editor of *The Household Magazine*.

In a more general way, I am indebted also to my colleagues of the Menninger Clinic with all of whom I have discussed the ideas herein expressed and some of whom read the manuscript in its first draft.

From the late Dr. William A. White we received in 1933 a grant of $2,500 for some special studies of suicidally inclined persons, a gift on behalf of an anonymous donor. These studies formed a part of the clinical basis for the general theory of suicide elaborated in Part II of this book.

Finally, I would acknowledge the invaluable assistance of Jeanetta Lyle, editorial secretary of our Clinic, who not only worked faithfully over every page of the manuscript, but herself pursued some special investigations on certain points, especially historical asceticism and martyrdom, and contributed paragraphs of the text in various chapters. The index was prepared by Margaret Linn, librarian.

K. A. M.

Acknowledgment is made to the editors of *The Psychoanalytic Quarterly, The Archives of Neurology and Psychiatry, The International Journal of Psychoanalysis, The Bulletin of the Menninger Clinic,* and *The Journal of Urology* for permission to reprint material first published in their pages.

Acknowledgment is also made to The Macmillan Company for permission to reprint from John Masefield's poem, "C.L.M.," to Houghton Mifflin for Henry Wadsworth Longfellow's poem, "The Children's Hour," to Alfred A. Knopf for Clarence Day's poem, "As the Worm Turns," to Farrar and Rinehart for Helene Magaret's poem, "The Trumpeting Crane," to the *New Yorker* for Milo Ray Phelps' poem, "Miss Elizabeth Bates," to Longmans, Green and Company for selections from *The Historic Martyrs of the Primitive Church* by Arthur James Mason and *Memories and Studies* by William James; and to the Nervous and Mental Disease Publishing Company for selections from *The Psychoanalysis of the Total Personality* by Dr. Franz Alexander.

Contents

PART VI: RECONSTRUCTION

PART I **Destruction**

ONE / Eros and Thanatos

Try as we may, it is difficult to conceive of our universe in terms of concord; instead, we are faced everywhere with the evidences of conflict. Love and hate, production and consumption, creation and destruction—the constant war of opposing tendencies would appear to be the dynamic heart of the world. Man runs the eager gamut of his life through hazards of sickness and accident, beasts and bacteria, the malignant power of the forces of nature, and the vengeful hands of his fellow men. Against these numberless forces of destruction, the long thin line of defense afforded by scientific intelligence ceaselessly battles in an effort to thwart the destruction of mankind. It is no wonder that frightened humanity looks wistfully to magic and mystery no less than to medical science for protection.

Time after time in the past few years, the swollen waters of the Ohio, the Mississippi, and other rivers have poured over the fields and cities of populous areas, sweeping away the homes and gardens, the books and treasures, the food and factories of a million people. Almost at the same time and in the same country, trees died of drought, grass withered in the heat, cattle perished of thirst and starvation; birds and little wild beasts disappeared and a brown-gray crust replaced the usual verdure of the landscape. And recently, again, the Pacific Coast was shaken with earthquakes which destroyed the patient labor of years, while the Atlantic Coast was swept with hurricanes and devastating storms.

While these spectacular rages of Nature were wreaking destruction upon defenseless millions, millions more lay in hospitals slowly or swiftly succumbing to the destructive inroads of bacteria, toxins, and cancer. And sprinkled here and there throughout these miseries were the daily occurring accidents in the ordinary pursuits of life bringing death and destruction in sharp, unexpected flashes.

One would expect that in the face of these overwhelming blows at the hands of Fate or Nature, man would oppose himself steadfastly to death and destruction in a universal brotherhood of beleaguered humanity. But this is not the case. Whoever studies the behavior of human beings cannot escape the conclusion that we must reckon with an enemy within the lines. It becomes increasingly evident that some of the destruction which curses the earth is *self*-destruction; the extraordinary propensity of the human being to join hands with external forces in an attack upon his own existence is one of the most remarkable of biological phenomena.

Men fly above ancient and beautiful cities dropping explosive bombs upon museums and churches, upon great buildings and little children. They are encouraged by the official representatives of two hundred million other people, all of whom contribute daily in taxes to the frantic manufacture of instruments designed for the tearing and ripping and mangling of human beings similar to themselves, possessed of the same instincts, the same sensations, the same little pleasures, and the same realization that death comes to end these things all too soon.

This is what one would see who surveyed our planet cursorily, and if he looked closer into the lives of individuals and communities he would see still more to puzzle him; he would see bickerings, hatreds, and fighting, useless waste and petty destructiveness. He would see people sacrificing themselves to injure others, and expending time, trouble, and energy in shortening that pitifully small recess from oblivion which we call life. And most amazing of all, he would see some who, as if lacking aught else to destroy, turn their weapons upon themselves.

Whether, as I suppose, this would perplex a visitor from Mars, it surely must amaze anyone who assumes, as perhaps we all do at times, that human beings want what they say they want—life, liberty, and happiness.

The doctor, for example, pursues his daily rounds in the steadfast belief that he is responding to the call of those who would prolong their lives and diminish their sufferings. He comes to place a great value on life and to assume that his is a universal attitude. He is at tremendous pains to save the life of a single insignificant child or a single useless patriarch. He subscribes naively to the absolute truth of the dictum that self-preservation is the first law of life. He feels himself a savior of mankind, a bulwark against the hordes of death.

Suddenly, or perhaps gradually, he becomes disillusioned. He discovers that patients often don't want to get well as much as they say they do. He discovers that their hovering and solicitous relatives often don't want them to get well, either. He discovers that his efforts are combated not alone by Nature, bacteria, and toxins, but by some imp of the perverse in the patient himself. An old professor of mine once remarked that the physician must devote most of his efforts toward keeping the relatives from killing the patient, and then trust God—occasionally the surgeon—for the rest; but the skillful physician really does more. He not only holds off the relatives but he tries to keep the patient from doing those things which favor the disease rather than the recovery.

It was such observations as this that led to the formulation by Sigmund Freud of the theory of a death-instinct. According to this concept, there exist from the beginning in all of us strong propensities toward self-destruction and these come to fruition as actual suicide only in exceptional cases where many circumstances and factors combine to make it possible.

But the question arises: If some great impulse toward death dominates all of us, if at heart we all want to die, why do so many of us struggle against it as we do, why do not all of us commit suicide, as many philosophers have advised? In some ways, it seems more logical to investigate why anybody lives in the face of the difficulties both external and internal than to prove why we die, because not all people do continue to live and all do ultimately succeed in dying. In other words, why does the wish to live *ever*, even temporarily, triumph over the wish to die?

Freud makes the further assumption that the life- and death-instincts—let us call them the constructive and destructive tendencies of the personality—are in constant conflict and interaction just as are similar forces in physics, chemistry, and biology. To create and to destroy, to build up and to tear down, these are the anabolism and katabolism of the personality, no less than of the cells and the corpuscles—the two directions in which the same energies exert themselves.

These forces, originally directed inward and related to

5

the intimate problems of the self, the ego, come ultimately to be directed outwardly toward other objects. This corresponds with physical growth and personality development. Failure to develop, from this standpoint, means an incomplete turning outward of the self-directed destructiveness and constructiveness with which we are—by hypothesis—born. Instead of fighting their enemies, such persons fight (destroy) themselves; instead of loving friends or music or the building of a house, such persons love only themselves. (Hate and love are the emotional representatives of the destructive and constructive tendencies.) But no one evolves so completely as to be entirely free from self-destructive tendencies; indeed, the phenomena of life, the behavior peculiar to different individuals, may be said to express the resultant of these conflicting factors. A sort of equilibrium, oftentimes very unstable, is achieved and maintained until disturbed by new developments in the environment which cause a rearrangement with perhaps a quite different outcome.

On this basis we can understand how it can be that some people kill themselves quickly and some slowly and some not at all, why some contribute to their own deaths and others withstand valiantly and brilliantly external assaults upon their lives to which their fellows would have quickly succumbed. So much of this, however, takes place automatically and unconsciously that it will seem at first blush like an impossible task to dissect the details of a particular bargain or compromise between the life- and death-instincts. It is for precisely this reason that the introduction of the psychoanalytic technique of investigation affords us an entirely new understanding of the process through the elucidation of its details. It enables us to recognize how postponement of death is sometimes purchased by the life-instinct at a great cost.

The nature of this premium paid for the postponement of death is quite variable both in degree and in kind.[1] In

[1] Ferenczi advanced this elaboration of Freud's theory in a remarkable paper entitled "The Problem of Acceptance of Unpleasant Ideas; Advances in Knowledge of the Sense of Reality" (*Further Contributions to the Theory and Technique of Psychoanalysis*, London, Hogarth Press, 1926).

Alexander has described the mechanism in detail: "From the moment of birth onward," he wrote, "the apparatus is continually encountering the painful experience that the world is no longer shaped so exactly to his subjective demands as was the maternal womb. The more independent the child becomes, however, the more he learns that the way to pleasure leads some cases the conditions are extremely narrow and restricted, in others more liberal. It is these premiums, these compromises between life- and death-instincts as we observe them in human beings, that form the subject matter of this book. It is an investigation, so to speak, into the price of living—"the high cost of living"—as one of my colleagues put it.

When a weasel or a mink gnaws off its own leg to escape from a trap it does so, so far as we can judge, consciously and deliberately and accepts, so to speak, the full responsibility for the self-preservative self-destruction. Some human individuals who are forced to similar sacrifices for the preservation of their own lives also accept the responsibility and defend their action with such logical reasons as they can command, sometimes correct, often fallacious, but usually quite plausible. This includes those whose suicide appears quite reasonable, the quiet taking of poison, for example, by an aged man dying of painful cancer. But it also includes such attenuated suicide as is represented by asceticism, martyrdom, and many surgical procedures.

In other cases the individual accepts the responsibility for the self-destruction unwillingly and only in part, and makes no attempt to explain or defend it, so that the acts seem purposeless, as for example the slow ruin of a life by chronic alcoholism or morphinism.

Still others can be recognized in which no responsibility for the self-destruction is accepted; the responsibility is projected upon Fate, enmity or circumstance; one sees this in some so-called accidents, which are frequently unconsciously intentional in their nature.

Finally, there is a fourth group in which the ego of the individual neither accepts responsibility for the self-destruction nor makes any attempt to explain or defend it. This is theoretically represented by certain physical diseases.

In all of these the self-destructive urge is implicit or explicit. Seen thus in series, it arrests our attention, and demands that we scrutinize analytically these various ways

---

through endurance, renunciation, and suffering. Whilst during the sucking period he only has to bear renunciation in the *passive* form of hunger, he learns later that he has often to seek out suffering *actively* in order to attain pleasure. And this active quest for suffering on tactical grounds, which often seems so paradoxical to us, is what is characteristic of the ego in its relations to reality and to the super-ego."—Alexander, Franz, "The Need for Punishment and the Death Instinct," *The International Journal of Psychoanalysis,* 1929, Vol. X, p. 260.

in which men commit suicide, sometimes without knowing it. Such an analytic study I have essayed.

PLAN OF THE BOOK

The plan of this book is as follows: We shall first take up the discussion of those failures in the attempt at compromise described above which result in immediate, more or less voluntary, death—in other words, suicide. We shall try to discover what underlying motives determine this choice, why in some individuals the wish to die so completely vanquishes the wish to live and does so with the full co-operation of the conscious intelligence. At the same time, we shall try to indicate to what extent these tendencies can be recognized prior to such a disastrous outcome.

We shall then examine various forms of the more successful compromises in which the impulse to destroy one's self seems to be diluted or diverted so that death is postponed, at least, even though at an unduly great expense in the form of suffering, failure, or deprivation. We shall be as interested to discover why such individuals do not commit suicide outright as to learn why they are so strongly impelled in the direction of self-injury and self-restriction.

This will lead us to the consideration of many forms of self-destruction—abortive forms, distorted forms, chronic forms—all those failures in life which seem to be directly related to obvious misconceptions and mismanagements on the part of the individual, rather than inescapable accidents of fate and reality. This includes that large number of people who demonstrate that they cannot endure success, who succeed in everything but succeeding, and that even larger number who seem to fail in everything except the consummation of failure.

And, finally, we shall consider to what extent and by what devices it is possible arbitrarily to deflect these malignant self-destructive trends and avoid the disasters and the sacrifices by which they are spontaneously, to these varying degrees, held in check. This entails a consideration of the techniques of which we may avail ourselves in strengthening the life-instincts in their defense against the destructive tendencies, with the aim of not merely preventing suicide in its crude immediate form but of meeting the far more extensive problem of diminishing the instances of handicapped living and of exorbitantly costly compromises in the struggle between life and death.

The first section of the book is, therefore, an analysis of

the deeper motives of suicide, suicide in the ordinary accepted usage. The next section will consider chronic forms of suicide in which the effect is diffuse. The third section will consider the more focalized type of self-destruction. The fourth section deals with an extension of the theory of self-destruction to the problem of physical disease, an extension which must be considered, as yet, largely hypothetical. The final section will deal with the available techniques of combating self-destruction and is, therefore, entitled "Reconstruction."

PART II **Suicide**

ONE / *The Taboo*

There are certain subjects concerning which we speak often in jest, as if to forestall the necessity of ever discussing them seriously. Suicide is one of them. So great is the taboo on suicide that some people will not say the word, some newspapers will not print accounts of it, and even scientists have avoided it as a subject for research.

Small wonder then that a friend and adviser was alarmed at the half a dozen suggested titles for the manuscript of this book. All of them involved this gloomy theme, a theme likely to repel the very readers that would most appreciate the final conclusions of the analysis. As I have already hinted, we shall come to the final conclusion that there are many ways in which the will to live may triumph over the wish to die, many devices for deliverance from self-destruction, but before we can assay these we must examine the dismal fact that men kill themselves and that playing the ostrich does not diminish this reality in the least.

During the last twenty-four minutes somewhere in the United States a man has killed himself. It happens about sixty times a day, every day; 22,000 times a year. This is only in the United States; it is twice as frequent in some European countries. It is everywhere more frequent than murder.

Under these circumstances one would expect that there would be a wide general interest in the subject, that many studies and researches would be in progress, that our medical journals would contain articles and our libraries books on the subject. Not so. There are novels, plays and legends galore which involve suicide—suicide in fantasy. But there is a surprisingly small scientific literature dealing with it. This, I think, is only another evidence of the taboo which

13

is associated with the subject—a taboo related to strongly repressed emotions. People do not like to think seriously and factually about suicide.

Indeed, my own interest in this subject began through my astonishment and curiosity at the operations of this taboo in connection with the relatives of some of my patients. This is what happened: Patients committed to our care in the depth of a temporary depression in which they threatened suicide would begin to improve, and relatives thereupon would seek to remove them, utterly disregarding our warning that it was too soon, that suicide was still a danger. Frequently they would ridicule the idea that such a thing might be perpetrated by *their* relative, insist that he was only bluffing or momentarily desperate, he didn't mean it, wouldn't do it, and so on. Then a few days or weeks later, the papers would carry an announcement of our former patient's death by hanging or shooting or drowning. I have a large file full of such clippings and, attached to each, the verbatim warning given the impetuous relatives.

For example, a very good friend of mine, who was being cared for during a depression, was awakened, roused out of bed, and removed from the hospital in the middle of the night by a relative against whom he felt hostile, but whom he was constrained to obey. We warned this relative that it was exceedingly unwise for her to remove him, that in the depths of his depression he might commit suicide; he himself was loath to leave the hospital and begged to be permitted to remain. He was taken by this relative from one place to another and finally back home to be nursed to health by her kind ministrations; shortly afterwards he killed himself. He was a scientist, a man of ability, a man of future.

I saw this thing happen so often that I became interested in the problems of why people did not regard suicide as a reality and whose responsibility it was to avert suicide. We doctors, who work so hard to save lives that sometimes do not seem to us to be worth saving, must also have some responsibility for the saving of these lives which are often full of promise and which are destroyed, so to speak, in a moment of impulsive bad judgment, a moment of predetermined misunderstanding, like that of Romeo when he found his sleeping Juliet and thought her dead. But we cannot do it alone. We endeavor to enlist the co-operation of the relatives in preventing the fruition of a potential suicide and the relatives must—if they are humane—take such warnings seriously and act accordingly. The fact remains that suicide continues to attract far less attention than its seriousness and its prevalence would seem to justify.

The subject is too big for comprehensive treatment in one book. I shall not attempt to present the historical, statistical, sociological, or clinical aspects of suicide, but shall put my emphasis upon the examination of the unconscious (and therefore usually neglected) psychological factors. *The Encyclopaedia Britannica, Hastings' Encyclopaedia of Religion and Ethics,* and similar reference books are replete with interesting accounts of various techniques, attitudes, consequences, and interpretations of suicide. Many of these change with the passage of time, and differ greatly in various countries. Statistical studies have interested numerous writers, particularly life insurance authorities, in spite of the fact that most such statistics have an acknowledgedly large element of error. So far as they go, the statistics would indicate that among civilized people suicide is much more common among males, although women try to commit suicide more frequently than do men. The frequency of suicide varies in men in direct proportion to the age; it is twice as frequent among men of 40 as among men of 20. There is no such variation among women. Suicide is more frequent in spring than in any other season, more frequent among single than among married people, more common in urban than in rural areas, more frequent in time of peace than in time of war, and more common among Protestants than among Catholics.[1]

Louis I. Dublin and Bessie Bunzel have given us a good general survey of the subject[2] including some historical, some anthropological, some psychological, and some statistical data. Clinical examinations of suicide have been few and on the whole quite unsatisfactory. Ruth Shonle Cavan wrote one of the earliest psychological studies of the modern era;[3] occasional articles have appeared in medical journals with such titles as "Differential Diagnostic Types of Suicide," [4] "Suicide and Mental Disease" [5] and "Suicide, Possibilities of Prevention by Early Recognition of Some

[1] For a vivid popular summary of statistics and theories, see Davidson, Henry A., "Beware of Loneliness," *Coronet,* March, 1937.

[2] Dublin, Louis I., and Bunzel, Bessie, *To Be or Not to Be! A Study of Suicide,* Harrison Smith and Robert Haas, 1933.

[3] Cavan, Ruth Shonle, *Suicide,* University of Chicago Press, 1927.

[4] Zilboorg, Gregory, *Archives of Neurology and Psychiatry,* 1936, Vol. XXXV, pp. 270-91.

[5] Jameison, Gerald R., *Archives of Neurology and Psychiatry,* 1936, Vol. XXXVI, p. 1.

Danger Signals." [6] In general, however, suicide has attracted surprisingly little attention from physicians.

One might have expected something from the psychoanalysts whose interest in the tabooed arises from acquaintance with the psychological powers of repression. But even they have contributed but little. In fairness, however, we must add that while the act of suicide itself has not been thoroughly investigated by them, the intention to commit suicide has been the subject of much study by Freud, Abraham, Alexander, and others. In the next chapter we shall follow their lead and break through the taboo which covers the subject and the even stronger repressions which guard the secret motives that seem to converge in impelling the act of suicide.

TWO / The Motives

At first it would seem gratuitous to offer an explanation of suicide. In the popular mind suicide is no enigma. Glib explanations are to be read with monotonous invariability in the daily newspapers, in life-insurance reports, upon death certificates, and in statistical surveys. Suicide, according to these, is the simple and logical consequence of ill-health, discouragement, financial reverses, humiliation, frustration, or unrequited love. What amazes one most is not that these simple explanations are continually offered but that they are so readily and unquestioningly accepted in a world where science and everyday experience alike confirm the untrustworthiness of the obvious. No such credulity or lack of curiosity exists, for example, with reference to the motives for murder. Mystery, murder and detective stories are turned out by the thousands in which the obvious explanation is pierced by the subtle persistency of the hero-sleuth. It is significant that it is almost never the explanation of a *suicide* which is sought in these stories, but that of a *murder*.

[6] Fairbank, Ruth, *Journal of the American Medical Association*, Vol. XCVIII, pp. 1711-14. See also the recent study by Merrill Moore, "Cases of Attempted Suicide in a General Hospital," *The New England Journal of Medicine*, Aug., 1937, pp. 291-303.

The slightest reflection is sufficient to convince anyone that such simple explanations as those referred to above do not explain anything.

The popular analysis of suicide might be simmered down to the formula: "Suicide is an escape from an intolerable life situation. If the situation be an external, visible one, the suicide is brave; if the struggle be an internal, invisible one, the suicide is crazy." This conception of self-destruction as a flight from reality, from ill-health, disgrace, poverty, or the like is seductive because of its simplicity. It parallels other escapes such as the taking of vacations or celebrating of holidays, falling asleep, wandering in delirium, or resorting to drunkenness.

But there is an essential difference between these escapes which are all in the nature of temporary substitutes, and suicide which is not temporary. One cannot substitute nothing for something, as Hamlet reflected in his celebrated soliloquy. It may be considered axiomatic that the human mind cannot conceive of non-existence, and hence, however agnostic or skeptical the person contemplating suicide may believe himself to be, his act betrays his belief in some kind of a future life more endurable than this present life. In itself this is not proof that the suicidal person has already begun to accept unreality for reality in an irrational way, because a belief in the future life is accepted by millions of people and constitutes the essential feature of many religions. And, although it is rejected intellectually by many scientists and others, emotionally an expectation of a future life or, rather, a continuous life is inherent in the unconscious of everyone. In the unconscious we are still animals, and there is no reason to believe that any animal fears death; with us humans it is our intelligence which "doth make cowards of us all."

The popular analysis outlined above would be more nearly correct, therefore, if it were phrased that suicide is an *attempted* escape from an intolerable life situation. This would call our attention more sharply to its irrationality and the power wielded for such individuals by fantasy. It would still leave uncorrected the fallacy lying in the implied assumption that the forces impelling the escape come wholly from without. Behavior is never determined only by external forces; there are impulses from within, the adjustment of which to external reality necessarily brings about stresses and strains which may be highly painful, but endurable except to a very few. Innumerable illustrations from

17

history and scientific clinical records could be marshalled to show that *for some persons no reality, however terrible, is unbearable.*

For we know that the individual always, in a measure, creates his own environment, and thus the suicidal person must in some way help to create the very thing from which, in suicide, he takes flight. If we are to explain the act dynamically, therefore, we are compelled to seek an explanation for the wish to put oneself in a predicament from which one cannot, except by suicide, escape. In other words, if for one's own unconscious purposes, one brings about an apparent justification in external reality for self-destruction, the unconscious purposes are of more significance in understanding the suicide than the apparently simple, inevitable, external circumstances.

This is very well brought out by many novelists who have described the way in which the man who ultimately commits suicide begins his self-destruction long beforehand.[1] The title of one of these[2] is derived from a famous legend; one version is this: A servant ran to his master in fright, saying that he had been jostled and threatened by Death in the market place and wished, therefore, to go as rapidly as possible to Samarra where Death would not find him. His master let him go and himself went to the market place and seeing Death there asked him why he had threatened the servant. To this Death replied that it was not a threat but a gesture of surprise that he should see in Bagdad the man with whom he had an appointment that night in Samarra.

The story has been variously ascribed some fifty origins, according to Alexander Woollcott, including Longfellow, Voltaire and Cocteau, and is, Woollcott believes, undoubtedly of very ancient origin. This would indicate that the idea that one inexorably keeps a rendezvous with death even while ostensibly engaged in fleeing from it is intuitively recognized as a common phenomenon of human experience, whether the propelling force toward death is projected upon Destiny or recognized as an autonomous impulse.

We all know by now that conscious motives cannot be relied upon to explain human behavior. There are too many instances where the motives cannot be confessed, cannot be interpreted, and, most pertinent of all, are not to the slightest

---

[1] See, for example, Thomas Mann's *Death in Venice*, Knopf, 1925.
[2] O'Hara, John, *Appointment in Samarra*, Harcourt, Brace, 1934.

degree recognized by the person himself. Psychoanalysis enables us in a particular case to overcome these obstacles because it gives us access to the unconscious motives. Therefore, it is from this source of study that we can change the apparent senselessness of suicide or its inadequate explanation into something intelligible.

Observations have now accumulated to a point where this may be done, imperfectly to be sure, but at least in outline. It is these conclusions which it is my purpose to lay before the reader in a systematic way. To do this, however, we must first of all dispose of the naïve notion that suicide is a simple act and recognize that from the psychological standpoint it is very complex, no matter how it may appear. Indeed, a considerable obstacle in the study of suicide is the popular assumption of its simple causal connections. Were it so simple, this book would have no justification whatsoever, but on the other hand, suicide would be infinitely more common.

A wealthy man is one day announced as having killed himself. It is discovered that his investments have failed, but that his death provides bountiful insurance for his otherwise destitute family. The problem and its solution, then, seem simple and obvious enough. A man has bravely faced ruin in a way that benefits his dependents.

But why should we begin our interpretations only at this late point in such a man's life, the point at which he loses his wealth?[3] Shall we not seek to discover how it came about that he lost it? And even more pertinently, shall we not inquire how he made it, why he was so driven to amass money and what means he used to gratify his compulsion, what unconscious and perhaps also conscious guilt feelings were associated with it and with the sacrifices and penalties its acquisition cost him and his family? And even those who have money and lose it do not in the vast majority of cases kill themselves, so we still do not know what this man's deeper motives were for this particular act. All we can really see from such a case is how difficult and complex

[3] There is a prevalent notion that loss of money is a common cause of suicide and of mental affliction. It has been scotched many times but persists none the less. My brother and Leona Chidester examined statistics and individual cases to show that financial losses, either actual or fancied, represented a very small percentage of the total number of precipitating factors of mental illness, and even such as did occur were *less* frequent during the great financial depression (1931-1934) than during better times.

Menninger, W. C., and Chidester, Leona, "The Role of Financial Loss in the Precipitation of Mental Illness," *Journal of the American Medical Association*, May 6, 1933. p. 1398.

the problem becomes as soon as we take more than a super-ficial glance at the circumstances.

Or further, take such a representative illustration as that of the cashier in a small town bank, a quiet, friendly, and generally-trusted individual, known to nearly everyone in the community. One afternoon after banking hours he locked himself in his office with a revolver and was found dead the next morning. A shortage in his books was subsequently discovered and it was proved that he had surreptitiously made away with thousands of dollars of the bank's funds. His friends refused for a time to believe it possible that such a well-known, trusted fellow could have done so; finally, however, it was the consensus that he had suddenly become irrational, yielded to overwhelming temptation, and then succumbed to remorse, to which suicide was the appropriate although tragic sequence.

A few weeks later, however, a new angle developed. It was disclosed that this man had engaged in "an affair" with a woman. Now the explanation of his suicide which had been so simple was upset; the question had to be reopened and a new solution found. "This, then, is the real explanation of the matter," said the townspeople: "When a sober, respectable married man with children becomes involved in an immoral affair he soon forgets all about honor." Another version was, "He simply had to have the money to support that woman. It was she who really killed him."

More thoughtful observers, however, would certainly investigate the real significance of a complicated sexual affair of this sort in the life of an apparently normally adjusted man, at least as to why such a fascination should have made him powerless against financial temptation. Only a few of this man's closest friends knew that his relations with his wife had been most unhappy, and only his physician knew that for twenty years of their married life they had been continent because of her frigidity.

"It was really his wife's fault," said these few. "She was always cold and unsympathetic."

But is it not apparent that this still does not explain the whole matter—the career of tragedy? Why did he marry such a woman? Could he not change her emotional reactions? Why did he go on living with her for twenty years?

And here one who had known this man as a child might raise his voice, "Oh, but you did not know his mother! She, too, was a cold hard woman, more interested in money than in her children. It is no wonder that he was incapable of making an intelligent marital choice or of dealing with a wife in a more competent and satisfactory way. Yes, if you only knew his mother—"

We have now carried the causal chain far back of the simple explanation which seemed so obvious to the man's fellow-townsmen. We see how fallacious and superficial the original explanation was. We must not assume that merely extending the links of the chain elucidates the motives any more fully. What it does do is to show how different the act appears in the light of each piece of additional evidence, but we are still in the possession of only the most obvious and external data. Our history is a little fuller than that given by the newspaper but it still falls far short of explaining why this man's life should have been so increasingly unsuccessful and why he should have terminated it in suicide. All that we can see is that this man *began to commit suicide long before he took the pistol in his hand and long before he took the money from the bank.* We still do not know why he could not mobilize his life instincts more successfully against these destructive tendencies that overwhelmed him.

We are justified, however, in assuming that this method of dealing with life is determined either by some inherent constitutional variation, abnormality, or weakness in the individual or by the acceleration or powerful reinforcement of the destructive tendencies of the personality during the formative period of life. In either case it is apparent that the self-defeating tendencies arose very early in the life of the individual and strongly influenced the entire course of his development in such a way as to overshadow and finally conquer the benign life-instinct.

Such a view of suicide completely disposes of those naïve judgments as to its "bravery" or "irrationality," and of all such causal explanations as appear in statistical summaries and the like.[4] Psychologically, I repeat, suicide is a very complex act, and not a simple, incidental, isolated act of impulse, either logical or inexplicable. The analysis of its

[4] Formerly, even the most scientific accounts of suicide made these naïve assumptions and it was assigned with simple finality to all sorts of causes. Modern authorities are more cautious but even yet there is a tendency to list "precipitating factors," "primary factors," and "secondary factors" and among these to list such units as "fatigue," "financial difficulties," "loneliness," "desire for attention," "poor methods of study," and "love affairs." A recent study (Raphael, Power, and Berridge, "The Question of Suicide as a Problem in College Mental Hygiene," *American Journal of Orthopsychiatry,* Jan., 1937, pp. 1-14) contains tables listing over 150 such "factors," each applied to an individual case. These are symptoms, not factors.

motives is made difficult not only because of the untrustworthiness of conscious and obvious motives but especially by reason of the fact that a successful suicide is beyond study, and (as we shall see later) the failure to achieve success—even in suicide—is apt to express accurately the mathematical resultant of component wishes—conscious and unconscious—acting as vectors. If the man described above were still alive and were willing to be made the subject of investigation we could analyze the early influences and experiences and determine what the specific tendencies were which caused his ruin.

This is an important point because it is quite logical to ask how one can talk about the motives of suicide when the person is dead and therefore cannot be psychoanalyzed. The answer is simple, however. Psychoanalytic studies have been made of many persons who have attempted suicide in a very determined and realistic way and who have been saved only through their accidental discovery by friends, relatives, or police before the full effects of the gas or poison had been exerted.[5] Again, some patients *would* commit suicide during their treatment were it not for the preventive measures taken by the physicians and nurses. The motives of these individuals are empirically familiar to us. Finally, incomplete but clearly defined tendencies toward suicide appear in the course of psychoanalytic treatment of many patients. It is a composite of the results of psychiatric and psychoanalytic observations in all such opportunities for research made not only by the author but by many predecessors and contemporaries, that forms the basis of what is to follow.

[5] Occasionally the victims of suicide recognize and confess *some* of the unconscious motives impelling the act, during the interval between the commission of the act and the moment of death. This is particularly vivid in such instances as are represented by the following press clippings:

DREAMER KILLS HIMSELF

LIVES ONLY LONG ENOUGH TO EXPLAIN STRANGE SHOOTING

Roseburg, Ore., March 13 (AP)—A pistol bullet fired during a dream was reported to state police here to have killed Phillip Pezoldt, homesteader in the remote Diamond Rock region.

Hearing a shot, Mrs. Louis Neiderheiser went to Pezoldt's room in his cabin and found him dying, she told officers. She said he gasped out that he had been dreaming, and had taken a pistol from under his pillow and shot himself.

—*Topeka Daily Capital*, March 14, 1935.

In Staunton, Va., Arthur Fournier fell asleep on a bus, dreamed he was asleep on the deep. Still asleep, he leaped to his feet, cried: "She's sinking! Jump for your lives!" No fool to remain aboard a sinking ship, Arthur Fournier jumped through the window, was killed.

—*Time*, Nov. 9, 1931.

THREE COMPONENTS IN THE SUICIDAL ACT

It is not difficult to discover in the act of suicide the existence of various elements. First of all it is a *murder*. In the German language it is, literally, a murder of the self (*Selbstmord*), and in all the earlier philological equivalents the idea of murder is implicit.

But suicide is also a murder *by* the self. It is a death in which are combined in one person the murderer and the murdered. We know that the motives for murder vary enormously and so do the motives for wishing to be murdered, which is quite another matter and not nearly so absurd as it may sound. For since in suicide there is a self that submits to the murder and would appear to be desirous of doing so, we must seek the motives of this strange submission. If the reader will picture to himself a battlefield scene, in which a wounded man is suffering greatly and begs someone to kill him, he will readily appreciate that the feelings of the *murderer* would be very different, depending upon whether he were a friend or a foe of the wounded man; those of the man who desires to be *murdered,* i.e., to be put out of his agony, however, would be the same in either case.

In many suicides it is quite apparent that one of these elements is stronger than the other. One sees people who want to die but cannot take the step against themselves; they fling themselves in front of trains, or like King Saul and Brutus, they beseech their armor bearers to slay them.

Finally, probably no suicide is consummated unless—in addition to this wish to kill and to be killed—the suicidal person also wishes to die. Paradoxically, many suicides in spite of the violence of the attack upon themselves and in spite of the corresponding surrender, do not seem to be very eager to die. Every hospital interne has labored in the emergency ward with would-be suicides, who beg him to save their lives. The fact that dying and being murdered achieve the same end so far as personal extinction is concerned, leads the practical-minded individual to think, "If a person wants to murder himself, or if he feels so badly about something that he is willing to be murdered, then he surely must want to die." But the illustration just given is only one of many indications that this is not so. Murdering or being murdered entails factors of violence, while dying relates to a surrender of one's life and happiness. A more complete discussion of both these elements will come later. For the present it is sufficient to make the point that in attempted suicide the wish to die may or may not be present or may be present to a quite variable degree, as may also the other wishes mentioned.

To summarize, then, suicide must be regarded as a peculiar kind of death which entails three internal elements: the element of dying, the element of killing, and the element of being killed. Each of these requires separate analysis. Each is an act for which there exists motives, unconscious and conscious. The latter are usually evident enough; the unconscious motives are now to be our chief consideration.

1. THE WISH TO KILL

The destructive instinct that slumbers within the heart of even the tiny child begins to be apparent as externally directed aggressiveness accompanied by rage almost from the moment of birth. Experiments by the behaviorist psychologists[6] and observations of the child-analysts[7] have made it clear beyond doubt that thwarting or a threat of it arouse intense resentment and protest in the youngest baby. We need no experimentation to show that this is also true of adults.[8]

The disturbance in a child's prenatal comfort by the violent act of birth is the first of such thwartings.[9]

More concretely apparent are the reactions of the child to the approach of a rival and the threat of deprival of satisfactions such as nursing. Such threats vigorously defended by attack promptly bring out the (previously self-absorbed) aggressive impulses. In essence the object of the attack is

[6] Watson, J. B., *Psychology from the Standpoint of a Behaviorist*, Lippincott, 1924.

[7] Klein, Melanie, *The Psychoanalysis of Children*, Norton, 1932.

[8] Only recently, however, has psychology investigated this matter experimentally and quantitatively. See, for example, Dembo, T., "Der Arger als Dynamisches Problem," Untersuchungen zur Handlungs und Affektpsychologie, Vol. X, ed. by K. Lewin, *Psychologische Forschung*, Berlin, 1931, Vol. XV, pp. 1-144; Lewin, K., *A Dynamic Theory of Personality*, McGraw-Hill, 1935; Brown, J. F., "The Modified Dembo Technique," *Bulletin of the Menninger Clinic*, July, 1937; Watson, J. B. and Watson, Rosalie Rayner, referred to in Watson, *op. cit.*; Rosenzweig, S., "A Test for Types of Reaction to Frustration," *American Journal of Orthopsychiatry*, Oct., 1935, pp. 395-403.

[9] Importance of the birth trauma first pointed out by Freud and later elaborated to the point of overemphasis by Rank is variously interpreted; there can be little doubt, however, but that it sets the pattern for all subsequent frustration anxieties, such as those connected with weaning, departure of the parents, etc.

the destruction of the intruder. Connected with it are feelings of resentment and of fear—fear of retaliation and of other consequences. The net result is the wish to eliminate the source of the threatened deprival, the object of the fear. (There may subsequently be fear of consequences arising in other quarters.)

Eliminating, driving away, disposing of, annihilating are all euphemistic synonyms for destroying. Such wishes represent in the more specialized practical language of the civilized adult simply the wish to kill—not in its pleasurable, sadistic aspects but in its primitive self-defensive purposes. Ordinarily, of course, except in the uncivilized society of savages, criminals, and psychotics, this wish is inhibited. It is inhibited by numerous factors, external and internal, which we shall discuss in detail later. The most powerful among these deterrents is a neutralizing impulse which likewise springs from the instinctual life of the individual. The aggressions become softened by the admixture of positive feelings; the hate, as we say, turns with more or less completeness to love. The intruder turns out to be not such a bad fellow after all, worth trading with, later co-operating or even joining hands with. The reader will think of many examples of this: the Greeks and the Romans, the Saxons and Normans, the American Indians and the Colonists, and a score of personal examples of the avowed enemy who became the warm friend. It doesn't always happen, of course; sometimes the hostility is too great to be overcome, and sometimes it is of such short duration that we cannot remember ever having had anything but the kindest feelings toward the individual from the beginning.[10] The principle is one pointed out by Freud, namely, that hostility usually leads the way to the contact with new objects, which the warm covering of love then gradually invests like vegetation progressively blanketing a stony hillside.

If the destructive impulses, the wish to kill, whether directed outwardly or back upon the self become sufficiently neutralized as to disappear completely behind the evidences of constructive positive feelings, the result is no longer destructive or murder but rather construction and creation, the making of life rather than the taking-away of life. In this sense procreation, the act of coitus, is the polar antith-

[10] An elaborate study of the importance of the unconscious motives determining the wish to kill, the selection of the person killed and of the method used in killing him, and of the final confession of the crime are contained in Theodor Reik's *The Unknown Murderer*, London, 1936 (English translation by Dr. Katherine Jones).

esis of murder. Constructiveness and creativeness may be directed to other than this immediate biologic form, of course. And in deference to the old morality which held that the more primitive a process, the "lower" it was, these "upward deflections" were called sublimations. A lateral deflection or displacement—for example, killing a deer instead of a member of the family—is, strictly speaking, not a sublimation although we sometimes speak of it so.

If the infusion of the erotic element, the "life-instinct," is not sufficiently strong to neutralize the destructive tendencies, it may nevertheless alter its character considerably so that while destruction is still the aim and the accomplishment it is less complete and less directly carried out. There may be an alternation of purposes; one sees this in the changes of mood and feeling between lovers, friends, enemies. One fancies that he can observe it in the alternate waves of cruelty and compassion shown by a cat toward a captured mouse and by some parents toward their children. But in its most familiar form partial erotization of cruelty appears as sadism—the ebullition of conscious joy in the act of destruction.

So unpleasant is this phenomenon in its balder manifestations that at first thought it would seem difficult to believe that it could represent any amelioration. One is apt to think that the erotization of cruelty adds to rather than subtracts from its virulence. The man beating a horse and giving evidence of sensual pleasure in so doing arouses us to greater resentment than the man who, even though in anger and for no other good reason, shoots his horse dead. We think the former is stimulated to his greater cruelty by what we call a perverse and abnormal sexuality. And in this we are partly correct. His sexuality is perverse because it is partial;[11] were it complete it would prevent him not only from killing the horse but from beating it at all. The man who killed his horse outright may have appeared to be more humane but logic compels us to regard him as less civilized and more destructive even than the sadistic beater.

[11] Technically, this is an incomplete explanation. In sadism there is not only an insufficient erotization but there is an incomplete fusion of the instinctual trends and the erotic trend becomes attached to the act instead of the object. For example, the whipping itself, partially irrespective of the particular horse, child, woman being whipped, becomes erotized, an end instead of a means. This implies some increase in narcissism, since the act is always more closely related to the subject (its author) than to the object. This whole matter is, however, still clouded in considerable obscurity, but the formulation above will serve for the purposes of this text.

This will be immediately apparent if for the horse we substitute a child. The man who kills his child from irritation or from any cause is counted by society as worthy of death. Partial erotization of such a man's uncontrollable aggressiveness might have substituted for murder a lustful whipping of the child which might have landed him in jail or in an asylum but certainly would not have been a capital offense.

A little more erotization and what we call sadism merges into those severe, ostensible kindnesses which characterize many school teachers, judges, and others in authority who lovingly administer what they assure their victims "hurts me worse than it does you." This is not always punishment. It may be a compulsive insistence upon rule and ritual in the name of some high ideal—law, education, religion, or character-building. The hypocrisy of it is usually entirely unrecognized by its perpetrators, but not by its victims.

Destructiveness turned back against the self may be erotized partially or completely. Sometimes this delight in torturing oneself, of which we shall speak again in the next section, appears to add to the motivations of self-destruction. Actually we must remember it always represents a saving grace—insufficient, to be sure, but enough to change the color and appearance if not actually thwart the total destructiveness of the act.

One frequently sees how, after such provocation, the backward ebbing flow of aggressiveness is prevented from effecting immediate suicide only by most valiant, persistent struggles on the part of the erotic impulses. Sometimes in a series of episodes the latter may be seen to lose ground and actual suicide ultimately occurs. Such a case I have related above (the defaulting bank cashier). At other times the life instinct seems to gain a little on the destructive tendencies and a series of episodes follows in which there is a diminishing malignancy. For example, a man whom I know became so angry at his brother that he consciously contemplated killing him; he restrained himself, however, not only on account of the law and other such consequences but because, for his mother's sake, he felt a deep protective obligation to this brother. He became so remorseful contemplating what he regarded as his criminal wishes that he made several attempts at suicide, all of which barely failed. For reasons not entirely clear to him, he then began to drive his car with a reckless abandon which seemed certain to result disastrously. But in spite of several serious accidents he was not killed. Next he conceived the notion of exposing himself to some disease that would kill him and deliberately tried to get syphilis by repeated exposures. He succeeded only, however, in getting gonorrhea, the treatment of which he completely neglected.

He turned then to alcohol in a series of debauches. In spite of all these things he had until this time continued in the good graces of his wife and his employer, both of whom knew his virtues too well to be blinded by his inexplicable behavior. He now managed, however, to get himself at outs with both of them, losing his position by deliberately provoking his employer in arguments and exasperating his wife to the point of divorce by announcements that he did not love her.

Long and varied as this list of self-directed aggressions is, it may be seen to represent a series of diminishing intensity. Actual suicide was averted. So were the serious consequences of most of the other episodes; he soon found another position and his wife returned to him.

A more complete fusion of constructive and destructive impulses results in those positive attachments to objects in the environment which make up normal love-life, evidence by a capacity for discrimination between real foes and real friends, between those things which should be hated and destroyed in the interests of personal and public weal and those things which should be loved. Growth of the personality, education, social capacity, and creative power become possible only as these aggressions are increasingly directed outward instead of inward, focused upon the proper objects of attack, and completely neutralized by love when those objects are desirable ones. In this way the self-love and self-hate, primary narcissism and primary self-destructiveness are drawn out from their primitive preoccupation with the self and fruitfully invested in the outside world.

Under certain circumstances, however, there develops a break in such a comfortable and satisfactory distribution of energy. The well-invested love and hate are loosed from their objects of attachment and require reinvestment. To some extent, of course, this is happening constantly, especially in the younger and more active years. But under various conditions sudden reinvestments of large amounts of energy are necessary—traumatic situations arise such that there is a forcible interruption in the previously comfortable adjustment. Or again, increasing difficulty may have been encountered in the maintaining of an apparently satisfactory readjustment. It is easy to imagine what sudden events would produce such a necessity for readjustment: the death of a loved one or, for that matter, of a hated one —the sudden curtailment in opportunities for work, the loss of a job, a false accusation or incrimination—anything, in short, which makes it suddenly necessary to reinvest love and particularly hate through the sudden interruption or threatened interruption of established investments. Later I shall go into more detail as to the specific nature of these precipitating events. For the present we are concerned with what happens to the interrupted stream of love and hate thus suddenly and forcibly detached from its outer moorings.

In the normal person, which is to say in most people, after a temporary period of grief and anxiety there is a gradual reinvestment in new objects. In certain individuals, however, whose predisposing peculiarities we shall discuss later, this does not—cannot—occur. Instead, the previously fused bonds of love and hate are now robbed of their object, become defused, and both return to their point of origin—the individual himself. Once more then, as in the beginning, the aggressive or destructive impulses lead the way followed *more or less* closely by the erotic impulses. If the lag is too great, the destructive impulses accomplish their goal—destruction. To the extent which the constructive tendencies overtake and neutralize their death-bent predecessors, suicidal effect is deflected, deferred, or completely circumvented.

In other words the theory of suicide is that the wish to kill, unexpectedly robbed of certain external occasions or objects of unconscious gratification, may be turned back upon the person of the "wisher" and carried into effect as suicide. This theory would correspond with the facts if (*a*) it can be shown that there actually is a reflection of the destructive tendencies upon the individual himself so that that self is treated as though it were an external object; if (*b*) persons prone to suicide prove upon examination to be highly *ambivalent* in their object attachments, that is, masking with their conscious positive attachments large and scarcely mastered quantities of unconscious hostility (the wish to kill); and if (*c*) is such individuals suicide is actually precipitated by occasions of sudden interruption in the object attachments corresponding to those suggested above.[12]

We shall apply these three tests in order, considering first the question how it is possible for an individual to treat himself as an external object, frequently identified with the very object toward which his love and hate and particularly his unconscious wish to kill had been directed.

We know from the fantasies of adult patients, from dreams, sensations, memories, and repetitious acts and behavior patterns, that in the unconscious, the primitive infantile layers of the mind, it is possible to regard one's body as not being a part of one and it is also possible to treat one's body as if it included the body of someone else. We call the latter *identification*[13] or, more accurately, *introjection,* because an identified person seems to be introjected into the self. Thus a mother who vicariously enjoys her daughter's pleasure in going to college, let us say, does so by a psychological process of identifying herself with the daughter, i.e., being in and of and around the daughter. A lover figuratively carries his sweetheart inside of him. Therefore, any desired treatment of the other person can now be carried out—logically—upon oneself. This turning back of hostile feelings upon the self, when such an introjection has been made (often unconsciously), thus serves a psychological usefulness. It is the well-known device called "kicking the cat" with oneself (one's own body) used as the cat.

For example, I used to play golf sometimes with a rather irascible but decorous friend who is unusually sensitive to the slightest noise or disturbance while he is putting. His caddy once unfortunately developed an attack of hiccoughs which distressed my friend increasingly. He managed to control his temper until near the end of the game, when he was trying for a very difficult putt, only to have the tense silence interrupted by the caddy's ineffectual efforts to restrain his diaphragm. My friend straightened up quickly, his face dark with anger, and was about to explode with profanity when some women players of his acquaintance,

---

[12] It is not necessary to show that this form of self-destructiveness is a direct expression of primitive instinctual trend; this is Freud's hypothesis which cannot at the present time be verified but which fits in well with the facts and has as yet no sustained contradiction.

[13] In psychoanalysis we speak of the feeling toward one person as if he were someone else, as "identification," and identification of someone else with the self is denoted "introjection."

leaving the next tee, passed nearby. He checked his words instantly, but in a gesture of wild exasperation, swung his putter in a wide arc, near the end of which the head of the club crashed into his own ankle with sufficient force to evoke a howl of pain and send him limping to the club house. Shortly after this I read in the newspaper of a man who had actually broken his leg in precisely the same manner. Is it not clear in such a case that the man's wish to strike the caddy was released against himself as a substitute?

Some people feel the intuitive truth of such a statement at once, and to others the whole thing seems fantastic. "It was just an accident," they will say. "He lost control of himself in anger and it happened that his club struck him. How do you know that was his intention?"

There are a number of reasons for our thinking so. In the first place, sometimes the victims will tell us so if we ask them. The trouble is usually that they do not know it. We can often infer it from the circumstances surrounding the act. Every man has noticed, for example, that he is more apt to cut himself while shaving if he is angry at someone and one frequently hears men say, "I took it out on myself this morning." A friend of mine, a doctor's wife at whose home I was a guest, became quite angry at her maid for botching up the dinner; to avoid a scene, however, she paid the maid off in silence but came into the living room charged with emotion and flung herself down in the chair from which she had arisen only a few moments before. In the chair she had left her scissors which now pierced her thigh for a distance of an inch or so. She leaped from the chair, and in pain and exasperation, exclaimed, "It's all the maid's fault!" Illogical as this reasoning sounds, it was, in a sense, quite true.

One frequently reads in the newspaper (for example, in one which I hold in my hand as I write this) that a young boy who had been scolded by his father for some minor dereliction hanged himself in the barn a few hours later. We are accustomed with intuitive accuracy to explain such actions on the basis of revenge. Every reader will be able to recall similar instances in his childhood which provoked similar feelings but which, fortunately, were gratified in imagination rather than in action. We imagined how sorry our parents would be for having mistreated us as they did. But this boy went further. His hate was so great that he was willing to sacrifice his life to vent it. To be sure, the act hurt his father but not nearly so much as it hurt himself. It must have been his father whom he really wished to kill. We know that some boys do kill their fathers under just such circumstances but evidently this boy couldn't do that; perhaps he loved his father too much to kill him; perhaps he feared him too much; perhaps he feared the consequences; at any rate, he couldn't do it. What he could do was to kill the father that existed within himself, technically, the *introjected* father. Every boy introjects his own father to some extent over the period of years that pass while he is growing up; probably many a man who is reading this can consciously recognize that he carries his father about with him in his heart. In the primitive thinking of the unconscious this is not a mere figure of speech.

A few years ago I ran across the following rather typical newspaper item:

STOCK LOSSES CAUSE SUICIDE

Leaving a note indicating that stock market losses had left him penniless, A. B. C., 32, a World War aviator, ended his life with poison yesterday in a room in the M. Hotel.

A maid discovered his body a few hours after he died. Near him was a glass and the bottle that contained the potion. A postscript on a note he left for a sister, Mrs. D. E. T., addressed G. Hotel, New York City, furnished the motive for his act. It read:

"I have given all I had to the brokers on the street this morning."

—*Chicago Herald and Examiner,* Nov. 17, 1930.

The interpretation which would ordinarily be given such an item by the casual reader or by the moralizing editorial writer would probably be that gambling on the stock market ruins some people and that some of them "can't take it."

Such facile explanations have just those deficiencies which we discussed earlier. They are much too simple and trite. They do not take into account the violent emotional conflicts going on in the heart of the victim. Of course, without more details than those given in the newspaper account we cannot be certain what these were, but the last sentence gives us a significant clue. It strongly suggests against whom this fellow's hatred flamed. It is not a mere explanation; it is a bitter accusation. One can almost hear this victim saying, "What a fool I was!" However true this may be, we must remember that fools do not kill themselves. They are more apt to kill those who have fooled them.

I should suspect, indeed I should feel quite certain on the basis of my clinical experience, that this man identified the broker with himself and by killing himself was really intending to kill the broker symbolically. I said so to a friend of mine who laughed at the idea. "I can even see," he said, "that this fellow might have halfway wanted to be a broker because he was so interested in the stock market and I can see how he might have hated the broker too, but if he wanted to kill the broker why didn't he kill him?"

In this particular case I do not know why he didn't kill the broker directly instead of indirectly. That could only have been ascertained from hours of patient investigation into all the intricacies of this man's mental life. But my friend was an intellectually honest fellow. A few weeks later he brought me the following clipping, dated, actually, a few weeks prior to the first clipping:

CUSTOMER KILLS BROKER AND ENDS OWN LIFE

Philadelphia, Pa., October 10. (AP) G. H. J., 32, member of a socially prominent family and a confidential clerk of C. Co., stock brokers, was shot to death today at the company's offices by a former customer, who then shot himself, dying later in a hospital.

S. was shot three times while he talked with the former customer. . . .

—*Chicago Tribune*, Oct. 11, 1930.

"I found this," he said, "and I am a little more inclined now to believe your explanation. You see this fellow *did* kill the broker! According to your theory, I guessed he killed him *twice*."

My friend assumed that I was merely theorizing, because he is not familiar with psychoanalytic literature. The illustrations I have given are, to be sure, entirely unconvincing to one who wishes scientific proof. I do not offer them as proof but only as available illustrations of what happens and how precisely they fit the explanation offered. Statistics could be marshaled to show the same thing—e.g., suicide and murder rates show constant inverse relationship. In Catholic countries there is usually a higher homicide rate, a lower suicide rate; in Protestant countries a higher suicide and lower homicide rate. But even statistics do not prove our point. The real proof depends upon patient investigation of examples that come under our observation during the treatment of individuals who are intensively studying their own motives. I shall cite some of these clinical examples later.

Let us consider more in detail now the question asked by my skeptical friend: Why don't these individuals who boil over with rage kill the other fellow? Why don't they attack the real object of their hate instead of venting their hate upon someone or something else in a roundabout way?

Numerous self-evident reasons will come to mind. For instance, the resistance offered by reality may be too great —the object attacked may be more powerful than the attacker.

Or again, the attack upon an enemy may be inhibited by various internal factors, chiefly fear. There is, first of all, the fear of the consequences, an intelligent, justifiable fear. One naturally dreads the penalty of going to the penitentiary or the gallows. But there are other fears which are even more deterring than this; for example, fear originating from the conscience. Probably some of us would commit a good many crimes if we could get away with them, but on the other hand no one can entirely escape his conscience, and in some cases it is tremendously powerful. To be sure, the conscience can be bargained with so that some individuals who cannot take a nickel from the street car company can cheat their competitor of hundreds of dollars without a pang. Such an individual, like the character in Aesop's fable who spared the snakes and killed the worms, may not hesitate to commit murder (so far as his conscience is concerned) if he be permitted to make a slight atonement in some other direction. But the fact remains that conscience is a strong deterrent and a harsh judge. Many a man finds it easier on this account alone to kill his victim indirectly, i.e., by attacking himself—like the Japanese creditor who kills himself on his debtor's doorstep.

But there are other fears aside from that of the consequences and the conscience. One of these fears which saps the strength of the aggressive drive by intimidation is a fear of hostile intention in the other person, a fear which magnifies the dangerousness of the opponent beyond the facts. One often realizes in himself that he overestimates the power or malignancy of the foe, because he is falsely attributing to the foe some of the hatred which only he himself feels. A little of this serves as an excitement but too much as an intimidation. Intimidation necessitates a deflection of aim and hence it is either some other person or, most conveniently, the self, which bears the brunt of the attack.

Finally, thwarting in the carrying-out of a direct aggression may be the result of weakening from the admixture of erotic elements. This simply means that we find it exceedingly difficult to kill someone we love. Love and hate always operate simultaneously, though the proportions may vary. I have already explained that a fundamental psychological principle is that love tends to follow hate and to neutralize it just as poisons in a river are gradually purified by oxygen from the air. Consequently, if the hate, i.e., the destructiveness, is not prompt or forceful enough in its action, it becomes impeded, thwarted by the development of this erotic infusion. One frequently sees this in wars, particularly long-drawn-out wars, and nowhere more clearly than in the Biblical record of the conflict between the Jews and the Philistines, where the constant anxiety of the spiritual leaders of Israel was that amicable relations might be established, customs exchanged, and arms laid lown. Samson, as a prototype of the Israelites, fought valiantly until the erotic element, i.e., his affection for the Philistines, one of them in particular, sapped his strength in a way which has been made diagrammatically clear by the well-known story.

We have thus led from the application of the test of psychological introjection to the consideration of the other two tests, that of the personality character of the individuals strongly given to introjection and that of the nature of the events precipitating it. We can scarcely separate these, but we shall try.

What is characteristic of a very large number of suicides is the apparent inadequacy of the precipitating event. We have already seen that these cannot be taken at their face value, but let us look at some of them. A girl killed herself because she became depressed after bobbing her hair; a man killed himself because he was forced to quit playing golf; a woman committed suicide after missing two trains; a boy took his life because his pet canary died. This list could be extended indefinitely. Every reader will be able to think of some examples.[14]

In these instances the hair, the golf, and the canary had an exaggerated value, so that when they were lost or when there was even a threat that they might be lost, the recoil of severed emotional bonds was fatal. But why should such

[14] Some of the above examples were taken from our own files. Some of them are mentioned in an article entitled "New Reasons for Suicide," *Current Opinion*, June, 1923, p. 728. The following instance was reported in *Time*, Dec. 7, 1936:

In Nadrljan, Farmer Jovan Bata, 60, bought his first cow. A week later he found the animal dead in her stall. "I can't get over this loss," wrote Farmer Bata before hanging himself on a beam above.

extravagantly exaggerated over-estimations and incorrect evaluations exist? We cannot dismiss the matter by saying they were foolish people; we must know why their folly expressed itself in this particular way, if we are to understand why aggressive tendencies can become self-directed.

Clinical observation has established the fact that such individuals are emotionally or psychologically immature in that they have never graduated completely from the infantile modes of love and being loved. The child loves with its mouth; the normal development assumes that to a considerable extent he substitute other modes of loving and receiving love.

And just as a suckling child resents weaning and feels that something is being taken away from him that it is his right to possess, so these people who are predominantly infantile and "oral" in their personality development cannot stand thwarting. It is, therefore, really not an exaggeration to say that for such individuals the over-evaluated objects in the cases illustrated above—the hair, golf, the canary, etc.—are equivalent to the mother's breast. The child feels he will die if it is taken away from him, as of course he would actually if something were not substituted for it. But not only that, he feels angry at the person who has deprived him. A study of the fantasy life of children, as has been made, for example, by Melanie Klein,[15] and the study of the customs of savage tribes, as has been made by Roheim[16] and others, indicate without doubt that sucking at the breast is not far removed from cannibalism and that the child would, if he could, drink up not only the milk but the breast and the entire mother. He would do so partly for the same reason that the man killed the goose that laid the golden egg, namely, his insatiable and imperative craving. But an equally strong motive is the hostile one, already discussed, some pages back, which is reflected in the fact that the child bites the nipple when the mother tries to withdraw. To believe this, one needs only to think of how a dog acts if one attempts to take his bone from him; he will certainly not hesitate to bite the hand that feeds him. Biting is only the first step to devouring, which the savages actually carry out. When we remember that in the calendar of time "civilized" human beings are only a

[15] Klein, *op. cit.*

[16] Roheim, Geza, *Social Anthropology: A Psychoanalytic Study in Anthropology and a History of Australian Totemism,* Boni and Liveright, 1926.

36

few seconds removed from the cannibals and a few minutes removed from the beasts, it will not be surprising to discover that in the unconscious, cannibalism is not yet extinct. Millions of devout Christians commemorate the death of their leader at frequent intervals during the year by a ceremony in which it is clearly announced by the pastor that the congregation will now eat the body and drink the blood of their leader. Even after Calvin won his argument with the organized church that the bread was not actually the body of Christ, it was clearly recognized to *symbolize* the body of Christ. Theologians would probably deny that this symbolic cannibalism had any aggressive content. It is to be sure a simple, primitive, biologically direct method of indicating love, but at the same time eating the body of another person may also be an expression of hate as, for example, in the childhood fantasies represented by such fairy tales as Jack the Giant Killer, the Gingerbread Man, and Red Riding Hood (in which the wolf disguises himself as the grandmother and seeks to eat the little girl). Both meanings are probably always implicit in the act, differing in proportions under different circumstances.

I have been at some pains to make clear the basis of this oral attitude because it seems probable that introjection is a favorite psychopathological technique of those individuals who have never relinquished their infantile oral propensities. Perhaps this is partly due to the fact that introjection is the psychological equivalent of eating another person.

One of the sources of our understanding of these oral personality characters is the disease known as melancholia. In its most typical form it is brought about by the loss of a loved one. The normal person reacts for a time with grief, that is, he feels as if something beautiful and desirable in the world has been taken away from him leaving life poorer for its loss. Time heals such wounds, however; every day the pain of bereavement grows less. But in melancholia the loss of a loved one, not necessarily by death, in fact more often by jilting, results in a different sort of reaction. There is the same brooding and sadness but with a different content which grows greater instead of less. It is not the world that seems poor and empty, it is something inside of the individual himself. He complains that he feels worthless, miserable, and wretched. He often says he ought not to be allowed to live and asks to be taken to prison or to the gallows. It is clear that he hates himself.

37

In such a person, it may be seen (now that the way has been pointed out by Freud, Abraham, and Ferenczi) that such an individual hates himself only a little more than he loves himself. In spite of his talk of how unworthy he is, he demands from those about him an inordinate amount of attention, sympathy, anxiety, and care. But this love and hate which he now directs toward himself in such a disorganized and unfruitful manner are directed back against himself for a very clear reason. They were formerly invested in the lost love-object, only at that time the hate was unconscious. When the love-object is lost his emotions are left, so to speak, extending out into space with nothing to rest upon. Such a state of affairs cannot continue any more than a man leaning across a chasm holding on to a tree on the opposite side can remain in this position if the tree gives way. If I may make a fantastic verbal diagram of what happens I should imagine an elastic bond of love between our patient and his love-object, a bond which completely hides an inner core of hostility. When the love-object is suddenly taken away, this bond of love, instead of being gradually absorbed and redirected as in the normal person, snaps back upon the self and in doing so breaks into its two components of love and hate. Two things have happened, then; the direction of the feeling has been changed of necessity and the two elements of the feeling have become defused and hence nakedly apparent. In this way the melancholiac patient can vent upon himself in bitter reproaches and attacks the formerly hidden hostilities which he once felt toward the beloved object but which are now directed toward himself because within his ego there is incorporated that object.

I promised that we should ascertain whether or not persons prone to suicide could be definitely shown to be characterized in their personality make-up by strong ambivalence. I have already referred to the empirical fact, a fact which is common knowledge as well as professional experience, that melancholiacs are strongly inclined toward suicide, but I have not demonstrated that melancholiacs are ambivalent. I shall not attempt to do so because this has been worked out repeatedly in the writings of psychoanalytic authors (see the names mentioned above; the reader may also consult the revised edition of my own book, *The Human Mind*, in which these theories are summarized under the discussion of the cycloid personality). It is now generally agreed among psychoanalysts that the intermediate

38

stages of psychosexual development between the earliest stage of complete intra-uterine self-satisfaction and the final stage of mature, normal, object-invested love are all ambivalent; that is to say they are all unstable, transitional stages in which both love and hate elements are active and incompletely fused. The melancholiac is a personality type strongly influenced by traumatic events (frustrations) which occurred in the oral stage of his development, the period of nursing and weaning. We do not know all of the reasons why some individuals are so strongly affected by these oral disappointments; some observers believe in a so-called constitutional or hereditary factor and others regard this as merely a way of hiding our ignorance behind vague concepts. We do know, however, and agree that those individuals who continue to be strongly influenced or determined in their relationships with the outside world by this stage in their development, instead of relinquishing this modality in favor of a more adult one, are characterized by strong ambivalence and an ambivalence which often takes the form of cyclic alternations of repression of one or the other element in the emotional relationship. Some people show their ambivalence by being kind and generous with one hand, so to speak, and stingy with the other, or striking a blow with one hand and soothing with the other. Others have long swings of generosity, of kindness, of manifest affection, but may suddenly switch to an entirely opposite type of behavior and attitude. Such swings may be a week, a year, or a decade in length. And if one examines closely the attachments of such individuals to their love-objects, one discovers evidences of the unconscious hostility betraying themselves subtly in the manner, conditions, or consequences of the love, and upon provocation, often amazingly slight, this hostility will emerge. Usually it emerges only in dreams, thoughts, impulses; the conscience is then quick to throw it back upon the self. A loving mother (of this type) is suddenly horrified at the thought which comes to her that she might harm her child; shortly afterwards her only thought is her own wickedness and self-destruction. (The normal person would reject such a thought as absurd and "forget"—repress—it.)

I can illustrate this ambivalence and its typical dependence upon oral character traits by a woman in whose early life there had been an oral thwarting of great seriousness. (So dramatically stark were her childhood days, and so severe her weanings from maternal dependence that her life was made the basis of a popular realistic novel.) She had nevertheless become a highly admirable, competent, and interesting woman, but one who was always unsatisfied. Unsatisfied is really too mild a term. She was actually voracious in her relationships with other people. People could not but like her, because she would make herself so agreeable, but they soon became aware of the fact that she was encompassing them with love—smothering them, as one person put it, like an octopus.

This cannot be better expressed than in the words of her own sister who wrote her at one time:

You must realize, my dear sister, that you frighten your lovers away by loving them so much. You love intensely and you want them to love you even more intensely. But your love is positively engulfing, devouring. You cannot eat your lover like a cake, you know. At least, if you do you can't expect to go on having him!

As is so often the case with such individuals, this woman had a propensity for electing lovers whom circumstances made it quite impossible for her ever to possess. One of these with whom she was deeply in love at the time she was under treatment had the given name of Allen, and was usually referred to as "Al." Shortly after her separation from him (at his instigation) this patient attempted suicide by taking an overdose of the drug Allonal and had a dream in which she and a group of men, which represented the analyst, the lover Allen, her father, her brother of whom she was very jealous, and others, were in a car and it was wrecked. They were all killed except herself. "Yes," she said, quite offhand, "they were all killed, Al and all." Spoken rapidly *"Al and all"* sounds much like Allonal. This verbal clue made it immediately apparent that in attempting to kill herself with the drug Allonal she was also devouring her lover and the other disappointing males. This devouring tendency was so apparent in all her actions that even her sister had detected it. Thus she obtained Al, in spite of his flight, by oral incorporation, and simultaneously destroyed him by the same method, i.e., by making a destructive attack upon herself in whom Al had been (was being) incorporated. In reality, as she well knew, killing herself would have been a tragic blow to Al, an unstable fellow greatly overwrought and distressed by the situation—and it would also have been a palpable blow at the analyst since the patient's analysis had been no secret to many observers and critics. But one sees here how these reality factors are not primary in such episodes—but merely over-determine them.

Persons of this undeveloped infantile or "oral" type of character organization are, therefore, prone to react with this splitting and rebounding of the instinctual trends when exposed to certain—for them unendurable—disappointments and frustrations. This is the most familiar type of precipitation of the reversal in ambivalent trends, appearing as suicide or melancholia.

But another type of precipitation is frequently observed in this same type of personality. (There are also other personality types prone to suicide which we shall mention later.) Indeed, precisely the opposite sort of event is capable of evoking the same response. Instead of committing suicide because of misfortune, some of these individuals react in this way to sudden good fortune. They cannot endure certain large successes. I have known men and women to become overwhelmed with depression and attempt or commit suicide immediately following a promotion, an increase in income, or a sudden realization of their importance and prestige in their community. I remember one man, who, owing in part to his good judgment and in part to some good luck, was able to make a considerable success of his bank at the same time that his competitor's bank and many other banks were failing, and he no sooner realized this fully than he became depressed and ultimately shot himself. I remember another man whose business sagacity had enabled him to succeed in a number of enterprises during the same period of national economic distress who reacted the same way. Indeed, the same woman described above, who became so depressed when she lost her lover "Al," subsequently led a fairly undisturbed life for several years under circumstances of considerable privation and loneliness. She then met a wealthy young man who asked her to marry him; and, although she loved him and wanted to accept him, her sudden good fortune again threw her into a depression with suicidal contemplations.

How shall we explain this? It is really not as paradoxical as it may seem. Some individuals, as we have seen, are fundamentally ambivalent, and however much some of them may assert their emotional independence, their detachment, and their objective judgment, at heart they want very much to surrender the necessity of such ambitious striving in favor of a more passive existence; in short, to be loved. They often resent very much indeed their inability to acknowledge or fulfill their wishes for passivity and for receptive gratification. One might say that such individuals were mature, accomplished, benevolent, and capable far beyond their real capacities. Alexander has aptly termed this "living beyond one's emotional means." But this still leaves unexplained why they should become depressed and suicidal in reaction to success. Freud was the first to point out that this was the reaction to the disapproval of an overgrown, "hypertrophied" conscience. Such a man lives his entire life under the dictates of a conscience which says, "You must work; you must renounce; you must sacrifice; you must earn; you must give; you must achieve; you must deny your expectation to be blessed with gifts, with love, with an easy life. This is what you want, to be sure, but you may not have it. For you to have it means the robbing or displacing of someone else, the failure of someone else, the usurpation by you of the position once occupied by your envied baby brother or someone else in the family. This you may not have, on pain of death."

Consequently, when reality comes into conflict with conscience, when good luck or the results of hard work bring the very reward which would seem to be entirely appropriate, the conscience reacts with a prohibition which disturbs the economy of the instinctual investments. The wish to be killed, which we shall discuss shortly, develops in response to the tyrannical conscience. Such individuals lose their objects and methods of sublimating hate, and they react to this interruption in the same way as those who are interrupted or frustrated in their program of loving. The frequency with which men, who retire from active work in middle age expecting to settle down for ten or twenty years of comfortable relaxation, succumb promptly to some illness suggests that when conscious and deliberate suicide is not enacted by this revolution, an unconscious accomplishment of the same end is instituted by the bodily processes. But this is anticipating the subject matter of a later section of the book.

We must say a final word as to other types of personality in which suicide may occur. Those individuals whose infantilism appears in their inability to do other than "want what they want when they want it," cannot brook any delay in their gratifications, may not be of the ambivalent oral type described. They may be of a little later, or of an even more primitive psychological organization, but ambivalence is still a characteristic. Again, there are individuals whose earliest experiences in life have been so terrifying and so disheartening and so prematurely convincing as to the starkness of reality and the lack of available love for them that they live in constant anticipation of the necessity and desirability of relinquishing all attempts to win love or happiness from the world. This is what we see in the schizoid personality type. For these persons all object attachments are exceedingly tenuous and faint; thwarting is, therefore, not so unexpected nor so revolutionary and is more apt to precipitate a complete reversion of all interest to the self and a surrender of their loyalty to reality in the form of a psychosis. Occasionally, however, suicide is resorted to instead of a psychosis.

To recapitulate; we have confirmed the theory to the extent of showing that introjection is a psychological reality and that it occurs to the realistic degree of suicide in individuals of certain immature personality make-up upon the occasion of sharp disappointment, frustration, or the reverse. We should expect from this that suicide might be more frequent in primitive society than in civilized society. This, some students of the matter have declared to be undoubtedly the case.[17] (Attenuated forms of suicide, we should expect, on the same basis, to be more frequent in civilized peoples.) Primitive people and persons of immature personality development are less capable of making positive object attachments relatively free from a high degree of ambivalence and are therefore more completely at the mercy of circumstances which rob them of their unstable love-objects.

That such interruptions in attachments, which may seem very ardent or may on the other hand seem trivial, precipitate an introjection of the wish to kill and a consummation of the act of suicide is attested by the long list of precipitating causes already referred to. If these are compared with the list of precipitating causes of suicide among savages, little difference will be detected. Westermarck,[18] for example, says: "The causes which among savages lead to suicide are manifold: disappointed love or jealousy; illness or old age; grief over the death of a child, a husband or a wife; fear of punishment; slavery or brutal treatment by a husband; remorse, shame, or wounded pride, anger or revenge. In various cases an offended person kills himself

[17] Zilboorg, Gregory, "Considerations on Suicide, with Particular Reference to that of the Young," *Am. Jour. Orthopsychiat.*, January, 1937, pp. 15-31.
[18] Westermarck, Edward, *The Origin and Development of the Moral Ideas*, London, 1906.

for the express purpose of taking revenge upon the offender. Thus among the Tshispeaking peoples of the Gold Coast, should a person commit suicide and before so doing attribute the act to the conduct of another person, that other person is required by native law to undergo a like fate. The practice is termed "killing oneself upon the head of another," and the person whose conduct is supposed to have driven the suicide to commit the rash act is visited with a death of an exactly similar nature'—unless indeed the family of the suicide be pacified with a money compensation.

"Among the Chuvashes it was the custom formerly to hang themselves at the doors of their enemies; among the Thlinkets (Savage islanders) an offended person who is unable to take revenge in any other way commits suicide in order to expose the person who gave the offense, to the vengeance of his surviving relatives and friends.

"Chinese do the same, not only because the law throws the responsibility of the deed upon him who occasioned it but also because the disembodied soul is supposed to be better able than the living man to persecute the enemy. The Brahmans also believed this."

That these unconscious mechanisms in suicide are intuitively perceived by many people is to be directly inferred from the publication of a cartoon in *The New Yorker* in the issue of November 17, 1934. The cartoon represents in the first picture a man sitting despondently beside the picture of a woman, a revolver held in his right hand. In the subsequent pictures he first raises the revolver and places it at his temple with an air of resignation. Then a thought seems to strike him and he lowers the revolver, while he takes another look at the picture of the woman. In the final picture he has thrown back his head and, pointing the revolver at the picture of the woman, fires, blowing the picture to bits while an air of triumph and satisfaction mingles with his evident anger.[19]

[19] Others than psychoanalysts have put emphasis upon the revenge motive in suicide. Bermann (G., *Archiva de Medicina Lega.*, Lisbon, April, 1931, p. 33) based what he regarded as an original hypothesis on personal interviews with persons who had attempted suicide and who were carefully studied psychiatrically and sociologically. His idea is that suicide is always a form of revenge against some one person or society as a whole. Revenge against a relative or lover is often obvious enough but he thinks the suicides of anarchists as well as of those who attack or feel vengeful against the human race as a whole because of their own inadequacy and resentment, exhibit the same thing.

All this conforms with what we know empirically about suicide—of its occurrence in unstable adolescents and rigid personalities of middle age, of its precipitation by reverses of fortune in love affairs, financial affairs, family affairs. In all these, the wish to kill is latent, covered up sometimes by the most ardent love making or the most tender maternal patience or the most scrupulous probity. Those who commit suicide are often among the most distinguished members of the community—the most generous, the most upright, the most intelligent. It may come as a shock, therefore, for me to ascribe to them, as to all suicides, any defects in personality structure, any emotional immaturity or psychological primitiveness. But actions speak louder than words. The man who kills himself has, after all, killed something and to that extent, by *prima facie* evidence, must have been dominated by an impulse—in psychological terms, a wish —to kill. All of us have such impulses, such wishes; this is not abnormal. But most of us can resist them and no matter what sophistry is invoked to attempt to justify or glorify suicide the fact remains that it is a murder, a climax of destruction, and has purposes, motives and consequences related to that inescapable fact.

So much, then, for *the wish to kill* arising from primitive destructiveness, invested with weak neutralization in one or several objects whose sudden removal or faithlessness dislodges the attachment, defuses the elements of the emotional bond and allows the murderous impulse, now freed, to expend itself upon the person of its origin as a substitute object, thus accomplishing a displaced murder.

2. THE WISH TO BE KILLED

We come now to the second element in suicide, the obverse of the killing motive, namely, the wish to be killed. Why does anyone wish, not to die or to kill, necessarily, but *to be* killed?

Being killed is the extreme form of *submission* just as killing is the extreme form of *aggression*. And the enjoyment of submission, pain, defeat, even ending in death, is the essence of masochism, i.e., the reversed or inverted reaction to the pleasure-pain principle. But it would be a misleading over-simplification to let it go at that. We must understand now why satisfactions may be achieved by punishment, that extraordinary phenomenon which we see

45

occurring on all sides in the persons who enjoy ill health and those who deliberately put themselves in predicaments in which they suffer.

Sometimes this passive search for a method of committing suicide without accepting the responsibility for it reaches absurd extremes. One patient, utterly miserable in mind, exploited the popular fallacy about catching cold and endeavored to get rid of himself by taking a hot bath and then standing in front of an open window in the hopes of getting pneumonia. Another patient who spoke constantly of the desirability of suicide and who had, indeed, been rescued from a very serious attempt at self-destruction from carbon monoxide in his garage promised not to attempt suicide in any overt way; however, he was convinced that he had a bad heart and so entered into athletics vigorously in the hope that he would collapse from heart failure. This would have had the double advantage (to him) of accomplishing his own self-destruction and of reflecting upon the bad judgment of the physicians in having allowed him to enter into these sports. Unfortunately for his conscious intentions, however, he did not collapse but, to the amazement of himself and everyone else, won the tennis tournament, including victory over several very much more experienced and proficient players. His reaction to this was to give up athletics entirely since they had failed him in his primary purpose.

The explanation of the wish to suffer and to submit to pain and even death is to be found in the nature of the conscience. Everyone knows for practical purposes what conscience is. We have an intuitive recognition of it; we are aware of it just as we are aware of the police system in a city where we do not actually see policemen. But such knowledge of the conscience is not very scientific. It has now been quite definitely determined that conscience is an internal, psychological representation of authority, originally and mainly parental authority but fused in later life with prevalent ethical, religious, and social standards. It is largely formed in infancy and childhood and seldom keeps pace with the changes in external environment. We all know that it sometimes makes us do things which we see no sense in doing and prevents us from doing other things which we should like to do and from which there is no good reason for our refraining. The conscience is often a good guide but it is sometimes a bad guide; and, good or bad, it is always to be reckoned with. As everyone knows, it can be bribed and bought off but it cannot be ignored. What is not so well known is that a part of the conscience is unconscious; there are some things about which we feel guilty without knowing it. Many people who think they disregard the conscience, or who insist that they never suffer from a sense of guilt, show by their actions that this is untrue. We are all familiar with examples of this, for instance, the minister's daughter who goes to Greenwich Village in a rebellion against her puritanical upbringing. By making a strenuous and obviously neurotic effort she manages to defy custom, convention, and morality; she does so with such vehemence and such obvious unhappiness, however, that she has become a standard type of character representing disillusioned and unsuccessful rebellion against the tyranny of the conscience.

The power of the conscience is believed to be derived from a portion of the original aggressive instincts which, instead of being directed outward to take destructive effect upon the environment, are converted into a sort of internal judge or king. Suppose a little tribe of people tried to establish themselves in a great unknown country; most of the adult males would be sent out as hunters and soldiers to fight with the elements in the surrounding country. A few would be retained at home, however, as policemen to enforce internal order. If we suppose that some of these policemen are in plain clothes, and hence unrecognized, we have a fair simile with which to compare the internal organization of the mind.

There are certain laws governing the activity of the conscience with which we have come to be familiar from clinical experience. One of them is that the ego must suffer in direct proportion to its externally directed destructiveness. It is as if that part of the destructive instinct retained within the ego had to carry on within the microcosmos of the personality an activity precisely comparable to that which the ego is directing toward the macrocosmos outside. If the individual directs an attack of a certain nature upon some person in the environment, the conscience, or super-ego, directs an attack of the same nature upon the ego. This formula is well known to us in social organization in the form of the *lex talionis,* the intuitive basis of all penal systems.

In the second place the ego has the difficult task of trying to adjust the strong instinctive demands of the personality not only to the possibilities afforded by the external world but to the dictates of this conscience. It has, for example, not only a man's hunger to deal with, and the fact that food is hard to find, but it must deal with the inward stipulation that certain foods that one finds may not be eaten. Now in this task of trying to adjust the demands of instinct, the demands of conscience, and the demands of reality, the ego finds some reality to be invincible, i.e., wishing will not change it; the instincts, likewise, are irresistible or at least relatively so. But the conscience can be traded with, and hence the ego devises all manner of ways in which to simplify the difficulties of its task and to mitigate its own sufferings.

Sometimes, however, the demands of the conscience are so great and so inexorable that there is no placating them. The relative power of the conscience, as well as the extent to which it may be bribed, varies greatly in different individuals and in the same individual under different circumstances. In melancholia, for example, the mental disease we were discussing a few pages back, there appears to be an enormous over-development of the conscience, so that one English psychiatrist (Glover) proposed that the disease should be called "chronic hyperplasia of the super-ego (conscience)." In this matter of conscience there is a wide divergence between the point of view of society in general and that of the psychiatrists. The world regards a highly conscientious man as a strong and admirable character. Hence people are sometimes a little shocked and disturbed to learn that psychiatrists regard the conscience of such a man as a neurotic stigma and incubus. "Why so?" they ask. "Because," we reply, "it makes inexorable demands upon an already over-burdened individual. This may result in many good deeds but they are done under an internal compulsion which robs them of their pleasure to the doer." "But what would you do?" they ask. "Would you have men throw away their consciences? Is not the term 'conscience-less' expressive of the menace of such a state?"

"No," we would reply. "In the first place no one can throw away his conscience. At best, he can only lose that overgrown part of it which refuses to be educated and makes unreasonable demands upon him. In the second place, to the extent that we can dispose of conscience, we can replace it with intelligence. This will commend itself to everyone as being, in the best sense of the word, more ethical. To refrain from a mean act or, for that matter, from a murder because it hurts our conscience is the weakest of all possible reasons; to refrain from it because there are more expedient and more sensible and more humane lines of behavior, denotes that one has, in that instance at least, attained conscious self-mastery, the greatest of man's achievements. And, finally, much evil is perpetrated in the name of conscience, because of its obtuseness, its cruelty, and its corruptibility: witness the savagery of conscientious Cotton Mather, John Brown Torquemada, "Bloody Mary," and many others.

One more fact or "law" about the conscience: a sense of guilt may arise from other than actual aggression; in the unconscious a wish to destroy is quite equivalent to the actual destruction with regard to exposing the ego to punishment. The Catholic Church recognizes this in demanding to know in the confessional even the *thoughts* of evil.

Dostoievski wrote a very famous illustration of this in *Brothers Karamazov* in which it will be recalled that Dmitri, who did not kill his father, nevertheless seemed to demand punishment for himself as if he had done so. He accumulated and displayed all sorts of circumstantially incriminating evidence. He put himself through the horrible torture of the trial and permitted himself to be sentenced to life-imprisonment, when he could easily have escaped it by the proper maneuvers in the courtroom. His brother, Ivan, was driven mad by the whole thing, and angrily denounced the court, saying that it was absurd for them to make so much over this affair, since everyone in the room was just as guilty as Dmitri. "Every one of you has wished for your father's death!" he cries to them. "Why do you persecute my brother, who has done no more than this?" But Dmitri knew that to have wished for his father's death as he had (he even went so far as to plan it) carried with it a burden of guilt almost as great as if he had indeed perpetrated the act.

Freud [20] has pointed out that it is a significant parallel that Dostoievski's own father was murdered by an unknown hand, and yet when Dostoievski himself was sentenced to prison for a crime of which he was innocent, he underwent terrific punishment without breaking down, probably because, like his character Dmitri, he suffered unconsciously from a sense of guilt with reference to his father's death and a corresponding need for the punishment. He not only

[20] Freud, Sigmund, "Dostojewski und die Vatertötung," *Gesammelte Schriften*, Vol. VIII and XII, Internationaler Psychoanalytischer Verlag, Wien, 1934.

did not kill his father but loved him and did not consciously want him to die; yet we know that in the unconscious it is as Ivan said. This is also the theme of the well-known tragedies of *Oedipus Rex* and *Hamlet*, and of many others since Sophocles, Aeschylus, and Shakespeare.

And so it is that one who nourishes murderous wishes also feels, at least unconsciously, a need for punishment of a corresponding sort. We see the truth of a statement made by Freud [21] many years ago that *many suicides are disguised murders*, not only because of the introjection which we discussed above, but for the reason that murder alone justifies in the unconscious the death penalty, even when both are acted out upon the self. In other words, melancholiacs very rarely kill anyone but themselves, although their driving motive is the wish to kill someone else.

The reader must be reminded that this wish to kill is usually unconscious; it may have been conscious once or occasionally and then have been repressed, disguised by a conscious attitude of love, protection, obedience. This, and the way in which the sense of guilt attached to the repressed emotion operates to determine the wish to die are well-illustrated in the following case of twice-averted suicide.

Mrs. Z. was a well-born Swedish woman whose father, a well-known lawyer and judge, was very autocratic. He sent his daughter to an expensive finishing school and then for a year's stay in Europe. Upon her return from abroad he insisted that she marry an old family friend, years her senior, who was even at that time dying of cancer. As always, she obeyed him without question.

Fifteen months later her husband died, leaving her a small fortune. However, although she had never professed to love her husband, she now became severely depressed. She developed the idea that *she* was very ill, demanded an operation, and obtained it! Following this she attempted suicide by turning on the gas in the kitchen but was discovered, taken to the hospital, and successfully revived.

She recovered and fell in love with another friend of her father's, also a lawyer, and also many years older than herself, and asked him to marry her which he finally did. Shortly after this her father died and she reacted to this with a second depression and a second attempt at suicide.

To one not familiar with psychiatric histories, this would appear to be the story of an unstable woman who over-

[21] Freud, Sigmund, *Collected Papers*, Vol. II, p. 220, London, 1933.

reacted with grief to the loss of loved ones. Careful study of the facts, however, supplies us with a better explanation of her suicidal urges. She felt very definitely that her marriage to her first husband had hastened his death. But even had this been correct, why should she have assumed the feeling of responsibility and guilt for it when it was well-known that she had married him at her father's insistence and not from her own desire? May we not suspect that her feeling that she had killed him was the expression of a wish? Such a wish might have come to anyone under such circumstances, and in this instance no doubt it was fortified by a deeper, more ancient death wish against the father whom she both loved and hated, hated because his autocracy had molded her life even to the point of forcing her into the tragic marriage. (A wish for someone's death is *unconsciously* equivalent, in determining conscience reactions, to the act of murder itself.) The feeling of guilt for the gratification of her death wishes accentuated by her inheritance of her husband's money brought about first of all a depression, then a compulsion to submit to surgical suffering, and finally, a more direct attempt at self-punishment by suicide. The suicide having been thwarted, she was impelled to relieve her sense of guilt by still another mechanism known technically as "undoing": she approached another father substitute and urged him to marry her, as if to say, "Please take me! Try me again. Let me repeat my relationship with a man without killing him. I will not be so destructive; I don't want you to die but I want to submit to you. Do with me as you like."

It happened, although I did not mention it above, that this second husband was a rather severe fellow, who unknowingly gratified her need for punishment in a mild but sufficient manner; with him she was very happy until her real father, the original object of her love but also of her deep unconscious resentment, died. This event revived again her sense of loss and at the same time her sense of guilt for her death-wishes; the latter impelled a repetition of the attempt at self-inflicted execution.

One depressed patient committed suicide the day after she had for the first time frankly expressed a long slumbering hostility for her mother in which the wish for her mother's death was more than implicit. Another patient attempted suicide after receiving a letter from his parents which particularly angered him. It is a technical comment of importance that psychotic patients strongly given to propensities of acting-out should be watched most carefully at such times as they apear to show clinical improvement with an increase in the outward expression of the hostilities so long repressed.

Such cases could be multiplied by any psychiatrist. There is, perhaps, a certain unexpected value in the less conclusive but more suggestive illustrations in the vivid and often succinct accounts of suicide given in the daily press. One lacks, of course, a clear view of the unconscious factors. But, on the other hand, one also lacks the complications of the analytic situation itself and sometimes the indications in the direction of analytic principles are extraordinarily clear. Consider, for example, the following suggestive account of a man who had made a business of killing others who finally turned his professional skill upon himself. The burden of guilt which such a man carries could not possibly be made more graphic.

CORONER SAYS EXECUTIONER KILLED SELF

Auburn, New York, February 23 (AP). The terse report of the coroner today clears the mystery surrounding the death of J. K. L., 55, former state executioner and long known as Auburn's "man of mystery."

"Death by suicide" were the cryptic words which Dr. W. E. W. used to report the finding of an autopsy. The retired executioner had been found dead in the cellar of his home yesterday.

The iron nerve which enabled H. calmly to send 141 men to their deaths in the electric chair during his career as executioner, stayed with him to the last, the physician's report indicated. Two wounds were found in the body, one in the left chest which, failing to bring instant death, was followed by another in the right temple.

—*Topeka Daily Capital*, Feb. 24, 1929.

Ossorgin illustrates something very similar in his beautiful novel, *Quiet Street*. Here the callous executioner becomes panicky at death threats aimed at himself, and actually succumbs to death as the result of an operation, to the recovery from which his body seemed unable to contribute.

THE PROBLEM OF HEREDITY IN SUICIDE

A circumstance of suicide frequently mentioned in newspaper reports and in popular discussions suggests a related problem which should be discussed at this point. The following is an example:

X., Kansas, January 30. (Special) News reaches here today of the suicide of M. N., 29, Professor of Agriculture in the Normal School at X., Nebraska. He was a graduate of the State University and had lived here until a few years ago. *His father committed suicide about six years ago.*

—*Topeka Daily Capital*, Jan. 21, 1932.

The question of suicide in families is one which has received almost no competent scientific investigation. Such newspaper accounts would indicate that in the popular mind the suicidal tendency is hereditary. In my own studies I have come upon several families in which it would certainly appear to be so. For example, one patient came to us at 61 on account of strong suicidal propensities which she had several times attempted to gratify. Three of the patient's sisters had killed themselves in an identical manner; the patient's mother, and the patient's mother's mother had also killed themselves in the same way. Moreover, the patient's mother was a twin and the twin brother had also killed himself!

In another instance, a highly-regarded family contained five sons and two daughters; the oldest son killed himself at 35, the youngest developed a depression and attempted suicide several times but finally died of other causes at 30, a third brother killed himself in a manner similar to that of his oldest brother, still another brother shot himself to death, and the oldest daughter took poison successfully at a party. Only two children remain living of this entire family.

I also have on file numerous instances where sisters or brothers have killed themselves. In one instance, three sisters killed themselves simultaneously.

Striking as these illustrations may be, there is no convincing scientific evidence that the suicidal impulse is hereditary and there is much psychoanalytic evidence to show that these cases of numerous suicides in one family may be explained on a psychological basis. Superficially there is the element of suggestion,[22] but deeper than this is the well-

[22] The method used is often identical and even the dates may correspond. The Countess of Cardigan, for example, is reported in the press to have struggled with suicidal impulses each year on the anniversary of her mother's suicide, remarking, "If I do not kill myself on this day, I know I shall have another year to live." Finally, on the eighth anniversary, at almost the same hour as her mother's suicide, Lady Cardigan succeeded in her efforts to kill herself. Even the most ardent believer in heredity would not expect the suicidal impulse to recur in annual cycles.

known fact that unconscious death wishes reach their highest development toward members of the family, and when a member of the family dies or kills himself, the unconscious death wishes of the other members of the family are unexpectedly gratified; this produces a sudden and overpoweringly strong wave of guilt feelings which replace the now gratified murder-wish. This wave may be so great and so overwhelming as to make it necessary for the culprit to be punished by death. Sometimes this is done, as every psychoanalyst knows, by dreams of being executed, hanged, killed in some other way, or sentenced to life imprisonment. In other instances, the element of suggestion points the way for the actual self-infliction of the death sentence.

Furthermore, in the case of suicide on the part of several siblings we cannot but suspect the existence of a parallel psychic structure resulting from a common background to account for the parallel behavior. Of course no two individuals, even twins, are exactly alike or have exactly the same environment but even widely-separated brothers (and sisters) can show similar effects of the treatment of a pathological father.

For these reasons, therefore, we can say that it is unnecessary to invoke heredity for the explanation of multiple familial suicide.

MEANING OF METHODS USED

In connection with the way in which the need for punishment and the wish to be killed is gratified by suicide we must give some consideration to the significance of the methods used. It is well agreed that, statistically, men appear to prefer shooting and women the taking of poison, gas, or water (drowning). These are obviously related to the masculine and feminine roles in life, i.e., active aggressive and passive receptive.

Very suggestive is the consideration of some of the more unusual methods. These illustrate clearly the need for punishment and frequently suggest by the form of punishment particular erotic values attached to certain symbolic acts. The following excerpt from an article[23] published thirty years ago cannot be excelled for clear exposition of these phenomena:

Nothing is more surprising in the records of suicide than the extraordinary variety and novelty of the methods to which man

[23] Kennan, George, "Problems of Suicide," *McClure's Magazine*, Vol. XXXI, p. 227.

has resorted in his efforts to escape from the suffering and mis-fortunes of life. One would naturally suppose that a person who had made up his mind to commit suicide would do so in the easiest, most convenient, and least painful way; but the litera-ture of the subject proves conclusively that hundreds of suicides, every year, take their lives in the most difficult, agonizing, and extraordinary ways; that there is hardly a possible or conceivable method of self-destruction that has not been tried. When I clipped from a newspaper my first case of self-cremation with kerosense and a match, I regarded it as rather a remarkable and unusual method of taking life; but I soon discovered that self-cremation is comparatively common.

. . . I have well-authenticated cases in which men or women have committed suicide by hanging themselves, or taking poison, in the top of high trees; by throwing themselves upon swiftly revolving circular saws; by exploding dynamite in their mouths; by thrusting red-hot pokers down their throats; by hugging red-hot stoves; by stripping themselves naked and allowing them-selves to freeze to death on winter snowdrifts out of doors, or on piles of ice in refrigerator cars; by lacerating their throats on barbed wire fences; by drowning themselves head down-ward in barrels; by suffocating themselves head downward in chimneys; by diving into white-hot coke ovens; by throwing themselves into craters of volcanoes; by shooting themselves with ingenious combinations of a rifle and a sewing machine; by strangling themselves with their hair; by swallowing poisonous spiders; by piercing their hearts with corkscrews and darning needles; by cutting their throats with handsaws and sheep-shears; by hanging themselves with grape vines; by swallowing strips of underclothing and buckles of suspenders; by forcing teams of horses to tear their heads off; by drowning themselves in vats of soft soap; by plunging into retorts of molten glass; by jumping into slaughter-house tanks of blood; by decapitation with homemade guillotines; and by self-crucifixion.

Once upon a time such extraordinary methods as these would have been regarded only as indicative of the insane nature of the act of suicide, but that was when we still ig-norantly believed that so-called insane behavior had no meaning. The work of Freud and, in this particular direc-tion, the work also of Jung[24] have long since sharpened the eyes and the understanding of psychiatrists to the meaning-ful nature of every word and act of the psychotic patient. Psychotic behavior is unintelligible to the uninitiated partly because it is so frank, and so clearly and undisguisedly re-veals the content of the unconscious. There are, of course,

[24] Jung, Carl G., *The Psychology of Dementia Praecox,* translated by Frederick Peterson and A. A. Brill, Washington, Nervous and Mental Dis-ease Publishing Co. Monograph Series, rev. ed., 1937.

other reasons, one of which is the more archaic type of symbolism used. All human speech is based upon the use of symbolism, but for the most part the symbols are arbitrary and mechanically standardized, whereas the language and behavior of the psychotic patient makes use of more primitive symbols which are unfamiliar in spite of their universality.

We have no right then to dismiss the significance of a particular method of committing suicide as being meaningless. In the light of clinical experience we know with a fair degree of definiteness what some of these symbols, and hence these methods, mean. Let us take, for example, the case mentioned above of suicide by hugging a red-hot stove. Such an act suggests, in addition to the motives which determine the self-destructive act, the existence of a pathologically intense wish to be loved, a feeling of such utter inner coldness that embracing a red-hot stove is like a final climax of destructive satisfaction, as if to say, "At last my heart is warm." One thinks of the humorous popular poem by Service, "The Cremation of Sam McGee," or of the popular song hit of some years ago, "Turn on the Heat." The clinician who works with neurotic patients is so familiar with this bitter complaint that the world is a frigid place that he will find this less incredible than the practical physician who is more sensitive to external suffering than to internal suffering.

Or again, suicide by self-crucifixion is a quite obvious identification with Jesus, and such Messianic aspirations in less extreme form are not regarded as anything but normal. The teaching in many churches is that one should try to be as much as possible like Jesus and in some forms of religious worship this is carried out as in the case of Los Hermanos Penitentes of New Mexico, to the extent of a pseudo-crucifixion of the most pious member of the sect. He is fastened to a cross and raised. It is really only a short step from this to a self-appointed and self-inflicted martyrdom of the same sort.

Plunging into molten glass, vats of soap, the craters of volcanoes, etc., represents of course, only more dramatic and more painful forms of drowning. The significance of drowning fantasies was one of the earliest of psychoanalytic discoveries, not only because of its frequency as a form of suicide, both contemplated and consummated, but because it is a common fantasy in disguised and undisguised form in the mental life of many people. When subjected to psychoanalytic investigation such fantasies seem to relate quite definitely to the wish to return to the undisturbed bliss of intra-uterine existence, a kind of reversal of the first great experience of birth. In my book, *The Human Mind,* I give numerous illustrations of this fantasy from the Bible, from poetry, from the casual conversation of the man on the street, from the church hymnal, from events in the newspaper, from patients in the sanitarium, and from the writings of Shelley and of Freud.

If the question be asked why the suicide chooses for the drowning such a horrible place, we need only remember that such fantasies may be accompanied by a strong sense of guilt and there is a well-known (concomitant) conception of the womb, or entry into the womb, as being something terrible. This we recognize in the nature of the mythological representations of entering the life hereafter —the dog Cerberus, the terrible river Styx, purgatory, and so on.

In this connection one recalls the extraordinary career of Harry Houdini (Ehrich Weiss) who was particularly fond of extricating himself from apparently inextricable situations, "straightjackets, all manner of manacles, chains, handcuffs, prison cells, chests, hampers, glass boxes, roll-top desks, and even iron boilers. With his arms thoroughly secured he leaped from bridges; suspended head downward by block and tackle he loosened himself from meshes of constricting apparatus. He allowed himself to be chained and buried in six feet of earth, to be locked in steel vaults, to be nailed in huge packing cases. Once, breaking free after an endeavor lasting over an hour, he said: 'The pain, torture, agony, and misery of that struggle will forever live in my mind.' His variations on the escape act were endless, nothing being too bizarre, tedious, or difficult so long as the principles of a constraining force were present." [25] His most dramatic escapes were from coffins buried underground and from chains while under water. Coupled with this, unconsciously, is the fact that he had an extraordinary attachment for his mother[26] which strongly affected his en-

[25] See Bragman, Louis J., "Houdini Escapes from Reality," *The Psychoanalytic Review,* Oct., 1929, p. 404.

[26] In his diary he wrote such things as this:

"Getting my Sainted Mother's letters ready to have transcribed so I can put them in book form. . . . Am having Darling Mother's letters written in good German on typewriter so that I can read them easily. Many a bitter tear I am shedding. In the entire lot of letters which I have saved since 1900, each is a love story, a prayer to God to protect his children, that we should be good human beings. . . . Had terrible spell after show on account of my Darling Mother."

tire life. One can here see the applicability of the above explanation. On the anniversary of his mother's death in 1925 he inserted in his diary a copy of Masefield's poem to his mother:

> In the dark womb where I began
> My mother's life made me a man.
> Through all the months of human birth
> Her beauty fed my common earth.
> I cannot see, nor breathe, nor stir,
> But through the death of some of her.

(From "C. L. M." in The Poems and Plays of John Masefield, Macmillan, 1918, p. 111.)

Bragman aptly remarks that "almost every stunt staged by Houdini represented a form of pseudo-suicide."

To return to the meaning of other methods, allowing oneself to be run over by a truck or steam-roller or train is so closely analogous to submitting oneself in a passive way to an irresistible power that it may serve as clear and further evidence of the validity of the second component of suicide discussed above (the wish to be killed).

Finally, because of its analogy with the taking of poison and shooting oneself, we should consider the significance of the methods represented by the example of thrusting a red-hot poker down the throat. Every physician wonders why some patients who wish to kill themselves with poison do so with such an uncertainly lethal but certainly painful method as drinking phenol. One of these patients calmly drank raw hydrochloric acid; it was vomited, of course; he tried repeatedly thereafter to accomplish suicide with this agent, diluting it with ginger ale. This resulted in a long period of surgical treatment for esophageal stricture resulting from the acid burns, in which it was necessary painfully to dilate the esophagus daily with a bougie. So long as the painful (intra-oral) treatment was continued, he seemed quite cheerful and in good spirits, refusing any psychoanalytic treatment as unnecessary. He was finally discharged, re-established his home and business, and then, about a year later, committed suicide successfully by eating fire-crackers!

These methods are very probably related to strong oral cravings, the origin of which we have already discussed, i.e., a great intensification of the erotic function of the mouth, connected with a pathological exaggeration of the need for love received in the infantile way, i.e., through the mouth. Those familiar with Freud's *Three Contributions to the Theory of Sex* will recognize the psychological relationship of these methods to persistent thumb-sucking in the child or fellatio in the adult. The same mouth which craves the forbidden pleasure with such terrific intensity is the locus for the experiencing of a correspondingly great punishment. A child whose mother scrubs out his mouth with soap because he used profanity, can well imagine that should he indulge in even more forbidden oral fantasies or activities such as occur to every adolescent, the punishment, were he detected, would be not less terrible than to have his throat burned out with fire or acid.

This preoccupation with fantasies of sexual pleasure by mouth always seems shocking and incredible to those not familiar with the intimate fantasy life of neurotic patients. Even doctors who know their patients quite well cannot believe that they would entertain such repulsive thoughts. It must be remembered that the patients themselves are more shocked than anyone else to discover them. It is exactly this terrific repugnance and the coincident fear of punishment that causes so much emotional tension in a patient whose early oral training was in some way defective or over-conditioned so as to predispose him, without his conscious knowledge, to such wishes. When such a conflict becomes unbearable it may, as in the cases cited, show itself in this terrible dramatic representation of the gratification and punishment *per os*.

Just what all these methods may have meant in full detail to these particular individuals we shall never know, but their similarity to neurotic fantasies and dreams with which we are very familiar in psychoanalysis leaves little doubt as to their general significance and reinforces what we have said as to the motives of suicide, viz., that it represents in one act a murder and a propitiation. We notice, however, that there is some new element in this murder and in the propitiatory submission, an element which is less violent and more romantic. This curious element, which upon analysis will prove to be far more important than might at first seem to be the case, is the erotic element.

THE EROTIC ELEMENT

Just as destructive activities directed toward another person become softened or even entirely cloaked by love, so the passive submission to violence may become, as we say, erotized, i.e., may offer certain opportunities for the constructive or love tendencies to develop and fuse with the aggressive tendencies, partially or completely. Erotization simply means, as we saw before, that these pleasure-giving constructive qualities are added or super-imposed. They may reach the point of partial fusion which appears as conscious sexual satisfaction in suffering. Obtaining pleasure from pain is technically called "masochism," a clinical phenomenon which has been the subject of a great many psychological investigations.[27] It is well known that some people like to be beaten and that this is accompanied by unmistakable evidences of sexual enjoyment, but it is difficult to imagine that even such individuals would care to have their pleasurable pain pushed to the extremity of being beaten to death. Nancy Sykes (of *Oliver Twist*) did this, however, and we all know others like her. Some of the martyrs of old are reported to have expressed the utmost joy and pleasure at the opportunity to die and to die in the most bloody and painful methods imaginable.

This can only be understood if we remember the principle that where the destructive tendencies lead, the constructive tendencies characterized by love and erotic feelings will follow.

One of these devices for increasing the pleasurable satisfactions in submitting oneself to the attack of others or in submitting oneself to a self-inflicted attack depends upon what we call exhibitionism. Exhibitionism is a morbid satisfaction in showing off before people, and while it is usually interpreted as an aggressive act toward people and is resented on that account, it is in the deepest analysis a passive pleasure. It represents, as it were, an extreme and dramatic submission to the eyes of the beholders—not aggressively, but masochistically. "For the thrill and satisfaction which my surrender to death may give you, I submit myself thus." And so the need for punishment is gratified dramatically and accompanied—softened—by the narcissistic pleasure of showing off and affecting other people's emotions.

Rare, indeed, are such clear-cut illustrations of this principle as the following:

HE "ILLUSTRATES" A SUICIDE

PARTY GUEST, ON DARE, DRINKS POISON SUCH AS KILLS GIRL

T., Penn., January 1, 1930. (AP) L. M., 26, died today from the effects of poison taken on a dare at a New Year's party here last night. Guests were discussing the recent suicide of Miss

[27] Freud, Rado, Horney, *et al.*

E. V., 19, when M. went to the kitchen and obtained a bottle of the same poison the girl had swallowed.

Reappearing among the guests, he asked if anyone dared him to drink it. Thinking he had placed water in the bottle and was joking, a member of the party called the dare and M. drained the bottle.

Oscar Wilde[28] understood this clearly in his *The Master:*

And when the darkness came over the earth, Joseph of Arimathea, having lighted a torch of pinewood, passed down from the hill into the valley. For he had business in his own home.

And kneeling on the flint stones of the Valley of Desolation he saw a young man who was naked and weeping. His hair was the color of honey and his body was a white flower; but he had wounded his body with thorns, and on his hair he had set ashes as a crown.

And he who had great possessions said to the young man who was naked: "I do not wonder that your sorrow is so great, for surely He was a just man."

And the young man answered: "It is not for Him that I am weeping, but for myself. I, too, have changed water into wine, and I have healed the leper and given sight to the blind. I have walked upon the waters, and from the dwellers in the tombs I have cast out devils. I have fed the hungry in the desert where there was no food, and I have raised the dead from their narrow houses; and at my bidding, and before a great multitude of people, a barren fig-tree withered away. All things that this man has done I have done also. *And yet they have not crucified me.*"

Closely related to the exhibitionistic motive in suicide is its connection with masturbation. It has been observed that suicidal attempts sometimes follow the interruption of an individual's habitual auto-erotic activities. This interruption may come in the form of a prohibition from external forces or from the person's own conscience. In either case the mechanisms by which the suicide is precipitated are the same: the masturbation occasions a heavy burden of guilt, because in the unconscious mind it always represents an aggression against someone. This guilt demands punishment and as long as the auto-erotic practices are continued, the punishment is bound up in the satisfaction, since masturbation is imagined by many to be a grave danger to health, and to one's life both in this world and the hereafter. Such a feeling of danger and desperate risk increases the masochistic pleasure in the deed. But when the process is interrupted the self-punitive and erotic satisfactions are abruptly terminated while the aggressions are stimulated by

[28] Wilde, Oscar, *Fairy Tales and Poems in Prose,* Modern Library, 1927.

the prohibition imposed. The self-destructive tendencies are then turned on the self, robbed of some of their erotic mitigation, and suicide is resorted to, not only because it represents a more violent form of sexual preoccupation with the self, but also because it affords a device for the punishment of those whom the victim feels to be responsible for his deprivation. As in childhood when his pleasure was interfered with by his parents, so now the individual can say, "You see where your hardheartedness, your prohibitions, your lack of love have driven me." The punishment accomplished on oneself (for the indulgence) is thus at the same time the punishment of the supposed interferers with this indulgence.[29] This aggressive sexual concern of the self with the self is the essence of masturbatory satisfaction and since this, as we have seen, is also true of suicide, we may regard one as sometimes representing a substitute for the other.

The psychoanalytic view of masturbation is that it is self-destructive, not in the ways ordinarily assumed, but in the sense that it represents a preoccupation with the self, based on aggressive feelings toward others.

An ingenious suggestion of Georg Groddeck[30] led me to the following thought as to the relation of the story of Creation and the conception of the life and death instincts. "It was to divert his love from his self-centered investment, his seeking only for his own pleasure, that he (man) was given a helpmate . . . someone who helps him . . . to find part of his pleasure elsewhere than his own body."

Of course Groddeck does not mean to say that Eve was created to save Adam. But he does raise the question as to why, from the philosophical standpoint, there should be two sexes in the world. The biologists have their explanations for this; the psychologists are entitled to theirs. From the standpoint of our theory of the instincts it may well be that the differentiation exists in order to permit the development of the life instinct through its cultivation in object investment—an object sufficiently similar to the self to be acceptable and sufficiently dissimilar to be complementary. This simply means that for the brief period that we love (other than ourselves) we live—which corresponds with

[29] This point was made by Stekel in a discussion of suicide before the Vienna Psychoanalytic Society in June, 1910, to which Freud and others also contributed.

[30] Groddeck, Georg, *Book of the Id*, Nervous and Mental Disease Publishing Co., 1926.

astonishing precision to numerous sayings attributed to Jesus and Plato.

In connection with masturbation as a factor in suicide we should not fail to mention those occasional suicides which are directly related to the fear of *examination*. It is well known that many people have an exaggerated and neurotic fear of examinations. This fear in the adolescent or in the school child can be traced in many instances as first suggested by Sadger[31] to fears of questioning concerning certain habits. Sadger pointed out that some suicides of school children incident to an enormous fear of examinations were undoubtedly due to the fear that their masturbation would be detected. He narrates a very representative case.[32]

There is still another way in which the life instinct finds satisfaction, paradoxically, in self-inflicted death. It depends upon that deadliest of erotic investments, narcissism. To kill oneself instead of being executed or slain by fate, is to retain for oneself the illusion of being omnipotent, since one is even by and in the act of suicide, master of life and death. Such omnipotence fantasies, for all that they have been extolled by poets and schizophrenics, are none the less to be regarded as infantile relics. They presuppose or assume the certainty of a future life, a reincarnation—so that such a suicide is not, in the conscious interpretation of the victim, a real death. The same dereistic fantasy is operative when suicide is elected to avoid death at the hands of others, or to demonstrate courage, devotion, intrepidity, etc. The narcissism already discussed under exhibitionistic suicide is here abetted by vain fantasy.

3. THE WISH TO DIE

Anyone who has sat by the bedside of a patient dying from a self-inflicted wound and listened to pleadings that the physician save a life, the destruction of which had only a few hours or minutes before been attempted, must have been impressed by the paradox that one who has wished to kill himself does not wish to die!

The popular assumption is that having yielded to a sudden impulse the patient has "changed his mind." It

[31] Sadger, J., "Concerning Fears of Examinations and Dreams of Examinations," *Internationale Zeitschrift fur Psychoanalyse*, Vol. VI, pp. 140-50, 1920.

[32] Cited in the author's *The Human Mind*.

leaves unanswered why the act should have brought about this change. The pain is usually not great. The prospect of death is actually less than before the attempt since "while there is life there is hope." One gets the impression that for such people the suicidal attempt is sometimes a kind of insincere histrionics and that their capacity for dealing with reality is so poorly developed that they proceed as if they could actually kill themselves and not die.[33] We have reason to believe that a child has some such conception of death—that it is a "going away," and that from such goings-away there is often a returning. Indeed the concept of a future life which is so real to many people is probably based upon this identification of death and going away. (So similar, as Freud pointed out, to the joyous glee manifested by the child with whom one plays peek-a-boo.)

One must distinguish between the *conscious* wish to die (or wish not to die) and the unconscious wish to die, the former being, as we have seen, the resultant of numerous co-operating and conflicting vectors. One suspects an unconscious wish *not* to die—or more correctly the absence of the wish to die—in the very frequent attempts at suicide which turn out unsuccessfully because of faulty technique. Many reports of such cases appear in the newspapers, e.g.:

Mr. Q. R. S., of Los Angeles, first tried "to hang himself from a chandelier. The chandelier came down. He cut his throat and still lived. He slashed his wrists and still lived. He opened veins at his elbows. When two detectives and a doctor came he was pronounced dead. Then Q. R. S. jumped out of bed, began fighting all three."

—*Time*, Nov. 17, 1930.

In Fort Lee, N.J., O. P. wrote two farewell notes, climbed up on the railing of a bridge, ready to jump 250 feet to death. As he teetered, Policeman C. K. shouted: "Get down or I'll shoot." Down got O. P.

—*Time*, July 16, 1934.

In Denver, T. S. burst out laughing when a $1 pistol he had bought to kill himself exploded, sent a bullet bouncing harmlessly against his chest. Calmed by police, T. S. announced he would try to go on living.

—*Time*, Dec. 7, 1936.

[33] Probably, as I suggested in the first chapter, this is always true—but, in some persons, it appears to have been almost consciously dealt with. My psychoanalytic colleague, N. Lionel Blitzsten, of Chicago, has emphasized this quality of conveying to the observer an impression of insincerity and histrionics in certain types of depression for which he has coined the term "Amphithymia." See Blitzsten, N. L., "Amphithymia," *Arch. Neurol. & Psychiat.*, Nov., 1936, pp. 1021-36.

Powerful self-destructive tendencies with conspicuous aggressive and punitive elements which were thwarted in every case by what appears to be a comparative weakness of the wish to die, are indicated in this account of the poet William Cowper, taken from Forbes Winslow's *Anatomy of Suicide* published in 1840, which so closely corresponds in general with the behavior of certain types of patients familiar to every psychiatrist that I cite it at length.

A friend procured him the situation of reading clerk to the House of Lords, forgetting that the nervous shyness which made a public exhibition of himself "mortal poison" would render it impossible for him ever to discharge the duties of his office. This difficulty presented itself to the mind of the poet, and gloom instantly enveloped his faculties. At his request, his situation was changed to that of clerk of the journals; but even before he could be installed into office he was threatened with a public examination before the House. This made him completely wretched; he had not resolution to decline what he had not strength to do; the interest of his friend and his own reputation and want of support, pressed him forward to an attempt which he knew from the first could never succeed. In this miserable state, like Goldsmith's traveler 'to stop too fearful, and too faint to go,' he attended every day for six months at the office where he was to examine the journals in preparation for his trust. His feelings were like those of a man at the place of execution, every time he entered the office door; and he only gazed mechanically at the books, without drawing from them the least portion of information he wanted. As the time of his examination approached, his agony became more and more intense; he hoped and believed that madness would come to relieve him; he attempted also to make up his mind to suicide though his conscience bore stern testimony against it; he could not by any argument persuade himself that it was right; but his desperation prevailed, and he procured from an apothecary the means of self-destruction. On the day before his public appearance was to be made, he happened to notice a letter in the newspaper which to his disordered mind seemed like a malignant libel on himself. He immediately threw down the paper and rushed into the fields determined to die in a ditch; but the thought struck him that he might escape from the country. With the same violence he proceeded to make hasty preparations for his flight; but while he was engaged in packing his portmanteau his mind changed, and he threw himself into a coach, ordering the man to drive to the Tower wharf, intending to throw himself into the river, and not reflecting that it would be impossible to accomplish this purpose in that public spot, unobserved. On approaching the water, he found a porter seated upon some goods; he then returned to the coach and drove home to his lodgings in the Temple. On the way he attempted to drink the

65

laudanum, but as often as he raised it, a convulsive agitation of his frame prevented its reaching his lips; and thus, regretting the loss of the opportunity, but unable to avail himself of it, he arrived half dead with anguish at his apartments. He then closed the door and threw himself on the bed with the laudanum near him, trying to lash himself up to the deed; but a voice within seemed constantly to forbid it; and as often as he extended his hand to the poison, his fingers were contracted and held back by spasms. At this time some of the inmates of the place came in, but he concealed his agitations; and as soon as he was left alone, a change came over him, and so detestable did the deed appear, that he threw away the laudanum and dashed the phial to pieces. The rest of the day was spent in heavy insensibility, and at night he slept as usual; but on waking at three in the morning, he took his penknife and laid with his weight upon it, the point being directed toward his heart. It was broken, and would not penetrate. At day-break he rose, and passing a strong garter around his neck, fastened it to the frame of his bed. This gave way with his weight; but on securing it to the door he was more successful, and remained suspended until he had lost all consciousness of existence. After a time the garter broke, and he fell to the floor, so that his life was saved; but the conflict had been greater than his reason could endure. He felt a contempt for himself not to be expressed or imagined. Whenever he went into the street, it seemed as if every eye flashed upon him with indignation and scorn. He felt as if he had offended God so deeply that his guilt could never be forgiven, and his whole heart was filled with pangs of tumultuous despair.

And what of those who, like the poets and philosophers, are convinced of the desirability of death yet cannot bring themselves to endure killing (themselves) or being killed? Leopardi, for example, "the greatest poet of modern Italy, who longed for Death in exquisite rhymes ever since he was a boy, was the first to fly in abject terror from cholera-stricken Naples. Even the great Montaigne, whose calm meditations on Death are enough to make him immortal, bolted like a rabbit when the peste broke out in Bordeaux." [34] All the pessimists, from Schopenhauer down, have been convinced of the desirability of death, yet could not escape the necessity of living on.[35]

[34] Quoted from Axel Munthe's *The Story of San Michele*, preface of American edition, Dutton, 1929. This preoccupation by poets and many adolescents with thoughts of death is referred to by A. A. Brill ("The Death Instinct in Relation to Normal and Abnormal Life," *Medical Leaves*, 1937, pp. 18-24) who recalls Bryant's *Thanatopsis* and poems by Goethe, Byron, Shelley, Keats, and Poe.

[35] A study made in Breslau, Germany, a few years ago showed that subsequent to the World War, attempted suicide had increased much more

Scientific studies have been made which would indicate that the consciousness of a wish to die is exceedingly widespread.[36] It is often particularly obvious in mental sickness, especially in that form of which Freud [37] said of the sufferer:

> . . . he has a keener eye for the truth. . . . When in his exacerbation of self-criticism he describes himself as petty, egoistic, dishonest, lacking in independence, one whose sole aim has been to hide the weaknesses of his own nature, for all we know it may be that he has come very near to self-knowledge; we can only wonder why a man must become ill before he can discover truth of this kind.

Such patients, especially those of superior intelligence and milder grade of affliction, will often marshal almost unanswerable arguments for the desirability of dying. They will point out with a passionate eloquence and with flawless logic, that life is hard, bitter, futile, and hopeless; that it entails more pain than pleasure; that there is no profit or purpose in it for them and no conceivable justification for their living on. I quote from one of my patients who wrote down some of her bitter reflections during a period when she was so melancholy as to necessitate her constant confinement and surveillance:

> Do not ask me why I should like to die. In a more energetic mood I would defy you to tell me why I should live, but now I only wonder, and even wonder is difficult when one has a preconceived conviction in favor of death.

> Objectively speaking, or at least so attempting, I am deluded but I am much distressed by the delusions I have and I am at a loss to know where delusion ends and reality begins. I live in a world where delusion leers in my face under a horrid mask which seems to me to hide reality.

---

than accomplished suicide. One might postulate that the Germans—as well as many others in the World War—had had their fill of death, vicariously. The abundance of it on all sides stimulated a greater-than-average resistance to the death instinct in favor of the life instinct—or love. The latter, as we shall see, is responsible not only for sexual activity, which was also increased in the years following the Great War, but is still closely linked up in the desire to kill and be killed, which as we have suggested, are important components of the suicidal act. We should expect *attempts* at suicide, therefore, to be more frequent, and frustration of these attempts—in the interests of self-preservation—also more frequent. This corresponds precisely with W. Oppler's findings ("Increase of Attempted Suicide and Their Reasons," *Archiv für Psychiatrie und Nervenkrankheiten*, Oct. 8, 1927, p. 95; Jan. 28, 1928, p. 335.

[36] Cavan, Ruth Shonle, *Suicide*, University of Chicago Press, 1928. Bromberg, W. and Schilder, P., "Death and Dying; A Comparative Study of the Attitudes and Mental Reactions Toward Death and Dying," *The Psychoanalytic Review*, Vol. XX, p. 133, 1933.

[37] Freud, Sigmund, *Mourning and Melancholia, Collected Works*, 1925, Vol. IV, p. 156, London.

I find no encouraging successes in recognition to lead me on to more strenuous effort. Far rather would I turn my back on such a world and mingle with the earth's insentient elements, to share no whit of responsibility for its ghoulish monstrosities.

The ego which once satisfied me seems now so paltry that I despise myself for being duped. An ego so useless as mine, without value to myself or others, might better drop from the world and make its last graceful gesture in a series of dimpling ripples in the surface of a river into which it might sink with a delicious finality.

Is this conscious wish for death ever an undisguised expression of the death instinct? I think not. Ernest Jones[38] says: "With the milder forms of cyclothymia we may often make the interesting observation that the patient in his depressed mood has a vivid sense of now being more normal, of perceiving life as it really is, and of recognizing that in his gayer mood he was merely being influenced by various illusions that distorted his perception of reality. Nevertheless, deep analysis constantly shows that even the philosophic pessimism about life is bound up with internal inhibitions of enjoyment and self-content which, from their origin and fate after analysis, can only be regarded as artefacts in the evolution of the individual."

The death instinct is probably much more evident in the activities of daredevils than in the pessimistic musings of the melancholy patients and philosophers. As Alexander points out, nothing else can so well explain the pleasure of mountain climbers,[39] automobile racers, building scalers in

[38] Jones, Ernest, "The Concept of a Normal Mind," *Our Neurotic Age,* ed. by Samuel D. Schmalhausen, Farrar and Rinehart, 1932.

[39] This refers, of course, not to mountain climbing in the popular sense, but to the death-defying ascents enthusiastically partaken in by members of numerous European and American clubs organized for that purpose. That this has taken some hold on popular imagination is apparent from the many magazine articles concerning it which have appeared within the last few years. One of these ascribes the increasing tendency to take incredible risks to the effects of the World War:

"Now [after the war] the typical climber was a boy of eighteen or nineteen, lean-faced and too grim-looking for his age. You saw that he was too young to have been in battles, but you knew that he had been through the war. He looked at the starvation around him and decided that there was but a meager future for his generation of youth. He acquired a fatalistic outlook on life, and as he saw little of beauty to strive toward, he devoted himself instead to the cultivation of hardness and danger [i.e., death].

". . . The essence of climbing is that, like life, it should be dangerous. He believes that the greatest satisfaction comes to those who not only climb to the limit of their capacity but, on occasion, are ready to take risks beyond that limit. As one of their spokesmen has put it: 'In the sport of climbing, it is worth while to stake one's life consciously, deliberately and meritoriously.'" (Muller, Edwin, "It's Foolish to Get Killed," *Saturday Evening Post,* June 9, 1934.)

exposing themselves unnecessarily to great dangers.[40] Sometimes this impulse to defy death becomes an outstanding character trait.[41] "The narcissistic gratification derived from one's powers of achievement may indeed play a part here but no one will fail to see the impulse, completely independent of this . . . to play with death, to expose one's life to serious risks . . . something like a fore-pleasure . . . to the ultimate gratification of the death instinct." [42]

It is my own view that we may also interpret as some evidence for the activity of the death instinct the observation that the physiological body-processes appear to be capable of acting either for or against the personality as a whole. The phenomenon designated by Freud as "somatic compliance" we may think of as a kind of biological acceptance of the instinctual tendencies as modified or directed by the psyche. One frequently sees such a thing as is illustrated by a case studied by Dr. Catherine Bacon of Chicago. This patient's conscious self-destructive activities went only so far as scratching herself with the deliberate intent of causing a skin infection, with the expressed hope of death. This is common in malingering. A patient of mine purposely sought draughty places to sit in, hoping to catch pneumonia and die. But what determines whether or not these infections shall prove fatal? Can we assume with the bacteriologists that it is entirely a matter of quantitative relationships between virulence and resistance or, in other words, mere chance? The possibility is that such infections become serious in just those cases

[40] What more dramatic illustration of this could be found than the incredibly hazardous (and fatal) balloon expedition of Salomon Andrée toward the North Pole—from whose diary I take these lines:

"I cannot deny that all three of us are dominated by a feeling of pride. We think we can well face death, having done what we have done. Is not the whole thing, perhaps, the expression of an extremely strong sense of individuality which cannot bear the thought of living and dying like a man in the ranks, forgotten by coming generations? Is this ambition!

"The rattling of the guide lines in the snow and the flapping of the sails are the only sounds heard except the whining of the basket." (See Andrée, The Record of a Tragic Adventure, by George P. Putnam, Harcourt, Brace, 1930, and particularly Russell Owen's review of it in the New York Times for Nov. 16, 1930, under the significant caption of Andrée, Who Dared the Impossible.)

[41] See for example the account of Mark Ridge (Time, March 19, 1934) who insisted upon testing a "stratosphere suit" he had designed by having himself shut in a steel tank packed with dry ice at a temperature of −100° F. "Daredevil Ridge, 28, has long been willing to risk Death for Science." Of course more discreet and no less courageous examples of this fill the pages of medical history but in these instances the benefits to society outweigh the purely autonomous impulse to take a long chance with death.

[42] Alexander, Franz, "The Need for Punishment and the Death Instinct," International Journal of Psychoanalysis, April-July, 1929, p. 256.

where there are strongly active self-destructive tendencies, of which there may or may not be other detectable evidence. It is possible that the available strength of the death instinct determines this biological acceptance of the extraneous opportunities for self-destruction.

There is another straw in the wind which I wish to mention. It has been suggested that the wish for death may be only another disguise for the frequently observed phenomenon commonly interpreted as birth fantasies or, more accurately, a desire to return to the womb. Suicide by drowning is, as I have said above, supposed to be particularly clear in its symbolic suggestion of this tendency. I think it is not impossible, however, that this interpretation is an exact inversion and that birth fantasies and the various phenomena interpreted as a desire to return to the peace of the womb may be only pictorial representations of what, at the deepest level, is the unconscious wish for death.

The whole theory of a death instinct and therefore also "the wish to die" element in suicide is only a hypothesis in contrast to the demonstrated facts of the existence of the other two elements. It is interesting, however, to speculate as to its precise relationship to the phenomenon of suicide.

To fully account for the clinical facts, we are obliged to postulate an undifferentiated portion of the original stream of self-destructive energy ("death-instinct") separate from that which has been converted, on the one hand, into externally directed aggression in the service of self-preservation and, on the other, into the formation of conscience. We may further assume, then, that this undifferentiated remnant of self-destructive energy finally accomplishes the death of the (normal) individual by gradual emergence from the state of latency to which it is (was) temporarily confined by the activities of the life instincts. In a person who commits suicide, on the other hand, it suddenly bursts its bonds, springs into power and puts an immediate end to the existence of the individual. Such a turn of affairs must be regarded as exceptional, accomplished only in the face of some relative weakness of the life instinct, i.e., some deficiency in the capacity for developing love, since it is the function of love (the erotic instinct) to convert destructive tendencies into measures of self-defense and socially useful adaptations, or into conscience. Gradually, to be sure, all these devices fail and death wins; but sometimes it threatens to win prematurely, aided often by incomplete or inefficient functioning of the neutralizing devices of love. In these cases, as we shall see in the chapters to follow, it is possible to purchase temporary immunity by sacrifice.

One finds an analogous illustration (which possibly depends upon some deep vitalistic parallelism) in the way in which vegetation develops and spreads, converting the hard and lifeless substances of the inorganic soil into soft and beautiful tissues, at the same time preserving this soil from the devastating erosion and dissolution to which it is otherwise doomed. While it grows and thrives, the vegetation can absorb and harness the elements of earth, air, and water and convert them into this temporary fruit. But sooner or later the inorganic elements win; winds erode and waters inundate, so that the nurturers of life become its destroyers. These inorganic substances destroy not only the vegetation, but as every farmer knows to his sorrow, they destroy even themselves; the soil washes away, moisture evaporates, air and sterile sand alone remain.

THREE / *Recapitulation*

It has been my purpose in this first section to make the following points:

First, that the destructiveness in the world cannot all be ascribed to fate and the forces of nature, but must be in part laid at the door of man himself.

Second, that this destructiveness of mankind appears to include a large amount of self-destructiveness, in paradoxical contradiction to the axiom that self-preservation is the first law of life.

Third, that the best theory to account for all the presently known facts is Freud's hypothesis of a death-instinct, or primary impulses of destructiveness opposed by a life-instinct or primary impulses of creativeness and constructiveness; it is various phases of interaction between these two which constitute the psychological and biological phenomena of life.

Fourth, that according to Freud's conception both the destructive and constructive tendencies are originally self-directed but become increasingly extraverted in connection with birth, growth, and life-experiences. In his contacts with others, the individual first reacts with extraversion of his aggressive tendencies followed by an extraversion of the erotic or constructive tendencies which by fusion with the former may achieve varying degrees of neutralization of the destructiveness from total to almost none.

Fifth, that when there is a forcible interruption in these external investments or when too great difficulty is encountered in maintaining them, the destructive and constructive impulses revert back upon the person of their origin, that is, are turned back upon the self.

Sixth, that here again, if defusion occurs, the destructive tendencies lead and may permanently prevail so that self-destruction to a lesser or greater degree supervenes; and that in this event one can trace evidences of the wish to kill and the wish to be killed, and also the eroticized forms of these two wishes.

Seventh, that in those instances in which the self-destructive impulses are overtaken and partially but not completely neutralized we have the many forms of partial or chronic self-destruction to be discussed in the subsequent chapters.

Eighth, that in those instances in which the self-destructive impulses too far precede or exceed the neutralizing constructive impulses, the result is that dramatic example of immediate self-destruction known as suicide.

Ninth, that the close scrutiny of the deeper motives for suicide would confirm this hypothesis in that there appear regularly to be elements from at least two and possibly three sources. These are, (1) impulses derived from the primary aggressiveness crystallized as a wish to kill, (2) impulses derived from a modification of the primitive aggressiveness, the conscience, crystallized as the wish to be killed, and (3) I believe there is evidence that some of the original primary self-directed aggressiveness, the wish to die, joins hands with the more sophisticated motives and adds to the total vectorial force which impels the precipitate self-destruction.

Tenth, that this is undoubtedly complicated by extraneous factors—social attitudes, familial patterns, community customs, and also by those distortions of reality incident to an incomplete personality development. The same individual whose childhood experiences so inhibited his emotional growth as to make it difficult for him to establish and maintain the proper external objectives for absorbing his loves and hates is likely to be one whose capacity for testing reality is so impaired as to make suicide only another game of "going to Jerusalem."

Eleventh, that we are certain that suicide cannot be explained as the result of heredity, suggestion, or any of the symptoms of maladjustment which so frequently precede it. Rather, we are frequently able to see the steady progression of self-destructive tendencies first appearing long before the consummation of the critical act.

Twelfth, that having thus examined the operations of destructive and constructive tendencies in the formula resulting in immediate suicide we may proceed to examine those instances of more successful neutralization represented by the chronic and attenuated forms of self-destruction.

PART III Chronic Suicide

ONE / *Asceticism and Martyrdom*

INTRODUCTION

In contrast to the sudden, acute manifestations of self-destruction represented by the act of suicide, those forms of self-destruction in which the individual commits slow suicide—suicide by inches as it were—could, I think, be called *chronic* suicide, or chronic self-destruction.

Asceticism, for example, with its varied and ingenious devices for prolonging existence for the purpose of enduring more deprivation, is the very refinement of slow death. Many instances of long neurotic invalidism also fall into this category of inhibited forms of suicide, the patient often appearing to cling tenaciously to a life that seems not worth the living. Alcoholic addiction is a somewhat more robust but certainly no less inhibited way of achieving self-destruction. Then there are other forms of chronic suicide which are more dramatic, such as martyrdom and so-called "chronic bad luck," in which the individual, perhaps by provocative means, instigates his own destruction and bears it nobly. Here the subtlety consists in the deftness with which the victim manipulates his situation to his own ends and then capitalizes upon it, all unconsciously of course.

We propose to study these chronic and attenuated forms of self-destruction psychologically and relate the motives discovered in them to those of direct undisguised suicide which have been discussed heretofore, namely, an externally directed aggressive component; a punitive drive, that is, submission to punishment from a sense of guilt; an erotic motive (achievement of pleasure, the essentially sexual nature of which is cloaked in elaborate disguise); and finally, a self-destructive impulse whose sole aim is the extinction of the individual.

77

There is a fundamental difference between chronic suicide and "acute" suicide. In the former the individual postpones death indefinitely, at a cost of suffering and impairment of function which is equivalent to a *partial* suicide—a "living death," it is true, but nevertheless living. In such persons, however, the destructive urge is often of a progressive nature, requiring larger and larger payments until finally the individual is, as it were, bankrupted and must surrender to actual death. Of course, this process of gradual renunciation takes place in everyone. In the words of Musonius:

> Just as a landlord who has not received his rent pulls down the doors, removes the rafters, and fills up the well, so I seem to be driven out of this little body, when nature, which has let it to me, takes away one by one, eyes and ears, hands and feet.

But in some individuals the natural processes are accelerated by active co-operation from the personality.

Nietzsche said that Christianity permitted only two forms of suicide—martyrdom and the slow suicide of the ascetic —and decorated these with the highest dignities and the highest aspirations while denouncing all others in a terrific manner.

It would seem from the accounts of the austerities of the early and medieval monks that many of them must have shortened their days by these two methods. St. Francis of Assisi is said to have declared in a transient burst of insight when he was dying that he had sinned against the body by subjecting it to privations. He imagined that, when at prayer during the night, he heard a voice saying: "Francis, there is no sinner in the world whom, if he be converted, God will not pardon; but he who kills himself by hard penances will find no mercy in eternity." However, he attributed this voice to the devil! [1]

It is apparent that the ascetic destroys himself to a greater or less degree by his self-imposed rigors, but it is more difficult to discern that martyrdom is *self*-destruction, since it is usually passively achieved. Unlike the ascetic who voluntarily condemns himself to a life of hardship, starvation, and flagellation, the martyr is mistreated by others while in pursuit of some ideal. It appears, therefore, that the punishment is incidental and unsought, and perhaps in many instances this is true. Martyrdom, like other

[1] Hase, Charles Berthond, *St. François d'Assise*, étude historique d'après le Dr. Karl Hase, pp. 137-38, Paris, Michael Levy frères, 1864.

kinds of greatness, is sometimes thrust upon one but in other instances it appears to be voluntarily (although usually unconsciously) sought.[2]

The heroic sacrifices of scientists who willingly incur the fatal risks incident to research, patriots who lay down their lives for freedom, saints of the church and other persons who give their lives for society, or for those they love, are usually not considered suicidal, because the social usefulness of the course chosen—the element of creativeness—denotes the victory of the constructive rather than the destructive elements in the person's nature. The individual may have wished to destroy himself or he may not—but if the social or reality value of his sacrifice is predominant, therein lies the evidence that the self-destructive forces were not triumphant. Charles Dickens' portrayal of Sydney Carton is thus psychologically sound for all its romantic departure from realities and probabilities. The martyr who wholly masters his aggressions and achieves redemption does so by virtue of an ultimate, though costly, victory of love.

For our exposition of self-destruction, therefore, I have chosen those instances of self-immolation where the wish to destroy the self is more clearly demonstrated, comparatively unmixed with neutralizing impulses toward life and love; those instances in which evidence can be adduced that the

[2] There are numerous examples of voluntary martyrdom in the history of the early church. "Direct and deliberate suicide," says Lecky (Lecky, W. E. H., *History of European Morals*, Vol. II, p. 49, Appleton, 1884), "which occupies so prominent a place in the moral history of antiquity, almost absolutely disappeared within the Church; but beyond its pale the Circumcelliones, in the fourth century, constituted themselves the apostles of death, and not only carried to the highest point the custom of provoking martyrdom, by challenging and insulting the assemblies of the Pagans, but even killed themselves in great numbers, imagining, it would seem, that this was a form of martyrdom, and would secure for them eternal salvation. Assembling in hundreds, St. Augustine says even in thousands, they leaped with paroxysms of frantic joy from the brows of overhanging cliffs, till the rocks below were reddened with their blood." St. Augustine and St. Optatus have given accounts of these suicides in their works against the Donatists.

Tertullian (quoted by Mason, Arthur James, *The Historic Martyrs of the Primitive Church*, London, Longmans, Green, 1905, p. 106) wrote:

"During the zealous persecution of Arrisu Antonius in Asia all the Christians of a city assembled and presented themselves in a body at his tribunal. He ordered a few of them to execution and remarked to the rest, 'Unhappy creatures! If you want to die, you can find precipices and halters for yourselves.'"

Such flagrant examples of provocative martyrdom of a large group seem to be rare. There are many instances, however, in which the martyr appeared to welcome his fate and even to draw great satisfactions from his suffering. Some of these will be described in this chapter but no attempt will be made to classify martyrs into such divisions as the purposeful and the accidental.

victim not only accepted his fate but gloried in it and capitalized it for his own purposes, or in which the individual deliberately sought out the means of his destruction; and those in which the element of social value, as indicated by the utility of his sacrifice, was absent or distinctly subordinate to the personal satisfactions.

Similarly, asceticism may in some instances be constructively used, according to the objectives which are consciously sought by this means. The discipline of the body for some ultimate purpose (as, for example, the asceticism of the athlete in training or that of the invalid who must temporarily forego customary indulgences) is practically differentiated from those forms of asceticism which destroy the body or neglect its claims entirely.

A. CLINICAL STUDIES OF MARTYRDOM AND ASCETICISM

While there are, on the one hand, many historical examples of asceticism and martyrdom with which we are all acquainted in a general way, there are also more accessible examples of asceticism and martyrdom with which psychiatrists are particularly familiar as clinical cases. The former are apt to be glorified by the public while the latter are looked upon with contempt or amusement and sometimes with indignation. In this materialistic age the martyr must justify his martyrdom more or less by its social usefulness, but there was a time when this was not necessary—when martyrdom existed for itself alone. These "clinical martyrs" afford us our most available material for the study undertaken in this chapter.

Psychiatry is not interested in justifying or condemning these individuals but rather in examining the structure of their personality make-up and the psychological mechanisms whereby their chief satisfaction in life is derived from suffering or deprivation. This paradox of joy out of pain is perhaps one of the crucial enigmas of psychology and has given rise to many theories and philosophies. When the joy is consciously recognized as sexual in nature we describe the phenomenon as overt *masochism* and the psychoanalytic view is that this erotic element enters to some extent into all such phenomena even when it is not recognized as such. Hence much psychoanalytic literature, particularly the earlier literature, proceeds upon the assumption that masochism is the chief characteristic of martyrdom, a supposition which newer discoveries in unconscious motivation do not support.

Repeated opportunities occur for the psychoanalytic study of clinical examples of asceticism and martyrdom in the form of neurotic invalidism characterized by an incapacity to accept or enjoy the pleasures of life and a compulsion to get into pitiable situations and derive comfort from the sympathy aroused by this plight. I shall review the main features in a few typical cases.

The first is a woman in which both asceticism and martyrdom were prominent as characterological symptoms. Although in many ways fortunate, she was to most of her friends an object of great pity because of the martyrdom she seemed obliged to endure at the hands of man and God. It was to a much smaller circle that she appeared in the ascetic role, which involved a complete inability to take advantage of opportunities for pleasure, an inability which seemed to them to be deliberate and senseless.

At great sacrifice on the part of her parents she was sent as a young woman to college where she played off her academic opportunities against her social aspirations and vice versa, cutting herself out of social life on the ground that she had to study, and neglecting her studies on the ground that a girl had a right to some social life. She withdrew from college and then, although unusually talented as well as beautiful, she insisted upon entering a petty, monotonous, business routine to which she held herself arduously until she became ill. A little later in her life she developed one of her talents and became a proficient musician, but after a few years began denying herself all opportunities for teaching or studying music and ten years later had apparently forgotten completely everything she had once known about music or its rendition. How similar this is to the medieval ascetics who cast from them their pleasure-giving talents, as for example, the gifted linguist who had mastered twenty languages but imposed upon himself the penance of silence for thirty years.

Some years later through a stroke of good fortune she had the opportunity of living in New York in fulfillment of a long-felt ambition. But having arrived there she consistently denied herself any metropolitan enjoyments. Such wells of pleasure as the art exhibits, the libraries, the concerts, the museums, all of which she had the intelligence to appreciate, were entirely eschewed. Nor should it be supposed that she spent her time in frivolous amusements instead; by no means. She worked laboriously at an uncongenial task to help her husband, who, as a matter of fact, did not need this help. By her consent, if not by her choice, they lived in dingy quarters; she made no friends, but led altogether a drab, colorless existence. Her only solace was the vast amount of pity she gave herself in thinking how miserable she was. In this particular, of course, she seems to depart from the ascetic character who is proud of his self-denials and rigors and pities himself only in secret.

Later this woman had still more opportunities for pleasure and social education poured into her lap. She lived for several years in one of the capitals of Europe and toured at leisure the Continent, the British Isles and the Far East. Here again, however, she repeated her curious self-immolation, at least as far as genuine pleasure was concerned. She made more acquaintances (no friends), did more drinking and party-going, but she enjoyed none of it. Her husband's official position with the American government gave her entrée to the highest social circles and his money and taste in clothes combined to make her, as I once heard her described by a friend, one of the best-dressed women in Europe. She was for a time much sought after but her curious inability to enjoy anything gave her friends such a feeling of futility in their relations with her that gradually she was deserted.

Her asceticism also extended to her marital relations. Not only was she sexually frigid in spite of a conscious wish to be otherwise, but she could not, with a clear conscience, permit herself any of the other pleasures of married life. She could not bring herself to believe, for example, that she should have a child, much as she wanted one. She became pregnant only after ten years of married life and no sooner did this occur than her rejection of her husband became complete, as if she felt that one person was all she had a right to claim. She took the child and went to England and lived in seclusion and loneliness for several years, rejecting or at least starving the friendship offered her by new acquaintances made there. Her husband sent her plenty of money, which she managed to spend with very little to show for it. She wore plain, unattractive dresses, lived in a small, uncomfortable house, neglected her appearance so that her former beauty was obscured, declined to entertain anyone even in return for occasional invitations she received from others and, in short, lived the life of an ascetic hermit.

Many other illustrations could be given of her asceticism but I shall illustrate now some of the ways in which she played the role of martyr. I distinguish this from the role of ascetic in that most of the self-deprivals and restrictions described above were self-imposed and the responsibility for them frankly acknowledged by her. In martyrdom the individual thinks himself, portrays himself as, or actually causes himself to be the victim of cruelty at the hands of circumstances or another person. In this sense the ascetic is a little more clearheaded than the martyr who accomplishes the same suffering for himself and, not realizing that it is to a large extent self-imposed, projects the responsibility. Some of the suffering this woman endured she was inclined to blame upon others. She did this more by inference than by direct accusation. For example, although she did not accuse her husband of sending her to this lonely English village, she let it appear that he had done so and she even acknowledged that he had good reason for doing so, that she had been so disagreeable, indifferent, and critical. While living alone she was repeatedly ill and on one occasion remained severely so for some months. At such times she was truly a pitiable figure, alone with her child, far removed from her husband or anyone she knew, self-excluded from any of the people in the country to which she had moved, sick, lonely, and miserable. The sympathy, not unmixed with perplexity, which this aroused in her relatives and the relatives of her husband was the only satisfaction from external sources which she derived.

In her subsequent psychoanalytic treatment she repeated, as psychoanalytic patients always do, the techniques which she had found successful in childhood but which failed her so miserably thereafter, namely, trying, on the one hand, to arouse pity by getting herself into deplorable predicaments or, on the other hand, attempting to make the analyst or someone else responsible for suffering that came to her. For example, she developed a slight infection of her throat. On account of it she rejected several invitations proffered by an acquaintance for some social activities. She wanted the analyst to examine her throat and prescribe for it. She was told that such treatments were not a part of psychoanalysis but that she should consult a nose and throat doctor whose name was given her. She consulted him but insisted that his treatment made her worse. The throat infection then actually did become severe, confining her to bed for a week. When she had recovered sufficiently to return to her analysis she accused the analyst of not having been interested in her because he did not examine her throat, of having neglected her by not prescribing for it, of having sent her to a doctor who made her worse, of having been glad to be relieved of her for a week and therefore really enjoying her suffering. Then she suddenly retracted all this, heaving a long sigh as if to resign herself to her fate, and insisted that she would take it all as her portion in life.

This martyrdom may not coincide with the reader's conception of martyrdom as cheerful suffering, just as her asceticism lacks the self-satisfaction that some notable ascetics evince, but it should be remembered that this woman was a *failing* martyr and a *failing* ascetic, that is, her martyrdom and asceticism were not quite able to sustain her. If they had she would never have come for treatment. (Real martyrs see no reason whatever for seeking *treatment* —treatment, of all things!) Psychiatrists would regard the extreme martyr and ascetic as individuals completely gone over to the acceptance of an unrealistic interpretation of life, a kind of socially-acceptable psychosis. A neurosis stands somewhere between normality and a psychosis in its hold on reality, and the fact that this woman's asceticism and martyrdom failed, while it made her a neurotic, saved her from a "polite" psychosis and opened the way to a return to normality which was achieved through her treatment.

With the knowledge that such adult behavior probably is determined by childhood experience, let us examine this woman's childhood with particular reference to the circumstances which led her to the adoption of the ascetic-martyr technique.

In her dreams she habitually represented herself as a Negress, as a hideous old woman, as a fat unattractive girl, or in some other unlovely role. As we have already seen, this is almost what she seemed to want to become. But as a child she had been very pretty, a fact which had been capitalized by her poor but aspiring parents who made many sacrifices in order to exploit her. They denied themselves and their other children in order to give her pretty clothes and such social opportunities as the small town in which they lived offered. An older sister, Gladys, was perhaps the chief sufferer both subjectively and objectively. For while our patient was never taught household arts nor required to do any household task but was expected only to live in pretty indolence, Gladys had it forced upon her that she was not as pretty or as likely to make a good marriage and was therefore expected to learn to cook and to deny herself in the matter of clothes for the sake of the prospects of the younger sister. The patient was literally made the queen of the family, to which end the mother, father, sister, and younger children all suffered.

Her unholy satisfaction in this honor was accompanied by such a sense of guilt that she ultimately became incapable of accepting the fruit of it and this is one reason why she was obliged always (in later life) to prove that she was *not* happy, *not* fortunate, *not* enviable, but just the reverse. Why she should have had such a sense of guilt is more apparent if one considers what happened to those whose sacrifices made her success possible. The older sister, Gladys, grew up a hard-working spinster in the home of the aging parents. The father went bankrupt and wandered away from home. The mother led a dreary, impecunious existence, subsisting on doles sent to her by the other children.

This accounts for the element of guilt and self-punishment which seems to be regularly one of the motives in martyrdom; but there are usually other motives, and they too were found in this patient.

Let us examine the way in which her martyrdom and asceticism were used as an aggression, i.e., a weapon of offense. This aspect of the matter was certainly clear enough to her husband. She almost ruined his career by so consistently thwarting the enjoyment and full utilization of his opportunities and by making it appear always that he treated her shamefully and was responsible for her misery. It was by reason of his ability and generosity that she was able to travel and to live as well as she did; he supplied her with many of the luxuries of life and it was through no fault of his that she did not enjoy them. In repayment, however, she not only did her best to make him appear to others to be a rascal but berated him and reproached him so bitterly and so unjustly for her sufferings as to make his home life intolerable. To secure help for her own self-imposed miseries she incurred bills for medical attention amounting to many thousands of dollars.

Now that we see the aggressive element in her martyrdom, we must seek an explanation in her childhood for this element also. It hangs in part upon the circumstances already related, with one addition. It might be supposed that

85

the patient enjoyed being made the belle of the town except for the prickings of conscience which it may have caused her—and certainly did cause her later. The family no doubt assumed so, but the fact of the matter was that, even as a girl, she was fully aware of the materialistic purpose back of the family sacrifices for her; she realized that they were seeking to exploit her beauty for their own financial and social redemption. The intense bitterness of her resentment became very vivid during her psychoanalytic treatment and was reflected in a curious way toward the end of it, in that for a time she stubbornly resisted the resumption of normal living on the grounds that to do so would only be to reflect credit on the analyst. She had been exploited by her family and shown off to the world ostensibly for her own future but in reality for the sake of the family. Now the analyst wanted her to recover not so much, she felt, because he was interested in her as that he wanted the world to see what a good analyst he was. For this reason she declined for a long time to return to her music, much as she consciously wished to do so and in spite of the fact that her performances were in demand. In this way she attempted to get revenge on the analyst whom she felt to be insincere just as she wreaked revenge on her own family for indulgences which she regarded (correctly) as insincere. So bitter had been her realization of her family's insincerity that she could never quite believe that those who professed to love her meant what they said. This was due in part also to the fact that she herself had never been quite sincere but felt that her insincerity was forced upon her.[3]

Finally, we consider the erotic motive in this woman's martyrdom which appeared very vividly in her analysis in the way in which she used or attempted to use suffering to win the love of the physician (as she had done with others before, but without insight). The incident of her sore throat has already been mentioned; there were dozens of such episodes. She recalled during her analysis such incidents as the following: While she was in grade school before the era of adolescent exploitation she remembered having discovered that she could make her own nose bleed at will by striking it with her hand behind the cover of a book or a desk and this nose-bleed would then serve as an excuse

[3] I am personally inclined to the opinion that this element of insincerity is possibly the most important and characteristic unconscious factor in martyrdom, and is reflected by the fact that the martyr always seems to be so intensely sincere.

from class-work and gain the sympathy of her teacher and classmates.

It became clear to her in the analysis that behind her apparent remorse was an ulterior motive. To put it in her own words: "While pretending to feel so guilty on account of my victory over my sister, and while apparently punishing myself, I was actually seeking to accomplish the same end by different means; I was trying to attract attention just the same, only now I did it by exhibiting my sufferings and my miserable looks instead of by exhibiting my pretty dresses and my curls." This use of exhibitionism in the service of the erotic life we have already discussed but there was a deeper erotic value and significance in the martyrdom which was one of the final discoveries in the course of her analysis. Beneath the veneer, the insincerity, the showing-off, the shallow pretense, and flirtatiousness, the patient had a deep longing to be loved and a feeling that she had been thwarted. For all that the family "promoted" her and dressed her up for the admiration of the outside world, it was the older daughter, Gladys, whom they, especially the father, really loved. The mother showed some preference for our patient but a preference which, as I have said, the patient felt to be insincere and hence not acceptable. But this rejection could not be quite wholehearted, because it left her quite without anyone to love her. For this reason she had to some extent identified herself with this mother toward whom she never felt or acted very kindly. The mother had denied *herself* and played the martyr to promote the patient. Although the patient felt this to be an insincere expression of love, it was all she had and so she clung to it in spite of her resentment. One can put all this quite simply by saying she was able to find erotic satisfaction only by identifying herself with her mother in her misery.

In these necessarily many words, we have seen how a woman's asceticism and martyrdom were related to buried feelings of guilt, revenge, and distorted love, all of which arose in childhood and remained in a latent or developmental form until their full flower in middle life. Stripped of the other data of her life and personality, they seem almost too obvious; they were by no means so obvious to her or to her friends. She was like all neurotics, an enigma to her friends, who wonderingly accorded her the pity which she seemed to demand.

Another very typical case of overtly neurotic martyrdom

can be briefly reviewed here to advantage because it indicates the essential similarity of pattern in these clinical martyrs. The case is taken from Stekel.[4] A 23-year-old woman came for treatment ostensibly because after three years of married life she remained sexually frigid. There were, however, many other symptoms. Her life was utterly joyless and she took no interest in anything. (This inability to become pleasurably interested in anything is a characteristic of the lives of many housewives and has been thought worthy by Myerson[5] of the designation "anhedonia.") She suffered constantly from headaches and from depression, weeping continually, sometimes for weeks. She was a devoted slave to her family, never leaving the family circle. She consulted her mother and sister before making any decision, however trivial. In her household affairs, the rearing of her child, the selection of her clothes—everything— she deferred to their opinion. She complained because her husband did not lay out certain tasks for her to do each day and that he did not keep her at the things she ought to do.

Although a Protestant by faith, this girl had been sent to a Catholic convent school until she was 18 because there were no good common schools in her community. She was very pious. Often, in repentance, she slept upon the bare floor with a single sheet under her. She had wished to become a nun but could not bring herself to confess her early sexual activities which had consisted of much sexual play with playmates, an older brother, and an uncle who had seduced her. In atonement for these sins she had taken an oath never to yield to any man and felt that it would be wrong for her to enjoy sexual relations.

The treatment brought to light that although she served her family devotedly she was fundamentally angry at every member of it. She hated her sister who had been held up as a model to her; she had strong death wishes toward her mother because of her jealousy and blamed her mother for her own unhappy marriage. Toward her father, the patient was very angry because of his infidelities.

Her aggressions were expressed most fully toward her husband. She was periodically seized with a buying mania, although generally she was quite economical. On these occasions she would squander large sums of money on worth-

[4] Stekel, Wilhelm, *Sadism and Masochism,* translation by Brink, Vol. II, p. 287, Liveright, 1929.
[5] Myerson, Abraham, *The Nervous Housewife,* Little, Brown, 1920.

less and unnecessary articles which she felt impelled to buy, and would later throw away. Her husband had reproached her for her extravagance and she would resolve solemnly never to do it again but would soon yield to the same temptation. There were many other indirect evidences of her hostile attitude toward her husband—her extreme dependence and lack of initiative, her candor about her fantasies and love from other men, her frigidity, and her dissatisfaction. She could not take care of her child because he made her so nervous. In the course of the treatment she confessed that she often wished to strike the child and had at times felt like choking him.

Psychoanalysis revealed that her extreme submissiveness and obedience were an infantile way of atoning for her inward hate and dissatisfaction, that her frigidity served as a self-punishment, an atonement, and an aggression against her husband. It was cured by the analysis, and her martyr-like attitude was undermined sufficiently to allow her to move away from her parents.

It is safe to say that thousands if not millions of such cases of household martyrdom are dragging out their dreary existences in this very country at this very hour.[6] Indeed, I should be very sorry if the extreme examples of asceticism and martyrdom which I have chosen to illustrate the essential similarity of such behavior to the more dramatic forms of self-destruction would lead readers to suppose that such things are occasional and freakish occurrences. Just the contrary is probably true, that is, that all of us to some extent indulge in self-destruction under the guise of martyrdom, defending ourselves from reproach or suspicion by various rationalizations. Indeed, we might well devote considerable time to the consideration of those chronic suicides which are apparent all about us in the lives of friends who do not regard themselves as neurotic or psychotic and, of course, under no circumstances as religious martyrs. The employee who is successfully promoted only to throw away his chances for the final and ultimate promotion toward which he would seem to have been striving, by what sometimes appears to be studied carelessness or even intentional neglect; the man who after steady progress and every indication of great future promise suddenly changes tack and veers off into what everyone considers to be a less fruitful direction; the man who without adequate justification sud-

[6] See Myerson, A., "The Neurosis of the Housewife," *Medicine and Surgery*, March, 1918, and also the book by this author, already cited.

denly becomes discouraged, throws up his hands, and resigns to the dismay of all of his well-wishers; the man who achieves a notable success only to nullify its benefits and the status of his own reputation by a series of acts calculated to inspire precisely the contrary attitudes in those about him—these and many other examples will come to mind. One of the readers of an early draft of this manuscript wrote me, "I have recently witnessed the impending destruction of the career of one of the most brilliant men I have ever known by a process so strikingly analogous to actual suicide that it bore out completely your main thesis. I spent several hours with him attempting to point out that while he had some slight reason in reality for his feelings, the feelings which finally led to offering his resignation were all out of proportion to the realities of the situation and were consequently neurotic, that what he should do was to attempt to adjust himself to the world instead of trying to make the world adjust to him. . . . These cases are common; the mechanism probably occurs to a greater or lesser extent . . . in every human being, and is usually not recognized either by the individual, his friends, or his physician."

Sometimes it is recognized by the friends though not by the individual. I once knew a woman who had great social ambitions; aside from her obvious ambitiousness she was a pleasant person with much to commend her. Upon a certain occasion she was invited to a small party which she did not consider particularly essential to her social rise and at this party behaved in an exceedingly rude, boorish fashion. In so doing she sealed her social doom as definitely as if she had committed a crime. Some of those present were among the social arbiters of the section and others were competent gossips. Between the two, the poor woman's fate was settled as a result of behavior which cannot be construed as a mere accident but as an expression of aggressiveness and essential hostility behind her usually sweet exterior. But that this particular episode was self-destructive and that it represented a trend in this woman's personality was by no means hidden from those acquaintances who witnessed it.

The same thing happens more frequently than we have any idea. Every reader can probably recall numerous instances when he succeeded in cheating himself out of a reward or a success which would certainly have been his save for his self-destructive activities.

It is only when such compulsive self-betrayal mounts

beyond endurance, however, that we get alarmed or seek help—sometimes not even then. Frequently one is able to detect in his own life waves of self-defeat, usually following certain set patterns. I recall a man who exemplified this in every department of his life. He was extraordinarily popular with women and finally won an attractive bride from whom, however, he became alienated and divorced.[7] He became a proficient golfer and won numerous tournaments, only in the height of his success to begin a progressive decline which no amount of practice seemed able to stem. He told me that he observed a peculiar feature of his golfing; he would often have a match practically won, so to speak, long before its end (four up and five to go, for example) only to lose every one of the final holes in a very unexpected manner. This, of course, was exactly what he did with everything else in life, that is, he threw away success when he once had it in his hands, thus corresponding to Freud's type of character which is unable to endure success because of a sense of guilt implicit in that success.

This particular man further illustrated this pattern by achieving great financial success within a few years after starting in business, only to lose not only every cent of his own money but the money of a number of other individuals which had been entrusted to his care.

The motives behind such everyday asceticism and martyrdom are probably the same as we have seen in the neurotic cases already discussed; no doubt we often do try to fail, try to destroy ourselves and actually are destroying ourselves at the very moment we think we are succeeding.

PSYCHOTIC MARTYRS

The unconscious motives of martyrdom (and asceticism) become very much more dramatic and at the same time more transparent as they are enacted in the lives of those individuals whose devotion to their convictions (or compulsions) is greater than their loyalty to reality. I refer to asceticism and martyrdom as they are observable in the psychotic. Every psychiatric clinic and every psychiatric hospital is familiar with them in many forms; for example, in the well-known Messianic delusions often carried to the extent of attempts at self-crucifixion.

It seems likely to be valuable to our exposition to include here a short account of two representative examples in

[7] This flight from love as a special form of self-destruction will be discussed more fully in connection with the historic ascetics.

which these elements of aggression, erotism, and self-punishment can be clearly discerned. We will then pass to the consideration of more distinguished individuals who lived too long ago to be in danger of psychiatric diagnosis but whose behavior is none the less susceptible of similar analysis.[8]

Patient K. was next to the oldest of eight children born to the union of a highly idealistic mother and a harsh alcoholic father. The patient was deeply impressed as a very young child by the religious training imparted by his mother with particular emphasis upon the suffering of Jesus and the dangers of hell-fire.

In spite of this, he indulged in a certain amount of adolescent rebellion including the use of some profanity, lying, and the average amount of pilfering; but at sixteen he was formally baptized and made a resolution to live "the life of a good Christian." He began to attend all the regular religious services and occasional revival meetings in which he took an active part.

The patient's father had founded a small manufacturing business which the sons, led by the patient, had expanded considerably, so that the family became quite well-to-do. Several of the brothers withdrew into other pursuits so that the patient came into practically full possession of a large business, which his ingenious schemes and genial personality combined to make very successful.

During the active period of his business success, the patient became increasingly religious, but at the age of 35 decided that he had made enough money and would devote the rest of his life to God rather than to the furthering of his own "selfish interests." He created popular enthusiasm for the support of certain public works at the cost of considerable personal and financial sacrifice, involving the expenditure of over a hundred thousand dollars. This he believed to be his duty "as a good Christian for the benefit of all God's people." His generosity had the effect of further increasing his own business, however, and this unexpected result made necessary greater efforts on his part to do some service which would really cost him something.

While in this mood, he became involved in a campaign against what he considered to be a derogatory representation of religion. He became very excited about this and

---

[8] I have made no attempt in the study of historical martyrs to distinguish those whom we would now regard as psychotic from the others.

spent several thousand dollars prosecuting his objections before he was forced to desist by the intervention of relatives. They were uncertain what to do with him, because, while he had apparently thrown away large sums of money foolishly (living meanwhile in an exceedingly humble and self-sacrificing way), his activities had thus far promoted the family business indirectly. Now, however, it became unmistakably clear that he had carried the idea of sacrifice, service, and submission to a pathological degree and a psychiatric study showed him to be mentally ill. He considered a private psychiatric hospital too good for him and went instead to a state institution. There he made repeated attempts to escape "in order to be apprehended and beaten" (to quote his own words). On one occasion he was gratified in this direction so severely that he was confined to his bed for several weeks as a result of his injuries.

When he was finally released from the hospital he went to a hotel room where he spent three days alone "crucifying himself." He deliberately burned his feet and hands on the radiator, gouged the soles of his feet and the palms of his hands and cut the figure of a cross on his forehead. He neither ate nor slept, but prayed constantly and fervently.

Septicemia and gangrene of his toes developed, so that several toes had to be amputated, and he remained critically ill for many months thereafter. His own explanation of the episode was that he felt that in order to live the life of a good Christian, he must punish himself to convince God of his sincerity. In this way he felt that he might eventually win the reward he sought, namely, the love of a pure, beautiful woman. This led to his confessing his distressing guilt feelings related to masturbation and fantasies about immoral women. Undoubtedly these feelings of unworthiness and sinfulness and his need for punishment on this score were powerful forces goading him to this and succeeding acts of self-mutilation.

The ascetic trend showed itself in this patient in many ways. He totally neglected and ultimately abandoned his business. He refused to accept money from his family even when he needed it; he one day gave his good clothes away to a tramp and accepted rags from the tramp for himself. He walked for miles in the snow and sleet without shoes, freezing several of his remaining toes; he starved on the road while hitchhiking to Chicago in order to help promote one of the public works in which he had taken an active interest. Over and over again he refused help that was offered him, insisting that he must live in the same conditions of privation that his fellow Christians did.

On one occasion while traveling by automobile he gave away his last gasoline ticket. When the car ran out of fuel, he calmly abandoned it and walked the rest of the way. While thus walking along the road dressed in rags, without food or money, he found a two-dollar bill. He regarded this as a miracle, an indication that God was watching over him, but since it was a gift from God he must return it to God. So he kept the money only until he found a church where he gave it away.

As has been indicated, the patient's erotic life was closely related to his religious conceptions. He claimed to have been the most passionate person in the world ever since the age of five. All of his life he craved the great love and passion of a pure girl, such as the Bible described, and was willing to endure any amount of pain and privation to attain this love. He spoke of his life as representing pain, peace, and love. During the years preceding his marriage he fell in love on numerous occasions but whenever the relationship approached intimacy the patient took alarm. He feared the terrible consequence of what he called "adultery." Those girls who refused to permit him to so much as touch them, he pursued fervently, holding them in reverence for their purity.

Once when he had dreamed that he had sexual contact with a woman his guilt feelings so oppressed him that as soon as he could get out of bed he plunged himself into a scalding bath and received severe burns. In recounting this episode he added, "The more I suffer, the more passionate I become." He said he had never experienced the height of his passion, but "God knows, I hope to some day, if not on this earth, then in the next one, or pray to God that he cut this passionate thing off because the suspense has pained me more than anyone will ever know, from my childhood up."

The dynamics of this patient's voluntary martyrdom may be partly inferred from what has been related of his background; his devotion to his mother and fear of his domineering father led him to adopt the submissive role of the "good child" as the only safe way for him to obtain love and erotic satisfaction. This position meant the denial of all sexuality and normal aggressive expressions as "bad." Because of his fear of and love for the all-powerful father he was led to identify himself with his saintly mother at an early age. (He himself dated his "passionate feelings" from the age of five, approximately the time at which the child, according to Freudian theory, is torn between his wish to take the mother from the father and have her all to himself, and his fears of the father's superior strength and his desire to propitiate him.) The identification was itself in the nature of martyrdom (since his mother was a martyr to his father); later the martyr-ideal became clearer in his identification with Jesus, as one who was also the son of a powerful, punishing father and who did not permit himself sexual expression. The patient, falling far short of his ideal, was obliged continually to make extravagant atonements for his indulgence in sexual fantasies, atonements in which he again identified himself with Jesus and derived masochistic pleasure from his attempts to crucify himself. In this he differed from the true masochist in that he did not demand that this torture be administered by a personal father-image and in that, like the martyrs and ascetics of old, he disguised even from himself the erotic satisfaction derived from his penances. The aggressive component of the patient's martyrdom was evident in his provocative behavior toward his family and friends, his neglect of them, his extravagant expenditure of funds which might have been used for their needs, and in his confessed fondness for fighting. His pursuit of women who did not welcome his devotion was also aggressive in that he often carried it to the point where it humiliated the women. He quarreled interminably with his wife, although he allowed her to beat him without making any attempt to defend himself.[9]

The case of Mr. Y. was even more dramatic. He was a rich and cultivated Cuban gentleman of 40. Two years before the following observations were made a certain episode had occurred to which he attached great importance. He had seen a woman on the streets of Havana who attracted him irresistibly and he followed her to her apartment. He watched her as she entered the door and disappeared. Just then he noticed a flower peddler sitting in the patio of the house with wreaths of flowers arranged on a long stick. The association of this mysterious and beautiful girl and the flower peddler suddenly seemed to him to have a symbolic significance meaning that he must make a choice between

[9] For a more detailed and more technical account of this case, see Reider, Norman, "Self-Mutilation in Paranoia," *J. Kansas Med. Soc.*, April, 1936, pp. 133-36.

life, represented by the girl, and death, represented by the man and wreaths. He decided to choose life and boldly knocked at the door of the apartment in which the woman had disappeared. It seemed a good omen to him that the door was opened by the woman who had fascinated him and she invited him in most graciously. He took his leave a short time later and returned home.

He was somewhat tired after his afternoon's experience and lay down to rest. In a meditative mood he reflected that his "choice" of "life" had been a happy one, so happy indeed that it seemed proper that he should make a sacrifice to forestall the vengeance of God. He decided he should give up his relationship with his wife although she had been all that a dutiful, affectionate wife could be to him, with no thought in the world but to make him happy. She could not give him children because of sterility, but he did not hold this against her. While musing thus he fell asleep and did not meet his wife for dinner as he had planned. He took the occurrence to be a sign from Heaven that his resolution to make the sacrifice was approved.

About this time he noticed that people began to look at him in a peculiar way, that some odd things were happening to him in his office, that his mail was being tampered with, and that people were saying queer things to him, all of which convinced him the more that he had been set apart in some way by a power over which he had no control and whose identity was not known to him. During this time he had noticed advertisements of the moving picture, "The Sign of the Cross," which he immediately decided was the symbol of the power or organization that had selected him for some great mission. Next, the patient began to be very much annoyed by people whom he described as "sissies," and in order to prove that he himself was not a "sissy" but a strong man he decided to take over the management of the business, discharging all of the employees except one, his close friend. He called up the directors of the company to tell them that he had postponed the regular meeting and would call one when it seemed advisable. Within the next few days he became increasingly disturbed, combative, and hostile toward his wife, ordering her out of his presence and threatening to kill her if she came into the room where he was.

As the patient looked back upon the period just described in later months he believed it to have been an attempt on his part to carry out such behavior as would guarantee his departure from Cuba to the United States. When brought to this country to receive psychiatric treatment, he felt that he had been selected by his government to populate the United States with millions of children whom he would have by thousands of girls. He was quite insistent at first that he begin immediately but when this was denied him he took the denial to mean that he had not made enough sacrifices to be worthy of so great a mission.

To prepare himself he burned his flesh with lighted cigarettes and made many appeals for a knife to inflict wounds upon himself. In spite of the fact that he was under the care of a special nurse day and night he burned his arm severely upon a steam pipe while pretending to be asleep, without even changing his expression. He would refuse to eat for several days at a time, although he was very fond of eating and every effort was made to tempt him with his favorite delicacies. Even when he was forced to eat, he would not take anything except a very unsavory mixture of milk, eggs, orange juice, cod liver oil, sugar, and salt. One period of fasting lasted three months, during which time he gave up smoking cigarettes, reading, dancing (which he had always enjoyed very much), picture shows and other outings, and, dressed in his old worn-out clothing, sat alone in his room, refusing to speak to anyone. When he was told that one of his sisters was probably fatally ill, he made no comment except to say that he had given up practically everything and now it appeared that it was necessary for him to give up this sister. He showed no interest in resuming his business responsibilities, saying that such affairs were of the world, and he had long ago forsaken everything of that sort.

Later on, Mr. Y. became more and more antagonistic to the people whom he called "sissies," saying that they were attempting to make him "soft" by setting him an example of easy living in the world, that they could not face hardships such as he had imposed upon himself, and did nothing creative. He felt that he represented an absolute contrast to these people because he had been chosen for a mission of inestimable good to the world which required a man of iron.

As one's experience with Mr. Y. broadened, it became apparent that his illness represented a struggle against homosexual impulses. In his own story he turned from the peddler, who had wreaths of flowers strung along a stick (probably a symbol of sex to the patient), to the strange girl. His choice of the girl was a flight from homosexual temptation to heterosexual activity. After this incident in which the perverse sexual temptation probably came close to consciousness, he reinforced his defenses by suddenly changing from an easy-going, passive individual whose greatest delight was to putter about the house, to an aggressive, drinking individual, who began to go to houses of prostitution and to fight with his friends. Later, in the sanitarium where he was confined, it was observed that he became disturbed when any attempt was made to substitute men for women nurses in taking care of him. His constant insistence upon his potency was also a defense as was his consistent hatred of anyone whom he called a sissy. This was further corroborated by material brought out in dreams; he dreamed that he was being married, but much to his astonishment he was a woman instead of a man, and a man, a friend of his, holding a long stick, persisted in attempting to thrust it into him.

In this case, the various elements determining the vivid martyrdom-asceticism picture are clearly visible. The erotic element was explicit; it was of a confused nature involving heterosexual façades for the denial of homosexual urges. The self-punitive element was also acknowledged frankly (and enacted unmistakably) by the patient. Least convincing perhaps to one who reads this rather than sees the patient, is the evidence for aggressive intention or action. But if it could be clearly represented how stubborn this fellow was in his refusal to accept any of the responsibilities of his home and business, how angry he became at the mention of certain people whom he defied or thwarted, how difficult he was to care for as a patient, such doubts would be fully dissipated. Martyr and ascetic he was—with defiant aggression, sexual confusion, and self-punishing guilt standing out in bas relief.

B. THE HISTORIC MARTYRS AND ASCETICS

Such instances as we have been citing have the disadvantage of seeming—to the average reader—too extreme. "Perhaps," says such a reader, "these extraordinary persons do exist, and do these extraordinary things for these extraordinary reasons. But it isn't what I know as martyrdom, which is a sober business with no crazy reasons attached." To the psychiatrist there is not this vast difference between the "crazy" and the sane, but only differences of degree and emphasis. The psychotic person—the "crazy" martyr—is more likely to neglect social values or subordinate them to his own instinctive drives, but he is also more direct in evincing the motives for his acts, whereas the sane person covers these with elaborate disguises.

How completely the underlying psychological factors in martyrdom, for example, have been obscured through rationalizations—"the great causes," the "inescapable circumstances"—becomes apparent when one contemplates the records of the historic martyrs and ascetics. These should be reviewed to appreciate fully the lengths to which socially approved self-destruction has been carried. The methods have varied widely from those forms in which the individuals with a view to spiritual perfection abstained from marriage, relinquished the pleasures of life, fasted, gave their property to the poor, and lived in utter simplicity but without withdrawing from human society, to those in which the persons seeking holiness retired completely from their fellowmen and lived as hermits in great privation and loneliness, often subjecting themselves to additional tortures of starvation, flagellation, exposure, and exhaustion.[10]

St. Jerome declares with a thrill of admiration how he had seen a monk, who for thirty years had lived exclusively on a small portion of barley bread and of muddy water; another who lived in a hole and never ate more than five figs for his daily repast; a third who cut his hair only Easter Sunday, who never washed his clothes, who never changed his tunic till it fell to pieces, who starved himself till his eyes grew dim, and his skin "like a pumice stone." . . . For six months, it is said, St. Macarius of Alexandria slept in a marsh and exposed his body naked to the stings of venomous flies. He was accustomed to carry about with him eighty pounds of iron. His disciple, St. Eusebius, carried one hundred and fifty pounds of iron and lived for three years in a dried-up well. St. Sabinus would only eat corn that had become rotten by remaining for a month in water. St. Besarion spent forty days and nights in the middle of thorn-

---

[10] The desert was a favorite retreat for ascetics. It satisfied their desire for solitude and the minimum amount of external stimulation. Furthermore, it was considered the home of the Deity (witness the retreats of Moses, Isaiah, Jesus, Mohammed). The Essenes, that interesting body of pre-Christian Jews who lived with extreme austerity and who were considered by Josephus to be the oldest ascetics known to historians, are said to have originated on the desert and to have returned there as hermits. The ascetic's longing to go into the desert is explained as a symbolic return to the peace and quiet of the mother's womb by Schjelderup (*Die Askese*, Berlin, Walter de Gruyter, 1928) who has assembled an impressive array of material on the subject of asceticism drawn from many source books, from his experiences in monasteries in Europe and the Orient, and from the analyses of two patients.

bushes and for forty years never lay down when he slept, which last penance was also during fifteen years practiced by St. Pachomius. Some saints, like St. Marcian, restricted themselves to one meal a day so small that they continually suffered the pangs of hunger. Of one of them it is related that his daily food was six ounces of bread and a few herbs; that he was never seen to recline on a mat or bed or even to place his limbs easily for sleep; but that sometimes, from excess of weariness, his eyes would close at his meals and the food would drop from his mouth. . . . Of another famous saint, named John, it is asserted that for three whole years he stood in prayer, leaning upon a rock; that during all that time he never sat or lay down, and that his only nourishment was the Sacrament, which was brought him on Sundays. Some of the hermits lived in deserted dens of wild beasts, others in dried-up wells, while others found a congenial resting-place among the tombs. Some disdained all clothes and crawled abroad like the wild beasts, covered only by their matted hair. In Mesopotamia and part of Syria there existed a sect known by the name of "Grazers," who never lived under a roof, who ate neither flesh nor bread, but who spent their time forever on the mountainside and ate grass like cattle. The cleanliness of the body was regarded as a pollution of the soul and the saints who were most admired had become one hideous mass of clotted filth. (Lecky, W. E. H., *op. cit.*, Vol. II, pp. 107-109.)

One of the ascetics of the New World is described with beauty and delicacy by Willa Cather.[11] Jeanne Le Ber, only daughter of the richest merchant in Montreal, was greatly indulged in her childhood. Her father, who was fond of society and entertained all of the distinguished visitors to Montreal, liked to present his charming daughter to his guests who showered gifts and attentions upon her.

Although warm-hearted and friendly, the child early displayed an ascetic trend. When she was at school she gave away the boxes of sweets that were sent her from home. Under the rich and beautiful gowns which her father bought for her, she always wore a haircloth shirt next to her skin.

When she reached marriageable age, her father, desiring a good match for her, fixed a large dowry upon her and many suitors came to court her, one of them being her childhood playmate. Jeanne, however, begged to be allowed to enter the convent. When her parents and even her spiritual directors begged her not to take the vows, she obtained permission to go into retreat in her home, taking the

11 Cather, Willa, *Shadows on the Rock*, Knopf, 1934, pp. 130-36, 150-53.

vow of chastity for five years, during which time she was not to speak to any member of her family. Her parents consented to such an arrangement in the hope that the resolution of the seventeen-year-old girl would soon falter, but from the day she went into retirement they did not speak to her or see her again except when she stole past them on her way to church. Her father, broken-hearted at the blow to his hopes, withdrew from social life and avoided his home. Her mother on her death-bed sent to her daughter, begging her to come to her side, but Jeanne refused.

When the five years were over, Jeanne renewed her vow and at the end of ten years of solitary hermitage in her parents' home, she took her dowry and with it built a chapel, in which she had a cell constructed for herself behind the altar. The cell consisted of three tiers: a grill in the first floor of the cell permitted her to be present, unseen, at mass in the chapel. Her food, which was plain and scanty, was handed her through a little window. The second floor was a sleeping room, just large enough for a narrow bed where she slept on the coldest Canadian nights with only one coverlid, but with her pillow only a few inches from the Blessed Sacrament on the other side of the chapel partition. On the third floor she embroidered beautiful altar-cloths and vestments, or spun yarn and knitted stockings for the poor.

This narrow stone tower was her living tomb from which she never came forth again, even for air and exercise, except at midnight of each day when she went into the church to pray for an hour. In the wintertime she had a small stove which she lit only in extreme cold weather so that her fingers might not become too stiff to work. With all this self-denial, she is said to have been so enraptured with her existence that she preferred her cell to all the rest of the world.

I shall leave it to the reader to decide just what details distinguish this magnificent example of asceticism and self-elected martyrdom from those clinical examples cited above. The elements of joy-in-pain, of love gratified by suffering, of self-denial if not "punishment," and of aggression against the parents and lover (in the form of disappointment and rejection of them) are clear enough.

Another historical example cited by the same author describes the martyrdom of an early missionary in Canada, Noel Chabanel, who perished in an Iroquois raid. He came to America from Toulouse, France, where he had been a professor of rhetoric. He was a person of refinement and delicacy, unfitted for the hardships of missionary life among the savages. In spite of this he went to live among them in order to learn their language and to win converts. In their smoky wigwams, sleeping and eating with dogs and savages, preyed upon by vermin, nauseated by the filth, the smells, and the dirty, poorly cooked food which consisted of dogmeat and other such delicacies, he suffered endless torture. Small wonder that he was unable after five years of study to master the language of this people who were so repulsive to him, although he spoke Greek, Hebrew, Italian, and Spanish in addition to his native French. The Indians looked upon the gentle young scholar with contempt and took every occasion to wound or shock him; once, so the story goes, they induced him to eat meat which they later informed him was human flesh and then jeered at his distress. He never became used to the privations and hardships as the other missionaries did but lived a miserable existence, sleeping in the snow to escape the dirty Indian lodges, eating uncooked cornmeal, serving as the butt of rude jokes, humiliated by his ineffectiveness in his chosen work, disgusted and sickened by the brutality and indecency of the savages, and subject to constant homesickness for France.

His superior, seeing his despair and his utter unfitness for his task, recommended his return to France, but Father Chabanel, with the means of his relief at hand, turned his back on the beauty and peace of his old life forever, by making a vow to remain in the Huron missions for the rest of his life. He died two years later while he was stationed in the wilderness, although it was never known whether he died of exposure or was murdered by the Indians.

Penances have been part of the religious worship of various sects even up to the present time. Best known of these, perhaps, in the United States at least, are those Mexican-American flagellants, known as Los Hermanos Penitentes de Sangre de Cristo, commonly called simply "Penitentes" and living in northern New Mexico and southern Colorado. According to ecclesiastical history this sect arose and flourished in Europe in the thirteenth and fourteenth centuries, practicing public flagellation to appease the divine wrath.[12]

Another curious sect of this sort is the Filipovtsi described by Baring,[13] who says that in the eighteenth century entire

[12] See Henderson, Alice Corbin, *Brothers of Light*, Harcourt, Brace, 1937.
[13] Baring, Maurice, *The Russian People*, London, Methuen, 1911, pp. 352-54.

families and even villages in Russia belonging to this sect barricaded themselves in order to starve to death. In the reign of Alexander II one peasant persuaded twenty others to retire into the forest and starve themselves to death.

Another Russian group described by Stepniak[14] called its members the *Christs* but outsiders derisively converted this name into *Chlists* which means "whips," since self-flagellation played an important part in their religious rites. They protested against family life and preached absolute continence. The Skoptsi or Castrati (to be discussed later) belonged to this group.

It must be emphasized that these rigors have not been practiced by Christian derivatives only. Most religions show the same phenomena. Ascetic practices are described among the Mohammedan devotees[15] as well as among followers of Buddhism and Brahmanism and many other faiths.[16] The Jews, the Greeks, the Romans and many others believed in sacrifice to forestall divine envy.[17] Juvenal describes how

[14] Stepniak, Michael Dragomanoff, *The Russian Peasantry*, Harper Bro., 1888.

[15] Miyan Hatim of Sambhal, who died in 1562, spent ten years roaming about bareheaded and barefooted, never sleeping on a bed. Muhamad Ghawth spent twelve years among the hills north of the Ganges practicing severe austerities, feeding on the leaves of trees, and sleeping in caves. Shaikh Burhan for nearly fifty years before his death abstained from meat and from most other articles of food and drink. . . . Toward the end of his life he abstained also from drinking water, spending his time in meditation in a small dark cell. (Hastings, James, *Encyclopaedia of Religion and Ethics*, Scribner, 1910.)

[16] "Hindu ascetics remain in immovable attitudes with their faces or their arms raised to heaven until the sinews shrink and the posture assumed stiffens into rigidity; or they expose themselves to the inclemency of the weather in a state of absolute nudity or tear their bodies with knives or feed on carrion and excrement. Among the Mohammedans of India there are fakirs who have been seen dragging heavy chains or cannon balls or crawling upon their hands and knees for years; others have been found lying upon iron spikes for a bed; and others again have been swinging for months before a slow fire with a tropical sun blazing overhead. Among modern Jews some of the more sanctimonious members of the synagogue have been known to undergo the penance of voluntary flagellation before the commencement of the Fast of Atonement, two persons successively inflicting upon each other 39 stripes or 13 lashes with a triple scourge. Among the Zoroastrian Yasts, 30 strokes with the Sraosho-karana is an expiation which purges people from their sins. . . . Herodotus tells that the ancient Egyptians beat themselves while the things offered by them as sacrifices were being burned and that the Carian dwellers in Egypt on such occasions cut their faces with knives. Among the ancient Mexicans blood drawing was a favorite and most common mode of expiating sin and showing devotion . . . 'they mangled their flesh as if it had been insensible and let their blood run in such profusion that it appeared to be a superfluous fluid of the body.' (Clavigero, *History of Mexico*.) Self-mortification also formed part of the religious cult in many uncivilized tribes in North America." (Westermarck, *op. cit.*, Vol. II, p. 353.)

[17] Schiller's famous poem, *The Ring of Polycrates*, epitomizes this sentiment. See also Money-Kyrle's *The Meaning of Sacrifice*, London, 1930.

the expiatory rites of the worship of Isis aroused great enthusiasm in Rome; women broke the ice of the Tiber River on winter mornings to plunge three times into the water, or dragged themselves on bleeding knees around the field of Tarquin, or undertook long pilgrimages to Egypt to propitiate the goddess.

The ascetic ideal is not confined to religious thought; the theory that the body should be kept in subordination to the spirit by self-denial was taught by many pagan philosophers, including Plato and Cicero.

Interesting as these widespread ascetic practices were, it would be impossible to establish the individual psychological motives for all of them. We should not overlook a certain logical justification for historical asceticism and martyrdom dependent on the social conditions in which they flourished. That men denied themselves ordinary comforts and even necessities or exposed themselves to what seem to us to have been unnecessary and foolhardy hazards may be interpreted to mean that their attitudes were determined by strong unconscious individual tendencies toward self-destruction, but, at the same time, these impulses were undoubtedly stimulated by certain popular influences of the age or culture which taught that, by these means, life in another—a larger—sense was saved rather than destroyed. Every culture contains many elements which tend to encourage and facilitate the individual's self-destructive trends. These influences may be mechanical, economic, philosophical, educational, sociological, or moral. We are not able to appraise objectively the destructiveness of some of these trends in our own civilization because we are too close to it to have a proper perspective. We now regard such voluntary martyrdom as has been described as self-destructive, but we probably overlook many of the suicidal aspects of our own culture, perhaps even considering them preservative. It may even be that in years to come our own period may be regarded as one in which man's self-annihilatory tendencies were at their maximum. (Consider, for example, our automobile traffic accidents, our militaristic activities, our waste of natural resources, and our neglect of human values.)

I may be justly criticized, therefore, if it appears in the citing of striking examples of this phenomenon that I have singled out, as peculiarly self-destructive, religious zealots who, within their cultural setting, may have been no more so than any other closely-knit group defending an ideal against a hostile society. It was not my intention to do so; rather, the painstaking and scholarly and often colorful records available concerning these early martyrs make them accessible to study as no other group is, and for this reason in gathering instances of asceticism and martyrdom to illustrate the factors of attrition, aggression, and erotism, already demonstrated in other forms of chronic self-destruction, I have drawn heavily upon religious chronicles, as well as upon historical accounts.

THE SELF-PUNITIVE COMPONENT

It has been reported that an Indian named Inepegut who lived on the White Rocks Indian agency in Utah killed his mother while he was drunk. He left the tribe and for the rest of his life, more than thirty years, did penance as a self-condemned criminal, living as a hermit on the little food that was left by those who pitied him. He wore no clothes and lived without shelter winter and summer, although exposed to extremes of heat and cold, so that at times as he slept on the ground his hair would become frozen in the ice and would have to be chopped loose.

The self-punitive motive so simply revealed in this story is not usually so clearly demonstrable in the lives of the martyrs and ascetics of legend and history, not because the penances were less severe but because the deeds for which they punished themselves were not so evident.[18] The holy men themselves said that they were sinners and that their suffering was an expiation, but one is inclined to dismiss these protestations as evidences of exceedingly tender consciences rather than as proof of guilt, forgetting that the need for punishment is not necessarily associated with heinous crimes or grievous sins. Extraordinary efforts to bring pain and ignominy upon oneself are *prima facie* evidence that the individual suffers from guilt feelings and seeks punishment to relieve them. The majority of people do not recognize that the average individual's conscience does not

---

[18] One may draw his own conclusions from the following: Hitler abstains from alcohol, tobacco, meat and marriage. (*Mein Kampf*, Munich. Eher Verlag, 1927.) Mussolini never drinks hard liquor or alcohol, is a vegetarian, has not smoked since the World War; takes neither tea nor coffee but only a beverage brewed from the leaves of the linden tree. (*Time*, Mar. 15, 1937.) Trotsky drinks no alcohol, eats meat only once a week, does not smoke and has forbidden anyone to smoke in his presence. (New York *Times*, Feb. 27, 1937.)

"A man's greatness appears to depend on his homicidal capacity," said Fielding in *Jonathan Wild*. Perhaps these powerful men maintain their psychological equilibrium by compensating for their aggressiveness by this asceticism.

correspond in its standards to the world of reality, being far more rigid and less amenable to reason. In the realm of the unconscious, fantasies of crime are as heavily weighted with guilt as actual crimes and must be punished. Even instinctual impulses, innocent in themselves, may be the source of agonies of remorse.

According to the psychoanalytic theory, self-condemnation and self-criticism are reflections of parental attitudes and functions incorporated by the child early in life and used as a guide for all his future conduct. Undoubtedly the restraints of civilization and the renunciations required by most religious creeds tend to reinforce these parental attitudes but they are not responsible primarily for guilt-feelings which are operative even among primitive peoples where creeds and philosophies, in a sophisticated sense, are unknown.[19]

History gives abundant testimony to the existence of the sense of guilt in ascetics. It is recorded that their mental suffering was so great that for all their self-torture they did not find peace but struggled with temptation in the form of imaginary demons and evil spirits[20] and were tormented by what they considered unholy thoughts, believing themselves seduced by the devil who (as they thought) came to them in their miserable cells in the dead of night in the form of a beautiful woman. Apparently, for all their atonements, they were still bowed down with an overwhelming burden of despair and fear. Of their grief over their sins, it is recorded of one saint that no day passed after his conversion without his shedding tears, and of another that his eyelashes dropped off from his continual weeping.

Some were able to project their guilt-feelings onto a part

[19] Westermarck (*op. cit.*) believes that asceticism "hardly occurs among nations who have no vivid sense of sin," and he infers that certain religions have intensified the sense of guilt in peoples formerly almost free from it and thereby made the need for expiation more urgent. Without denying the truth of this, psychoanalytic study has quite conclusively refuted the notion that the sense of guilt springs fundamentally from religious teachings. Rather, the religious concepts have sprung from deep psychological needs of mankind and are designed to allow expression of some of these, including the sense of guilt.

[20] In the pictorial representation of the temptation of St. Anthony by a follower of Hieronymus Bosch, in the Metropolitan Museum, grotesque forms are used to symbolize the temptations and evil thoughts. While the symbolism appears obscure at first, closer scrutiny reveals many familiar ideas. The eye and the ear of an old man, for example, probably represent the ever-watchful parents, and the beautiful nude woman surrounded by gross bestial figures represents the degradation of sex. The lascivious postures of some of the weird creatures further illustrate the nature of the temptations. It is not necessary to assume that the artist was aware of the symbolic meaning of the figures, however.

of themselves (the body) and, by mistreating and neglecting it, satisfy their conscience. They maintained that the body was evil, that it was antagonistic to the spiritual things of life and by its demands kept man from attaining perfect holiness. If it failed under the cruelties visited upon it, so much the better. (Compare this attitude with that of the psychotic patient described above who wreaked vengeance upon his body in various ways.)

Self-punishment of this sort was necessary not only to ease the conscience but to relieve the fear of greater punishment (and possible extinction) by a higher authority. Why the idea should have arisen that suffering is pleasing to God is difficult to understand unless one accepts the theory that it was supposed to appease and disarm an avenging power. The question then arises why fear of punishment was linked with such acts as eating, drinking, and sexual pleasure, and why abstinence from these was thought to avert vengeance. The psychoanalytic explanation of this is that originally in the individual's life the superior powers to be propitiated are the parents and that ascetic practices are determined by their attitudes. The child has many resentments against the parents because of their interference with his wishes but he is usually at great pains to conceal these because of his fear of their displeasure. Sometimes he indulges in forbidden acts and on this score, as well as because of his unspoken rebellion, he feels guilty and afraid. To allay his conscience and to avert more severe punishments from his parents, he may punish or deny himself in some way. Since sexuality is surrounded by so many taboos and is absolutely forbidden to the child, it is apparent how that may fall under a ban so severe as to persist throughout adulthood.

The tendency to starve oneself is more obscure in origin unless one dismisses the matter by saying that fasting is merely an effective way of suffering and for that reason commends itself to the individual who wishes to punish himself. It is known, however, that in the unconscious the punishment is usually connected very closely with the crime. For a more specific explanation of the tendency to deny the appetite for food, then, we must again go back to the childhood situation. The ascetic trend has frequently been noted in children who refuse nourishment. Here a mixture of motives which exist for such behavior tend to confuse the issue. The little child may wish to secure attention, excite pity and concern, to exert power over his parents, or to defy or exasperate them by not eating. But deeper than all these motives is the child's anxiety because of imagined danger connected with the act of eating. For him it has acquired a peculiar psychological significance connected with infantile fantasies of eating people. Psychoanalysts[21] and other students have found evidence that in the unconscious, cannibalism is not relinquished to the extent to which social custom has abandoned it since our aboriginal days. I have already referred to this in discussing the oral character (pages 36 ff.). If the entire act of eating becomes too heavily freighted with the fantasy of eating someone or with the fear of being eaten, the child's uneasiness, guilt, and fear lead to an inhibition. It may be set down as axiomatic that where there are fear and guilt in connection with an object, there an inhibition will develop.

Devouring one's enemies is an essentially infantile fantasy (phylogenetically and ontogenetically), but it must not be forgotten that many infantile modes of thought persist unchanged in the unconscious and dominate the adult's behavior, although, as Melanie Klein has pointed out, the normal adult can rationalize his dislikes in all sorts of ways whereas in a child, habits of this kind are attributed to naughtiness or eccentricity. Thus the adult can rationalize an abhorrence of meat on the grounds that fruit and vegetables are a more hygienic diet or that it is in bad taste to eat flesh or that his stomach is so constituted as not to digest meat or that he honors God by abstaining.

Special aversions to food, sometimes extended to the point of refusing to eat anything, are commonly found in the disease melancholia (the manic-depressive syndrome) where this symptom frequently assumes major importance. This affliction is also characterized by feelings of guilt and unworthiness and by self-punitive measures. Infantile cannibalistic fantasies play an important role in this illness,

[21] See especially the following references: Freud, Sigmund, *The Future of an Illusion*, Liveright, 1928, p. 17; Freud, Sigmund, *Inhibition, Symptom and Anxiety*, Psychoanalytic Institute, Stamford, Conn., 1927, p. 23; Abraham, Karl, *Selected Papers on Psycho-Analysis*, London, Hogarth, 1927, pp. 251, 257, 276, 420, 488; Malcove, Lillian, "Body Mutilation and Learning to Eat," *Psychoanalytic Quarterly*, 1933, Vol. II, pp. 557-61; Eder, M. D., "On the Economics and the Future of the Super-Ego," *International Journal of Psychoanalysis*, 1929, Vol. X, p. 251; Jones, Ernest, "Recent Advances in Psychoanalysis," *International Journal of Psychoanalysis*, 1920, Vol. I, p. 165; Fenichel, Otto, *Outlines of Clinical Psychoanalysis*, Norton, 1934, and Psychoanalytic Quarterly Press, Albany, 1934; Lewis, Nolan D., "The Psychobiology of the Castration Reaction," *Psychoanalytic Review*, 1928, Vol. XV, p. 53; Klein, *op. cit.*, pp. 219-20.

which is usually precipitated by a disappointment in a loved object. The patient reacts to this disappointment not by an actual attack upon the object but by an unconscious fantasy of revenge by devouring it. In this way he kills the disappointing one and at the same time keeps him lovingly within him.[22] It is for this great "sin" that the melancholiac reproaches himself with the characteristic bitterness. The aversion to food is at once a denial and a punishment of the fantasied act.

THE AGGRESSIVE COMPONENT

In addition to the more obscure elements of guilt which martyrs and ascetics seem compelled to gratify, there appear to be certain positive satisfactions in martyrdom which we should be prepared to analyze. One of these is the familiar instinctual urge toward destructiveness and aggression which we uncovered in the analysis of the hidden motives of suicide. Indeed, since civilization requires us to control or conceal it, we must expect it to be hidden. It certainly is not usually associated in the public mind with those who serve great causes, and in the case of martyrs, while frequently noted, it is usually discounted by critics as well as by admirers, because of the tremendous price paid for the privilege. In a scientific consideration of the psychological motives of behavior, however, we cannot overlook an important determinant because of the cost to the individual of gratifying it. Furthermore, the great sense of guilt implicit in the need for punishment, discernible in ascetics and martyrs as illustrated in the foregoing pages, implies an aggressiveness and a destructiveness either of intention or accomplishment, for which we must systematically search.

Sometimes it is quite evident; hunger strikes, for example, have an openly avowed aggressive intent. It seems at first contrary to human nature that one individual could force another person to do his will simply by compelling

---

[22] Cf. Longfellow's fantasy:

> I have you [his daughters] fast in my fortress,
>   And will not let you depart,
> But put you down into the dungeon
>   In the round-tower of my heart.
>
> And there will I keep you forever,
>   Yes, forever and a day,
> Till the walls shall crumble to ruin,
>   And moulder in dust away!

from "The Children's Hour,"
Houghton Mifflin, 1899.

his antagonist to witness his suffering and thus force him to assume the moral but illogical obligation for it. Yet this appeal has often proved effective where more direct aggressions have failed. It is said to have been used frequently by the victims of the Conquistadors. The mass suicide attempt of the starving Hungarian miners is another case in point. Creditors used to sit down before the doors of their debtors threatening to starve themselves to death if they were not paid. An Indian legend [23] tells that once when a Raja ordered the house of a Brahman destroyed and his lands confiscated, the Brahman retaliated by fasting at the palace gate until he died and then became an avenging ghost who destroyed the Raja and his house. There is a remarkable likeness in such a legend to the behavior of the child who says to himself (as what child has not?) when he is angry at his parents, "They'll be sorry when I die."

From such consciously directed aggressive suffering to that form in which the sufferer is unaware of his desire to hurt others is not a long step. It has been remarked frequently that unnatural curbing of instinctual impulses tends to shrivel the personality and to weaken its capacity for social adaptation. Thus the ascetic often became a hermit, severing all ties of affection with his family and fellowmen. It is generally believed that severe restriction of normal physical pleasures leads to an impairment of the qualities of good humor, generosity, frankness, and energy, and to a certain extent this is true. The psychoanalytic theory, however, places more stress upon developmental etiology, believing that the original failure to develop the softening love-instincts that would neutralize the hostile drives and result in the development of tolerance, kindness and generosity, is responsible for the severity and rigidity of the personality. The iron control which the ascetic imposes upon certain forms of activity in himself (and oftentimes upon almost every form of activity, destructive and creative alike) is not sufficient to hold in check the aggressions which are extraordinarily powerful in the person whose love-development has been thwarted or choked, but it is sufficient to change the form and direction of their expression. The expression, for example, is usually a passive one in which the inconvenience or hurt caused someone else appears to be incidental to the sufferer's own greater pain; or it is made to appear that the damage occasioned others is brought about impersonally through the cause which the

[23] Related by Westermarck, *op. cit.*, Vol. II, p. 649.

ascetic or martyr has espoused. Thus the responsibility for the aggression is shifted from the conscience.

The nature of the martyr's aggression has never been more concisely stated than in Clarence Day's four lines:

AS THE WORM TURNS

When lovely woman weds a Tartar
And learns too late that love is grim,
How sedulously she plays the martyr,
And meanwhile makes one out of him.
—*The New Yorker,* March 2, 1935.

It is strikingly apparent in a study of the typical aggressions of the martyr that they are generally directed toward the persons most closely bound to him, usually the members of his family. It was said of one saint that he was so benevolent that he was never known to be hard or inhuman to anyone *except his relatives.* This is not so strange as it may seem at first thought, since to a certain extent this tendency to be cruel to those one loves best is present in everyone. The necessity to hate is as fundamental as the necessity to love and the two emotions are combined in our feeling for the people about us. Usually the need to love and be loved is sufficiently well developed to dominate one's relationships with his family, although the frequent breakdown of close relationships bears witness to the underlying hate. But in the martyr, as we have suggested, the love-instincts are poorly developed and the hate impulses thus gain an overwhelming strength.

One of the heroes of my state, John Brown, led a famous fight against slavery; for twenty years he went about in poverty, exhorting, pleading, fighting, burning, and killing before he himself was finally hanged, convicted of treason and murder. His was the true martyr spirit; several times before the day of his sentence he said, "I am worth now infinitely more to hang than for any other purpose." It was as if his bent from the first had been to die for the cause to which he had devoted his fierce, hawk-like spirit. His lawyer wrote of him, ". . . . He answers that he would not walk out if the jail door were left wide open. . . . Yes, I believe it best to give up hope of rescuing our old friend. For he wants to hang! Heaven save his soul, the old man *wants* to hang!"

While Brown wandered about the country, pursuing his vision with intrepid and fanatical zeal, his patient wife struggled with cold, hunger, and wretched poverty on a bleak Adirondack farm. There were thirteen children in the family, nine of whom died. They lived in a leaky, un-plastered house and came close to starvation in the long hard winters without money or food. When the sons were old enough to be of use to their father he sent for them and bid them sacrifice themselves in his holy war. Their mother's mild protest at giving up the son who had man-fully tried to take his father's place as head of the house, assuming responsibilities too heavy for his young shoulders, was ruthlessly thrust aside before the demands of what Brown considered the right. At one time this son wrote his father that his brothers were busy with their own families and would not fight in such a bloody, hopeless cause any more. They had known what it was to be hunted for their lives in Kansas, to be browbeaten by their stern father, "the most dreaded man in the territory," to go to prison for their father's murders, deeds which sickened them. One son had gone mad. Another had been shot. But still their father held them grimly to his purpose. "Tell my sons de-spite they are set strong against me I do not release them," he wrote. Nor did he, for two of them died terrible deaths at Harpers Ferry under siege. When a thousand men sur-rounded the town and the odds were hopelessly against Brown's handful of men, he refused to surrender but sent one of his young men out to treat with the enemy to put a stop to the firing. The man was promptly taken prisoner. Brown then sent out his own son, the lad whom his mother had depended upon and tried to keep with her, to nego-tiate with the troops. He was shot down, fatally wounded before his father's eyes, and dragged himself painfully back to the arsenal to die a lingering death. Still the old man refused to surrender and was taken by force. There seemed to be in him no pity for his sons, no softening when they begged him to let them go and live in peace.[24]

Over and over again in the histories of the martyrs one finds this insensitiveness to the suffering of loved ones. Great explorers and scientists have thrown aside the closest family ties and responsibilities to undertake lonely expedi-tions and dangerous missions. We are familiar with the "slave" to business who sacrifices his family's happiness as well as himself to his ambition. There are countless ex-amples of the unconscious aggressions of the person who sacrifices himself—artists who give up their lives (and

[24] For further details see Ehrlich, Leonard, *God's Angry Man*, Simon and Schuster, 1932, from which this material was taken.

desert their families as Gauguin did) for the sake of art; revolutionaries who imperil their own lives and bring their families and friends into danger through their flaming devotion to an ideal; housewives who make themselves martyrs to their families or to their household duties and by so doing make all those about them unhappy. Our psychological investigations refuse to allow us to accept the naive assumption that such gross indifference to the comfort and welfare of others is always entirely incidental and unavoidable.

Many early accounts of saints deal with flight from the mother, and not only flight from her but actual rejection of her. The mother (or sister) is often represented as following the ascetic into his retreat and begging to see him, while the saint hardens his heart and refuses to have anything to do with her. The element of pleasure in defeating the mother is plainly evidenced in these stories. Sometimes the mother prevailed upon a superior to command her son to see her and the son resorted to such ingenious devices as going to see her in disguise and with his eyes shut so that the mother did not recognize him and he did not see her.

St. Poemen and his six brothers had all deserted their mother to live the ascetic life. The old woman went alone into the desert to see her children once more before her death. She caught sight of them as they were about to leave their cells for the church but they immediately ran back into the cells and slammed the door in her face. She remained outside weeping bitterly and calling to them to let her see them. They refused to open the door, however, telling her that she would see them after death.

The story of the famous Simeon Stylites is even more revealing in his aggressive attitude toward his mother. Of him Lecky has this to say: "He had been passionately loved by his parents, and, if we may believe his eulogist and biographer, he began his saintly career by breaking the heart of his father, who died of grief at his flight. His mother, however, lingered on. Twenty-seven years after his disappearance, at a period when his austerities had made him famous, she heard for the first time where he was, and hastened to visit him. But all her labor was in vain. No woman was admitted within the precincts of his dwelling, and he refused to permit her even to look upon his face. Her entreaties and tears were mingled with words of bitter and eloquent reproach. 'My son,' she is represented as having said, 'why have you done this? I bore you in my womb, and you have wrung my soul with grief. I gave you milk from my breast, you have filled my eyes with tears. For the kisses I gave you, you have given me the anguish of a broken heart; for all that I have done and suffered for you, you have repaid me by the most cruel wrongs.' At last the saint sent a message to tell her that she would soon see him. Three days and three nights she had wept and entreated in vain, and now, exhausted with grief and age and privation, she sank feebly to the ground and breathed her last sigh before that inhospitable door. Then for the first time the saint, accompanied by his followers, came out. He shed some pious tears over the corpse of his murdered mother, and offered up a prayer consigning her soul to heaven . . . and then, amid the admiring murmurs of his disciples, the saintly matricide returned to his devotions."

This was that saint whose penances exceeded those of almost every ascetic of his period for ingenuity and painfulness. "A horrible stench, intolerable to the bystanders, exhales from his body, and worms dropped from him whenever he moved, and they filled his bed. Sometimes he left the monastery and slept in a dry well, inhabited, it is said, by demons. He built successively three pillars, the last being sixty feet high and scarcely two cubits in circumference, and on this pillar, during thirty years, he remained exposed to every change of climate, ceaselessly and rapidly bending his body in prayer almost to the level of his feet. A spectator attempted to number these rapid motions, but desisted from weariness when he had counted 1,244. For a whole year, we are told, St. Simeon stood upon one leg, the other being covered with hideous ulcers, while his biographer was commissioned to stand by his side, to pick up the worms that fell from his body, and to replace them in the sores, the saint saying to the worm, 'Eat what God has given you.' " [25]

Unconscious pride and satisfaction in defying and wounding a loved one is discernible in the diary of the remarkable martyr, Perpetua,[26] a young woman of good birth and education, the only daughter of an indulgent father and mother. Although she was only twenty-two years old her firmness of purpose distinguished her among the little band of early Christians who were imprisoned with her. She records her struggles with her aged father, telling how she resisted all

[25] This and the quotation in the preceding paragraph are quoted from Lecky, *op. cit.*, p. 134.
[26] See Mason, *op. cit.*, pp. 85-105.

his attempts to dissuade her from what he considered a dangerous faith. On one occasion he became so stirred by her defiance that he flung himself upon her to pluck out her eyes but "went away conquered" as she complacently says, adding, "Then for a few days I thanked God for being left without my father and I was refreshed by his absence."

The journal, supposed to have been written by her shortly before her martyrdom, while she lay in jail, describes several painful scenes with her father in which he came to her worn out with sorrow, calling upon her to pity his gray hairs, reminding her that he had preferred her to all her brothers, and begging her not to ruin her family by exposing them to scorn and suspicion, "for not one of us will be able to speak like a free man, if anything should happen to you." He came to her trial, carrying her infant son in his arms and begging her to pity the child, "who cannot live when you are gone." Hilarian, the procurator, who was conducting the trial, was touched by the sight of the old man's frantic grief and urged Perpetua to spare her father's hoary head and her boy's tender years, but she would not listen. Finally, she says, as her father persisted in trying to persuade her, Hilarian ordered him to be turned down and someone hit the poor old man with a rod. She was not finished with him however, for as the day of the sports in the arena drew near he came to see her again and began to tear out his beard and to dash himself on his face on the ground and to "say such words as might move all creation." Perpetua, however, was unmoved from her purpose.

The account of Perpetua's death is given by Tertullian who reports that she retained her spirit to the end, arguing with the tribune about certain arrangements for the sports with such force that she won her point; later she aroused the admiration of the crowd by her courage in the arena; and at the last, after she had been tossed by a savage cow, she was still able to take the faltering hand of the young novice of a gladiator and move the sword point to her own throat. "Perhaps," says her chronicler, "such a woman could not otherwise have been killed . . . if she had not wished it herself." [27]

PROVOCATIVE AGGRESSIONS

Differing somewhat in purpose from the aggressions already

[27] Quoted from Mason, *op. cit.*, pp. 85–105.

described are those in which the chief aim seems to be to provoke persecution or chastisement to obtain self-punitive or masochistic gratification. In the early days of the Christian church the fanatical zeal of some of its followers broke out in sallies against the pagans in which they burned temples, broke idols, overturned altars, and fought with the peasants who tried to defend the shrines of their gods. These insults infuriated the people and endangered the lives of all the Christians. The Council of Illiberis, one of the early Church councils, found it necessary to make a canon refusing the title of martyr to those persons who were executed for such provocative offenses. Nevertheless, martyrdom obtained as a result of enraging the people by rash and defiant deeds was still sought after as a high honor by some zealots, as the story of Apphian and Aedesius[28] illustrates. These young men were brothers, members of a distinguished family in Lycia. Apphian became a Christian and ran away from home to Caesarea where he joined a community of students and lived a life of stern asceticism for nearly a year when an edict was received requiring the attendance of the whole population at sacrificial rites. The governor was in the act of pouring a libation to the gods when Apphian slipped through the band of soldiers and officials and seized the governor's hand, bidding him desist. He was arrested and put in the prison stocks over night. Other forms of torture were resorted to to make him recant, such as wrapping rags soaked in oil about his legs and setting fire to them. Finally he was thrown into the sea.

His brother Aedesius was determined not to be outdone. He was well educated, familiar with Latin literature as well as with Greek. Soon after his brother's death he was condemned to hard labor in the copper mines of Palestine. When he was released he followed the austere profession of a philosopher, until one day when the governor of Egypt pronounced sentence upon some Christian girls in Alexandria where Aedesius was sojourning, he stepped up to the governor, slapped him in the face first with his right hand and then with his left, throwing him to the ground. Like his brother, he was given a course of tortures and then thrown into the sea. The fact that neither of these young men carried out their parents' high ambitions for them, that one of them is reported to have run away from home because he found it intolerable, and their almost identical assaults upon a person of high degree, indicate a conflict

[28] *Ibid.*, pp. 290-92.

about authority, for which they paid with their lives. This defiance and provocation of authority is characteristic of many ascetics and martyrs, as we have seen. What should not be overlooked is the evident desire to struggle with authority and to be overpowered (as was certain to be the case). The defiance has the purpose of stimulating swift and sure punishment.

Many times the magistrates seem to have been aware of this element of provocativeness and to have tried to avoid gratifying it. They had the difficult task, on the one hand, of trying to control the people who had been stung to fury by the militant methods of the Christians, and on the other hand, of subduing without satisfying the frantic desire of the fanatical members of the Christian community for martyrdom. Rivalry between candidates for martyrdom seems to have been a common phenomenon.[29]

One author states that the judges might have been ex-

[29] This element is illustrated in the legend of the aged ascetic, Leo, who lived on the southern coast of Asia Minor (Mason, op. cit., pp. 200-01), who had lost a friend by martyrdom and felt despondent that his own life had been spared. He dreamed one night that he saw his martyred friend ahead of him in a great flood of rushing water. By struggling against the current, he was able to reach the point where his friend stood. The next day he started for the grave of his friend to pray. Passing a pagan temple, the old man dashed in, throwing down the lighted lanterns and tapers and shouting defiance. He was arrested and brought to trial, where instead of answering the charges, he harangued the judge. It is recorded that the judge was patient with the elderly man but finally yielded to the clamor of the outraged crowd and ordered him thrown in the river, to the great joy of the prisoner.

A similar case is that of Theodore, a native of Syria and a soldier. He made it plain that he was a Christian and was accordingly brought before the governor of the province for examination. He condemned the worship of pagan gods in no uncertain terms, but the authorities were inclined to be lenient with him and did not place him under arrest. That night Theodore took advantage of his liberty to go and set on fire the temple of the Mother of the gods (for whose worship this district was famous) which stood in the very center of the city. He did not conceal his deed, but rather gloried in the destruction. But even then the authorities were loath to punish him and offered him not only pardon but promotion if he would sacrifice. (This custom of burning incense before the statues of the emperor, which was the usual form that the Christians who came into conflict with the law were required to honor, was according to some authorities more of a test of loyalty to civil authority than a confession of any particular belief, and the refusal of the Christians to comply with it aroused feelings of impatience somewhat akin to those produced many years later by the refusal of the Quakers to take an oath in court. [Lecky, op. cit., Vol. I, p. 405.] The Jews refused to sacrifice to the emperor, also, but were rarely molested because their religion, while exclusive, was unaggressive and consequently they were conceded liberty to abstain from official national rites.)

Theodore, however, continued to answer this offer with words of outrage and insult against the gods and against the emperor. When he was finally tortured to break down his resistance he began to sing. His biographer says, "A short but merry imprisonment ended in a death by fire." (Mason, op. cit., pp. 233-34.)

cused if they had lost their tempers with the martyrs, so provocative were the answers to the questions of the court as related in the *Acts of the Martyrs,* but on the contrary it is recorded in many instances that the judges showed great patience and kindness in their endeavors to save the martyrs from the doom they seemed intent upon. Such answers as "We bear the authority of the eternal King; therefore we pay no regard to the authority of mortal man," were calculated to defy the authority of the civil court. The executioners and the judges were often weary of their gruesome task and sought to shorten it by moving to let the prisoners go. Often the judge, moved by the youth and inexperience of some of those brought before him, offered to parole young Christians to relatives. In some cases the advocates hired by friends of the prisoner, against the martyr's will, saved the prisoner by misrepresenting the case to the judge, who was only too willing to listen to them rather than the prisoner. But the martyrs defeated these kindly efforts in their behalf over and over by rashly shouting their contempt for authority and their desire for a glorious death.

THE EROTIC COMPONENT

We have spoken of satisfactions of another order in martyrdom—satisfactions of a positive nature which tend to mitigate the bleak suffering and to transform it into an ecstasy of pain. Our clinical experience and also some study of the historical accounts would give us the impression that in some instances there is physical pleasure even in this kind of suffering which is akin to, if not a direct representative of, the pleasure associated with gratification of the sexual instinct. That some men and women will go to incredible lengths to submit to cruelty, deriving conscious sexual satisfaction from ill-treatment, is well known, probably better known than that the phenomena of masochism may also be operative (although unrecognized and unacknowlededged) in the passion for suffering, and the mystic and ecstatic experiences which come to many through deprivation, degradation, and physical torture in the service of a cause. These experiences are often described in sensuous terms in the historic records.

In addition to this satisfaction, there are other gratifications, which, although derived from the same instinctual element, are more serviceable in making the fate tolerable than in electing it. Some of these are expressly described in the writings of the day. They include the exploitation of suffering to gain power and prestige in this world or in the next, and exhibitionism, both conspicuously represented in the accounts of the lives of many martyrs.

Whether the erotic satisfactions obtained from suffering are primary (motivation), or secondary (capitalization), it is often impossible to tell because the possibility of the subsequent *exploitation* of the situation acts as a determining *motive,* although probably a less powerful one than the more direct instinctual derivatives (neutralization of aggression by erotic infusion). That the paradox of pleasure from pain existed and influenced the martyrs is not difficult to show from the historical accounts; I have attempted to go further and to select several instances which indicate the possible nature of the satisfaction in certain situations.

Many martyrs were sustained in their suffering by the expectation of attaining power, knowing that their prayers were held to be far more efficacious than those of ordinary people. Recorded dreams and visions show a childlike regard for the distinction and special privileges supposed to be secured through martyrdom. In this unworldly but nevertheless impelling thirst for power the degree of suffering was held to be important in determining the degree of exaltation. As Cyprian wrote to four Christians who had been in prison in Rome for many months: "The very delay of your martyrdom elevates you to yet greater heights and the length of time, so far from detracting from your glory, does but enhance it. . . . Each day adds to you a new distinction. Your deserts grow greater with each month as it rolls over you. The man who suffers outright, gains but one victory, but he who remains under constant inflictions, and meets pain without being conquered, receives a daily crown." [30] (This argument may shed some light on why chronic forms of self-destruction are frequently elected instead of more direct forms.) [31]

Somewhat akin to the thirst for power is the satisfaction obtained from exhibiting one's fortitude under cruel treatment. The erotic root of exhibitionism is easily discernible. Vanity (narcissism) in undisguised form is frowned upon

[30] Mason, *op. cit.,* p. 153.

[31] See St. Anthony's boast in Flaubert's account (Flaubert, Gustave, *The Temptation of St. Anthony,* translated by Lafcadio Hearn, Harper Bro., 1932): "Lo! for these thirty years and more I have been dwelling and groaning unceasingly in the desert! . . . and those who are decapitated, tortured with red hot pincers, or burned alive, are perhaps less meritorious than I, seeing that my whole life is but one prolonged martyrdom."

by society, perhaps because of its antisocial nature but also because of its erotic significance. The act of showing oneself off in its classical and undisguised form, i.e., exposure of the naked body, is forbidden by law and flagrant display of personal egotism is universally disapproved. An actor or entertainer becomes unpopular when his self-love pierces the disguise of his art. But in indirect and socially acceptable forms exhibitionism is admired, providing its subjective motive is sufficiently disguised. Asceticism and martyrdom, more particularly the latter, are two of the most effective of all such disguises, because they carry with them the element of great, often quite disproportionate, suffering.

The satisfaction experienced need not be accompanied by any conscious feelings of pleasure. In fact the accounts would lead us to believe that the ascetics in general carried on their "pious calisthenics" (as one writer calls their fatiguing compulsive rituals) dismally enough. Their activities seem obsessional rather than consciously pleasurable, although some holy men testified to mystic ecstasies in connection with their privations. The martyrs, however, are often described as having been joyful, even merry, as they impulsively threw away their lives.

An instance in which the exhibitionistic element seemed strongly indicated was that of a young Christian who was condemned to death for his faith and was sentenced to be thrown in the river immediately. The young man, much disappointed, is reported to have said, "I thought I should have all those tortures that you threatened me with and then, at the end of them, be put to the sword; but you have treated me with none of these things. Do it, I beseech you, that you may learn how Christians through their faith are schooled to despise death." The governor is said to have relented (!) to the extent of adding to his sentence the death by sword and the young man thanked him for extending the range of his sufferings.[32]

One may argue that the martyr's desire for self-effacement seems in many instances to deprive him of every opportunity for exhibitionistic satisfactions; but this is to assume that he requires a large audience; oftentimes his sufferings are displayed to one person alone; and in other instances he appears satisfied with his own self-regard (although, technically speaking, this is pure narcissism instead of secondary narcissism or exhibitionism), as was Narcissus in the Greek legend. In religious self-immolation the ex-

[32] From Mason, *op. cit.*, p. 351.

hibitionism may be directed toward a god. The custom of humiliating oneself before a god—a means of exalting the god and publicly demeaning oneself—is widespread. Westermarck alludes to the Moorish practice of tying holy men and throwing them into a pond in order that their pitiful condition might induce God to send rain. One might expect, therefore, that one motive in the martyr's suffering would be to arouse pity and concern in the god he serves, as well as in beholders. We have already mentioned the genesis of this attitude in the child's desire to arouse concern in his parents. Pity, being akin to love, is sometimes accepted in lieu of love and is as eagerly sought after.

Apart from exhibitionism, however, the suffering of the martyr and the ascetic would appear to have no relation to the gratification of erotic impulses, to be indeed associated with the renunciation of all sexual interests. The tendency to renounce sex was as marked in the early Church adherents as it was in the clinical cases we have cited. To give a few illustrations of this tendency:[33] St. Nilus, who had a wife and two children, longed to join the ascetics and finally induced his wife to consent to a separation; St. Ammon, on the night of his marriage, greeted his bride with an harangue upon the evils of the married state and they agreed to separate at once; St. Melania convinced her husband, after long and earnest argument, to let her go to devote herself to the ascetic ideal; St. Abraham ran away from his wife on the night of his marriage.[34]

Although the less fanatical leaders of the church viewed with alarm the spread of such teachings and ruled that married persons should not enter into an ascetic life except by mutual consent, it was still popularly regarded as a proof of sanctity to abstain from sex relations.

One may well ask what erotic gratification can be afforded by such an obvious flight from sexuality. One is rather impressed by the harshness of the conscience which forbids such individuals not only erotic but all other pleasure in life. This element is the only one perceived by the

[33] Taken from Lecky, op. cit., Vol. II, p. 322.
[34] Among the numerous legends in this spirit is one cited by Lecky (II, p. 323), ascribed to Gregory of Tours, which tells of a rich young Gaul who was passionately attached to his young bride. On their wedding night she confessed to him, with tears, that she had vowed to keep her virginity and that she regretted that her love for him had betrayed her into marriage. He promised her that she would be free to observe her vow, although they would remain united. And it is recorded that when she died several years later her husband declared that he restored her to God as immaculate as he had received her.

martyr, just as it is remarked by the rest of the world, while the masochistic pleasure he derives from the situation is usually entirely overlooked and can be inferred only by observing the behavior of the suffering individual with more than ordinary care.

Among the legends of those saints who fled from marriage is that of St. Alexis who left his bride on their wedding night. Many years later he returned to his father's house where his wife still mourned her desertion. There he begged a lodging in the name of charity and lived unknown to his family until his death. The erotic capitalization possible in this arrangement is apparent; the situation enabled the lonely, loveless man to live among his loved ones; to be homeless and yet at home; to be cared for and fed by his father as he had been in infancy and childhood; to be the object of veneration and devotion and yet to be free from the burdens of maturity and marriage; thus it permitted him a singular amount of gratification under the guise of great deprivation, since he denied himself the pleasure of revealing his identity to his family.

The story of Polyeuctus and Nearchus,[35] which has been made the subject of a play by Corneille, illustrates an almost undisguised erotic motivation in the choice of martyrdom. Whether historically true in all its details or not, it

[35] Polyeuctus and Nearchus were soldiers and close friends in the same Roman legion. Nearchus was a Christian and when an edict against Christians was published he shunned his friend in order not to bring him into suspicion and danger. Polyeuctus was greatly disturbed by this and even more grieved when he discovered that Nearchus believed that their friendship must cease at death, since unbelievers were lost. He decided that he would cast his lot with his friend. Nearchus was pleased at this decision but feared that his friend's faith was not sufficiently well founded to stand the terrible tests to which it would be put; Polyeuctus, however, felt no such misgivings; he feared that he would be put to death before he received baptism and thus be separated from his friend. When he was reassured on this point he was on fire to demonstrate his good faith, and drawing his friend to the place where the edict against Christians was posted he read it through with scorn and then tore it down and destroyed it. A few moments later they met a procession carrying idols back to the temple and Polyeuctus dashed the idols to the ground and trampled upon them. The two were arrested and brought before the local magistrate who was Polyeuctus's father-in-law. He was grieved at the turn of events and begged Polyeuctus not to commit himself further until he had seen his wife but Polyeuctus remained obdurate, saying wife and child were nothing to him unless they would take the same step he had. He rebuked his father-in-law for attempting to turn him from his course and refused to be moved by his wife's tears. His father-in-law was left with no choice, under the code of the times, but to sentence him to death. Polyeuctus accepted the sentence to be beheaded calmly, saying he saw a young man leading him on (his fellow Christians assumed this was Christ). His last words were ones of encouragement and affection for his friend, Nearchus. (Abstracted from Mason, *op. cit.*, pp. 120-22.)

is interesting because it shows the author's intuitive perception of the intensely personal (erotic) gratification which an individual may seek and find in suffering for an abstract cause.

Most forms of masochism demand that the punishment or mistreatment be administered or, at least, sanctioned by a loved being, although in the religious masochist this necessity may be veiled in mystic ecstasies of the spirit. For example, Father William Doyle, a member of the Society of Jesus, a modern martyr, killed in action in 1917, inflicted upon himself great personal discomforts, including a hair shirt, chains, exposure to nettles and thorns, and to freezing water at midnight; he lay on the cold chapel stones; he flagellated himself and he denied his hearty appetite the satisfaction of all but the barest necessities. His notebook records in detail the temptations he had in connection with sugar, cake, honey, jam and other delicacies: "Violent temptation to eat cake, resisted several times. Overcame desire to take jam, honey, and sugar. Fierce temptation to take cake, etc. Drank cold tea. Tempted to take sweets."

That these sacrifices were dedicated to God in a very personal sense is evidenced in such entries in his journal as, "God has been urging me strongly all during this retreat to give up butter entirely," and "Towards the end of the retreat a light came to me that, now that I have given Jesus all the sacrifices I possibly can in the matter of food, He is now going to ask retrenchment in the quantity." This personal relation with a severe but loving God is further indicated in his own words: "I long to get back to my little room at night to calm and quiet and yet I dread it, for He is often so loving there. . . . It is such a helpless feeling to be tossed about, as it were, on the waves of love, to feel the ardent, burning love of His heart, to know He asks for love, and then to realize one human heart is so tiny." ". . . at times I feel half mad with the love of God." And again, "Every fiber of His divine nature is thrilling with love for me . . . every beat of His gentle heart is a throb of intense affection for me. . . ." One cannot doubt the intense erotic gratification of such mystic experiences.[36]

There is another form of masochism, however, in which the suffering itself seems to be the entire source of gratification, quite apart from the agent administering it. Freud

[36] Campbell, Charles Macfie, *Human Personality and the Environment*, Macmillan, 1934, pp. 25-28. (Abstracted from O'Rahilly, Alfred, *Father William Doyle, S.J., A Spiritual Study*, Longmans, Green, 1925.)

calls this the "moral form of masochism." The suffering is the important thing, whether it comes from friends, foes, or an impersonal fate. The gratification afforded by such masochism is apparent in the eagerness with which the person seeks situations in which he must suffer and in the relief of tension which the suffering always brings him. That what is significantly called the "lust for pain" may overwhelm the individual and lend a peculiarly "unmoral" coloring to his excessive morality has been noted again and again by sober observers. Thus the ascetic is "tempted" to sin in order that he may do greater penances and the martyr "provokes" his persecutors in a frenzy that goes beyond the bounds of righteous zeal.

This was recognized and regretted by the early Church fathers who came to attach penalties to too excessive indulgence in suffering among the faithful. Those who volunteered for martyrdom were reproved, even though they came well out of the trial. "It is not Christ's will that we should present ourselves of our own accord to the attendants and men-at-arms of the devil, and bring upon them guilt of additional deaths, compelling them to be more cruel than they would otherwise have been," said the bishop of Alexandria.[37] He attached no blame to those who paid money to be left unmolested in their religion; he urged his followers to protect themselves by withdrawing into hiding when danger threatened, even if others were apprehended instead of them, and he exempted from all blame those Christians who were compelled by violent force or while unconscious to accept sacrifice.

Nevertheless, the white-hot fervor of the martyrs continued to transport them. During the epidemic of martyrdom which swept the early Christian church, "men seemed indeed to be in love with death." [38] Ignatius, bishop of Antioch in Syria, was said to have been in a state of unearthly exaltation before his martyrdom. He had been condemned to fight with wild beasts at Rome and while on his way from Antioch he wrote seven epistles. His one fear was lest some powerful Christians at Rome should procure his pardon. "I dread your very love," he writes them, "lest it should do me a wrong. . . . Oh, that I may enjoy the wild beasts that are prepared for me. I will entice them to make short work of me. . . . If they will not do it of their own accord, I will make them do it. Come fire and cross

[37] Quoted from Mason, *op. cit.*, pp. 312-14.
[38] Lecky, *op. cit.*, Vol. I, p. 391.

and grapplings with wild beasts, wrenching of bones, hacking of limbs, crushings of my whole body, cruel tortures of the devil, only let me attain to Jesus Christ." It is said [39] that nothing that had yet happened did so much to enhance the glory of martyrdom as "the intoxication of spirit with which this fiery Syrian prophet shot like a meteor from the East to the West to die."

Religious history is full of accounts of similar passionate martyrdoms. Of an English martyr, many years later than the early Christians, it is said [40] that he was so merry during the three months of his imprisonment that many wondered at him for he had always been shy at home. When he was brought out for execution it was remarked that he reached the scaffold before the sheriff "as if he were a bridegroom going to his nuptials." Edward Burden, another English martyr, suffered from tuberculosis and lay ill upon his prison bed, when a summons came for him to come into court. Invigorated by the prospect of a speedy martyrdom (which was not denied him), he rushed into court with so much alacrity that the judges upbraided the jailer for having said he was a sick man.

SUMMARY

In this chapter we have considered the fact that the behavior of many martyrs and most ascetics is essentially self-destructive, whether the victim is regarded as a saint, a hero, a psychiatric patient, or a foolish friend. Upon examination, the components of the self-destructive urge in asceticism and martyrdom are apparently identical with those which we found to determine actual suicide—the self-punitive, the aggressive, and the erotic. Evidently, however, these are in different proportions. For that death is postponed is evidence of some greater degree of neutralization of the destructive element by the erotic element, a neutralization which would seem to vary greatly in different instances. The precise nature of the interplay between these vectors can be studied in a few examples, insufficient in number to permit of generalizations beyond those already implied: in chronic suicide the erotic elements are stronger, the destructive elements relatively weaker, than in direct and immediate suicide. But the battle is a fierce and bloody one, even in those in whom, by dint of great sacrifice, a

[39] Mason, *op. cit.*, pp. 17-20.
[40] Pollen, John Hungerford, *Acts of English Martyrs*, London. Buns and Oates, 1891.

little flame of life is kept burning for a relatively long time.

It may be argued by the philosophically-minded that every individual who conforms to the requirements of civilization in restricting his appetites and controlling his aggressive drives, has developed an ascetic trend. In this train of thought, education appears a training in asceticism —an asceticism which comes to its full flower in the unselfish, day-by-day sacrifice of the individual for his children and the social welfare of his community. The parallel between the sacrifice of the individual to the common good and the phenomenon we have described in the foregoing chapter cannot be carried far, however, without an important point of difference becoming apparent; in the normal individual the renunciations made are dictated by external reality requirements—the laws of health, of society, and of economic necessity—and are designed to bring him reality rewards. In other words, they are accepted as conditions of life. In the victim of chronic suicide, on the other hand, the renunciations are dictated more by inner necessities than by external reality and, although the individual, himself, may regard them as a means of perpetuating life, they appear to the objective observer as explicit self-destruction.

TWO / *Neurotic Invalidism*

There are certain forms of martyrdom which do not meet with the same popular approval as the conventional forms which we have been describing. They appear to lack the *voluntary* element and yet they can scarcely be described accurately as involuntary sacrifice because they do not develop in the service of any ideal but seem rather to be purely personal—even selfish—affairs. For this reason they lack the approbation accruing to self-sacrificial martyrdom dedicated to a cause.

These martyrs of whom I speak are not so forthright, either, in their avowal of their intentions. The orthodox martyr faces his fate with a full recognition of the necessity of sacrifice; the victims of the chronic self-destruction which we are about to describe deny to the end that the destruction which they achieve for themselves is in any way sought by them. I refer to the martyrdom of chronic invalidism.

Naturally, I exclude from consideration such chronic invalidism as arises on a fortuitous or extrinsic basis; a victim of cancer, of an automobile accident brought about by someone else, or of an hereditary disease certainly could not be regarded as a self-appointed martyr. I have in mind chiefly those cases ordinarily described by physicians as *neurotic* invalids and hypochondriacs, but I do not mean to exclude the occurrence of physical symptoms and actual physical lesions. We know how some individuals capitalize any illness and distort its importance and seriousness; the greater susceptibility of such individuals to sickness is also well known. As Forsyth[1] has well stated, these patients are usually treated either by being submitted to unnecessary medical or surgical treatment, thus intensifying the neurotic condition, or by being told that the physician does not *think* anything is the matter but suspects some organ or system which needs watching and care, or, finally, by being told that they show no evidence of organic disease and that the whole thing is "functional," "imaginary," "all in the head," with the implication that they are liars or malingerers or "damned neurotics" deserving the unfortunate kind of care that must necessarily go with such a characterization. All of this plays into the hands of the unconscious needs of these patients, and justifies their feelings of being misunderstood, neglected, mistreated—in short, *martyred*.

These chronic invalid martyrs are so familiar, at least to physicians, that it would be carrying coals to Newcastle merely to recite symptomatic descriptions or case histories of such persons. Probably the majority of all the patients who consult physicians and others for relief fall into this category. Hence I think it devolves upon us to study some representative cases minutely from the psychological standpoint for the sake of showing the similarity of psychological motivation in these cases to that in the more conventional and less disguised forms of chronic self-destruction discussed in the previous chapter.

I shall cite two examples, the one so extreme and long established that while it could be observed and fairly well understood psychiatrically, the patient was entirely impervi-

[1] Forsyth, D., *Place of Psychology in Medical Curriculum*, Proceedings of Royal Society of Medicine, 1932, Vol. XXV, pp. 1200-12.

ous to any kind of treatment; the other one, a case once also regarded as hopeless but ultimately cured, is of importance here not so much because of this result as because the treatment used threw so much light on the determining motives for the illness. Both patients happened to have been women; perhaps women are more frequently addicted to this form of self-destruction than are men.

The first patient was married, sixty years old, but well preserved despite her innumerable woes. She had had a life-long preoccupation with her body. In addition to exaggerating the severity of every ordinary physical illness—and there were comparatively few such illnesses—she had always had fears of various diseases and many times imagined that she was suffering from various malignant conditions.

In spite of her neurosis, she had been able to hold many jobs successfully. Each position, however, she had quit of her own accord, because of a real or fancied illness. Aside from the usual childhood diseases, the first illness which she could remember was an attack of grippe when she was 24. In her latter years, she was frequently inclined to blame all of her subsequent maladjustment and misery on this attack of grippe. It was characteristic of her always, however, to ascribe everything to her latest illness, and to say that she was getting along all right until *that* had to happen and give her a "backset."

Her entire history was a succession of incidents running somewhat as follows: After slowly recovering from the last previous illness, she would manage to get a job, work compulsively but with many neurotic difficulties and considerable unhappiness for several years, when there would occur another illness—even so slight a condition as an ear abscess, or an attack of the grippe—whereupon she would quit her job, exaggerate the symptoms tremendously, demand attention, complain and worry constantly, irritate her relatives and doctors and nurses almost to distraction; then improve, get another job, and repeat the whole process.

She quit a good job to marry an impecunious ne'er-do-well whose intellectual and cultural status was many grades below her own. This neurotic marriage was a failure from the outset. She had been married less than a year when she began a round of constant worry, bickering, and complaints of various bodily symptoms which gradually came to focus about a supposed "chronic appendicitis," a condition now regarded by most physicians as mythical. She finally got herself operated upon, but the intense hypochondriasis and invalidism which finally brought her to the state hospital began then in earnest. As ever, she blamed everything onto this operation. She should never have had it in the first place, she said; the doctor let her go home from the hospital too soon; she should have gone somewhere else than the place she did go to. Always it was, "If that hadn't happened, or if I had done something else instead of what I did, all this trouble and sickness could have been avoided."

Once in the hospital, she considered herself weakened and exhausted, too weak ever to recover. She felt her pulse dozens of times every day and was apprehensive about the slightest real or fancied increase or decrease in its rate; she noted every new sensation in the heart-region or elsewhere in the chest, interpreting it as a sign of malignant heart disease; she was intensely concerned for a time about her thyroid, thinking it was enlarging and that she would have to have an operation which she wouldn't survive; she was never free from concern about her bowels, being very finicky about her diet in an attempt to prevent a bowel movement, worrying because she feared one was impending, and when it finally occurred, being seized with weakness and exhaustion so that she had to lie down for several hours to recover. When some water was accidentally spilled on her head and ear, she complained and worried for days about a possible ear infection; when she bumped against somebody and hurt her eye a little, she cried and whined for several days that she was blind, and was almost disappointed when she found she was not. When she was taken to the dentist to have a badly abscessed tooth extracted, she moaned and mourned for days, going around holding a towel or handkerchief to her mouth, refusing to have her mouth examined, and saying that now she could never get well, whereas she was getting along all right before, and should never have had it done. She contracted a slight cold during a wintry spell, and stayed in bed, the picture of misery and suffering until the cold disappeared, and thereafter this slight illness was another irreparable injury. When she could be encouraged to go out for a short walk, or to sit in the sun for a while or to go down some steps to hydrotherapy, she complained bitterly upon returning, saying that she had overdone and had injured herself, for which events those who had urged her to go were wholly to blame.

Let us now look more closely into the origin and development of these symptoms and afflictions. This patient was the second of three sisters, being three years younger than the eldest, and nine years older than the youngest. Her father, who was a paranoid, irresponsible man, preferred the oldest sister until the youngest sister was born, and then he showered all his attention upon her, always treating the patient with disdain, spanking her for various offenses but never spanking the sisters. The patient slept between her parents in bed until she was about six years old, and recalls that she could not fall asleep unless she held onto the lobe of her father's ear, or held her hand against her mother's cheek. Afterwards, when she slept alone, she would often awaken in the night, find everything quiet, and listen with strained ears for the breathing of each member of the family. If she couldn't hear it, she would be terror stricken and would have to get up, make the rounds and see for herself that each one was still alive; only then could she go back to sleep. She had conscious death-wishes for her younger sister which filled her with horror, and even had impulses to attack her with a knife. At the same time she was filled with fears of injuries to her own body, and was afraid she would not be able to pray enough to avert destruction for herself and the rest of the family. In this we see how she feared punishment in the form of the injury or illness she wished to see fall upon others.

The patient was very prudish about sex all through childhood, but began to masturbate at thirteen and concurrently developed the most marked fears about injury to her own body. She would frequently examine herself closely in the mirror, especially her face and her genitals, to see if there were any sign of injury. She feared she would go blind, or would injure herself internally in some way. Her masturbation was accompanied by fantasies of violent attack upon herself, and of injury and death for the other members of the family. She felt she had never gotten any affection from her parents but only censure and punishment, especially from her father, and she had undoubtedly provoked her parents to punish her in order to get at least that form of attention.

After she conquered her erotic feelings at the age of eighteen, she felt very pure and chaste for five years. Later, however, she noticed that when something went wrong in her work, she would have a feeling of anxiety followed by an involuntary sexual climax without any genital stimulation. Thus it was apparent that masturbation and sexual relief had become associated with anxiety and punishment. She did not marry until 37, and immediately after marriage developed an intense syphilophobia and felt she was being destroyed by this dread disease.

In the hospital, she many times vowed she would kill herself as the only way out; when anxious and disturbed, she would fantasy cutting her throat or her wrists with a piece of glass or a knife, then going to the bathroom to sit by the tub and die in her own gore. She often fantasied hanging herself or inserting poison into her rectum. Afterwards, however, she would often be seized with terror that by indulging in them (the fantasies) she had irreparably injured herself—her heart, her thyroid, her general bodily health, and would become so disturbed that she would feel again that the only thing left for her was suicide. Thus the patient destroyed herself hundreds of times in fantasy, the fantasy having the symbolic meaning of a sexual assault which she both desired and feared. Her self-destructive fantasies were provoked by rage against the nurses or the doctors because of certain slights or fancied mistreatment. How this repeated the early childhood situation is obvious.

Her frequent but transitory improvements were always traceable to some show of affection on the part of the doctor, especially if she could read into it some sexual element. For example, after she had discussed sexual matters with him and he had explained some sexual matter to her, she felt relieved for a whole afternoon sometimes; then she would begin to fantasy about sex in her usual way, as an attack, and would become frightened, especially when she experienced pleasurable genital sensations. On one occasion the doctor hitched up his trousers and adjusted his vest as he rose to leave her room after a visit. She thought he had done this to arouse sexual feeling in her, and felt a warm glow of pleasure and contentment for a number of hours, until something happened that she could interpret as a rejection, when she became again disturbed, resentful, and obsessed with sado-masochistic fantasies. Throughout she remained impervious to all treatment.

One sees in such a case all the elements of self-destruction laid bare in the analysis of the deeper motives of suicide—but with a saving or sparing element which finds refuge in chronicity. This poor woman died a thousand deaths, and while her death wishes for others probably killed no one, they certainly rendered many people very unhappy. Such patients every doctor knows to his sorrow.

They are, literally, martyrs and at the same time they make martyrs of others. Their martyrdom has the same unconscious motives as those pointed out in the historic martyrs discussed in the previous chapter—aggression and self-punishment, both eroticized. The conscious motives, however, in these invalid martyrs are obviously very different; instead of a great cause, a religious or romantic purpose, their entire preoccupation would seem to be with themselves and, if their suffering accomplishes anything beyond this, it usually escapes their knowledge or is interpreted belatedly like a postscript. One recalls how smugly Job's friends were able to explain the virtues of and reasons for his afflictions. I remember a more modern saint, racked with rheumatism, who refuted his own doubt by the brave declaration, "It isn't everyone that God can trust to suffer." Others get greater satisfaction out of the effect they produce upon the doctors and upon their friends than in contemplating the extent to which it pleases God.

Next, I want to present in somewhat greater detail the history of a similar patient, somewhat younger but equally ill, equally hopeless-appearing, equally resistant to the many treatments she had had. This was the daughter of an aristocratic Californian "native son" whose horses, orchards, and wealth brought him no relief from his constant anxiety about his invalid daughter.

She was first seen in bed, prostrate, a slight, delicate, ethereal-looking girl unable to walk and scarcely able to talk. She suffered constantly from severe and torturing pains. In addition to the pain which shifted from one part of her body to another, she was troubled with constant headaches; she could not eat; her digestive and menstrual functions were exceedingly irregular; she slept only with large doses of sleep-producing drugs. All this had begun rather suddenly sixteen years previously, acute episodes alternating with partial remissions ever since. Her entire adult life had been a pilgrimage from one doctor to another, from one hospital to another, in a search for relief from her prostrating invalidism. Her pilgrimages were unsuccessful, however, for she remained unimproved and had been told by several physicians that she would be a cripple and an invalid for the rest of her life. Others held out hope in this treatment or that; there had been more than a dozen major and minor operations, to say nothing of other kinds of treatment—medicines, dietary régimes, etc. She herself had abandoned all hope—she no longer expected anything from any treatment. She was brought in an ambulance and carried on a stretcher to a bed where for days she scarcely moved. When it was absolutely necessary that she do so her face would contort in agony, she would writhe from side to side, arch her back, press her hand upon her abdomen or her back and groan softly as if struggling to control a more disturbing expression of her great suffering. She described the pain in her side as a feeling that something "tender and swollen" were inside it, as if hot knives were thrust into her.

Physical, neurological, and laboratory examinations revealed insufficient structural or physiological basis for the pain. There were the many operative scars, but nothing organic to account for her suffering. A chronic invalid, a "martyr" of this type, whose condition had defied medical (and religious) efforts for sixteen years, who after all that time is still suffering too acutely to even speak, could certainly not be regarded as promising or even likely material for therapeutic success. Yet this woman, two years later, was well, clinically and socially. This is important not as an evidence of the value of the psychoanalytic method which was used, but as evidence that under certain conditions an unprofitable, wasteful type of martyrdom can be surrendered and, most important of all, the motives for such phenomena can be laid bare and compared with those we have previously examined.

Naturally there are many factors in her history which I cannot, with respect to professional discretion and the economy of space, include in this narration. Nor shall I recite in detail how she was gradually led to regard the psychological factors in her case as worth consideration, especially since she protested loudly from the beginning that her symptoms were physical and that those who ascribed them to psychological causes misunderstood her and were impugning her motives and her honesty by implying that her pain was imaginary. It is sufficient to say that she was assured that her symptoms were not imaginary but also assured that she could be mistaken in believing that such pain and suffering could not be psychological in origin. Instead of pointing out the satisfaction she was obviously getting from her illness, a procedure which would only have aroused her resentment, it was suggested that, since she did not know the meaning of her illness, perhaps such an explanation could be found in the unconscious which could be explored by the psychoanalytic technique. Finally, she began a psychoanalysis, not with any personal hopes but, as she said, "only for mother's sake."

Whenever patients talk in this obviously (but unconsciously) hypocritical way about getting well for someone else's sake, we suspect that their hostility is so great toward that person that they can overlook such commonplaces as the fact that nobody gets well or stays well for anyone's sake but his own. On the other hand, we know that they often get sick in connection with a wish to hurt someone else and the quoted statement is a hint of a partial recognition on the part of the patient that she is using her illness as a weapon against the person for whose sake she now says she wants to get well. In other words, it is a partially true statement, meaning "I will try now to give up some of my hostility against So-and-so."

This suspicion of ours proved to be well founded in this case; it was not very long before this patient was saying quite frankly, first, that she wished her mother had brought her up differently, then that she felt resentment and bitterness toward her mother, and finally that she recalled childhood fantasies of her mother's death.

There were good reasons for this. For one thing, her mother had reared her with an extreme degree of repression and restriction; she had told her daughter nothing about sex except that she was unfortunately a girl and would have to take the consequences of this fate, that like all females she must submit in long-suffering patience to the ruthless dominance of men. Fear and resentment toward men were the greater because this patient was the only girl in a family of five children and her parents gave many privileges to the boys which the patient was denied. To make matters worse, at the age of twelve, just as she began to menstruate (which frightened her greatly), she was sent to a very strict girls' school in Switzerland and denied all contact with boys for six years.

The patient soon abandoned the saintly long-suffering mask of hypocrisy by means of which she had permitted her illness to appear to be involuntary martyrdom. She began to realize quite clearly as a result of frequent repetitions of the formula that her waves of illness were expressions of her own hate. As a result of resentments felt against the parents, particularly the mother, she retaliated with the only means of aggression of which she was master, namely, passive resignation (she would exemplify this in the sanitarium by a refusal to help herself in the slightest way, depending upon the nurses for even the smallest services). Then because of its aggressive hostile intent, this passive resistance would lead to a bad conscience and a sense of guilt for which she would try to atone by an increase in religious formalities, and more particularly by an increase in painful symptoms. In order to prove to herself and to the world that she was actually atoning for her sense of guilt she had to convince the doctors and nurses that she was really suffering. By this means she reinforced the aggressive accomplishments of her passivity and idleness. This, in turn, led to conscious feelings of discouragement, despair, self-reproach, and guilt, and the entire cycle was then repeated, each time growing larger and larger like a snowball pushed down a hill. She entirely reversed the normal feminine method of attracting attention from "See how pretty I am, how attractive, how intelligent," to "See how sick I am, how miserable, how full of pain." This substitution of pity for love has been shown by much psychoanalytic experience to depend upon a sense of guilt arising from powerful but inhibited aggressions.

We cannot go into all the details of this patient's analysis but it is necessary for purposes of clarity to carry the explanation far enough to account for the tremendous involvement of physical symptoms and the repeated submission to surgery. The first clue as to this came in a dream in which

she and another person were in a house. The other person seemed to be a part of herself and at the same time seemed to be a man. She was afraid someone would see the man so she jumped into bed and pulled the sheet over her head but then said, as if speaking to the man who was a part of herself, "What does it matter if they do see you? Why try to conceal it any longer?"

This dream foreshadowed an increasing realization of the resentment she felt at her own femaleness and the envy she felt toward men. She recognizes (in the dream) that she thinks of herself as part man, part woman—but tries to conceal the "man" part. In fact, it could be said that her entire life centered about the wish to become a boy like her brothers and the feeling of guilt implicit in the idea of becoming a boy by robbing them of their masculinity. It proved to be the unconscious motive back of her repeated submission to surgeons. One day while in church to which she had gone compulsively as a part of her atonement ritual, it suddenly came to her that perhaps she wanted to suffer like Jesus as she had obviously been doing for a long time, even to the point of having the same pain in her side that Jesus had, for the following reasons: Jesus was a man; hence, by being Jesus, even though one suffer, one can be a man.

Such an "irreligious thought," as she termed it, disturbed her very much, but later she returned to a realization that it was the basis of much of her religious fervor. It explained her wish to believe in miracles, her faithfulness to her devotions, her feeling that some day she would get her reward and that God would answer her prayers. She felt that perhaps if she suffered greatly she might be granted the privilege of becoming a man. This began to appear very clearly in her analysis. She kept complaining that she was getting nowhere. It was not clear what she wanted of the analysis but she evidently expected something wonderful to happen. She expected the analysis to gratify her lifelong quest for masculinity. To this end she assured the analyst of her belief in miracles and implied that she expected a miracle to happen in her analysis. In every way she showed that unconsciously she was taking the position that if the analysis would make her into a man it was worth the suffering it cost her.

From this we can see that this girl's symptoms had a direct relation to the brother hatred and masculine envy and the guilt connected with this. Because the parents were responsible, as she felt, for discrimination against her because she was a girl instead of a boy, it was logical that she should take out her resentment against them indirectly and this she could do by exploiting the illness. In this way the symptoms served to gratify her fantasy, punish her for the fantasy, and enable her to obtain a reality value in place of or in addition to the fantasy. The family had spent many thousands of dollars upon her and she had enlisted the attention and services of literally hundreds of doctors and nurses. She had sacrificed parts of her anatomy time after time, always with some apparent physical justification. As is so often the case, this method of sacrificing a part of the body over and over is frequently insufficient to relieve the emotions provoking it.

During the latter months of her psychoanalytic treatment the material was concerned with a process called restitution. She not only repudiated in her dreams, fantasies, free associations, and conscious thoughts her masculine ambitions, her envy of her brothers and, in particular, of their physique, but there was a definite tendency toward giving instead of taking. For example, she would dream of making gifts to her brothers instead of the earlier type of dream in which she was always taking something from them; instead of eating her little brothers or some part of them and having that portion lodge in her side and cause pain, she began to dream of feeding her brothers and other people and acting in a more maternal way. The analyst, her parents, and others who in earlier stages of her analysis were symbolized in her dreams and fantasies as tyrants, Negro servants, or kings, she began to portray in more naturalistic colors as friends of hers, toward whom she could feel as an equal and be similarly regarded. This increasing degree of objectivity was reflected in her generally improved social adjustment.

It may be of interest to the reader, although not particularly pertinent to the theory, to outline the subsequent history. Under psychoanalytic treatment insight into the origin of these phobias and compulsions was gained and the original situation relived to an extent sufficient to correct the feelings of disappointment and resentment. So far as the physical symptoms themselves were concerned, the patient gave them up entirely. Her pains disappeared and her physiological functions assumed the periodicity and the painlessness common to the normal woman. In external behavior, she developed into a quite different person. Her physical appearance changed for the better to an incredible degree. From preoccupation with her sufferings and new proposals for their treatment, she became increasingly concerned with normal feminine interests and pleasures. She went back to college and took some courses in which she was interested; she developed an active social life; she gave and attended parties. Shortly afterwards she met a mining engineer and became engaged and subsequently married to him, and is now the mother of two children.

I have cited the outcome of this case in no spirit of patent medicine testimonial. Psychoanalysis has its therapeutic failures as well as its successes, but neither one of these is our present consideration. These are the facts: this woman, from reasons that were entirely removable, had been for nearly twenty years crucifying herself upon a cross of invalidism, nailed to it by repeated well-meant but futile attempts to relieve her by surgical and medicinal techniques. This is no reflection upon those treatment techniques nor upon those who administered them; a part of her self-destructiveness lay in the persistency with which this patient flung herself upon these physicians and demanded that type of treatment. The first step in her salvation was made by one of these physicians, who himself pointed out to her, at the temporary cost of her friendship, that she was demanding a treatment which was not appropriate for her case, and insisted upon a fair consideration by her of the possibilities of psychiatric study and treatment.

SUMMARY

To summarize, we can see that elements of aggressive envy and corresponding self-punishment with erotization were primarily responsible for the chronic piecemeal self-destruction of these invalid martyrs. The secondary utility of the illness in both cases contained these elements of aggression, self-punishment and erotic capitalization. This, it will be recalled, is precisely the same formula as we found to be present in martyrs and ascetics. The practical result differs in one respect, namely, that the martyr and ascetic are more successful in obtaining popular favor through the espousal of a cause which has some broader social appeal. The neurotic is, as everyone who deals with him senses immediately, more self-concerned, or to use a more psychoanalytic term, more narcissistic. At least his narcissism is more closely wrapped up in body sensations and cannot be gratified as in the case of the martyr by the more intangible element of social approbation. This seems like a greater difference than it really is, because some neurotic individuals are successful in enlisting the sympathy and interest of vast numbers of people aside from the doctors and nurses, while others antagonize everyone, including the doctors and nurses.

In chronic invalidism we have a manifest conflict between the wish to live and the wish to die. Sometimes this is evident in the conscious productions of such patients; they say frankly that they "would rather be dead than go on suffering this way"; they often speak of their condition as a living death; sometimes it is the relatives and friends who realize that such an affliction is little better than death and might even be relieved by death. The fact is, however, that chronic invalids of this type seldom die young, and despite frequent threats of suicide, rarely resort to it.

How shall we interpret this psychologically and psychodynamically? We can, of course, continue in the naive assumption so often made by the patient himself (or herself), namely, that he is the unfortunate victim of a cruel fate. But the material we have just submitted, to say nothing of the experience of every practicing physician, convinces us that this "fate" is in some large degree elected and self-appointed. Now it is easy to dismiss the whole matter by saying it is simply masochism. But masochism is by no means a simple condition. It is a very complex resultant of many factors. The extraordinary fact that a person should enjoy suffering or should prefer pain to pleasure cannot be easily explained. It can be understood only when one sees that the visible sufferings are far less than the invisible sufferings of such a person, or rather the invisible fears of suffering. To put this very simply: for some individuals it is better to be pitied than to be ignored; it is more terrible to be cast into outer darkness, either in the sense of being left alone and unloved or in the sense of being castrated or dead than to suffer any conceivable amount of pain. Therefore, for such individuals love is obtainable only in the form of pity, but as such it is better than death or desertion.

But these are only general principles and they understress the fact that such a bargain, such a compromise with fate or with imagined fate, involves a terrific price, a costly sacrifice, the sacrifice of a considerable portion of the personality. In that sense the price paid for life by the chronic invalid is so great as to be virtually a self-destructive one. The theme of paying too dearly for one's whistle is far older than Benjamin Franklin's well-known story. One must see, however, that such a conception or rather misconception of one's fate, such a misinterpretation of one's whole life situation, could not be persisted in were it not cemented by more than a single experience or misapprehension. It is cemented there, as it were, by some satisfaction involved in it and this satisfaction must depend in part, I believe, upon the opportunity for carrying out a measure of instinctual self-destruction.

In other words, I think we can interpret chronic invalidism as a drawn battle between the forces of destruction and of erotization, i.e., the will to live and the will to destroy (and die). Were the death-instinct a little stronger or the defense a little weaker, the patient would die of his disease. Were the erotic capacities a little greater, they would overcome the destructive tendencies and the patient would find other techniques for living and loving without the involuntary martyrdom of invalidism which, costly as it is, remains his only satisfaction in life.

THREE / *Alcohol Addiction*

Only a few years ago, were a psychiatrist to approach the subject of alcohol, it would be assumed immediately that he would deal chiefly with the celebrated syndrome, delirium tremens. As a student at Harvard Medical School twenty years ago, I was minutely instructed, along with my classmates, in the details of differential diagnosis that would distinguish delirium tremens from a half dozen other psychotic pictures that somewhat resembled it. And this is all I learned of alcohol and its function in the disruption of mental health.

Today, in the active practice of psychiatry, with patients before my eyes daily, including many whom alcohol has ruined or nearly ruined, I have not seen three cases of delirium tremens in as many years. Not that this affliction has disappeared from the earth, for in the wards of public hospitals or behind the bars of city jails new cases are, I am sure, admitted daily.[1] But they do not interest psychiatrists now so much as those cases which give a better opportunity to discover why they drink rather than the results of their drinking.

I do not think this represents any change in the effects of alcohol on the human being. I think, rather, that it is the best possible illustration of the change in emphasis, interest, and concept in psychiatry. Once we looked curiously

[1] "Dr. Karl M. Bowman, director of the department of psychiatry of Bellevue Hospital, New York City, in a recent address at the New York Academy of Medicine discussed the need of more effective means for the treatment of chronic alcoholics. He stated that at Bellevue Hospital his department was treating 1,000 cases of alcoholism a month and pointed out the fact that temporary treatment or fines or other jail sentences would not cure these inebriates. He recommended the establishment of State institutions for long-term treatment of chronic drunkards and psychopathic alcoholics. Mild cases of alcoholism should be treated by shorter periods of hospital care. He called attention to the fact that at present only those alcoholics whose families can afford to pay for private hospital treatment are receiving proper attention." (*Mental Hygiene News*, N.Y., Jan., 1937.)

—and, to be sure, tenderly and humanely as well—at the end-results of men whose brains were finally reacting in a dramatic spectacle to a cumulative over-dose of poison. Those inestimably more numerous persons whose self-poisoning produced symptoms less vividly tinctured with hallucinations and terrors were regarded as sociological—not psychiatric—problems. The psychology of the man impelled to ruin himself by self-poisoning, in spite of disaster, remorse, and resolutions to abandon it, some way or other escaped the consideration of the psychiatrists and was left to the clergy, the social workers, the prohibitionists, or to the devil.

Drunkenness is as old as Noah, but drunkenness is not alcohol addiction. Many become drunk who never become addicts. Furthermore, an occasional alcoholic addict is seen who is never, or rarely, "drunk" in the popular sense (because he is partially intoxicated all the time, and the effects are concealed for want of a comparative background). It is not my intention to discuss the function of alcohol in the life of a normal person, or the amenities of social drinking. There is much to indicate that in our civilization alcohol has a very useful function to perform, and may be a source of increased happiness and decreased hostilities.

But there remains the phenomenon of self-destruction by irresistible addiction to repeated, excessive drinking of alcohol.[2] Everyone knows examples of this—individuals who suffer from what seems to be an irresistible impulse to throw away all obligations and opportunities and bring their house of cards tumbling about their heads by getting drunk. Every social worker could testify to homes filled with bitterness and despair because of an addiction to alcohol on the part of a father, husband, son, or even a mother. Furthermore, every psychiatrist (and others, too, of course) could, with the author, cite case after case of prominent and formerly successful men, together with many others who are potentially successful, whose lives are literally ruined in this peculiar way. I say "peculiar" because it is paradoxical that a substance which gives and has f centuries given pleasure, relief, and stimulation to man, should, for a few, become an instrument of self-destruction.

Someone may be tempted here to make a jocular response, that if, indeed, it be self-destruction, it is at least

[2] Addiction to drugs is psychologically similar, but differs in that all narcotic habituation is socially taboo, while alcohol ingestion is socially approved and hence immensely more dangerous and frequent as a basis of addiction.

a pleasant form of it. With this no one intimately acquainted with the suffering of an alcoholic addict or his family could agree. Funny it may seem to the casual observer, but to the drinker's family and ultimately to him, too, it is a tragedy past jocularity.

Yet, at the same time, there is a little truth in that joke. It is an example of what has been called "gallows humor" —as in the case of the condemned man who remarked, on the way to his execution, "This is certainly going to be a lesson to me."

Since it is true that alcohol has the quality of giving some degree of relief from the pain of facing reality and also from other psychic pain resulting from emotional conflicts, to the extent that it is sought for the purpose of relieving pain, the use of alcohol can be regarded as an attempt at self-cure. Some alcoholics recognize this but many others cannot be persuaded that their periodic bouts are more than jolly little affairs which, for all they may end in a rather untidy and tiresome mess, with a few disappointments all around, no one should hold against them. This wish to be treated like a child and to have one's most serious aggressions overlooked is very characteristic of the type of personality which finds excessive indulgence in alcohol so irresistible.

This leads us to wonder what type of personality or what predisposing experiences in any personality lead to the election of this kind of suicide. In order to arrive at some conclusions about this let me describe some of the typical situations.

In tracing back the history of drinking in those individuals who later become its victims, we usually find it difficult to say when socially and relatively harmless drinking was superseded by a more malignant and compulsive type of drinking. In fact, this is one of the insidious dangers of alcohol for unstable individuals. A typical history of the early period would run somewhat as follows: George is the oldest son in a prominent family. He is successful in high school, both socially and in athletics. He is not brilliant but his teachers like him as do all the students. He is sent to the state university. Up to this time he had little to do with alcohol; his parents were opposed to it in any form. At the university he sees considerable drinking but takes little part in it, at first; then, with increasing frequency, he finds one or another group of companions with whom he can spend the evening or the week-end and drink more and more. His parents get wind of this and there is a family scene. He is very humble and penitent, promises not to do it any more. Three months later there are reports of repeated drunkenness and threats of suspension, and there is another family scene and more penitence and promises.

Occasionally (actually rather rarely) parents will at this point consult a psychiatrist and what they say, if their words, gestures, attitudes, and behavior can be synthesized and summarized, is something like this: "We are rather important people, you know, and we have a very fine son, in fact, an extraordinary fellow, now attending the university, who has been in a little trouble recently about drinking. Of course, we realize that it is somewhat absurd to regard this as anything serious or anything in which a psychiatrist might have any interest, because the boy isn't crazy; in fact, there's really nothing the matter with him but bad companions. We don't think he needs any treatment but maybe you could scare him a little, and perhaps threaten to lock him up for a day or two if he doesn't quit drinking. Tell him he will get delirium tremens. He has just been spoiled by too much fun down at the university."

Although there are exceptions, as a general rule the parents of alcoholics, for reasons that we shall understand better later, are peculiarly unseeing with regard to the sufferings of their children. They think because their child is popular in high school or because he makes a fraternity or an athletic team in college that all is well with him, that peace and contentment fill his heart. Such parents little realize the suffering silently endured (often unconsciously) by well-appearing, well-regarded children. Once let these sufferers discover the temporary assuaging powers of alcohol, and it will take more than family scenes, reproaches, and threats to deter a repetition. We psychiatrists know this from repeated experiences but most of us have discovered that it is totally useless to convince such parents that we are other than alarmists who want to frighten them into a more radical treatment program than they see the slightest necessity for. They align us with the most rabid prohibitionists whose sweeping denunciations of alcohol have probably done more harm than good in deterring people from its expedient use.

Usually the parents do not consult us; they do not consult anyone. The boy shortly leaves the university and gets a job. The parents may hear some rumors of week-end sprees but these are discounted. News that the son has lost his position because of drinking comes then as a great shock.

Very likely he comes home, then, very disheartened. His father is provoked, denounces such behavior, and expresses himself as disgusted. The mother weeps. The son is thoroughly humiliated, obviously remorseful, resembles nothing so much as an overgrown child, and knows it. Again he makes apologies, resolutions, and promises. A few months pass and again the relatives feel justified in assuming that their good boy is relinquishing his bad habit and will live happily ever afterwards.

Of course he does not. I could pile case history on case history and make a composite record which would show that the career of the alcoholic is one such episode after another. More jobs, more drinking, more dismissals, more scenes, more promises, more disappointments. To be sure, there are many variations. Marriage usually occurs early and often involves financial help from the parents. There may be children to complicate the picture. Sometimes the wife is helpful, more often not; frequently she herself joins in the alcoholic sprees. I remember one instance in which the wife of an alcoholic patient went on a spree while her husband was taking treatment for alcoholism, and taking her two frightened little girls with her, drove five hundred miles to the sanitarium where her husband was confined to demand that he abandon his treatment and join her.

There is another complication to be mentioned, that in spite of their addiction to occasional orgies these victims sometimes do fairly well, even surprisingly well. Some only begin to drink seriously after they have achieved considerable success. This the reader will recall is exactly what we have observed in connection with suicide; some only kill themselves or attempt to do so or feel like doing so after success or reward. We will not repeat the explanation but only mention the parallelism here.

Sooner or later, however, most alcoholics get themselves into a hopeless impasse. They lose all their friends, they estrange their wives, they drive their parents to repudiate them,[3] or they come into conflict with the law, because of automobile accidents while drunk, sexual scandals while drunk, check forging, indecent exposure, etc. (the latter, of course, are not necessarily impasses, but there is usually

---

[3] One father, in exasperation at innumerable attempts to help his son, said in my hearing, "He can lie in the gutter and rot before I lift a finger to help him again!"

an accumulation of circumstances which make it so). Novelists have described this—Ernest Hemingway, Scott Fitzgerald, John O'Hara, John Dos Passos.

I don't know what usually happens after that. Naturally the psychiatrist sees only a small proportion of them. We know that some land in jail, some in the asylum, and that some commit suicide. We also know that many others go from one sanitarium or so-called "cure" to another. Those whom we finally do see have generally come to us because relatives and friends have become exasperated and provoked beyond endurance. It is very rare indeed that an alcoholic addict comes to a psychiatrist voluntarily. It is usually by reason of medical, legal, or moral—sometimes physical—compulsion from without. The spasmodic attempts to save themselves, to relinquish their intemperate demands for periods of drunken insensibility, are usually bogus; they are insincere, half-hearted, often flagrantly hypocritical. The reason for this does not lie in some wicked perverseness but in the deep hopelessness and despair from which every alcoholic secretly suffers. For him the efforts of any person or institution to relieve him of his alcohol habit is as if they would rob him of the only relief he has from unendurable suffering—expensive, disastrous, and disappointing as the relief has been to him. For this reason these patients usually dodge psychiatrists and psychiatric hospitals, where the underlying basis of the alcoholism might be approached, and play with the idea that a fishing trip, a dude ranch, a nursing home, a so-called "cure" or just "a rest" will do the trick.

If and when alcoholics do come to a psychiatric hospital, their admission is regularly accompanied by certain peculiar circumstances. In the first place they are apt to be drunk, even though they were sobering up from a previous bout at the time of the decision to take psychiatric treatment. The anticipation of deprival pain, the "last chance" philosophy and sometimes a wave of resentment against "well-meaning but mistaken friends" impels a final fling. This is apt to be followed by a period of remorseful shamefacedness. In this the patient shares, on the one hand, the attitude of the stricter religious groups that drinking is a sin to be abstained from on the basis of moral conviction, and, on the other hand, the mixture of resentment, disappointment and pity manifested by his relatives and friends.

At such a time the patient will promise anything and comply with any rules or expectations. This, however, gradually gives way to increasing assertiveness and truculency—everything about the hospital is "terrible" and the patient is "entirely cured and ready to return to work immediately" (this even when no work exists any longer, the patient having completely destroyed all of his opportunities).

In this connection, I must mention another curious but almost invariable phenomenon. This is the characteristic pathological optimism from which both the patient and all members of his family seem regularly to suffer. The word "suffer" is chosen advisedly because as a rule this attitude is the most serious obstacle to the successful treatment of the affliction. No matter how desperate the case may seem at first or how dismal or tragic the history, it is usually only a matter of a few weeks or months until the patient and (what is really much more strange) his relatives are convinced that he is now perfectly well, has made a radical change in his psychology, will never fall into such a habit again, and should accordingly be trusted and expected to resume his full share of responsibilities in life. Even when this same trick, this same formula of promise and disappointment, has been repeated over and over, it still works because the members of the family *want* to believe it. It is the vicious circle of interaction between the mutual aggressions of patient and family.

It would seem almost too obvious to require mention that such an optimism and such a false sense of security are only self-deception used for the purpose of escaping the necessity of effecting a thoroughgoing change in the underlying psychopathology. The alcoholic suffers secretly from unspeakable terror which he cannot bear to face. He knows only the device of drowning the fear by drinking and this "cure" (drinking) then becomes worse than the disease, at least so far as outside evidences are concerned. When his hand is called he temporarily repudiates the attempt at self-cure rather than confess or face the reason for the need of it and accepts a more promising scientifically-applied cure which he soon runs away from, as described.

Some alcoholic patients, however, if properly approached can be engaged in an attempt to discover what lies back of the alcoholic compulsion, what great anxiety drives them to this suicidal comfort. That it arises from external life difficulties is an alibi no alcoholic patient gives to a psychiatrist who has won his confidence. Troubles there are in the world, to be sure, and some insoluble problems that would vex the soul of the most enduring, but it is not these, or at least not these alone, which impel alcoholic solution. (If it were so, we should all become alcoholics.) No, the victim of alcohol addiction knows what most of his critics do not know, namely, that alcoholism is not a disease, or at least not the principal disease from which he suffers; furthermore, *he knows that he does not know* the origin or nature of the dreadful pain and fear within him which impel him, blindly, to alcoholic self-destruction. It is like some poor beast who has been poisoned or set on fire, and runs blindly into the sea to court one death in fleeing another.

Indeed, we frequently see patients who start out with *conscious* suicidal intentions and end up by getting drunk (or who get drunk first in order to make a suicidal attempt), as if this was (as it is!) a less certain death than shooting. Many of the patients treated for alcohol addiction are preoccupied in their sober moments with thoughts of self-destruction, sometimes coupled with realization of their own unworthiness, sinfulness, and incompetence. Some patients partially carry out these suicidal intentions even, as it were, in spite of getting drunk. One, for example, slashed his face repeatedly with a razor. Another jabbed himself with a knife. Several jumped or attempted to jump off high places and it scarcely seems necessary to speak of the thousands of instances of persons who head for suicide by getting drunk and then attempting to drive their own cars.

Thus alcohol addiction can be thought of not as a disease, but as a suicidal *flight from* disease, a disastrous attempt at the self-cure of an unseen inner conflict, aggravated but not primarily caused (as many think) by external conflict. It is literally true that the alcoholic, as he himself says, does not know why he drinks.

We do know now, however, from painstaking psychoanalytic investigations into the unconscious mental life of a goodly number of alcoholics by numerous psychoanalytic workers,[4] why some of them drink. Why is it?

[4] Rado, Sandor, "The Psychic Effects of Intoxicants," *International Journal of Psychoanalysis,* 1926, Vol. VII, pp. 396-402; Rado, Sandor, "The Psychoanalysis of Pharmacothymia" (Drug Addiction), *Psychoanalytic Quarterly,* Vol. II, pp. 1-23, 1933; Simmel, Ernst, *Zum Problem von Zwang und Sucht,* Bericht V. allg. ärztl. Kongress f. Psychotherapie, 1930; Knight, Robert P., *The Dynamics and Treatment of Alcohol Addiction,* read at the Fourteenth Congress of the International Psychoanalytic Association, Marienbad, Czechoslovakia, Aug. 4, 1936, and published in the Bulletin of the Menninger Clinic, Vol. I, pp. 233-50, 1937; Knight, Robert P., "The Psychodynamics of Chronic Alcoholism," *Journal of Nervous and Mental Diseases,* Nov., 1937, pp. 538-48.

Knight believes that there are at least two main clinical varieties of

Let us begin with the more superficial aspects. "Alcoholics" are almost invariably jolly, sociable, talkative fellows who make themselves very popular, who indeed seem *obliged* to make themselves well liked and are very skillful at doing so. It takes very little penetration to discover, however, that this inordinate wish to be loved which compels them to be at such pains to be charming and to win popularity in one circle or another bespeaks a great underlying feeling of insecurity, a feeling which must constantly be denied, compensated for, or anesthetized.

From clinical experience also we know that such feelings of insecurity and inferiority depend less upon actual reality comparisons than upon unconscious, "irrational" reasons—generally feelings of great frustration and rage, and the fear and guilt which the rage induces. All this is, of course, now unconscious. But once it was *fully* conscious, only too conscious. In fact, a supplementary function of the alcohol-drinking is the further repression of such feelings and memories which threaten to emerge, to become again conscious. Such individuals, as children, have endured bitter disappointment, *unforgettable* disappointment, *unforgivable* disappointment! They feel, with justification, that they have been betrayed, and their entire subsequent life is a prolonged, disguised reaction to this feeling.

It is true that every child meets with disappointment and frustration; this is inevitable in the nature of reality. We are born into a world where we must change from directing our existence according to the pleasure principle to a program of directing our existence according to a reality principle which we discover by painful testing, step by step. We all had to be weaned, we all had to give up our dependence on our parents, we all had to relinquish our belief in Santa Claus. In this respect, then, the alcoholic probably does not suffer in childhood anything qualitatively different from what the rest of us suffer, but apparently there is a quantitative difference. In the case of the alcoholic the disappointment has actually been greater than he could bear. It was so great that it definitely affected his personality development so that in certain respects he re-

alcohol addiction: (1) That in which alcohol addiction appears to be a reactive symptom in the course of a neurotic illness developing in adult life, and (2) that in which alcoholism is the most conspicuous of numerous devices utilized by a developmentally deformed character arising from earliest childhood. Such a distinction is extremely valuable clinically. The former naturally has a much better prognosis; but while the total personality development is quite different, the psychological motives are essentially the same in both types mains all his life what we call an "oral character." We have already referred to this in the discussion of melancholia; I shall only repeat that an oral character is one characterized by conspicuous residua of the stage of psychological development in which the child's attitude toward the world was determined by his wish to take it in through the mouth and to destroy with his mouth anything which resisted his demands.

Drinking (in the sense in which we are now using it) is a typical infantile revenge reaction. In the first place, it is performed with the mouth; in the second place, it places a fictitiously high value upon the magical virtues of the substance desired; more important still, its practical aggressive values are indirect. An adult reaction of revenge would be more directly aggressive. For example, a mature person, angry for good reason at his father, would state the issue and discontinue further dealings instead of grieving and embittering his father by debauches. But the alcoholic cannot risk giving up the love objects to which he clings, angry and resentful as he may feel toward them, consciously or unconsciously. Furthermore, like all neurotics he confuses his friends and his (theoretical) enemies and treats those whom he thinks he loves as if they were identical with those whom he hates or whom he *once* hated. Thus, the alcoholic suffers at the same time from the wish to destroy his love-objects and the fear that he will lose them. He also fears the consequences of the aggressions which he is constantly impelled to make against them and from which he deters himself only by fierce internal restraint which in time accumulates to the point of leading him to seek a form of anesthetization which indirectly achieves the very aggressions and other consequences which he so feared he would succumb to.

In this strong ambivalence of the alcoholic, this conflictual and confusing attitude of love and hate, one sees an epitome and therefore a partial explanation of the nature of the great disappointment which he once suffered. Rather than derive it logically, let me depend again on empirical observations. We have noted time after time in those cases which have been subjected to penetrating anamnestic and psychological investigations that the parents of alcoholics increased the inevitable disappointment of the child tremendously by artificial, however unintentional, means. Apparently they did this usually by leading the child to expect more gratification than they were prepared to give or than

149

reality made it possible to give. A few examples of this will illustrate specifically what I mean. The mother of one alcoholic nursed her child until he was nearly three years old because she herself was so fond of the experience; she then became desperate because of the difficulty she encountered in weaning him and achieved her aim finally by painting her breasts with stove blacking in order to frighten and repel the child. The mother of another alcoholic made of her child a pet and darling, almost ignoring the other children, a role which naturally had to be relinquished when he grew a little older. The father of still another alcoholic habitually did such things as this: he sent his son to the corner drug store repeatedly for cigars and household supplies, instructing him to say to the clerk only the magic words, "Charge it." One day the son used this same formula to obtain some candy, seeing nothing wrong in extending his knowledge to this new need. When his father learned of it he whipped the boy severely to the child's astonishment and resentment.[5] Still another father encouraged his son to work and develop a savings account; then he, the father, appropriated the account.

This inconsistency in attitude toward the child bespeaks an ambivalence on the parents' part and explains why these patients are so often described by their friends and relatives as "spoiled"; "a spoiled child that never grew up," and similar expressions which imply reproach to both the "child" and his parents. Such appellations are partially correct, but err in the assumption that such children are "spoiled" by having been given too much love. I doubt very much if any child is ever spoiled by too much love. What passes for excessive "love" on the part of the parents is often only thinly disguised hate or guilt, and this fact is perceived by the child, if not by the neighbors. Over-solicitous, over-protective mothers and fathers who bestow large gifts to avoid the necessity of spending time and thought on the child; parents who exploit, promote, or smother their children with their own personalities, for the gratification of their own narcissism, cannot be said to be "loving" their children however much they themselves may think so. And for all these aggressions against him the child will certainly some day, perhaps at great cost to himself, take full and terrible revenge.

All this theory becomes very much more understandable when studied in a particular case:

[5] Cited by Knight, *op. cit.*

Jonathan Richardson was the son of one of the most distinguished men in the United States in his generation and in his particular field. We saw him—the patient—first at the age of thirty-five. The preceding fifteen years of his life had consisted of a dismal series of failures and the decimation of an opportunity for a career such as is offered to few men. The ostensible cause of all his failure was alcohol; indeed, the tragedy of his life was of just the sort which those opposed to the sale and use of alcohol use as an example with telling effect.

He was a very handsome man both in feature and in figure. He had perfect manners and good, if not superior, intelligence. These things, with his family's prestige and money, combined to make him exceedingly popular wherever he went. He had been a leading socialite, a prominent athlete, and a popular leader in the student body of the large and well-known eastern university to which he was sent. Nor did he carry his popularity with a bad grace; he was not arrogant, snobbish, or ostentatious. Indeed, his only fault during the earlier years of his life might be said to have lain in a certain passive acceptance of his good fortune rather than any energetic effort to gain it or make the best of it. He did not drink at all during his freshman year.

He left the university, where his father thought he was not working hard enough, and went to another school to obtain training in his father's business specialty in order to be equipped to take over the large responsibilities that would devolve upon him as the ultimate head of the firm —his father's great ambition for him. But here he showed a strange reaction to his opportunities which no one could understand. It was first a lack of enthusiasm about the work and later an out-and-out aversion to it. Finally, in spite of what seemed to be a conscientious effort, he failed completely in all the subjects related to the professional course.

It was in connection with this failure that he began drinking. Repeatedly, on nights when he should have been studying, he would go out for a few hours' relaxation and end up by becoming dead-drunk, and would then miss his classes the next day. In desperation his father insisted that he transfer to still another school but here the same thing happened. He had decided by now that he did not want to go into his father's business, that he had no interest in it or liking for it, that the apparently great opportunity meant nothing to him. His father could out-argue him and he would always admit that his father was probably right and then lapse into silence and (at the first opportunity) into another drunken spree.

He had some talent for drawing and pled that he be allowed to cultivate this talent, but his father thought it ridiculous that a son with his opportunities in the business world should dabble in art, for which, moreover, he seemed to have at best only a mediocre gift.

Then several things happened almost simultaneously: The World War broke out, and disregarding the opportunity for advancement which his father's prestige would have given him, he enlisted as a private and worked his own way up to the rank of commissioned officer. He married a beautiful woman and one who subsequently turned out to be as intelligent, levelheaded, and patient as she was beautiful. At that time, however, she was the cause of repeated penalization for him because he would absent himself from the army without leave in order to see her. He continued to drink surreptitiously and after his discharge more than ever.

The father in the meantime had become fully reconciled to the fact that his son would never come into his business and was anxious only to have him stop drinking and get into some work at which he would be self-supporting. During the next ten years he financed project after project, lending the son thousands of dollars, setting him up in one business after another, only to have him make a failure of every one of them. In each case the failure would be of the same character. There would be a burst of enthusiasm, an initial spurt of hard work, the establishment of many contacts, a period of good will and popularity and the promise of success, then increasing disappointments of customers on account of absences from the store (drinking), increasing drinking, and decreasing sales, the latter causing discouragement and thus more drinking, the whole thing ending up in bankruptcy, arrest and threatened or actual imprisonment, sudden disappearance, or some other dramatic finale. Throughout all this he would preserve an amiable, conciliatory, earnest manner that had the effect of convincing everyone that surely he had repented all his dissolute ways and had turned the corner toward reform.

"I have thrown away everything," he would say. "I have broken my mother's heart, turned down the best business opportunity a man ever had, wasted my youth, neglected opportunities for education, encumbered myself with the responsibilities of a loving wife and children whom I can't support, and what have I got out of it? Nothing! A lot of drunken brawls which I didn't even enjoy at the time."

Now to look into the psychology of this boy's drinking. He had what we feel to be the typical set-up for alcoholism. He had a powerful, money-bestowing, but vacillating (i.e., ambivalent) father; he had an indulgent and undiscriminating (therefore also ambivalent) mother; he had a sister whom the parents definitely preferred.

A word of explanation about these. The father, whom every son unconsciously strives to emulate, was in this instance on a very high pinnacle. This alone made a difficulty for the boy, because the greatness of his father seemed to him to be unattainable. But added to this was the fact that the father used his position cruelly. He was high and mighty with his son, at times savage with him, and at other times sentimental to the point of being maudlin. A consistently harsh father gives his son something to fight against. A father who, as this one, ridicules and humiliates the son with sarcasm until he leaves the table sobbing, and at other times boasts of him to others in his presence and overwhelms him with gifts, excites terrific antagonism and at the same time inspires its suppression. The son is not only embittered by the harshness but forestalled by the occasional kindness from normal attempts at retaliation.

Another resentment of this son against the father was the father's preference for the sister. Normal as this may have been on the part of the father, it aroused in the son—as it always does—unconscious envy of the feminine position because the father's attitude toward her was more consistently kind. The normal solution of the emotional conflict caused by this family set-up would be for the boy to turn toward his mother for such help as he needed during his growing years and then graduate from the family to more hospitable and less conflictual fields. But there are certain difficulties about this. The wives of such superior men as this boy's father are apt to have their own private neuroses, a very common one being the tendency to turn from the husband to the son as a love-object. This leads to further complications; it overwhelms the son with love from a source which either tends in the direction of keeping him a spoiled child who need make no manly effort to win love, or increases his fear of the powerful father in whose domain he is trespassing. One might say that such boys, incensed at being slighted by their fathers and by the preference shown their sisters (or someone else), turn toward the mothers for affection inordinately, but because of the fear of the powerful father, accept this love from her only in the infantile mode and remain sucklings.

Exactly this happened in the patient I have been describing. How it was reflected in later life can be clearly seen in the brief history of him given above. The boy was forced by his feelings of inferiority toward his father, his envy of the sister, and his oral dependence upon the mother into the acceptance of an extremely passive role in life. All the characteristics of the typical alcoholic which I described above can be related to his essential passivity and the wish to win love from people by excessive friendliness and essential subservience rather than by masculine achievement. But while passive in method, alcoholics are by no means lacking in aggressiveness.[6] Indeed, they use their passivity in the most aggressive way against those who thwart them. It is for this reason that alcoholism so often develops or increases to a pathological degree shortly after marriage. The predisposed individual seeks more maternal gratification from the wife than the average or normal woman is prepared to give, characteristically accuses her of not being affectionate enough, and is himself reluctant to assume his masculine responsibilities toward her. The result of this feeling of thwarting is a return to the bottle which serves at the same time as a gratification to him and as an aggression against her.

In the case of Jonathan Richardson, it will be recalled that the drinking began before marriage at a time when the father insisted upon a change in universities. He wanted the son to follow in his business. This the son could not do for many reasons. It implied an undesired identification with his father. Moreover, it would have put him in an unendurable position of comparison and rivalry with his father of whom he was so afraid. (It is characteristic of oral characters that they are poor winners and poor losers; they cannot bear to do either and hence usually sidestep competitive activities of all sorts.) Jonathan wanted rather to be an artist, another feminine identification (no aspersion upon artists is intended; I refer now to art as *he* conceived of it, which was in imitation of his mother). In this his father tried to thwart him and he tried in turn to thwart his father's ambition for him. He did so, however, in the way characteristic of alcoholics. He went through the mo-

---

[6] It is a common error to think of passivity as the opposite of aggressiveness. Passivity is often very aggressive in intention and effect.

tions of trying to comply with his father's wishes and appeared to fail only through succumbing to the temptation of drink (which is symbolically equivalent to the childhood retreat to his mother).

There is one other element in this case not invariably characteristic of alcoholics but very common. That is the fact that the patient's father himself drank very heavily. The older psychiatrists regarded this as a very important point because they considered alcoholism to be an hereditary trait. Of course, scarcely any scientist believes so today, although it is still a popular theory. Alcoholism cannot possibly be an hereditary trait, but for a father to be alcoholic is an easy way for the son to learn *how* to effect the retaliation he later feels compelled to inflict. Many alcoholics, as everyone knows, have parents distinguished for their sobriety and self-restraint. Of course, in such homes the alcoholism of the son carries the greater power as a weapon.

Such a case illustrates as well as any one case can some of the various psychological functions of alcohol addiction. What strikes some as most apparent in such cases is the feeling of inferiority which the alcoholism seems to relieve; many people have made this observation introspectively and the case just cited seems to be a good example of it. However, one should remember that such a great sense of inferiority usually depends upon guilt feelings arising from envy and hostility. The mild elation which releases inhibitions after a few drinks of an alcoholic beverage cannot be compared directly with the feelings of a person addicted to alcohol. For one thing, the alcoholic never stops in the stage where such feelings of release can be advantageously enjoyed but carries the drinking to a point where these feelings are annulled, and usually to a point where his behavior is such as to actually increase rather than decrease his social or intellectual disability or "inferiority." This, plus the most casual observation of the behavior of such individuals, is sufficient to convince anyone of the unconsciously aggressive function of the drinking. It would seem scarcely necessary to prove this point; everyone is familiar with the obnoxious behavior of drunken boors at parties, public gatherings, and in private life. Alcoholic patients give psychiatric hospitals more trouble than any others, not because of any consistent disagreeableness or belligerency but rather because of the contrast between their superficial attitude of amiable, courteous compliance and the petty grumbling and occasional impulsive and un-expected obstreperousness which any denial of their incessant importunacy evokes. They simply cannot endure the privations incident to life in a real world (or even in the specially modified world of the sanitarium). Indeed, an alcoholic may be considered as beginning to "get well" when he discovers that getting drunk is not the only way in which he habitually makes himself disagreeable. William Seabrook[7] in his amazingly candid account of his experiences while under treatment for alcoholism describes this faithfully and accurately. For anyone interested in the problem this book is an indispensable source of material in spite of the fact that what the author may have regarded as a deep psychological study of himself was quite obviously interrupted at a relatively superficial stage, at least so far as the recorded account goes.

I have stated that the inferiority feelings of the alcoholic frequently arise from a sense of guilt. In some individuals this consciously precedes the drinking but in the majority of instances it is often erroneously ascribed (by them and by some physicians) to the physiological effects of the drinking (hangover, katzenjammer, etc.). But this sense of guilt pertains not so much to the immediate aggressiveness implicit in the drinking as to the fundamental aggressiveness back of it, the partially but never successfully repressed hostility which, I believe, is one of the chief determinants of the alcoholic neurosis. This is apparent in some cases only after considerable study but in others, as in one now to be cited, it strikes one immediately.

This was a thoughtful, intelligent young fellow of twenty-three who looked and acted as if he were thirty and who, after outstanding success in the preparatory school from which he graduated with honors, was dismissed from the university on account of excessive drinking. Subsequent to this he lost position after position on account of drinking and dissipation with women. He came to the clinic in a serious frame of mind, determined that he must get help or face the consequences of becoming a hopeless drunkard. He was the more ʻhoughtful and earnest about it because his father had recently died, throwing considerable responsibility upon his shoulders as well as increasing feelings of remorse which had never been entirely absent but which, on the other hand, had never been effective in inhibiting his drinking.

He was considerably disturbed by recurrent dreams of

[7] Seabrook, William, *Asylum*, Harcourt, Brace, 1935.

being in the penitentiary. He recalled that shortly after his father's death he had been awakened several times by a nightmare in which he saw his father's corpse arise from the dead, angry and threatening. His father, a successful, intelligent, far-seeing man, had been greatly disappointed in this son, and had been stern and reproachful with him. The patient admitted that he could not escape the conviction that his drinking had so distressed the father as to have actually been a contributing factor in causing his death. This explains the patient's nightmare dream and penitentiary dream. "I realize I killed my father," said he; "small wonder I dream of going to the penitentiary."

The patient continued to dream of being hanged or put in the penitentiary which disturbed him so much that he would get drunk and then remorseful again. "I am nothing but a drunken bum and a degenerate," he said. "Let me drink myself to death. I am not worth saving."

He broke off his treatment and left the institution (toward which, however, he retained the kindliest feelings) in a determined effort to carry out this intention of self-destruction. He continued to drink, became involved in an automobile accident in which a man *was* killed (as in his "prophetic" dream) and he was actually put on trial for manslaughter (also conforming to his dreams) but was acquitted.

He went to another psychoanalyst for a while but again broke off the treatment and entered business, in which he was moderately successful. He had meanwhile discontinued drinking as the result of his fright in connection with the automobile accident but in its place he suffered now from an array of almost paralyzing neurotic symptoms, fears, anxieties, inhibitions, physical symptoms, and morbid ideas. The substitution of one type of neurosis for another is here strikingly illustrated.

This case also demonstrates the rather typical sexual pattern in alcoholism relating the aggressiveness and guilt-feelings to the erotic value of the drinking. The terrific sense of guilt with reference to the father, the almost studied provocativeness toward him combined with a deep attraction to him led to a conflict between his wish for passive erotic dependence upon him, and his rejection of this wish. It is almost axiomatic that alcoholics in spite of a great show of heterosexual activity, have secretly a great fear of women and of heterosexuality in general, apparently regarding it as fraught with much danger. They often realize that they do not possess normal sexual powers or interests, frankly avowing that it is not sexual gratification they seek from women so much as affection, care, love—by which they mean maternal solicitude. This, ultimately, the normal wife rebels against giving to a grown man supposedly her protector and master. The outcome is inevitable. The patient then assumes a grieved or contemptuous or utilitarian or even consciously hostile attitude toward her and all women and turns toward men with a mixture of friendly and provocative behavior, with temporary jollity and popularity but ultimate misery and personal loss. At the same time that he is drinking with boon companions who appear to be substitutes for his father, he is defying and grieving his real father and rejecting his real mother or her substitute. This, in turn, gives rise to remorse which leads to self-depreciation and self-injury. Meanwhile the exasperated wife considers or applies for divorce. Immediately, the little-boy husband rushes back to her with tears, prayers, and promises to which she very likely succumbs and the whole cycle begins again.

The self-destructive consequences of alcoholism which are so obvious would seem to be in part incidental, that is, they are the untoward consequences of self-administered efforts at obtaining relief from internal dangers. As soon as these internal dangers threaten the destruction of the individual by his own impulses, alcoholism is chosen or substituted as a kind of lesser self-destruction serving to avert a greater self-destruction.

We have commented that the same problem faces many if not all people and the same solution is also available to everyone. The question is, what particular problems obsess the potential alcoholic and why is this particular method chosen by him to solve them. The cases recited illustrate some of the conditioning experiences which favor the development of the alcoholic's emotional problems and also favor this method of attempted solution. They relate to the thwarting of the early oral receptive cravings of these individuals, i.e., their need of love and the fearful resentments which these thwartings create with a corresponding anticipation of punishment or annihilation as the consequence of indulging or even fantasying these retaliations.

The alcoholism solves the problem neatly because it enables the individual to carry out these retaliations and aggressions, often against the very person toward whom they were originally directed; in addition, however, it incurs liability for a certain amount of punishment which is not so dreadful as that feared under the original circumstances.

Furthermore, it supplies the oral love—*symbolically,* in the form of a precious liquor taken by mouth, the "mother's milk" which was so much craved; and *actually,* in the form of conviviality and sentimentality which accompany social drinking. To be sure, this sometimes seems to be a substitute for heterosexual object love, but the alcoholic, like all oral characters, is not very discriminating between the sexes. Indeed, his chief resentment may be against women rather than men on account of thwarting propensities ascribed to his mother so that he discriminates against them, not so much on account of their sex, as on account of their similarity to her, i.e., not so much on a sexual basis as on a personal basis. Many alcoholics indulge in homosexual (or in heterosexual) relations only when they are drunk but these various facts confirm our proposition that all forms of self-destruction are partially (incompletely) eroticized, i.e., used as a source of pleasure.

The general problems of treatment I have consistently deferred for special consideration in the final section. Alcohol addiction is, however, such a widespread affliction and one in which present modes of treatment are so notoriously inadequate that I have thought it worthwhile to insert a brief summary of the treatment methods indicated by the conception of it as a form of self-destruction as outlined above.

Given this view of the problem of alcohol addiction, one can see that the general principles of its successful treatment must necessarily follow very different lines from those based upon the old conception that it represents a bad habit or an unfortunate inheritance. The effective treatment of alcohol addiction is, of course, the treatment of that which impels it. This means the gradual elimination of the tendency of over-reaction to frustration, and the progressive relief of those deep, inner feelings of anxiety, insecurity, and of childlike expectation and resentment which so regularly determine it.

Inasmuch, however, as the persistence of these traits represents a definite character deformity of very long standing, the modified results of childhood injuries, the accomplishment of their elimination implies a complete and thoroughgoing reconstruction of the entire personality.

So far as I know, there is only one treatment technique

which even attempts to accomplish this, and that is psychoanalysis. I do not say that alcoholism cannot be cured by any other means. I have seen it happen in one instance as the result of a prolonged vigil of several years in a lonely spot by a very intelligent and determined man; I have known it to occur as the result of religious conversion; and I am sure it is occasionally possible in not too severe cases as the result of psychiatric conferences and counsel. We all know that "cure" is occasionally accomplished as the result of substituting another neurosis for the alcoholism; alcoholics, for example, sometimes cease to be alcoholics and become hypochondriacs or religious fanatics. And, finally, in justice to the facts, one must add that it sometimes happens suddenly following intense emotional experiences and also following apparently trivial incidents; the explanation of the metamorphosis in these cases remains entirely obscure.

But, on the other hand, I have never seen an alcoholic addict cured by confinement alone, even though alcohol is withdrawn completely during that period. This applies to long-time commitments as well as short-time "cures." I have talked to superintendents of numerous state hospitals where alcoholics have been treated and their observations have been the same as mine. In fact, one of our friends, who is the superintendent of such an institution, has recently refused to approve the admission of any more alcoholics to his hospital, not because of any scientific disinterest in them, but because of his conviction that residence in a state hospital is a state expense which accomplishes nothing for them or for the state.

It is not difficult to see why such treatment does not change the character or allay the underlying desires. Just as soon as the alcoholic is released he is once more exposed to the same opportunities for relief with just as much inner distress clamoring to be relieved.

To bring about the character revision necessary to relieve alcohol addiction requires psychological "surgery," i.e., psychoanalysis. *Theoretically,* it is the treatment of choice. *Practically,* there are many serious difficulties in the way. In the first place, psychoanalytic treatment cannot be accomplished in a few months. It is a typical alcoholic fantasy that the reconstruction of a character which has been thirty-odd years in forming (or, rather, deforming) can be accomplished in three, six, or even twelve months. The treatment of alcohol addiction, like the treatment of tuberculosis, is a long-time affair. This means that it is expensive in money as well as time. This is unfortunate but it is true. To encourage relatives or patients to believe that a few weeks or months are likely to bring about a fundamental change (with or without analysis) is only to disappoint them with certain failure.

Furthermore, most persons addicted to alcohol are too "far gone," too far removed from loyalty to the reality principle, to be treated by psychoanalysis under the ordinary circumstances. In other words, they must be treated in a specially adapted environment and for practical purposes this means that they must be confined, and opportunities for alcohol removed from immediate availability. Provision for increasing freedom, as their general behavior justifies it, is implicit in this plan. The proper direction of the aggressive tendencies as they become more and more direct and less and less circumvented by the neurotic inhibitions can be made to contribute to the therapeutic effectiveness of the treatment régime. Athletic and competitive tendencies are encouraged, and as soon as possible business or other sublimated aggressions engaged in.

Hence, confinement, *plus* psychoanalysis, *plus* the proper direction of the increasing capacity for externally directed aggressions constitute in our opinion and experience the best program of therapy for this affliction. Even this is not always successful but by means of it a few individuals have been cured and have stayed cured, not only of drinking but of the infantilism which accompanies it and the character deformities which produce it. This cannot be said, so far as I know, of any other treatment of alcohol addiction at the present time.

SUMMARY

Alcohol addiction, then, can be considered a form of self-destruction used to avert a greater self-destruction, deriving from elements of aggressiveness excited by thwarting, ungratified eroticism, and the feeling of a need for punishment from a sense of guilt related to the aggressiveness. Its further quality is that in a practical sense the self-destruction is accomplished *in spite of* and at the same time *by means of* the very device used by the sufferer to relieve his pain and avert this feared destruction.

FOUR / *Anti-Social Behavior*

It has long since become common knowledge that many persons relinquish their loyalty to reality and their consideration of their fellow men to a degree short of "insanity" but not short of self-destructiveness nor of the obvious need for psychiatric help. In what is called sexual "perversion," for example, the victim is overwhelmed by infantile tendencies which he has never been able to bring under the restraining influences of society to the point that he can find satisfaction in acceptable ways. He is forced rather to remain sexually immature, to impress these immaturities upon others for his own sake, so that a society reluctantly tolerates him with contempt or ostracizes him altogether. There are also those in whom the uncontrollable aggressive urges exceed the demand for erotic satisfaction and break through the restraints of judgment and conscience and social prohibitions to accomplish an immediate end regardless of the ultimate loss. This we call "criminality"; for it society has traditional methods of treatment, more dramatic than effective, originally designed to punish and to deter. Finally, there are individuals who are driven by their impulses no less than the criminals and sexual perverts but who, on the other hand, do not leave their punishment to the state or to organized society but manage to inflict it (indirectly) upon themselves. This disorder has gone by various names in the course of psychiatric history; I, myself, suggested the term "perverse personality" and used this designation in *The Human Mind*. The most recent designation for it is "neurotic character." The neurotic character is distinguished from the neurosis in that the symptoms of the former appear in behavior, the latter more often in feelings and physical complaints.

All three of these overtly aggressive types of behavior react like boomerangs upon their unfortunate authors, driven as they are to these unsatisfactory goals usually to suffer in the end what it was their original intention (often successfully) to make others suffer. The net result is thus self-destruction.

Perhaps it is unnecessary to point out that not all external aggressiveness is self-destructive in its effect; a man fighting in his own right in defense of infringement upon his home, his happiness, his reputation, his ideals cannot be said to reap self-destructive rewards; rather the contrary. A man who does not fight under such circumstances is passively self-destructive. In the clinical forms I have described, the aggressiveness is a two-edged sword and destroys the individual no less certainly and often more nearly completely than anyone else and hence falls into the general category of self-destructive behavior.

I realize that one can become involved in a logical or philosophical argument over the teleological assumption made here that the result (self-destruction) was the intention. If the intensity of (a positive) desire is simply overwhelmingly great and outweighs all other considerations, some of which lead *or may lead* to death, one might hold that the self-destruction was a chance taken, or even a penalty accepted unwillingly but incidentally. My position is the pragmatic clinical one, based not so much on the deductive hypothesis that what happens was elected (psychic determinism) as upon my experience with the psychoanalytic study of these persons. Almost invariably the patient discovers and confesses that his uncontrollable desire included elements of hostility and guilt which demanded punishment and hence contributed to the urgency of the impulse, and the tendency to minimize the probability of dangerous consequences. The temporary faith in a saving "luck," and the disregard of reason and judgment are a part of the technique of self-destruction.[1]

I shall defer, for the present, special consideration of psychotic self-destruction, and take up separately the three clinical forms of cloaked self-destruction just mentioned— neurotic character, criminality, and sexual perversion, in

[1] Does anyone suppose, for example, that to risk ten or twenty thousand dollars—or more—for one dollar, with a possible penitentiary sentence thrown in, could be other than a self-destructive impulse, no matter how urgent it may have seemed? Yet—

POOR BARGAIN

New York, May 18, 1935 (AP)—For 29 years and 10 months, T. W. has been a postal clerk. In July he was to retire on a pension.

But today he was convicted of stealing a $1 bill from an envelope. One dollar cost him a $1,200 yearly pension for life and a year and a day in jail.

—*Topeka Daily Capital*, May 19, 1935.

this order, citing some representative examples and indicating the ways in which the self-destructive elements are discernible upon closer scrutiny long before they become manifest.

A. NEUROTIC CHARACTER

This form of chronic self-destruction, disguised by aggressive behavior, is quite similar to alcoholism except that the individual ruins himself by inexpedient conduct instead of by drinking. I do not refer to a single injudicious act but a certain consistent *addiction*, as it were, to "bad" (i.e., aggressive) behavior, the net result of which is disaster to the individual. Such individuals may assume the role of alcoholics, of neurotics, or of out-and-out criminals, but they always fail. They are, so to speak, always successful in failing. If, for example, they pursue the career of crime, their crimes are stupidly executed, they seem to rush to be arrested rather than to escape it, they frequently do everything possible to obstruct their attorney's measures for their defense and seem, in short, to invite punishment. If, on the other hand, they aim higher and seek, ostensibly, some more worthy attainment, they skillfully manage to bring it to catastrophe time after time.

In the older psychiatric categories these patients were called *psychopathic personalities* and by this term they are still known to the majority of psychiatrists. Many elaborate descriptive studies have been made of them but it was not until the introduction of psychoanalytic concepts that they were understood in a dynamic way. It is fair to say that on account of their provocativeness, aggressiveness, and inexplicably bad judgment, they are apt to arouse so much emotion in the physician (as in all others with whom they come into contact) that it is very difficult to take an objective attitude toward them long enough really to understand them. Nevertheless, this has been accomplished in a sufficient number of cases to enable the general pattern of their lives to be now fairly well understood. Unlike the neurotic invalid and the alcoholic, they are quite able to express their aggressions directly but they are not able to do so discreetly, or shall we say, with sufficient discrimination to exempt them from the penalties of conscience. Society they may, for a time, fool; their own consciences, never. They are, therefore, impelled instinctively, on the one hand, to commit aggressions which the neurotic person would inhibit, and, on the other hand, they are driven by their consciences to bring about a punishment which a more normal person would avoid. For this reason the aggressions often assume the nature of provocations like those of a child who, feeling guilty on account of some secret transgression, provokes his father by an obvious and petty aggression to a punitive retaliation.

Alexander[2] deserves the credit for the most thorough exposition of the neurotic character in various writings. Many of Alexander's studies were made of criminals, or as we should say, neurotic characters who got themselves incarcerated as criminals, but it should not be forgotten that many neurotic characters, particularly those whose social or economic standing protect them, elude these legal consequences for long periods if not indefinitely. A typical example of such a case follows:

This fellow was the son of wealthy and aristocratic Bostonian parents who were the chief victims of most of his aggressions. These had begun at an early age; one of his earliest memories was of setting fire to one of the outbuildings on the family estate. By the age of seven he had already done considerable petty stealing of money, jewelry, and other objects from his parents, sometimes destroying them or pawning the jewelry to obtain money and spending it on candy.

He was sent to a private school where, although he was at first called a "sissy" because of his curls and feminine appearance, he proceeded to establish himself as the school bully by beating up every other boy in it and intimidating each new one as he came. He used to take particular delight in cruelly torturing and teasing some of the physically handicapped children in school. He was expelled repeatedly. He began sexual activities at a very early age, intriguing numerous girls with whom he had casual affairs in a highly caddish and contemptuous fashion. He was finally sent away to a preparatory school in Virginia where he violated the rules to the point of expulsion and when admitted to a second preparatory school defied the authorities and his parents by refusing to study and so failing to pass. That this was not on account of any intellectual defect was clearly shown by subsequent psychometric tests which indicated his intelligence to be definitely superior.

[2] Alexander, Franz, *Psychoanalysis of the Total Personality*, Nervous and Mental Disease Publishing Co., N.Y. and Wash., 1930; *Ibid.*, with Staub, Hugo, *The Criminal, the Judge and the Public*, Macmillan Co., 1931; *Ibid.*, with Healy, William, *Roots of Crime*, Knopf, 1935.

At his own insistence he was permitted to accept a position in a bank obtained for him by his father's prestige and high business standing, but lost it through repeated episodes of drinking, car smashing, arrests and notoriety for dangerous driving. He burglarized the homes of some of his relatives, taking jewelry, money, and liqueurs. He became involved with some gangsters in Philadelphia and opened up a private gambling establishment but lost heavily on this venture and in order to recover money to meet his losses, committed forgeries in which he was detected. His family's influence enabled him to escape prosecution.

These are a few of the main events in his life sufficient to indicate his behavior pattern. The interstices were filled with innumerable petty crimes against his parents and society in general which it would take pages to relate.

His appearance, however, belied it all. He had a fresh, boyish expression and a courteous, dignified manner which instantly stamped him as a person whose social advantages had been superior. He admitted with engaging candor that he did not know why he persistently got himself into so much trouble by these actions and hoped we could enlighten him. Psychoanalytic study, upon which he embarked with "honest" skepticism and at times a somewhat cynical amusement, soon revealed definite reasons for his behavior which were a great surprise to him.

Externally the circumstances under which he had been reared would seem to have been almost ideal. His mother and father were upstanding and respected citizens, his only sibling was an elder sister who would not appear to have offered much threat of early rivalry and there was no external pressure from economic or social difficulty. Despite these fine appearances, however, the early childhood situation was fraught with insuperable obstacles to normal development. There had been instilled in this patient very early in his life a feeling of inferiority for which much of his subequent behavior was an attempt at compensation. This appeared clearly in a dream which he related shortly after he had begun his analysis.

I was in a bicycle race such as one often sees in the newsreels. I was leading. A fellow behind me began a spurt as if to catch up and pass me. It has always seemed absurd to me for the leader to allow himself to be passed as he so often is in the pictures, and I thought to myself, "I'll show them." I made a terrific effort and kept ahead of the whole gang. But I guess it cost me my life because I got to going so fast that I couldn't take the curve and the last I remember was a crash as I shot out into space.

This dream vividly portrays the pattern of this boy's self-destruction. He had always to be first in everything and in his vain effort to achieve this impossibility he disregarded all reality and so crashed.

What was it that so threatened his self-confidence as a child as to impel him to these destructive efforts at self-assertion?

In the first place, his earliest rival had been this sister, who, after the initial interest which the birth of a baby brother created in the family had somewhat abated, robbed him of this position of importance by studied efforts. That these passed the bounds of ordinary childish rivalry was indicated by the increasing deceptiveness, meanness, and underhanded trickery which she used to secure her position as favorite. Probably she, too, felt greatly threatened in her position and felt obliged to resort to such methods but she is not the subject of our investigation. It was freely admitted by the parents to be a fact that she became increasingly their favorite child, while her brother became a black sheep who did nothing to please and everything to distress them.

If his parents had had the benefit of modern child-guidance information and instruction they might have recognized that much of this boy's behavior was provocative as well as retaliatory, i.e., he was not only taking revenge because he felt slighted but was trying to obtain in this subversive way the love he felt was denied him. This they did not see, however, and they played directly into his hands by punishing him severely, a method of discipline which, of course, only increased his feeling of being wronged and stimulated him to greater aggressiveness.

Even the forms of punishment used by the parents were unfortunately chosen. The father would sometimes beat the boy but more often he would enact a dramatic but insincere threat, the emptiness of which was immediately detected by the child. For example, he several times took the boy to the police station by pre-arrangement with the officers. The mother, on the other hand, was given to severe pinching which she would inflict upon him under such circumstances that to scream or cry would have exposed him to the indignity of public observation. She humiliated him by obliging him to wear dresses quite late in life and to attend grammar school wearing curls. Quite early, therefore, he was forced to defend himself against terrific blows to his self-esteem and to his masculinity while at the same time he was exposed to daily demonstrations of the fact that to be a girl meant to be the recipient of favors and to have one's trickery, unfairness, and deceitfulness overlooked. From psychoanalytic studies we know that every boy is sorely tempted by some of the advantages which seem to accrue to girls and is for that reason torn between his natural masculine strivings and the temptation to surrender these in favor of a passive receptive feminine attitude. When, in addition, he has parents whose insincerity and cruelty are readily detected by the child and greatly increase his feelings of helplessness and insecurity, there is little left for him except to succumb to supine passivity or outright homosexuality or else to deny these by violent gestures in the opposite directions, at the same time secretly seeking such passive gratifications as can be surreptitiously stolen behind the aggressive façade.

The latter course was chosen by this boy. Unconsciously he took the position that nothing he did would please the parents anyway, that they had been unfair and unkind to him and that there was therefore no reason to please them, his only purpose in life being to get, in the most convenient way, whatever he happened to want. Consciously this was represented by the inexplicable disinclination he felt for everything which the parents wished him to do and the extraordinary proclivity he showed for doing everything the parents did not want him to do. Some of his parents' ideals corresponded with those of society in general and the fact that the patient's aggressions against his parents fell to some extent upon society was an unfortunate complication.

Thus far I have shown only how a boy was so wounded by the treatment received in childhood from his well-meaning parents that he became first a "bad boy" and then a "bad man." This would explain how he became what could be regarded as a *criminal* but not what we would call a *neurotic* character. The distinction is that a neurotic character does not permit himself to profit by the aggressions which he makes, but on the other hand seems to head directly into punishment regularly. This was precisely true in the patient I have been describing. All of his drinking, stealing, forging, raping, car smashing, fighting, and so on, failed to achieve for him any substantial gain. The money he stole he lost; the forging he did was promptly detected; the drinking he did made him sick; the girls he got into trouble worried him nearly to death; the friends he thought he had made by generous splurges and sympathetic friendliness always deserted him. He was constantly in trouble, actually very unhappy. Time after time during the period of my observation of him he would reach an oasis of relative peace which he would shortly disturb by an aggressive act toward someone, the natural reaction against which he would use as a justification for a more serious aggression of a sort which, it would seem perfectly obvious to anyone, could not fail to get him in trouble. Then when the blow had fallen and his punishment was full upon him he would, after a preliminary flurry of blustering and recrimination, settle down to a mood of despair and a half-hearted inquiry into the possible reasons why such senseless behavior should have seemed so sensible to him only a few days before. When it was pointed out to him how he deliberately arranged to punish himself, he would vigorously deny that he had even so much as a sense of guilt about it. This is typical of the neurotic character.

Alexander and Healy (*op. cit.*) have described an unforgettable example of the neurotic character which so vividly represents the way in which these individuals yield, on the one hand, to their feelings of aggressiveness and hostility and, on the other hand, to their need for self-punishment *projected into the hands of an official agency* that I think to round out the picture I shall cite this case.

This was a boy, the eldest of five children in a fairly well-to-do family where he had all normal advantages. No other members of his family were delinquent nor did there appear to have been any untoward circumstances in his upbringing. From the time he was eight years old he had stolen articles and this propensity led to his being committed four or five times to correctional institutions where he made friends readily because of his courteous and industrious behavior. He stated frankly that something, he did not know what, drove him to steal and that his behavior was a puzzle to himself.

When he was sixteen, while on parole from a boy's correctional institution, he stole a suitcase and was brought into juvenile court where he told the judge that the correctional institutions to which he had been sent had failed to cure him and that he needed more severe punishment. At his own request he was sent to the reformatory for adults where he again made a good record and was paroled. He speedily got into more trouble, but then settled down for a year or so, did well in business, and married. After the birth of his first child, however, he returned to his delinquencies, repeatedly making long trips in automobiles which he had stolen. He joined the navy but soon deserted and continued to steal until he was arrested and placed in another institution. He escaped and returned to his criminal career. During all this time he wrote affectionate letters to his wife, declaring that he acted under some strange impulse which he could not understand and begging her to forgive him. His father and his wife's parents, who had a genuine affection for him because of his winning manners, spent a great deal of money getting him out of difficulties, only to have him plunge into more serious escapades. He was finally arrested for burglary and was given a long sentence in the penitentiary. Here he made a fine record and eventually, by distinguishing himself as a hero in a prison catastrophe, obtained a pardon. A few days before the pardon was to become effective, however, after his wife had come for him and plans for a new start in business had been made, he ran away and soon was implicated in a series of thefts and burglaries in another state. He was given a long penitentiary sentence and once again people became interested in him because of his unusual qualities. A psychiatrist who studied him at this time reported that this was not an ordinary criminal type but rather a man who committed criminal acts because of an inner compulsion. All attempts to have the case studied by psychoanalytic methods were frustrated, however, and in the course of time the young man made his escape from a road gang and established himself in a city far away under an alias. Here he contracted a bigamous marriage and continued to steal, committing many bizarre crimes which seemed calculated to call attention to himself and which finally brought about his capture. Altogether the record of this young man, not half told here, included ten or twelve incarcerations, many arrests, punitive as well as kindly treatment at the hands of many authorities, beginning with his own parents, and still he remained a puzzle to himself as well as others; an intelligent, healthy, gifted young man "strangely optimistic about the possibilities of the future for him."

PASSIVE NEUROTIC AGGRESSION

Sometimes instead of blustering, fighting, and trouble-making, the individual accomplishes his aggressions and his self-destruction by a more passive technique. Passivity can be just as provocative as active aggression. In fact, perhaps those who exasperate their associates by laziness, indifference, and ineptitude are more numerous even if less conspicuous than those of the type illustrated above. In such cases the punitive effect is likely to be more insidious and to appear more definitely as if the individual were the victim of fate or of inexorable forces such as economics rather than of the vengeance of those whom he has injured.

For want of a better name, we might call this kind of neurotic character the "helpless" type. A child, thwarted and outraged at every turn by indulgent but sadistic parents who used him as a plaything and a foil, could submit passively to the indignities that were put upon him and remain supine and receptive through life or he could react with belligerence and hostility leading to provocations of punishment. It is this latter type which is usually described as the typical neurotic character, but I think this passive type which I mention is of the same genus and perhaps no less abundant, although, so far as I know, it has not been previously recognized. Its representatives are able to hide much of their aggressiveness as well as their punishment by ascribing their plight to blind fate. The case of another man whom I knew very well will serve to demonstrate the kind of neurotic character who makes a vast amount of trouble for other people, as well as for himself, by constantly failing at tasks well within his scope.

This young man was referred by the dean of the college where he had gone for six years without completing the necessary amount of credit hours for his degree. Like the holy men of old who did penance by taking one step backward for every two steps forward, he had managed to complete only one-half to two-thirds of the work for which he enrolled each year. The records and our examinations showed that this was not due to any inability to do college work, but in each course he failed to complete part of the prescribed assignments. He failed to write a certain theme in one course, in another he left a drawing unfinished, in another failed to turn in a book review or a bibliography, in still another neglected to complete a little laboratory work and was absent from class too many times. He was an amiable young fellow who confessed that he got nothing done and couldn't seem to catch up in his work but did not know what to do about it. In his hopeful pleading for help or "advice" he was like a good child who seeks approbation, and, like a child, he came at regular intervals to see the physician, not to report progress in the accepted sense, but rather to bring further examples of his failures and ineptitude.

One day he brought his program of activities. The doctor went over it with him and pointed out that he was aimlessly wasting a great deal of time which might be devoted to his studies. A few days later he came proudly presenting a theme which he said he had written in a few hours and which had prevented him from receiving credit in a certain course for more than two years. At the same time he ingenuously explained that that very morning he had awakened and, finding that it was raining, had turned over and slept all morning, cutting a class in which he was on the verge of failing. Such naive attempts to extricate himself from the morass in which he was floundering were characteristic of this patient.

He was the only son of a domineering, tyrannical but indulgent father and a strict mother. A sister, two years younger, was lame and the patient's early play was molded around her illness and that of his best boy friend who died a lingering death at eight years of age. He became known as a "sissy" and was bullied and teased by the other boys in the neighborhood who made him cry often. He was forced to pull the other boys in his wagon or to ride them on his back and was made the butt of practical jokes. At home and at school he was punished severely. He was inept at all sports partly because his mother refused to allow him enough freedom to learn how to play rough and ready games. When he received roller skates as a present he could not use them and was finally shamed into learning because his little sister learned first. Until he was ten years old he slept in his baby-bed, even though he grew so tall that his feet stuck out at the end. He had no room of his own but slept with his mother and sister.

When he was twelve his mother took the two children and left the powerful father whom the patient loved and feared. A little later the father kidnaped the boy, who then became the unwilling bone of contention between his parents. His father sent the boy to military school where he was knocked about and mistreated by the other boys, hung from the windows by his ankles and subjected to other indignities and was miserably unhappy. The boy grew up ill-at-ease, clumsy, lethargic, unable to do any kind of work successfully. His father ordered him to attend college and the boy did so, enrolling year after year with discouraging results. He remained dumbly attached to his energetic father in spite of his father's active displeasure over his successive failures. His whole interest was bound up in this parent whom he apparently sought to please, but whom he actually disappointed and thwarted daily by his infantile dependency and his refusal to try to be a man.

A somewhat similar case of successive failure was that of a certain middle-aged farmer who came to a clinic with a large collection of physical ailments which we shall dismiss for the present and cite only some of the manifestations in behavior of his self-destructiveness.

When he married, his father and father-in-law had each given him a farm. During the first few years of his married life he mortgaged these and in 1917 (at a time when no farmer was hard pressed because produce prices were very high) he lost them both. With some funds advanced to him by his father he moved to California where he invested everything in a vineyard and lost it. Then he purchased (with what funds I do not know) an orchard, but this too he lost. By doing various odd jobs he earned enough money to buy some trucks, expecting to go into trucking on a large scale but failed to make the payments and lost them. His father again advanced him money, a thousand dollars, which he invested in a filling station and was making some success of it when his expansive notions led him to construct a large garage in connection with the filling station. He failed in this venture and lost both the garage and the filling station.

A few years later his father offered him a farm if he would return east to live on it, which he did, soon placing heavy mortgages on the land. During the busy season on the farm when he should have been working very hard, he suddenly decided to take a trip back to California. He planned to pay for the trip by charging fares to other people who wished to make the trip with him. Fourteen people agreed to go with him but in spite of this he lost money on the trip because some of those whom he took failed to pay and he failed to collect. He bought cars in the east, and drove them to California with the idea of selling them there at a profit but this scheme failed, also, and he sold the cars at a loss. He returned to his home to find many mortgages on his farm due. In order to pay them he sold some cattle which belonged to his wife but instead of applying the money on the mortgages he yielded to an impulse to return to California.

From there he went to New Mexico and rented 14,000 acres of land for some large-scale farm operations but he used up so much money in the down payment for the rent that he did not have enough cash to buy sufficient seed to plant this, so gave up the whole deal and returned east, to find that the bankers and relatives were utterly out of patience with him and were demanding payments on the farm mortgages, which he was unable to make. This man's aggressiveness, which was great, was carried out very largely in his work, but unlike the normal man who uses this drive as a means to success, this man made it his business to fail, losing not only his own money but that of everyone who trusted him.

All of this sounds so absurd and extreme that it is difficult to realize that such individuals live and breathe and carry on business relations without being generally regarded by their friends and neighbors as self-destructive, even when things come to a climax. They may be accused of stupidity, or knavery, or of courting bad luck. But these descriptive terms fail to discern the underlying psychology. A few might perceive in this fellow that feelings of inferiority resulted in over-compensatory gestures in the form of business aspirations so far beyond his ability as to be predestined to failure, but even this is not sufficient to account for the string of successive failures; over-compensatory striving is usually to some extent successful. Apparent stupidity, on the other hand, is a frequently used weapon of aggression. Such consistent failure, however, associated with the many physical complaints which have not been discussed but which were a part of the clinical picture combine to indicate that in this man there was a dramatic exemplification of self-destruction thinly masked as ineptitude and ill-fortune.

These cases, like the foregoing ones, leave little doubt as to the dynamic power of irrational and unconscious motives which determine the repetitious behavior of the neurotic character. The net result is uniformly self-destructive in a high degree—self-destructive in the sense that martyrdom, asceticism, neurotic invalidism, and the other conditions discussed in this chapter are self-destructive. It is true that the neurotic character saves his life—he may even save some crumbs of normal pleasure, and more often than not he has the mad satisfaction of many a wild, impulsive fling. But for all this he pays too dear a price—a price of suffering, restriction, deprival, the destruction of hope and joy. By all reality standards it is a fool's bargain, a throwing-away of life for momentary satisfactions.

Let it not be thought, or said, that in the wild joys for which he pays so dearly the neurotic character gets his heart's desire, his money's worth—and is, therefore, to be envied, not pitied. Such brave words every psychiatrist has heard time without number from the lips of these victims themselves, attempting betwixt defiance and despair to hold high a head "bloodied but unbowed." But he has seen, also, the hollowness of the pretence. Reality cannot be flouted with impunity, and the burden of punishment and consequence accumulates until wistfulness and sorrow replace blitheness and arrogance. Not until then will the self-destructive program permit the approach of effective therapy; unfortunately the self-destruction has, by that time, often passed beyond the point of reversibility.

B. CRIMINALITY

The scientific study of criminality has progressed to a point such that, granted its relevancy, the inclusion of even the bare outline of the subject would be impossible in this book. I shall consider, therefore, only that aspect of criminality which bears on our thesis, namely, the self-destructive motives in the psychology of the social transgressor.

There has been some attempt to disseminate among the American public the slogan, "Crime never pays." Motion pictures of crime-detection, the punishment of criminals and, particularly, criminals who (chained to the arm of the sheriff) loudly proclaim this slogan are presumably intended to impress tempted youth to abstain from the lure of criminal shortcuts across the rules of society. Nevertheless, crime goes on and the very fact that such a slogan has to be *preached* at us by design is an indication that its truth is not self-evident. Large numbers of American citizens show by their behavior that they believe that crime *does* pay. How it pays them might well deserve some psychological analysis because, obviously, different people want different rewards. But even assuming that the paying refers to material acquisitions, the American public has had constantly before its eyes for a long time the magnificent successes of individuals ranging from bank presidents and utility mag-

nates to organizers of beer joints and brothels who successfully elude apprehension or conviction.

Furthermore, almost at the same moment that crime prevention agencies are assuring the public that crime never
pays, the police departments of many of our largest cities
openly proclaim their intention of using criminal methods
in handling criminals. The police commissioner of one of
our large cities, for example, announced, "There'll be pro-
motions waiting for the men (police) who muss them
(gangsters and suspects) up. I'll promote the men who kick
these gorillas around and bring them in."[3] In the same
week, a lynching was defended by a district attorney in the
South and only a few years ago Governor Rolph of California made his celebrated defense of lynchings. The American public is periodically shocked by such frank confessions
on the part of prominent individuals that criminal acts are
permissible, providing favored individuals commit them.
This mental reservation that others should not commit
crimes but for me it is all right is a characteristic element
in American psychology. Indeed, only a little reflection is
necessary for us to realize that our country was founded by
a group of people who defied and violated the laws of England persistently from the outset. Furthermore, most of the
financial fortunes and the so-called economic stability of
our country in the early days depended upon a criminal
destruction and waste of natural resources, the iniquity and
sad results of which we are only now beginning fully to
realize. Even yet, there are millions of American citizens
who feel it to be their God-given right to destroy timber,
to kill and maim wild birds and wild animals, to pollute
streams, and to exploit land without any regard to the anti-
social consequences of such ruthless destruction.

If I have wandered somewhat afield from the topic, it is
because I am somewhat dubious about the possibility of
convincing the average American reader that criminality is
actually self-destructive. Our whole national ideology disputes it. As Alexander and Healy[4] say in their recent book,
in comparing the psychological investigation of criminals
in Germany and in the United States:

The most impressive of these [differences] is the heroic exhibitionistic evaluation of criminal deeds in America; this much
more than in Europe plays an important part in formation of

[3] *The Nation*, Nov. 13, 1935.

[4] Alexander, Franz, and Healy, William, *Roots of Crime:* Psychoanalytic
Studies, Knopf, 1935, p. 283.

motives for breaking the law. In spite of official condemnation, not only instinctively but even consciously, the [American] public views criminality with a sort of adolescent hero-worship. At the same time machine civilization with its mechanizing and leveling tendencies strangulates individuality and compels the individual to become a part of the collective unit. Criminality remains one of those few outlets left through which the individual can express his spite against this pressure and emphasize his masculine sovereignty. . . . The ideological basis of American democracy, an individualistic philosophy of life, is personified in the ideal of the self-made man, who is independent of external help, who is successful in the free competition of equal chances.

In other words, rugged individualism implies the right of the individual to disregard social rights and this, in essence, is criminality.

The truth of the matter is that we Americans believe that crime does not pay if you get caught. The moral of this, and the working program of many Americans, is, "Be a rugged individualist, get along with your neighbors the best you can, and commit such offense against them as is necessary in such a way that you do not get caught." If one is skillful one can do much of it and receive financial rewards and public acclaim. If one is clumsy or stupid or makes a mistake, then one is no longer in the game but receives official condemnation as a criminal and is asked to testify before the puzzled youth of the country that crime does not pay.

This excursion into certain political implications of the study of criminality should not lead us from the scientific consideration of how criminal behavior may result in self-destruction, even though *in America* it frequently does not. There certainly is such a thing as normal criminal behavior in the sense that some individuals do away with any hypocrisy about it, with any attempt at loyalty to higher ideals or higher social standards, and take what they want when they want it, and defend themselves against capture or punishment. The Missouri Crime Survey[5] showed that only one out of a thousand crimes committed in the area surveyed led to actual punishment of the offenders. Any study of criminals, therefore, in this country should distinguish between criminals captured and criminals not captured. Almost all of the studies that have been made have drawn conclusions about criminality based on the study of those

[5] Moley, Raymond, *The Administration of Criminal Justice in Missouri*, St. Louis, Missouri Association for Criminal Justice, 1926.

who have been captured; when it is so well known that the vast majority are not captured this does not seem to me to be a proper "sampling" in the statistician's sense of the word.

The Gluecks[6] have shown that those who do get captured continue to commit crimes and continue to be captured again. That their aggressions against society lead to self-destruction in the sense of imprisonment, misery, and deprivation is obvious.

But, as I have already indicated, I do not feel sure that we should call these people criminals, if we are to apply the same word to those who never allow themselves to be caught. It may be that we should refer to them as neurotic criminals. Some of them are undoubtedly stupid and are caught for this reason, some of them are unfortunate; a few of them may be normal criminals who erred in technique. But perhaps the majority of them will fall into a group which has been carefully studied psychoanalytically.[7] In many individuals the impulse to commit crimes, which we can assume is a universal tendency, is irresistible, but such individuals cannot, on the other hand, escape the vengeance of their own consciences. Such individuals, therefore, having yielded to their aggressive impulses, are obliged to surrender in the end to the threats of their own consciences if not to the intimidations of the law. This leads them, then, to seek punishment, to allow themselves to be caught, to commit provocative offenses or even to "break into jail."

These motives have been studied at greater length in a more recent study of the psychological motives in crime by Alexander and Healy, referred to above. About a dozen criminals were subjected to psychoanalysis. In all these cases this deeper psychological study showed somewhat the same general formula, namely, a great wish to remain a dependent child and great resentment against the social, economic, and other forces which thwarted their satisfactions, with the consequent combination of mixed feelings of revenge, self-assertion, and guilt. "They treated me mean, I hate them, I don't need them any more, I will pay them back, I will take what I want from them; but I am sorry, I feel guilty, I will be punished for this. . . ."

That this conforms in general to the formula for other methods of self-destruction is obvious. It might be simmered

[6] Glueck, Sheldon, and Glueck, Eleanor T., *Five Hundred Criminal Careers*, Knopf, 1930.

[7] Alexander, Franz, and Staub, Hugo, *op. cit.*, Reik, Theodor, *op. cit.*

down to the following: Some criminality is the result of overwhelming hate developed in childhood, which the individual can express only at the price of intimidation by his own conscience to such an extent that he unconsciously fails to carry through his aggressions and allows himself to be detected, captured, and punished.

This was made very vivid to me by one of the most extraordinary individuals, sane or insane, criminal or non-criminal, that I have ever met. From fully a thousand pages of notes about him, I shall try to condense into a few pages enough of the record of his life to indicate the emotional origins of his terrible criminality.

Before me lies a manuscript written by this remarkable man, later executed by order of the federal court. It begins as follows:

I am John Smith, No. 31614, United States Penitentiary, at ——.

I am a liar.

I am a thief.

I am a murderer.

I am a degenerate.

But that these things are so does not detract a bit from the truth of what I have here written.

I am now 38 years old. Of these 38 years I have spent 22 years in jail, reform schools, and prisons. In all of my lifetime I have never done any good to myself or anyone else. I am a first-class A-1 skunk. . . . But what I am the law has made me.

I feel now that I shall soon be dead, that is the reason that I write this. . . .

All of my life I have lived destructively. In these writings I am going to attempt to prove that it was possible for me to have lived constructively and to have been the means of much good both to myself and my fellowmen if I had been properly taught and treated right in the beginning by the law. . . .

I am fully aware of the fact that I am no good and that no one likes or respects me, which worries me not at all because I don't like or respect anyone else. I despise, detest, and hate every human being on earth, including my own self. . . . My only feelings now are hate and fear. I have practically lost all the power I ever had to enjoy life. I can only suffer. . . . Every decent feeling that I may have had in my nature has been brutalized and knocked out of me long ago.

The manuscript then proceeds to an unflinching self-analysis in which the prisoner spares neither himself nor society. He frankly confesses that he has murdered twenty-three men and has no regrets about it. (Most of these murders were substantiated by investigation.) He does not pretend to have had immediate justification for these murders but says that he killed because he enjoyed killing, that it gratified his hate and his wish for revenge, although the revenge was displaced from the original object of his hatred.

It is really impossible to convey in the compass of a few pages the uniqueness of this man. He had an almost total lack of formal education but had schooled himself to a surprising extent and was possessed of superior intelligence and an amazing lack of repressions. I have never seen an individual whose destructive impulses were so completely accepted and acknowledged by his conscious ego. He outlined to me in detail a plan he had conceived for bringing about the destruction of *the entire human race,* a plan which was by no means absurd in its conception and compares favorably with the ingenious devices patented by inventors pandering to the munition manufacturers who are so proud of their devices for increasing official murderousness.

No one can read this manuscript in its entirety without an emotional thrill. On the one hand, there was the terrific hate, bitterness, and incredibly sadistic cruelty of the man; on the other hand, his clear evaluation of himself, his wistful faith in and affection for one federal official, who as a younger man had once shown the prisoner some kindness and who had kept up a correspondence with him long afterwards, his curious interest in bettering the world in spite of his feeling that nearly all human beings were so bad that it would be better if they were all killed. It was an incongruous picture of stark reality which produced an effect comparable to that of gazing into the interior of a human body torn open in some horrible accident, with all the vital organs laid bare, the person retaining consciousness with a superhuman ability to endure pain so that he could calmly discuss the accident and his approaching death.

For this man knew quite well how and why his destructive tendencies had been wrought to such an overwhelming height. In early childhood he had had, on the one hand, stern religious teaching and, on the other hand, economic pressure and extrusion from the home so that at the age of eight he had already been arrested. At twelve he was a prisoner in a boys' Industrial School where official cruelty added to the bitterness of his childhood fears. Subsequently, his life was simply one incident after another of revenge, recapture, punishment, release and more revenge, more punishment, more bitterness.

The same psychological factors later discovered in the psychoanalytic investigation of the prisoners referred to above were recognized in himself by this extraordinary fellow and set down by him in these comments about his own psychology, the psychology of mankind and of criminals in particular. They are, in short, that hate breeds hate, that the injustices perpetrated upon a child arouse in him unendurable reactions of retaliation which the child must repress and postpone but which sooner or later come out in some form or another, that the wages of sin is death, that murder breeds suicide, that to kill is only to be killed, that there is no real atonement but suffering, and that bitter suffering bears no fruit.

This prisoner demanded that he be executed for a murder he committed in prison. Inasmuch as he was tried in Kansas in which there has long been a law and a sentiment against capital punishment, a strong effort was made to prevent his execution, but by insisting upon certain technicalities, refusing all counsel, skillfully refuting the testimony of psychiatrists and others, the prisoner obtained his wish to be executed and this was carried out, the only instance of capital punishment in Kansas in over fifty years.

On the day of his execution, he ran eagerly forward, climbed to the gallows with alacrity, urging his executioners to hurry the thing up and get it over with. It was remarked by everyone how eager he was to die. His execution was, in essence, a suicide, a direct accomplishment of what he had indirectly sought for all of his thirty-eight years.

C. PERVERSIONS

It is beyond the province of this book to go into a discussion of how and why society establishes certain norms or acceptable forms of behavior with reference, for example, to the expression of sexual impulses, or to show how and why changes in these standards take place from time to time and from country to country. The fact remains that several forms of sexual activity which were once officially approved of in civilized countries are now taboo, while, on the other hand, numerous taboos which once existed have now been removed. From the social or legal standpoint, therefore, sexual perversion is a variable concept. From a psychological and biological standpoint, it is much more definite and refers to a dominant persistence of infantile modes of obtaining sexual pleasure to the exclusion or thwarting of normal modes. Every psychiatrist is consulted by individuals who are in love with things instead of persons, or with persons of their own sex instead of the opposite sex, or for whom being cruel or suffering pain or just looking at or listening to something sexual replaces normal sexual activities.

We realize from the epoch-making studies of Freud, beginning with his famous *Three Contributions to the Theory of Sex,* that such perverse trends exist in everyone but are submerged in the normal person in favor of more adult forms of gratification. In some individuals the struggle to give up these infantile modes in favor of adult modes is for one reason or another a very difficult one, and one of several things may happen. Sometimes they are given up only at the expense of sacrificing all sexual life; sometimes they are given up only in the direct form and continue to be gratified in numerous indirect, disguised ways. In still other instances they are not given up at all but are gratified either openly or surreptitiously. If the latter are detected the afflicted ones are punished by society for indulging these forbidden sexual impulses just as those who undeservedly gratify their aggressive instincts (criminals) are, if detected, punished by society. One side of the picture is that certain people seem compelled from within to attain their sexual satisfaction perversely. But there is another side to this which is not so obvious or so well known. That one who in this way clings to infantile techniques instead of adult techniques must come to grief and ultimately lose even these satisfactions, would seem to be evident enough to anyone to act as deterrence. Since, however, these things go on we must assume that either the impulses are too strong or the supposed deterrence is ineffective, if not actually an incentive. In either case one must conclude that the consequent self-destruction is knowingly accepted if not actually sought. (The blocking-off of the voice of intelligence has already been mentioned.) To present this idea and show how completely disintegrating and demoralizing sexual perversion could become was apparently the purpose of Gide in his novel *The Immoralist.* No better illustration of the self-destructiveness of perversion could be found than the experiences of Oscar Wilde and Lord Douglas. The terrific hate for one another smoldering beneath the vaunted love culminated in the treachery resulting in Wilde's incarceration and Lord Douglas' ultimate disgrace.[8]

The resentment which society feels toward overt homosexuals as expressed by violent attacks proudly made upon them by solicited individuals expresses, to be sure, a certain amount of unconscious fear of and over-reaction to unrecognized homosexual impulses within the attacker himself. It also expresses something more explicit, something which psychiatrists in their attempt to understand and explain the behavior of homosexuals are apt to overlook. This is the aggressive element in the seduction. Sometimes this is very obvious. I studied a girl once in the State Prison for Women who made no attempt to conceal from me the deliberate seduction she had made of dozens of high school and grade school girls. Her technique of seducing them was to tell them that men were bad and hurt little girls, counseling them never to allow themselves to suffer the cruelties men inflicted upon women, never, in short, to let a man even touch them; that women, on the other hand, were nice and soft and sweet, could love one another and make one another feel very happy and pleasant by certain techniques. If anyone can doubt the aggressiveness (withal unconscious) of such seductions he will be more convinced to learn that this girl, who had an indescribable personal charm and the apparent softness and tenderness of a delicate flower, was in prison *not* on account of these seductions but for the crime of having beaten her husband to death with a hammer, leaving him thereafter locked in their apartment while she drove fifty miles to a bridge party!

That this aggressiveness is tied up with self-destruction may not be so explicit. Perhaps it is not always the case, but in some instances it is very strikingly so. A single woman of thirty-two gave a long history of sexual irregularities, both heterosexual and homosexual, beginning with an experience with her older brother when she was six. Such experiences are, of course, very common and do not ordinarily predispose or lead to homosexuality. In this case, however, homosexual impulses and experiments began in adolescence, consisting of physical intimacies with another girl. This, too, could still be regarded as within the range of normal experiences had it ceased there; instead, however, during the succeeding ten years, she had had many

[8] See André Gide's autobiography, *If It Die*, Random House, 1935, pp. 296-304.

homosexual affairs, always without any real feeling of affection and almost invariably with consequent damage to herself. Her work brought her in close contact with younger girls—her choice of profession (she taught aesthetic dancing) being presumably motivated by her homosexual propensities. In the course of her teaching jobs, she was invariably indiscreet or exhibitionistic in her homosexual behavior and so got a bad reputation for herself, and lost her job as a result. She would make sudden homosexual advances to girls whom she had only recently met. Naturally, she would usually be repulsed, reported, and then discharged. Again, she would kiss girls openly and excessively and thus provoke unfavorable comment. She was always afraid, on getting a new job, that her reputation would catch up with her and cause her to lose her new job, and this it frequently did.

Thus she constantly defeated herself through yielding to impulses which she considered sexual in nature, but which were actually aggressive and self-destructive. She had no feeling of affection for any of her sexual objects. Her aggressive motivation was also shown by a fear from which she suffered that she had injured or would injure physically or socially the girl to whom she was attracted. Instead, she injured chiefly herself—bringing about her own disgrace and punishment, virtual self-destruction.

Such behavior can be better understood in the light of her familial and developmental history. She was the youngest of seven living siblings, with four elder brothers and two elder sisters. One brother, eleven years older, seduced her in childhood many times, and frequently gave her spending money only if she would permit him to indulge in sexual play with her. Her next elder brother, three years her senior, was her idol. Her next elder sister, eight years older, was still single, a cranky, complaining trouble-maker, still living at home, and so obnoxious that the mother had almost had her arrested on several occasions. The father was an irresponsible ne'er-do-well, who had always openly consorted with other women, and frequently left home for weeks at a time without explanation. He once sent one of his daughters to his brother's home for the brother's sexual enjoyment.

The patient had always been regarded as a tomboy, and many times wished she actually were a boy. Her interest in athletics and physical education, her mannish haircut and clothes all gave evidence of her masculine identification.

On the other hand, she had had sporadic heterosexual experiences and interests but had always avoided marriage, or any prolonged heterosexual affair. Apparently her early seduction by her brother and other boys emphasized for her the masochistic conception of the female role and rendered it frightening and unacceptable. Also, her father's irresponsible behavior prevented her from having any acceptable ideal of a man. Early envy of the freedom and genital endowment of boys caused her to flee from her role as a girl and try to imitate and identify herself with boys. But her actual mistreatment by her parents and older siblings caused so much resentment, that her sadistic conception of the masculine role was increased by resentment and rage consequent to this mistreatment. Hence she acted out in her sexual behavior aggressive, destructive impulses against girls—substitutes for her sisters and mother—but with so much guilt about this destructive behavior that nothing could prevent her from using techniques which got herself into situations leading to her own ruin.

SUMMARY

It has been the import of this chapter to demonstrate that anti-social behavior may mask self-destructive intentions. That it has self-destructive consequences does not prove this, but the study of such representative forms of overtly aggressive behavior as neurotic character, criminality, and sexual perversion seem to point to the substantiation of the hypothesis in many cases. Analysis of the motivations back of the behavior indicates close parallelism—in different arrangement—with the motives behind suicide, lacking, of course, the complete dominance of the death-instinct.

FIVE / *Psychosis*

That one virtually destroys himself if he so far abandons his loyalty to reality as to yield to impulses contrary to natural laws or social standards is perhaps obvious. If such a departure is extreme, if the impulses are so powerful as to escape all inhibition and express themselves in a chaotic, disorganized fashion without regard to any reality, we have what is designated medically as "psychosis" and, legally, as "insanity." These terms, particularly the latter, imply that as a matter of common knowledge these conditions represent a state and degree of helplessness such that, despite the offensiveness, the aggressiveness, the external as well as the self-directed destructiveness, society tolerates such individuals without retaliation and seeks only to protect itself by quarantining them. It was these unfortunates who formerly made up the bulk of psychiatric case material.

I shall not attempt to portray all the forms of mental disease which regularly or occasionally reach the degree which we call psychosis (the word which is sometimes used in the definitive sense given above, and sometimes to mean any particular one of the recognized psychiatric disease pictures). I shall limit myself to two conditions in which the self-destructive aspects of the psychosis are clearly recognizable. As can be inferred from the definition above, one element common to psychoses of all forms is the dereism, i.e., the rejection of the reality principle as a determinant of behavior in favor of the pleasure principle.[1]

Whatever we may think about certain religions,[2] the fact that they are socially accepted even by a small group puts them beyond our consideration as a form of psychosis by definition, since a part of reality is social reality, social customs, social attitudes. However, the psychiatrist sees many patients whose rejection of reality is so definite, so extreme, and so individualistic that there can be no dobut in anyone's mind but that they are using infantile modes to protect themselves from the inhospitality of a world toward which they feel hostile, and that they protect themselves

[1] In cases of depression where suffering is intense, it may seem strange to think of the pleasure principle as being in control, but it is, for reasons explained in Chapter One of this section, nevertheless true.

[2] It is true that many religions also reject reality to a greater or lesser extent. Some repudiate it entirely, some only misinterpret it. But so long as such repudiation is jointly agreed to by any considerable number of people, it is always possible for them to say that it is they who detect the "real reality" and others who live on illusion. In this connection, I remember an amusing incident from hospital practice. A very queer, maladjusted farm boy in the early thirties who had undoubtedly had a mild form of the disease called schizophrenia for many years and who heard voices, saw visions, and otherwise betrayed his mental unsoundness, sat hour after hour steadfastly reading *Science and Health.* I asked him one day if he understood it, and he replied that he did understand it and believed it. "But," he added, "the world doesn't believe it. The world doesn't believe this and it doesn't believe science, either. But you understand science and I understand this." He implied that it was he and I against the world, he with his peculiar religion and I with my peculiar science (psychiatry). To him they seemed strictly comparable.

by a rejection of it which may reach the extreme of destruction. There are those who cannot maintain satisfactory object relationships with the outside world, whose loves and hates were not easily transplanted from the childhood soil in which they grew to the new requirements of a changing world. Those thus handicapped in this capacity are called schizoid personalities and I have dealt with them descriptively and dynamically elsewhere.[3]

The schizoid personality which fails in the attempt at transplanting becomes the schizophrenic psychosis. Recognizing and dealing effectively with reality is synonymous with establishing properly distributed investments of hate and love in the parcels of reality, human and non-human, which surround us, and failure to do so results in a return of the love and hate, which should be externally invested, upon oneself. We have already discussed that form of mental disease characterized by the return of large quantities of suddenly released hate. In this condition (melancholia) sufficient contact with reality may be maintained so that the individual, for all his self-destructiveness, does not endanger the lives of others, and may even co-operate in efforts to redirect or reshape his own life. For this reason, melancholia is sometimes described as a neurosis rather than a psychosis. But some victims of melancholia abandon all loyalty to reality and may be extremely deluded and even homicidal. The mechanisms are the same as in the so-called neurotic form, but the surrender of object attachment and of reality testing here is much greater.

This departure from reality standards enables the psychotic person to destroy himself in a unique way not available to anyone else. He can *imagine* himself dead; or, he can imagine a part of himself to be dead or destroyed. This fantasied self-destruction, partial or complete, corresponds in its motives to actual self-mutilation and suicide. It is sometimes described technically as a negative hallucination, or (more accurately) as a nihilistic delusion, and there are those who prefer, especially for one form of this fantasied destruction, the impressive-sounding but not very well-defined term "depersonalization." [4]

In the following illustrative case there had previously been some actual suicidal attempts; these were followel by

---

[3] See *The Human Mind*, revised edition, Knopf, 1937.

[4] The most penetrating psychoanalytic study of this phenomenon is that of Oberndorf (Oberndorf, C. P., "Depersonalization in Relation to Erotization of Thought," *International Journal of Psychoanalysis*, 1934, Vol. XV pp. 271-95).

fantasies of non-existence, then by the fantasied destruction of a *part* of the body (the eye), and then by actual attempts to destroy that part of the body—a series of self-destructive phenomena progressing toward reality (and therefore toward greater dangerousness, but also greater "sanity").

This was a middle-aged spinster who had always lived with her father. The father died after a lingering illness, and left the patient a comfortable fortune. But no sooner had the father been laid away than the patient developed a series of kaleidoscopic symptoms which perplexed various internists but eluded diagnosis or relief. Gradually the affliction assumed more and more definitely the form of a fluctuating depression, a characteristic phase of which was the patient's· gloomy insistence that things were not real, or rather that she could not feel them to be so.

"I just don't think anything; I don't feel anything," she would say, rocking back and forth in her chair; "I am nothing—just right here, that's all, this little room around me —you're sitting there and I see you but you don't mean anything. I wouldn't recognize my own home if I saw it. Nothing interests me or means anything to me. I don't love anyone.

"I haven't got any face," she would say, feeling it with her hand, "I haven't any face, I haven't anything." She would then do a few multiplication problems for the examiner quite accurately, would give the name of her home-town and would respond to questions of a general nature appropriately. Then she would say disparagingly, "But that means nothing; it has nothing to do with me. I think one is in a pretty bad way when you're just nothing."

Three months later, after a period of increasing agitation and physical restlessness, the refrain of her complaint had changed somewhat. "I have no eyes. Those are just two holes. No, you don't understand. I have no eyes, no ears, just nothing except this [touching her face]. That isn't it. I haven't been able to see or hear as long as I've been here. There's nothing but two holes." She would continue thus without cessation except when she fell asleep or was forcibly fed.

She became quite pugnacious, striking at the nurses or doctors when attempts were made to feed her. Then she began to pick at her eyes and on one occasion tried to stick a tack into the corner of one eye. She explained this by saying that there were no eyes there in the first place so she couldn't do any harm. Frequently she said the only thing to do was to wrap her up in a sheet and send her home because she couldn't see or hear.

Nearly a year passed, during which she had periods of seeming cheerfulness and mental health. These would be followed by recurrences of the depression and the conviction that she was no longer alive. When reminded of her comfortable home, her friends, her resources, she would pay no attention. Over and over she would repeat her insistences that she was dead.

There was evidence to suggest that the cycles of depression were dependent upon recurring acquiescence in auto-erotic cravings. She was apparently able to resist these for moderately long periods but would finally yield and then be overwhelmed with a sense of guilt because of her association of auto-erotism with illness and the association of illness with the death of her father. The delusions of being dead then followed as punishment. The component elements of aggressions, punition and erotization with which we became so familiar in the previously described forms of self-destruction here reappear in connection with this singular and literally "fantastic" form of *partial* (ego) self-destruction.

The phenomenon of phantasied self-destruction (so-called depersonalization) is so interesting that I shall cite another example reported by a colleague.[5]

This woman was a very neat little person who kept her house so immaculate that after fourteen years of married life her furniture still looked brand new. This necessitated a great many prohibitions which she enforced upon her family and upon visitors. Her life moved in rather narrow circles; outside of her home, her only interest was in the church.

A few years after the birth of her second child it was felt necessary to perform a surgical operation from which she seemed to recover but which was followed in turn by recurrent attacks of influenza which would leave her very nervous and upset. She would go in tears to her sisters. It would require several days for them to comfort her. These crying spells became more frequent; it was noted that she left unfinished many things she started; she felt convinced that she was developing a goiter and that she

[5] Wholey, Cornelius C., *Depersonalization*. Read before the annual meeting of the American Psychiatric Association, Pittsburgh, Pa., May 11, 1937.

was going to lose her mind. Finally, she attempted suicide by taking a tablet of poison. A doctor was called who used a stomach pump immediately and she was saved, but from that time on *she insisted that she was dead.*

She declared that she did not know her name, that the person whose name they ascribed to her was dead, that she remembered that person very well, and knew that her behavior was nothing like that of hers. In this indirect way she described much of her past life but she insisted always that "that person" was dead and that she did not know who she herself was. All sorts of questioning were used, all sorts of logical fallacies were presented, but the patient remained steadfast in her belief.

For example, one of the doctors said to her, "If you are not Mr. X's wife, he is paying for keeping another woman here." She replied, "I will tell you what he is paying for; he is paying for keeping something evil living on this earth for years and years. Every part of my body feels like Nellie; I *imagine* it feels that way. Oh, imagination is an awful thing." The doctor pointed out that she had the same scar that Nellie had on her hand. "Oh," said the patient, "that, too, is imagination."

Her behavior was not entirely consistent with the delusion, because she attempted several times to commit suicide. Once she dropped out of a fourth story window with the avowed purpose of reaching an open grave into which she could crawl because she said that was where she belonged. She was dead and ought to be buried. She seemed to have no appreciation whatsoever of the fact that anything harmful could befall her.

These evidences of self-destruction were probably intuitively used by the physicians in the selection of a form of treatment which was rationalized as justified on entirely different grounds. The patient was subjected to an operation for the removal of "infected teeth and tonsils." She promptly recovered, resuming her normal frame of mind.

Time was when such fortunate occurrences, which are not infrequent, were held to be proof positive of the toxic nature of mental disease and of the therapeutic value of removing the foci of infection. Many thousands of persons were subjected to the removal of teeth, tonsils, prostates, colons, and other organs in a blind acceptance of this theory. One large state institution formerly employed a staff of surgeons who worked unremittingly along these lines. Great claims were made and bright promises held forth. And while occasional good results followed, for reasons which we think can now be explained quite otherwise than by the original theory, there were many disappointments. Medical opinion slowly relinquished its early hopes in the method and the theory of focal infection, and the toxic origin of functional psychoses is now almost forgotten.

That it is possible to explain some recoveries after surgical operations on entirely psychological grounds we shall see in greater detail in the next section. The case just described illustrates quite clearly how a woman who repeatedly tried to destroy herself in various ways, who in a part of her mind already believed herself dead, suddenly got well when instead of continued kind custodial treatment she received painful and bloody handling, even though we know it to have been skillfully and humanely applied.

Such cases as the one just cited in which self-destruction is phantasied but, as a rule, not actually carried out lie somewhere between the classical and frankly suicidal melancholiacs and the classical schizophrenics who are rarely self-destructive but frequently self-mutilative. Several examples of this will be cited in the next chapter; here I should like to refer only to that indirect self-destruction which results from the phantasies typical of schizophrenia, that they can destroy, or have destroyed, the world of reality and re-created a world of their own. The extreme result, as we commonly see it clinically, is a group of patients so completely self-absorbed, so indifferent to the laws of gravity, physiology, economics, and good taste that they seem totally incomprehensible and totally uncomprehending. (As a matter of fact, they are neither incomprehensible nor uncomprehending. Those who have the patience to work sympathetically and understandingly with them are often the means of their salvation.) There are, however, many cases less extreme than this, patients who in their fantasies destroy reality but who conceal them quite successfully and sometimes even turn them to good account (sublimation). One of my associates[6] has described a man in whom destructive fantasies of this type accompanied by gradual recession from the hated and feared world nearly overwhelmed him; he was able to recover his equilibrium with the physician's aid and gradually converted these

[6] Tidd, Charles W., "Increasing Reality Acceptance by a Schizoid Personality During Analysis," *Bulletin of the Menninger Clinic*, Vol. I, pp. 176-83, 1937.

phantasies of destroying the world with a secret invention into more and more plausible mystery and adventure tales and sold these tales to magazines. Ultimately, he gave up such fantasies and began writing serious and less fantastic tales.

One might say that those forms of mental illness in which the person denies his personality or heaps deprecations and abuses upon it represent self-destructiveness focused upon the ego. This can be contrasted with a very different syndrome in which not the ego but the super-ego is the object of the attack. To paralyze or narcotize the super-ego is often the ostensible purpose of getting drunk, and the condition to which I refer is one which bears many external resemblances to drunkenness.

It is called—unfortunately—"mania" (also "hypomania" and the "manic phase" of "manic-depressive psychosis"). From such designations the uninformed may be led to visualize a wildly disturbed, frenzied person, "raving" or screaming. Such a picture is rare. The more familiar example is almost indistinguishable in appearance from a "happy drunk," or a very gay, uninhibited person at a lively party. Chatter, pranks, preposterous proposals, laughter, and ceaseless expenditure of energy are characteristic. As in acute alcoholism, also, such individuals are extremely irritable if crossed or hindered in their extravagant, absurd, and often extremely injudicious behavior.

The condition differs from acute alcoholism in several important respects: in the first place, it does not subside after a few hours but continues for days, weeks, or months —occasionally for years. More important is the fact that a kind of intense seriousness is apt to be developed with reference to certain proposals and plans, and the individuals become engrossed in enormous self-imposed tasks which have innumerable ramifications. At first these may appear so sensible, even so admirable, as to command the respect and envy of others, but one soon detects in the average case the unreasonable and irrational excesses to which the plans are going. There are a few individuals who are able to control themselves at this stage and whose achievements in the world have made them famous, the world little recognizing that these prodigious achievements actually represent the prolific productions of mentally unsound individuals. Even in these cases, however, the laws and feelings of society may be outraged and such individuals frequently go to prison. They may become fearfully enraged if thwarted and appear to regard themselves as answerable to no one, not even to their own consciences.

This brings us back to the theoretical formula represented by this psychiatric picture: the conscience has been destroyed. Prior to an attack such individuals may be exceedingly sober, retiring, dignified, cautious, unassuming persons, who would be highly mortified by such behavior in themselves or anyone else. Suddenly the conscience is, so to speak, struck dead. We know from our previous discussions that the conscience is an internalized representation of authority formed in childhood, presumably from the parents. To kill the conscience is then equivalent to a destructive blow aimed at the internalized parents.

A case illustration will perhaps make this more definite.

John Smith was the eldest of five children in a middle-class Minnesota family. The father had been a small merchant, a good provider, but a very sober, moody man; he committed suicide when the patient was twelve. This necessitated the patient's taking over many responsibilities at that early age. By diligence, faithfulness, and the exertion of tremendous energy, he had—by the age of 30—worked himself up to the position of department manager in a sizable manufacturing company. Relatives and other members of the family looked upon him with great pride; he was pointed out by them as the "poor boy who made good" and who never forgot to help his dependent mother and sisters.

His employers likewise regarded him with favor, not only because of his energy and capabilities but because of his cooperative and deferential manner toward his superiors. In the course of his work numerous questions arose in which his judgment came into conflict with that of the general superintendent, a cautious, conservative man who in many respects resembled the patient's father. Frequently Mr. Smith's ideas prevailed over those of his superior officer and worked out to the great advantage of the company. Upon one occasion, however, he had promoted a project which had involved his company in serious financial loss He felt exceedingly regretful about this mistake, although he was not censored or penalized in any way by the company. His own sense of guilt about the matter was considerable, but it was also observed that he felt guilty and uneasy even when the projects which he put across in spite of the plant superintendent's disapproval turned out more fortunately.

One day he did not come to his office which was very unusual as he was a methodical, reliable worker. It was assumed that he was ill and no investigation was made for several days. When inquiry was made at his home, his wife was surprised. He had told her that the company wished him to go to New York on business and, as his word was absolutely dependable, she had not questioned this. The president of the company communicated with their New York representative, who reported that Mr. Smith had called him on the phone the day before from a hotel and seemed nervous and somewhat excited, mentioning numerous expansive plans for the business of which the representative knew nothing.

Smith was finally found in a large, expensive hotel suite where he had installed five stenographers and had a waiting room filled with representatives of wholesale houses and with prospective employees with whom he proposed to make contracts related to the new business which he planned to bring the company. In fact, he was so busy discussing these plans with his callers that the representatives of his organization could not get him aside for some private words. When they did get his attention, he told them in a loud and excited voice to come back when he had more time, and, quite contrary to his usual nature, he added many words of profanity to the effect that they had been unnecessarily tardy in arriving.

They finally managed to get him in hand and after listening patiently to his extremely complicated, somewhat incoherent but not entirely senseless plans for a great expansion of the business, they tried to persuade him to return home with them. This proposal he rejected violently, denouncing them in a loud voice for being stupid, meddling fools incapable of grasping his grand ideas for the development of *their* business. He became so furious that he attacked one of the men physically and would have done him bodily harm had he not been restrained. In a final flare of rage he threw bottles and pieces of furniture through the hotel window and then stamped out of the room in a fury of righteous indignation. On the way out he passed some of the hotel servants to whom he administered a lecture on the dangers of communism with a few cuffs and kicks. Before the astonished servants could recover their senses he had descended to the lobby, had helped himself to a handful of cigars from the counter and was challenging all comers to a wrestling match in the middle of the floor.

These challenges were couched in vulgar and profane language utterly foreign to him in his normal condition.

When he was finally apprehended he was at a public bar surrounded by strangers who were highly amused at his jokes and extravagant proposals. He had bought drinks for everyone in the place and had given several girls twenty-dollar bills, promising them more if they would come to his hotel. It should be borne in mind that under ordinary circumstances he was a man of very strict morals who never drank liquor or used profanity, and always spent money sparingly.

The company, anxious to prevent the indignity and publicity of arrest and detention in jail, sent for the patient's family, who came to New York and placed him in a sanitarium immediately. There his excitement subsided to a considerable degree. He looked upon being placed in a sanitarium as a great joke and insisted that his company was making a serious mistake in not carrying out his proposals for expansion, but said if they were too thick-headed to take advantage of his excellent ideas and join in his fun he was perfectly willing to "play along" with them on a "two by four" basis instead of on the larger plan he had outlined. He said he had just about worked himself into a "state of nervous collapse" over the "damned business" and that he would enjoy having a nice long rest in the sanitarium. He assumed a highly patronizing air toward the institution, praising the physicians, the nurses, and everyone connected with it, declaring that he had met more interesting people in a short time than he had met outside in years. His new plans for the business were entirely forgotten; he had, he said, done his best for them and now they would have to worry along without him until he had rested as long as he felt inclined to rest.

This is only a short sketch of a single case; such cases are always so colorful that each one abounds in details which makes it unique, but they all have the characteristics described above and illustrated here.[7] I have related this one more to show the typical psychological structure than to detail the variable symptoms.

In this case one is immediately struck by the fact that the patient's father committed suicide, throwing responsibilities upon the patient to which he reacted in an over-

[7] Not all patients with this affliction are so consistently amiable when hospitalized, and even this patient was at times irritable and demanding in a highly autocratic, aggressive way.

compensatory way. It was as if he had determined not only to emulate his father as a successful business man but to surpass him, and in this he succeeded. This success, however, was apparently not sufficient to gratify the insatiable craving for greater success and this uncontrolled expansiveness is apparent in his psychosis. One is reminded of the little frog, who, attempting to excel his father in the eyes of his observing mother, inflated himself larger and larger until he burst.

This victory over his father was one source of guilt; the envy of his immediate superior, the plant superintendent, added to it; the errors which he had made which entailed so much expense for his company increased the burden still more. Finally, a state of tension developed which was no longer bearable and self-destruction threatened. But instead of killing himself outright, as his father had, he demolished (for the time being) only his own super-ego. It is as if he could say, then, "It is *not true* that I feel guilty about the death of my father, it is not true that I feel guilty for trying to surpass him, it is not true that I feel guilty for my dependence upon and at the same time envy of and conflict with the superintendent, it is not true that I feel guilty about the losses which I have incurred for my company, nor do I need to feel guilty if I swear or drink or pursue prostitutes. I do not feel guilty about *anything!* On the other hand, I feel entirely untrammeled by inhibitions. I have none of the ordinary restrictions in thinking or acting which make others stupid or lazy. I am a free, powerful, happy man, who can do anything he likes, who has no troubles, no regrets, no fears." This is the typical psychology of this disease.[8]

We perceive immediately that a considerable portion of his super-ego escaped death, however, because, in spite of his freedom from the real anxieties and the sense of guilt from which he had formerly suffered, he still restrained impulses which in a totally uninhibited person would have been expressed. A man with no conscience at all, similarly stimulated, might truly run amok, killing, stealing, and otherwise misbehaving as the fancy struck him. This rarely happens. We must qualify our statement, therefore, that

[8] It may have occurred to the reader that in acute alcoholism also one sees a partial paralysis or temporary destruction of the conscience, but this, while a *conscious* purpose of some drinking, is a secondary and pharmacological effect, whereas the self-destruction of the conscience represented in the manic syndrome we have been discussing is spontaneous and primary and takes place without conscious participation of the personality.

the manic psychosis represents the destruction of the super-ego, and say, rather, that it represents a *partial* destruction or paralysis of the super-ego. That it is related to the other forms of self-destruction by analogy and expresses aggressiveness and self-punishment with a palpable degree of erotization needs, I think, no further demonstration.[9]

Since one of the therapeutic aims in psychoanalytic treatment consists in freeing the ego from the dominance of the tyrannical super-ego, and replacing conscience by intelligence, one might question whether the concept here proposed does not seem to equate the manic syndrome and the successfully psychoanalyzed patient. In both instances, the super-ego is, according to theory, eliminated. And if it leads us to an absurdity, something must be faulty with the theory.

One answer to this lies in the point already made, that in the manic syndrome only a part of the super-ego is destroyed, since such plain evidence exists that a part of it remains toward which the patient reacts with terror. There is, however, a further explanation. In psychoanalysis the super-ego is not suddenly destroyed; it is only rendered increasingly unnecessary and therefore useless because the ego freed from its constant oppression is permitted to grow and assume greater power, replacing prejudice with objec-

---

[9] The following case is dramatically illustrative of this same phenomenon:

A very conscientious, hardworking stenographer was the sole support of her frail, deaf old mother with whom she lived. When she was about 27 she had met a business man with whom she gradually developed a steadfast love affair, but her lover had insisted that he could not tolerate the idea of keeping her mother in the home with them and since the girl felt she could not leave her mother, the marriage was postponed from year to year with the expectation that the frail mother would shortly die and the girl's responsibility be lifted.

But the mother did not die and the girl's hopes grew fainter and her life drearier. Suddenly one day she developed a very curious mental condition. For a few days she seemed to be unconscious and when she awoke she seemed to have developed a radical change in personality. Instead of her usual patience with her mother she was bitterly and outspokenly resentful. "I have waited ten years for that old fool [her mother] to die so I could live a normal life." Instead of her usual modesty with respect to men, typical of a prudish spinster, she was shockingly frank in her words and gestures whenever a man (for example, the physician) approached. She announced frankly that she wanted to get married and did not care when or to whom; she called her mother names, swore at her doctor, jeered at her lover and, in short, acted as if she had suddenly discarded all of the restraints and ideals which had previously molded her character.

She suddenly recovered with a total amnesia for this moral vacation and was again a woman of such sweet, soft-spoken, patient kindness that it was incredible to those of us who had witnessed the episode that she could have been even temporarily so uninhibited, her conscience, for the time being, destroyed.

tive reality evaluation. In the manic syndrome, on the other hand, the super-ego or a part of it is suddenly eliminated and a feeble ego is expected to handle powerful impulses which come so rapidly and irresistibly that it is overwhelmed. A small child suddenly presented with a hammer or a pair of scissors could not be expected to use these with the propriety and safety characteristic of an adult carpenter or seamstress. The ego of the manic patient is always childlike; that of the successfully psychoanalyzed person is relatively mature.

SUMMARY

In this chapter I have tried to show that a repudiation of the ordinary standards of reality constitutes mental illness of the degree and form known as psychosis, and that this may sometimes be interpreted as a form of self-destruction. The self-destructiveness may be directed against the ego itself, as in those cases in which the psychotic person reproaches or depreciates himself, or even declares that he no longer exists. Again it may be focused rather upon the super-ego as in those whose sudden freedom from the restraints of conscience would indicate that they have temporarily destroyed that part of themselves which ordinarily exerts the necessary and unnecessary inhibitions. I have also referred to the fact that in schizophrenia, the classical syndrome of reality repudiation, the self-destructiveness is, as a rule, limited to occasional bodily self-mutilation, rather than to any more general self-destruction; the destructive impulses are converted into fantasy and remain directed toward objects of the outside world, sometimes embracing the entire universe, while the individual, instead of attacking and hating himself, seems to love himself, sometimes to love himself, literally, to death.

ONE / *Definitions*

In contrast to those forms of partial suicide discussed in the preceding section in which the self-destructive activity although attenuated in time is still generalized in its focus are those in which it is concentrated upon the body, and usually upon a limited part of the body. I have designated this localized self-destruction "focal suicide."

Certain clinical phenomena familiar to all physicians belong—I believe—in this category. I have in mind particularly self-mutilation, malingering, compulsive polysurgery, certain unconsciously purposive accidents resulting in local injury, and sexual impotence. I shall define and then discuss each of these, and I believe it will be possible to demonstrate that they are determined in general by the same motives and mechanisms outlined for suicide proper, except in the degree of participation of the death-instinct.

That certain organic diseases may also represent forms of focal suicide I shall leave for discussion in a subsequent chapter. For the present we shall consider only those self-destructions which are mechanically or manually produced in ways which are consciously recognized and directed by the patient.

By "self-mutilations" I refer to (1) those deliberate destructive attacks upon various parts of the body with which we are most familiar in the extreme, bizarre forms occasionally manifested by patients in mental hospitals. In the same category, also, we cannot omit (2) the various forms of self-inflicted bodily injury to which neurotics are addicted. Biting the fingernails, for example, is a degree short of biting the fingers, and some individuals have a compulsion to bite themselves more or less severely in various other parts of the body. Others scratch and dig at their flesh incessantly, pluck out their hair or rub their eyes or skin to the point of inflammation. Finally (3), we will consider the self-mutilations which are authorized, encouraged, or dictated by social custom and by religious ceremony.

"Malingering" is a word of obscure origin of which the earliest definition appears in Grove's *Directory of the Vulgar Tongue:* "A military term for one who under pretense of sickness evades his duty." As early as 1820 the observation was made that "formerly it was ulcers of the legs which were most easily produced by artificial means by soldiers disposed to malinger." [1] From this strict application to soldiers, however, the word has been extended to all forms of fraud relating to sickness and injury. The particular form of malingering to which I wish to direct attention is self-mutilation with the conscious intention of deceiving someone for a so-called ulterior purpose.

By "polysurgery" I refer to those persons who seem addicted, as it were, to surgical operations, who successively develop conditions, sometimes with a considerable show of objective justification, which make it necessary, or at least make it *seem* necessary, that an operation be performed and that something be cut from the body. It is often clear that such a patient submits himself to surgery repeatedly as a neurotic compulsion.

By *purposive accidents* I refer to those occurrences in everyday life by which the body suffers damage as a result of circumstances which appear to be entirely fortuitous but which, in certain instances, can be shown in their natures to fulfill so specifically the unconscious tendencies of the victim that we are led to believe that they either represent the capitalization of some opportunity by the unconscious self-destructive wishes or else were in some obscure way brought about for this very purpose.

"Sexual impotence" is a categorical designation for relative or complete inadequacy in the sexual act; in the female it is sometimes called "frigidity." I have included impotence and frigidity here as a form of focal self-destruction because, as a self-determined inhibition of the function of one part of the body, they are in effect a repudiation or functional destruction of that part.

[1] Luscombe, quoted by Jones and Llewellyn, *Malingering,* Blakiston's, 1917, p. 55.

TWO / *Self-Mutilations*

I must warn the reader that what follows in this chapter is not very pleasant subject matter. Our experience with pain makes the thought of self-mutilation even more repugnant than the thought of suicide, in spite of the great reality differences in favor of the former. We physicians, familiar from our daily experiences with these unlovely sights, often forget that for most persons the barriers imposed by these taboos are quite high, to be set aside only by the more intelligent, objective, and mature. It is certainly not reading for children (although one of the stories in the third grade reader, adopted by the textbook commission of the state in which I live, contained an illustrated story of mutilation [of an animal] as vivid as any of the clinical examples which I shall mention).

It is absolutely essential to the development of our theory, however, that we demonstrate that the suicidal impulse may be concentrated upon a part as a substitute for the whole. Self-mutilation is one of the ways in which this is done and we must examine it.

A high school principal of thirty developed a severe depression with the delusion that all life was full of sorrow for which he was chiefly responsible. He was confined in a hospital and showed some improvement, whereupon his mother came one day and removed him against advice, insisting that she understood her own son better than did the physicians and knew that he was well. She took the patient home where a few nights later he quietly arose while the rest of the household slept, and murdered his own two-year-old child by beating it in the head with a hammer, saying that he wanted to spare the baby the suffering that he himself had endured. This led to his commitment to the state hospital. While in the hospital he repeatedly made attempts to injure himself and one day succeeded in thrusting his arm into some machinery in such a way as to bring about the amputation of his right hand. After this he made a rapid and complete recovery.

Although this case was not studied psychoanalytically it is possible to make certain general reconstructions on the basis of clinical experience regarding the unconscious mechanisms back of such behavior. This is always more nearly possible in psychotic persons than in neurotics for the reason that in the psychoses the unconscious tendencies are acted out or spoken out with less disguise, i.e., with less distortion.

It is strongly presumptive here that this patient was driven to make a spectacular atonement for an equally spectacular crime. By injuring himself in this terrible way, he paid the penalty for having murdered his child, that is, he cut off the offending arm, faithful to the Biblical command, "If thy right hand offend thee, cut it off." But the child whom he murdered was apparently his chief love-object, and, in spite of the poet's comment that "each man kills the thing he loves," we know that he does so only if that love has become too strongly tinctured with (unconscious) hate. Destruction is not the fruit of love but of hate.

Then what is the explanation for hate so great as to drive this father to murder? Sometime after his recovery I talked with him. He seemed singularly unconcerned and unabashed about his fore-arm stump. But when I asked him about the death of his child, he showed more emotion; with tears gathering in his eyes he said, "You know, I shall always feel that my mother was partly responsible for that, some way. She and I never got along together."

This, I think, was undoubtedly the correct clue. The patient's mother was a very aggressive, and unsympathetic woman who had been apprised of the patient's condition and yet disregarded experienced advice. It is easy to understand how a person with such a mother would feel hatred toward her. But we know from everyday experience that when such hatred cannot be carried out toward the person who has given rise to it, it is often transferred to someone else. We know, too, from psychiatric and psychoanalytic experience that in melancholia, the disease from which this patient was suffering, the victims stew in the caldron of their own hate, turned back upon themselves from some unrecognized external object.

Whether this external object was more immediately the mother or the baby daughter is really of secondary importance here. What we clearly see is that this fellow hated someone so much that he committed murder, for which he then offered propitiation by mutilating himself. In his unconscious thinking and feeling, this man's mother, daughter, and self were all partially identified. If he killed his child to punish his own mother, he also cut off his own arm to punish himself.

The psychological mechanisms of this instance of self-mutilation, therefore, are like those of suicide to this extent, that hate directed against an external object was turned back upon the self and reinforced with self-punishment. It differs from suicide in that this punitive self-attack, instead of being concentrated upon the total personality, as is the case in suicide, was divided into two parts, one part upon the baby and one part upon the arm, each of which was played off against the other.[1] Lacking, also, is any convincing evidence for a wish to die, which we found reason for believing to be dominant in the case of suicide.

"But," the reader may object, "this is a very interesting speculation, logical enough but quite unsusceptible of proof. How can one be sure that these interpretations are correct? Other explanations might be constructed that would seem equally convincing, at least in a particular case which one might select."

Such a demurral is entirely justified. I cannot support the application of these explanations to this case except by analogy and inference because it was not accessible to study. It is appropriate, therefore, to proceed immediately to a consideration of self-mutilations in more accessible material.

A. NEUROTIC SELF-MUTILATIONS

It is convenient to begin with self-mutilation as it appears in the course of or as a part of a neurosis, first, because such cases are frequently seen by psychiatrists, and have been reported upon by various authors,[2] and secondly,

---

[1] Compare the following item:

"In Gavardo, Italy, having signed promissory notes for several friends, Giuseppe Mazzolini, 36, was obliged to pay them when his friends defaulted. When the last defaulted, he laid on a table the hand with which he had signed the notes, pulled out a pruning knife, hacked the hand off."—*Time*, Oct. 3, 1932.

Here again apparently we have hate of another reflected upon a part of the self.

[2] The following are only a few of the psychoanalytic reports on the subject: Stärcke, A., "The Castration Complex," *International Journal of Psychoanalysis*, June, 1921, p. 179; Horney, K., "On the Genesis of the Castration Complex in Women," *Ibid.*, Jan., 1924, pp. 50-65; Farrow, E. P., "A Castration Complex," *Ibid.*, Jan., 1925, pp. 45-50; Oberndorf,

because the behavior of neurotics is always much more closely akin to that of so-called normal people and therefore more easily understandable by them. Psychoanalytic treatment of neurotic patients affords us the advantage of using the combined aid of the subject's intelligence and the observer's experience to pierce the disguises which cloak the motives and the methods.

I say "methods" because it is actually true that neurotics often disguise the method by which they accomplish the self-mutilation; in this particular they are like malingerers rather than like the psychotic patients who make no effort at such concealment. This arises from the fact that the neurotic is far more loyal to reality than the psychotic patient. The neurotic patient rarely mutilates himself irrevocably. Substituted and symbolic forms of self-mutilation are, however, very common and neurotics frequently demand and obtain mutilation at the hands of a second party, for example in the form of surgical operations which we shall discuss later.

The explanation for this, according to our psychoanalytic conception, lies in the very nature and purpose of the neurosis, namely, that it is a compromise device intended to save the personality from such direct and serious consequences of the demands of the instincts and of the conscience. The ego, i.e., the discriminating intelligence, has the task of adjusting these demands and if it finds itself failing it makes the best bargain possible. It concedes as little as possible to the insistence of the conscience upon self-punishment. The result may be silly and it may be serious but it represents the best that the ego of the neurotic can do. The psychotic patient, on the other hand, ceases to attempt any such bargaining, and hence one sees the extreme and bizarre self-mutilations common to them.

The element of bargaining—making the best possible compromises—is the essence of the whole matter. The normal person is normal because he can make so much better a bargain than the neurotic; he can do so because he is not so much at the mercy of his stern or cruel conscience and this in turn is partly due to the fact that he is not so

C. P., "The Castration Complex in the Nursery," *Ibid.*, July, 1925, pp. 324-25; Bryan, D., "Speech and Castration: Two Unusual Analytic Hours," *Ibid.*, July, 1925, pp. 317-23; Lewis, N. D. C., "Additional Observations on Castration Reaction in Males," *Psychoanalytic Review*, April, 1931, pp. 146-65; Alexander, Franz, "The Castration Complex in the Formation of Character," *International Journal of Psychoanalysis*, Jan.-April, 1923, pp. 11-42.

strongly moved by destructive urges. Compared to him the neurotic makes a bad bargain but compared to the total surrender of the psychotic person the neurotic's bargain is not so bad.

In the case cited above, for example, the man whose right arm had killed his child would have been obliged, had he been wholly dominated by the demands of his conscience, to have killed himself in atonement. Indeed, this very thing happens daily, as we know from observation and also from the study of suicide presented in the first chapter. In the vernacular, this patient was "not so crazy" as to do that. There is no use in punishing one's self if one ceases to live, since the ostensible object of self-punishment is to enable one to live thereafter in peace. When the priest assigns to the Catholic penitent a certain task he defeats his own aim if he makes that task impossible of performance. His object is to make life tolerable and endurable without the dragging sense of guilt which the unatoned-for offense arouses.

What this person did, therefore, was to substitute a self-mutilation for suicide; instead of offering up his life he offered up his arm, which was quite logical since it was the guilty organ. It was logical if one assumes the personification or autonomy of various organs of the body, and this, as we shall see, is one of the devices of the unconscious for unloading guilt. "It is not I but the arm that was guilty, therefore I shall sacrifice the arm, my guilt is expiated and I have saved my life." (It will be recalled that he got well promptly after this event.)

But it must be obvious that the more normal person would have made an even better bargain with his conscience than this. He would have said, "I regret what I have done more than I can say but to injure myself would not make matters any better. I cannot bring my baby back to life but I can raise another child or I can provide out of my earnings enough to make some other child happier, or I can do something to promote the prevention of such ignorance concerning mental disease as my mother exemplified and I will do so and so or give such and such." This would have been the more intelligent solution but it would only have been possible to one far more normal, that is, less burdened by hate and less tyrannized over by conscience than the strict and serious-minded high school principal.

The compromises made by neurotics are usually not so

extreme as the one just cited, nor are they, on the other hand, so intelligent as the normal examples I have suggested. Sometimes—and this is what we are now interested in—they are self-mutilations. As I have already indicated, these mutilations are apt to be disguised or indirectly achieved, they are also subject to the confusing element of the patient's false explanations of them.

We can observe this in such a familiar clinical example as "nail-biting." Such a mild degree of self-injury may seem scarcely to merit such a formidable designation, but after all, it is the nature of the act rather than its degree of seriousness which determines its classification. For that matter all of us have seen quite severe and even serious mutilation from nail-biting. I have had patients who gnawed off every vestige of nail from every finger; some actually gnaw the fingers themselves.

A little girl of my acquaintance had developed the habit of biting her fingernails severely. From this she went to her toenails, which she bit so savagely that she twice tore a nail completely from the toe. An infection resulted and she was taken to a surgeon for treatment which was necessarily painful. The child, however, bore the treatment stoically without tears or struggle. She appeared entirely absorbed in watching the physician's head, which was quite bald, and when he had finished the treatment her only comment was: *"I don't like your haircut."*

One outstanding fact about the case is the extent to which this child carried the common habit of nail-biting. There is no doubt that in this case the biting resulted in a severe mutilation. A second interesting feature is the child's apparent indifference to pain, both in regard to the original mutilation and its treatment. This is surprising because it seems to correspond to the indifference to pain of adult hysterical people such as we have described in previous sections who were moved so strongly by psychological motives as to be unmoved by physical sensation accompanying their self-punitive acts.

Finally, the child's apparently unrelated remark to the surgeon leads to some interesting conjectures as to the connection which the child may have made between her own denuded toe and the surgeon's hairless head from which, be it noted, the child thought the hair had been *cut.* The child, who did not flinch from bearing the full consequences of her own act, looked with fastidious distaste upon the havoc which the surgeon, as she evidently thought, had wreaked upon his own head.

One need only recall the distress, the anxiety, the impotent rage, which the habit of nail-biting on the part of their children creates in mothers, to realize how great the satisfaction of the child must be, and how correct the unconscious intuition of mothers. Nothing but a satisfaction of a sort about which the mother herself feels guilty could possibly excite the uneasy and irritable intolerance with which they view this and similar habits.

The fact that the child *bites* its own fingers and fingernails suggests that it represents a punishment no less than an indulgence. The mother cannot see or welcome this evidence of contrition, however, because she senses that such self-punishment must be in much the same spirit as that of the little girl who slapped her own hand before she stole candy from the buffet. (Brill.) The punishment actually permits the continuance of guilty indulgences and in this way becomes in itself a kind of indulgence.

Clinical investigation has shown quite definitely that there is a close association between nail-biting and a less conspicuous but similar "bad habit" of childhood—masturbation. Mechanically the parallelism is obvious; the fingers instead of being applied to the genitals are now applied to the mouth, and instead of the genital stimulation there is the labial stimulation accompanied, as we have already pointed out, by the punitive (mutilative) element of biting.

How do we know this? In the first place, we know it from the observations of many clear-headed, intelligent mothers who have observed their own children without panic. In the second place, we know it from the scientific observations of children made by the child-analysts and by those engaged in child guidance work.[3] Finally, we know

[3] Wechsler (Wechsler, David, "The Incidence and Significance of Finger-Nail Biting in Children," *Psychoanalytic Review*, April, 1931, pp. 201-09), from observations on some 3,000 children between the ages of one and 17 years, deduced that there is a close relation between the incidence of fingernail biting and the various stages of psychosexual development and that it varies in intensity according to these phases, reaching its peak at the onset of puberty, when the Oedipus situation is revived and the guilt feelings reactivated. Two years later there is a sudden and significant drop, corresponding to the adolescent's final disposition of the Oedipus situation. He found that more than forty percent of girls between the ages of 12 and 14 and of boys between the ages of 14 and 16 were nail-biters. In boys and girls two years older the proportion of nail-biters dropped abruptly to less than twenty percent. The rise occurs at different ages for boys and girls, the difference corresponding to the age difference in the onset of puberty for boys and girls.

it from the study of adult neurotics who in the course of analyzing their own childhood are able to recall clearly the details of and the connections between their nail-biting and their masturbation.

One patient of my own, for example, during the course of her analysis suddenly felt impelled to pursue a course of piano study which required arduous finger exercises. She practiced assiduously for many hours a day, giving her fingers the most severe discipline even to the point of pain. At the same time she became greatly worried because her little daughter persisted in the habit of nail-biting. She became increasingly excited over this and spoke much of the danger of letting a child develop bad habits. Also, she feared—she felt sure—that this child was masturbating!

I asked her why she jumped to this conclusion. She replied by confessing, or recalling, that she, herself, as a child had had an intractable nail-biting habit which her mother had vigorously combated, not knowing of her masturbation. Then she added reluctantly, and only after evident resistance, that only recently she had yielded to a strong impulse to masturbate. This I pointed out must have been closely associated in point of time with the vigorous finger punishment she had been indulging in; she was startled to realize this, and intelligent enough to see immediately that the association was more than chronological.[4]

Common as nail-biting is, we do not yet know all the unconscious meaning of it by any means. David Levy[5] has recently shown, for example, by experimental work with dogs and babies that those who get an insufficient amount of suckling are prone to substitute, later, oral gratification of the type of thumb-sucking, and possibly also nail-biting. It is as if the child who does not get enough gratification at the mother's breast seeks to find it from any source, without discrimination. This does not contradict the connection

[4] I owe the suggestion to Dr. Robert Knight that nail-biting may sometimes have a quite different origin and significance. We know that among all primitive carnivores the association of claw and fang is very close, and that what would correspond to the nails are used, in conjunction with the teeth, in the tearing and rending of food or the enemy. That the child has fantasies of destroying his enemies by the similar use of his nails (claws) and teeth is indicated by the observations of Melanie Klein (op. cit.) and other child observers. In this sense, then, the biting of the nail would be the destruction or punishment of one weapon by another.

[5] Levy, David, "Finger-sucking and Accessory Movements in Early Infancy," American Journal of Psychiatry, 1928, Vol. VII, pp. 881-918 and "Experiments on the Sucking Reflex and Social Behavior of Dogs," American Journal of Orthopsychiatry, April, 1934, pp. 203-24.

with masturbation, because masturbation is a later and entirely natural stage in the child's pleasure development. In other words, the normal child gives up sucking as a chief form of pleasure and learns to masturbate; the neurotic child because of his fear of punishment stops masturbating and substitutes nail-biting or some other similar substitute, which is regressive in the sense that it harks back to the earlier days and ways of pleasure, using the mouth instead of the genitals. It is then a substitute kind of gratification and a concomitant punishment simultaneously, both of them enacted in attenuated forms.

More vigorous attacks upon the body than that of nail-biting are frequently to be observed in neurotics, particularly attacks upon the skin which the dermatologist calls neurotic excoriations. These are cases in which the individual seems impelled to pick or dig at his skin with the finger nail sometimes ascribed to an uncontrollable desire to relieve itching or to rid the skin of what he believes to be a parasite, but more frequently for no reason which the patient can explain. In one case Dr. Joseph V. Klauder of Philadelphia was able to ascertain that the intolerable itching, which the patient relieved by digging out these chunks of flesh, occurred chiefly on the two days of the week upon which her husband had lain in a dying condition.

The most remarkable case of neurotic self-mutilation I have seen was that of a steamfitter's assistant of thirty-five. He had as early as twelve or fourteen exhibited some twitchings and jerkings of his arms which were at that time regarded, at first, as chorea. When, however, they grew gradually but steadily worse, this diagnosis was doubted by subsequent consultants and by most of them contradicted. (It was probably *Gilles de la Tourette's Disease.*)

When seen twenty years after the onset of the affliction he presented a most extraordinary clinical picture. He had developed an amazing variety of sudden jerks, twists, lunges, grimaces, kicks, waggles, and even barks and whoops, which came suddenly in the midst of a period of calm during which he gave an intelligent account of his affliction. For a few moments he would be at rest and continue his conversation only to be insufferably interrupted by involuntarily spasmodic misbehavior of the sorts indicated. His arm would fly up, his leg would kick out, his head would twist halfway around, his diaphragm would apparently contract sharply, so that in the midst of the conversation, which, however, he bravely attempted to carry forward, he would be thrown out of his chair, or he would be obliged to gasp, grimace, or shout in a totally irregular and unpredictable way. He would also ejaculate irrelevant, vulgar and profane words apparently unintentionally.

Such, at least, was our first impression. It gradually became apparent, however, that his involuntary movements, in spite of their wide variation, had one very definite point of agreement. As he himself had long recognized, they all seemed directed against himself, i.e., either against his body or against the carrying out of his conscious wishes. Thus his arm jerks, carefully observed, proved nearly always to be body blows; in kicking it was his own leg and foot that suffered; frequently he kicked the other leg. Often he would slap or jab his face with his thumb; there was a large open lesion on his forehead of which he remarked, "It seems like if I get a sore started, I pester it nearly to death," and as he said this he punched it a half dozen more times in rapid succession. Three of his front teeth were missing as the result of backhand blows given himself in the mouth while working with heavy wrenches. (In spite of his affliction he held a position in a steamfitter's shop in Chicago.) His hands were covered with the scars of minor injuries. "Whenever I get a knife in my hand," he said, "and naturally I have to do that a lot, I always cut myself; it never fails."

This patient certainly fulfills all of the requirements of the characteristic motives of the suicidal act. His attacks were fierce, his submission heroic. And as to the contribution of the sense of guilt, it is rather significant that in the course of the one brief conversation with him he remarked spontaneously that he and his mother had never gotten along very well because she was always reproaching him, particularly for his propensity for going out with girls, of which he rather modestly boasted. In spite of his affliction, he said, he had many friends and was active both socially and sexually. "But she says I'm getting my deserts . . . that I would never have gotten this way if I hadn't run around with girls so much!"

We can only surmise what the connection was between his compulsive acts and the sense of guilt he betrayed by his boasting and his citation of his mother's threats. We know that the affliction began in childhood, when the sexual activity is not "running around with girls" but masturbation. It is this for which some mothers scold, punish, and threaten their children, and that this was such a mother we have the patient's testimony. The assumption might well be made that his physical self-abuse began as a punishment for his genital "self-abuse." I have since heard that this man, who is a member of a respectable family, has for some time been living with a prostitute and also that in the course of a number of involuntary attacks upon himself he has nearly blinded himself. We see how inexorable the demands of the conscience may be.

Less spectacular cases I have seen frequently. I recall a successful young woman who had suddenly developed a compulsion to pull out handfuls of hair[6] immediately following the marriage of her younger sister of whom she had always been jealous. The expression "snatching one baldheaded" was literally descriptive of what she did—not to her sister, but to herself. In a personal communication, Dr. Henry W. Woltman, of the Mayo Clinic, mentioned seeing a case of *trichotillomania* in which the act was directly and consciously associated with masturbation, which it accompanied, as if to atone for the "sin." (Compare this with the interpretation of nail-biting given above.)

It will convey a better idea of the irresistible nature of the compulsion to perform this type of self-mutilation if I quote verbatim from a letter which, unfortunately, I have been obliged to condense somewhat.

"All my life I have been steeped in timidity, self-depreciation and a consciousness of physical unattractiveness. I have never had many friends nor any male attention; but here is my real problem, my greatest worry, the most important reason for my life being a nightmare. At eight I developed the habit of pulling the hair from my head, caus-

---

[6] This affliction (*Trichotillomania*) is sometimes epidemic in the same way the other hysterical affections are. (See David, H., "Pseudo-Alopecia Areata," *Brit. J. Dermat.*, May, 1922, p. 162.)

Dr. Holden-Davis (*British Journal of Dermatology*, 1914, Vol. XXVI, pp. 207-10) said that in 1914 he had reported an epidemic of hair-pulling in an orphanage in which two or three genuine cases of *alopecia areata* had occurred. The children who had *alopecia* became the central figures in the orphanage and the others in order to obtain attention took to hair-pulling.

Burrows (*Proceedings of the Royal Society of Medicine*, May, 1933, pp. 836-38) has reported a case of infantile *trichotillomania* in which a three-year-old child wet its fingers, plucked out a hair, examined the plucked hair and threw it away. He had continued this conduct over a period of fifteen months. Dr. Burrows wrote the superintendent of the Zoological Society Gardens inquiring if the habit was present to any extent among the higher apes or monkeys and received the reply that nothing of the same nature had been observed among the primates.

ing great bare spots. Then shame and remorse would seize me until a new growth came to cover them; but in a few months the habit would steal upon me and in a night, or an hour, I would be a despairing, bald-topped little girl, going my isolated way to an unfriendly, snickering school. My family were also despairing, never having heard of anything of this sort and not knowing what possessed me. But they were never unkind but only went about silently—occasionally pleadingly—trying to do what they could to help me. I suffer a great deal from thoughts of how my mother and father and brothers and sisters must have been humiliated by their odd sister.

"Mine was the only true golden, the only really curly hair, that any of us sisters had. But now the mistreated scalp produces only black, stiff bristles over the top. For I still have this dreadful habit! For three years I almost dared to believe it was conquered. Then all in a night my hopes flew and I had an ugly bald spot, as large as my hand, that only deft concealment hides. I manage to comb what is left of my hair over the scalp but there is no telling how long I can conceal it. No will of mine seems able to control my fingers once they start plucking; and I enjoy eating it— chewing up the stiff hair and root!

"I was quite brilliant in my early years in school and showed fine intellectual promise but now I don't concentrate well nor remember. I only wish I could be fervently interested in religion or anything else. Has this habit impaired my mentality irreparably? affected the delicate brain? I fear I will soon be so enslaved as to find satisfaction in nothing but this habit—for think!— For almost twenty years now I have been pulling out my hair at intervals, oblivious at those times of everything else in the world.

"Do you believe I have insanity in store? I have been told to 'forget it,' to 'keep busy'; one physician said, 'have a baby.' If I could only hope to! But it wouldn't be fair to any young man to take a chance on me, and it wouldn't be fair to any child, either."

Notice that this girl herself mentions the fact that she had prettier hair than her sisters, that the treatment she has given her head has spoiled this beauty, and that she is remorseful about the effect of her illness on her sisters. To a psychiatrist these things point to a sense of guilt with reference to these sisters and an unconscious wish to punish herself and make herself less beautiful than they. This in turn must have arisen from some unknown resentments against them.

A case of self-mutilation, which I had the opportunity to study over a period of many months and in great detail, also was concerned with hair. This well-educated business man of twenty-seven used to seize a shears and chop away at his own hair until he produced a repulsively grotesque effect, with splotches here and there where he had come close to the scalp. The reason that he at first assigned for this was that being very poor he had to economize and could not waste money going to a barber but had to cut his own hair. Since in reality he was well-to-do, he acknowledged the necessity of a better explanation than this, admitted his stinginess, but could give, at first, no better reason for his rash self-barbering. He was positive that his hair was falling out and he shared the popular view that if one kept cutting hair its growth would be stimulated. This was a comforting rationalization in line with the previously observed phenomenon of forestalling punishment by punishing oneself, i.e., in order that his hair not be taken away from him by external agencies he cut it off himself.

Further analysis revealed the real reasons for his hair-cutting compulsion. As a boy he had had luxuriant black hair. But he had a blond brother whom everyone preferred and of whom, therefore, he was exceedingly envious and jealous. Because of his hatred of this younger brother he would tease him and at times violently mistreat him, and as a result would be beaten by his father. In these beatings the father would seize the boy by his luxuriant hair and so hold him while he administered the blows.

His entire adult life had been a series of disasters, the rough formula of which was this: He would enter a new project with high hopes and great promise. He made a good impression and because of his intelligence and likability he would advance rapidly. But once established in someone's favor he would pick a quarrel, or make himself the object of justified retaliation so that in the end he would be thrown out, abused, sometimes attacked, and always disliked. This had happened many, many times. In other words, he kept repeating over and over the formula of attacking his brother, defying his father, and incurring for himself punishment. He either punished himself directly, or saw to it that he got himself punished for the aggressions he carried out on various people in lieu of his father and brother.

215

Cutting off his hair represented not only a re-enactment of his wish to escape from his father but also, in a more realistic sense, a punishment of himself. It was the one physical asset of which he had had reason to be proud but it had not prevented him from being jealous. His savage self-administered hair slashing had another meaning. His family was Jewish, but his brother was not interested in religion and was of such a disposition that he was freely accepted socially by Gentiles. For this reason the jealous brother, my patient, did everything possible to accentuate and exploit his Jewishness. Although not so reared, he espoused the orthodox form of the faith which, as is well known, entails leaving the hair unbarbered. He was for a time very meticulous in all the prescribed observances but his interest, as we see, was not dictated by piety so much as by less worthy motives, chiefly that of rebuking and shaming and being different from his brother. When he saw that it had no effect on his brother or upon his father he renounced it: he had been disappointed again. He could indicate such resentful renunciation very understandably by mutilating and discarding his hair.

A classical case of neurotic self-mutilation involving the nose and teeth is the celebrated Wolf-Man case which was partially analyzed by Freud and reported in his series of case histories in 1918 [7] and later during a recrudescence of the neurosis further analyzed by Dr. Ruth Mack Brunswick.[8] This second neurotic illness had as its presenting symptom a fixed hypochondriacal obsession in regard to a supposed injury to his nose which he thought had been caused by treatment he had obtained from a physician.

The symptom had begun as follows: His mother had come to visit him and he noticed a nasal wart which he urged her to have removed surgically. She refused. He then began to worry about his own nose, recalled the dissatisfactions he had had about it as a child when he was teased and called "pugnose," and comforted himself with the thought that his nose had no blemish. How terrible it would be, he thought, were he to have a wart on his nose; he then began to examine it and discovered some obstructed sebaceous glands. His mother departed from his home about this time. Two weeks later he discovered a

[7] An Infantile Neurosis, Freud, Collected Works, op. cit., Vol. III, pp. 473-605.
[8] Brunswick, Ruth Mack, "The Infantile Neurosis, Further Analysis," International Journal of Psychoanalysis, Oct., 1928.

small pimple in the middle of his nose and recalled that in addition to his mother he had also had an aunt with such a pimple and later insisted on his wife being treated for a pimple. He extracted the pimple with his finger nails, then repaired to a dermatologist, whom he had formerly consulted, and persuaded him to open some obstructed sebaceous glands in his nose, thus making several holes in it instead of one.

Within the month he also developed trouble with his teeth and had several extracted; he now returned to his dentist and managed to have another tooth pulled, not the one which had pained him but a sound one.

This episode turned him against dentists entirely and his attention was redirected to his nose. He gazed at it all day long and went from doctor to doctor for their opinions. One dermatologist told him he suffered from vascular distention which could be treated by electrolysis. The patient then consulted more dermatologists, one of whom recommended diathermy. Immediately he returned to the one who had recommended electrolysis and then began to worry lest this cause scars. He went to another dermatologist who told him the scars would never disappear. This threw him into a state of bottomless despair.

This is enough of the very long story to show how he first mistreated his own face (nose) and then went to physicians to get them to mistreat it, and then put the blame for the mutilation entirely on them; he did the same with his teeth.

If we summarize this we see that he first made a hole in himself and then got dermatologists and dentists to make more holes in him; we remember that his mother, his aunt, and his wife all had pimples which worried him. All three of these people were women and his conception of himself as having a lesion like them which must be removed is his symbolic way of saying, "I feel that I must be like they are, i.e., I want to be female instead of male." Deeper analysis of the case made it clear that this arose from a sense of guilt toward his father, who had left him a great deal of money, and toward Professor Freud from whom he, the patient, had taken money under false pretenses. For this taking of something from the father to which one is not entitled, the conscience demands the talion punishment of being similarly deprived of something oneself. Here we see that this "something" refers basically to the organs of sexuality.

The meaning of neurotic self-mutilation, its aggressive, erotic and self-punitive functions, and its relation to other forms of self-destruction are all neatly set forth in these few lines of poetry:

Once a man she knew had cut his thumb
Off at the base, lest the millennium
Arrive, and he be found unpunished for
One adulterous night. Remembering him
She smiled, and wondered if he entered heaven
Perhaps through such a self-inflicted whim;
Surely to her eternal life was given
For she had cut her whole life at the core.[9]

B. RELIGIOUS SELF-MUTILATION

Self-mutilation appears to have been practiced as a form of religious observance since the earliest times. If we include also mutilations which, while not actually self-inflicted, are submitted to willingly and even eagerly by religious aspirants, one is safe in saying that all religions contain this element. Precisely what its significance is we shall attempt to determine.

These mutilations represent sacrifice and usually, as we have seen in the preceding section, the sacrifice demanded of the holy man was that of his sexual life. It is sometimes alleged that this condemnation of the erotic life as incompatible with religious worship is a Christian innovation,[10] but this is erroneous. Christianity made use of conceptions and attitudes implicit in religious faiths which were already many hundreds of years old at the time of Christ. Even in the mythology with which the Mediterranean religions were so closely associated there existed to some extent the conception that the religious leader must be asexual. The Phoenicians believed, for example, that Eshmun, the beautiful God of Spring, castrated himself in order to escape the erotic advances of the goddess Astronae and that his priests were obliged to do likewise. Similarly the Galli, self-castrated priests of Attis, according to Frazer[11] were com-

[9] Magaret, Helene, *The Trumpeting Crane*, Farrar and Rinehart, 1934, pp. 121-22.
[10] Origen (185-254 A.D.) castrated himself that he might be unhindered in his zealous devotion to Christianity, especially in the instruction of women. He was one of the foremost leaders and teachers in the early Church but his self-mutilation was given by the synod of bishops as one reason for depriving him of the honor of being a presbyter.
[11] Frazer, Sir James George, *The Golden Bough*, Macmillan, 1923.

mon sights on the streets of Rome before the days of the Republic.

The worship of Cybele and Attis[12] was introduced into Rome where its orgiastic rites and bloody ritual became popular. From a description of these rites[13] one gets a very clear impression that the self-mutilation served the purpose of offering the supreme sacrifice of the sexual life in favor of the devotion to the highest (known) good. In essence these ceremonies, actually or symbolically, consisted in the

[12] There are numerous legends about the cult of Cybele and Attis which originated in Phrygia after the sixth century B.C. I am indebted for this investigation of the folklore and literature of the cult to Mrs. Bernice Engle of Omaha, Nebraska, who gave me permission to abstract the material from her paper, "Attis: A Study of Castration," *Psychoanalytic Review*, October, 1936, pp. 363-72. The gist of several of them is that the Mother-Goddess Cybele (or in some legends, Agdistis) was originally hermaphroditic and that the gods performed a surgical operation, cutting off the creature's external, i.e., male, genitals, and leaving the female genitals. She is represented as being related to Attis, either directly or indirectly representing his mother. Attis grows to manhood and is beloved by Cybele, but is persuaded by his friends to marry a king's daughter. At the wedding the mother-lover appears and drives Attis mad with frenzy. He castrates himself and his bride kills herself. Cybele mourns the deed and obtains from Jupiter the promise that Attis's body shall not decompose but that his hair shall continue to grow and his little finger to move.

Ovid, in his *Fasti*, gives a slightly different version of the legend. He relates how Attis, a Phrygian youth of great beauty, attached himself to the goddess Cybele. She made him keeper of her temples, pledging him to a vow of chastity. He sinned with the tree nymph Sagaritis whom Cybele destroyed. Attis then fell prey to fears, thinking himself attacked by torches, scourges, and furies. He lacerated his body with a sharp stone and cut off his genitals, crying out, "Such are my deserts: With my blood I pay the deserved penalty; perish those which in me have been the sinning parts!"

Priests of Attis regularly castrated themselves on entering the service of the goddess Cybele. Catullus wrote his poem *Attis* not about the god of the legend but about a chief priest of the cult. Like the original Attis whose name he bears, he castrates himself in a mad frenzy from (in the words of the poet) "utter abhorrence of love."

Other examples of self-castration in ancient religions are found in the legends of Zeus and Hecate in Caria, Artemis in Ephesus, Atargatis and Adonis and Astarte (Hierapolis), Adonis and Aphrodite in Cyprus, Osiris in Egypt and Angustudunum in Gaul.

[13] ". . . The third day was known as the day of blood; the Archigallus, or high priest, drew blood from his arms and presented it as an offering. Nor was he alone in making this bloody sacrifice. Stirred by the wild barbaric music of clashing cymbals, rumbling drums, horns and flutes, the inferior clergy whirled about in the dance with waggling heads and streaming hair, until, rapt into a frenzy of excitement and insensible to pain, they gashed their bodies with potsherds or slashed them with knives in order to bespatter the altar and the sacred tree with their flowing blood. The ghastly rite probably formed part of the mourning for Attis and may have been intended to strengthen him for the resurrection. The Australian aborigines cut themselves in like manner over the graves of their friends for the purpose of enabling them to be born again. Further, we may conjecture, though we are not expressly told, that it was on the same Day of Blood and for the same purpose that the novices sacrificed their virility." (Frazer, *op. cit.*)

sacrificing of virility, under the influence of religious fervor, in a bloody and painful manner.

Such orgies of public self-torture have been adopted as a part of the religious worship of various sects since those early days and even up to the present time. In I Kings xviii, 28, there is a description of how the priests of Baal engaged in a rainmaking ceremony, gashing themselves with knives and lances until the blood gushed out upon them. The Syriac word *ethkashshaph,* which means literally to "cut oneself," is the regular equivalent of "to make supplication." In some cases human sacrifices have been succeeded by religious practices involving the shedding of human blood without loss of life.[14] For example, in Laconia the scourging of lads at the altar of Artemis Orthia was substituted for the sacrifice of men which had previously been offered her. Euripides represents Athena as ordaining that the festival of Artemis be celebrated by the priest holding a knife to a human throat until blood flows.

The ceremony called "Tootoo-nima," said to be common among the Tonga islanders, is also cited by Westermarck (*op. cit.*). It consists of cutting off a portion of the little finger as a sacrifice to the gods for the recovery of a sick relative and was asserted to have been such a prevalent practice in former days that "there was scarcely a person living in the islands who had not lost one or both little fingers or at least a considerable portion of them."

In Chinese literature there is frequent mention of persons cutting off flesh from their bodies to cure parents or paternal grandparents who were seriously ill. "Often also we read of thigh cutters (in China) invoking heaven beforehand, solemnly asking this highest power to accept their own bodies as a substitute for the patients' lives they wanted to save" (De Groot). Bleeding as a means of propitiating the gods was used in Bengal and among the Peruvian Indians.

In America we have the Flagellantes or Penitentes, previously mentioned (page 102). Their beatings are sometimes equivalent to self-mutilations. The late Dr. T. P. Martin of Taos, New Mexico, informed the writer that he had frequently been called to save the life of an over-vigorous self-beater who had severed a blood vessel or otherwise injured himself quite seriously during these ceremonies.[15]

---

[14] Westermarck, *op. cit.,* Vol. I, p. 649.

[15] Dr. Helen McLean of Chicago in a personal communication to the writer laid emphasis upon the joy in suffering which these devotees exhibited during their self-lashing as observed by her in New Mexico. The

A religious body which is also nearly contemporary with us and in which essentially the same rites are carried out as in the ancient Phrygian and Syrian worship described above, including actual self-castration is the Skoptsi sect of Russia.

The Skoptsi constitute a Russian religious sect of considerable size, founded about 1757. While its actual extent is not definitely known because of the secret character of the sect, it has been estimated to have included over 100,-000 members. For our purpose it is necessary only to establish the fact that its ceremonies were not limited to a few psychotic or eccentric individuals but fulfilled the psychological needs of a considerable community of people to the extent of self-castration.

The Skoptsi believe that Adam and Eve, our first parents, sinned by entering into sexual relationship, and that the only way to atone for this evil and avoid further sin is to destroy the potency of human beings. They quote the passage, "If thy right eye offend thee, pluck it out, and cast it from thee: for it is profitable for thee that one of thy members should perish, and not that thy whole body should be cast into hell. And if thy right hand offend thee, cut it off, and cast it from thee: for it is profitable for thee that one of thy members should perish, and not that thy whole body should be cast into hell." (Matt. v, 29-30.) The offending member, according to their founder, Szelivanov, was the organ of procreation.[16]

Szelivanov "baptized himself by fire," mutilating his body with a blazing iron. He baptized hundreds in the same way and worked untiringly to gain new converts. When the world contained 144,000 Skoptsi the millennium would be at hand. At one time it appeared to be not far distant for the membership was rapidly increasing. Everyone was urged to secure new converts. He who brought in twelve mutilations was given the distinction of apostleship. In eastern Russia, entire communities went over to the Skoptsi. One such mass conversion consisted of 1,700 souls. The missionaries worked among the beggars and other lowly

rule is that they take one step with each lash, and our familiarity with symbolic utilization of climbing to represent sexual activity in the language of the unconscious would confirm the interpretation of this religious ceremony as a simultaneous symbolic sexual indulgence and actual self-punishment.

[16] Goldberg, B. Z., *The Sacred Fire*, Liveright, 1930, pp. 345-50. See also Wall, O. A., *Sex and Sex Worship*, Mosby, 1919, pp. 211-12; Leroy-Beaulieu, Anatole, *The Empire of the Tsars and the Russians*, Part III, London, Putnam's, 1896, pp. 422-37.

elements of society convincing them or bribing them to accept the new religion. Some were even forcibly mutilated. An appeal was also made to the curious, the adventurous element.

This very fact that there were wholesale conversions to the sect and that each convert was to be mutilated, made it quite impossible for these operations to be performed with that great care and precision required to insure their effectiveness. . . . A good many of the converts performed the operation on themselves and halted in the process because of pain or fear. In fact, the Skoptsi religion took cognizance of this condition by establishing two degrees of mutilations, those of the Greater Seal and those of the Lesser Seal. (Goldberg.)

Self-castration as an expression of the moral sentiment of the community may be incorporated into legend and tradition instead of into religious practice, but its significance is thereby all the more easily discovered. For example, in his elaborate study of the sexual life of the savages of the Trobriand Islands, Malinowski[17] has collected numerous erotic dreams and fantasies of these people, some of which show the theme of self-mutilation and self-castration as a form of punishment and misdirected aggression exactly comparable with what we have seen of it in other places.

For example, there is the story of Momovala (Vol. II, p. 411) who yields to an incestuous impulse toward his daughter. The girl, in her mortification, persuades a shark to eat her. To this the father reacts by attacking his wife sexually so violently that she dies also, whereupon Momovala castrates himself and dies.

A longer and more specific tale is the legend of Inuvayla'u. Inuvayla'u was supposed to have been a great chief whose lecherousness led him to take sexual advantage of all the women of the village during the absence of their husbands. The men of the village finally caught him *in flagrante delicto* and punished him by the disgrace of being ducked. This filled him with great shame and sorrow and he ordered his mother to prepare their belongings for moving to another village.

When all was packed he came out of his house in the central part of the village wailing aloud; he took his ax and cut off the end of his penis wailing and lamenting it as he did so. He threw this part of his penis to one side and it turned into a large stone which the natives believe

[17] Malinowski, Bronislaw, *The Sexual Life of Savages in Northwestern Melanesia,* Liveright, 1929.

to be still observable. Crying and wailing he went further, from time to time cutting of a piece of his penis and throwing it to one side where it turned into stone. Finally he cut off his testicles which became large white coral boulders and are still visible. He went to a village far off and lived there with his mother making gardens and fishing. There are some variations of the myth but the essential part, as Malinowski states, is the expiatory self-castration. He adds that the stones described in the myth still exist although "the similarity to their anatomical prototypes has worn' away with time, while their size must have enormously increased."

In spite of the fact that self-castration is, as I have just recorded, an essential part of certain religious cults, ancient and modern, the practical-minded, present-day person can scarcely conceive of it as the act of a normal man. It is too much like the self-mutilations of psychotic patients which we shall consider shortly.

For the present let us examine what it is about them that seems insane. Is it that the sacrifice is so great or that it is so unnecessary?

I think we could easily agree that it is the former since the idea of renunciation of the sexual life is present in all religions, with greater or lesser emphasis. But the fact that self-castration as a religious rite exists and has existed for centuries is of the utmost theoretical importance, because it shows us what the extreme form of sacrifice may be. Of course it is not the only extreme form of sacrifice. We know religions have existed in which children were burned alive, property confiscated or ceded to the church, and martyrdom of various types expected and approved. But in these other sacrifices it is not so much the sacrifice of the sexual life as the submission to pain or deprival which is emphasized. These we have already discussed. Many believe, however, that this renunciation of the sexual life, and in particular the infliction of some kind of self-mutilation upon the genitals, is the fundamental form of all sacrifice. There is some clinical evidence to support this.

It is common knowledge that surgical mutilation of the genitals is practiced as a religious rite by millions of people, both savage and civilized, including the Jews, the Mohammedans, and many of the native tribes scattered over Asia, Africa, and Oceanica. We also know that the circumcision of boy babies has become exceedingly prevalent in the United States, being a routine procedure in the practice of many obstetricians, pediatricians and general practitioners. A vast number of theories have been advanced to explain the origin of circumcision.[18] But most of them are what psychoanalysts call rationalizations, i.e., they attempt to explain something on the basis of some utility which has been secondarily discovered. We can only expect to understand the origin of circumcision if we can understand the dynamic principles which impel people to want to sacrifice a part of their bodily flesh.

We already have a clue as to what this may be derived from, taken from the more radical religious rites described above. If instead of cutting off the entire genitalia one can satisfy the religious requisites equally well by cutting off only a part of the genitals, namely, the foreskin, he has managed an exceedingly practical substitution. That this general principle of a part for the whole operates in our lives is apparent on every side. The Children of Israel offered up a bullock to the Lord indicating their willingness to give him everything, but very prudently they kept the majority of the herd for the maintenance of the tribe. When we call upon certain friends, we leave a calling card which represents not just our name but ourselves. It is a part of us which stands for the whole.

The point is that almost all religions which have survived have learned to make liberal use of symbolism and all the evidence points to the fact that circumcision is a symbol of a more radical mutilation. It is, however, a particular type of symbolism, that of a part for the whole, which is characteristic of unconscious thinking and conscience-bribing which we have already discussed.

We obtain evidence for this from clinical data. I could cite many illustrations from psychiatric practice to show how, in the unconscious, circumcision and castration are equated. Because the fear of cutting in connection with the genitals is so widespread and apparently so basic in the

[18] Hygienic considerations (Steinmetz), protection against sexual dangers (Crawley), test of courage (Zaborowski), sacrifice and hallowing of the sexual life (Barton, Jeremias, Valeton, Lagrange), intensification of the sensual pleasure (Burton), expression of the belief in resurrection (Frazer), have all been advanced as causes for the origin of circumcision. Most scholars, and among them those who have studied the question most intensively, R. Andree, H. Wilken, Ploss-Renz, and L. Gray, consider circumcision to be a custom of initiation, serving as an introduction into the sexual life and to make procreation more certain by the removal of foreskin, which is considered to be a hindrance." (Schmidt, W. and Koppers, W., *Völker und Kulturen,* Part I, Regensburg, 1924, pp. 239-43.) See Gray's article in *Hastings' Encyclopaedia of Religion and Ethics,* Vol. III, p. 664 ff.

formation of character,[19] any surgery in connection with the genitals is apt to be associated with strong emotional feeling which psychoanalysts, on the basis of their daily experiences with the language of the unconscious, ascribe to the "castration threat," i.e., the fear that the genitals are to be irremediably injured. How intense this can be is rather well-illustrated by the following incident from the earlier life of a patient whom I recently saw. He had discovered at an early age that he had what he called a "rupture" (which, of course, has nothing to do with the genitals although this fact is not known to all laymen). He felt that he must keep it a secret from his parents and did so until he was seventeen. Becoming convinced by that time that he must have an operation, he broached the matter to his father for the purpose of obtaining money. The father became agitated, fearing that such an operation might ruin the boy "in some way," but after brooding over it for some days consented and that evening mentioned the matter to his wife. His wife, in turn, flew into a terrific tantrum, saying that he had concealed something from her, that he had plotted something dreadful with reference to the boy, that he was a monster and a villain. She ended by *shooting and killing her husband that same night!* Upon examination many years later we found the boy to have no "rupture," no hernia, but an atrophied testicle on one side.

That circumcision, like the threatened hernia operation in the case just described, represents symbolic castration is intuitively perceived by some people and remains quite inconceivable to other people. Actual castration, according to early Roman law, could be performed with the consent of the castrated person or with that of his legal guardian. Later, however, when castration was prohibited by the Romans (Domitian) both for free men and slaves even with the consent of the person involved circumcision was also strictly forbidden.[20] Mommsen states that "Hadrian was the first one, not apparently for religious reasons, but because of the superficial similarity of the operations, to equate circumcision and castration, which was one of the reasons that led to a serious Jewish insurrection at that time. His successor granted it to the Jews and also the Egyptians.

[19] See for example Alexander's article, "The Castration Complex in the Formation of Character," *International Journal of Psychoanalysis*, Jan.-April, 1923, pp. 11-42.
[20] Theodor, *Römisches Strafrecht* in K. Binding, *Systemat. Handbuch d. Deutsch. Rechtswiss.*, I Abt., 4. Teil, p. 637, Leipzig, quoted by Bryk, *op. cit.*

Otherwise, however, circumcision was considered equal to castration and equally punished."

It is a common assumption that circumcision rites belong only to men but this assumption is contradicted by the facts, since circumcision of women is widespread among savage peoples and the unconscious motives are apparently the same as in males. The conscious motives, however, are quite different, as are also the techniques. All parts of the female genitals are attacked by the circumcisors of various primitive tribes, sometimes the clitoris, sometimes the labia majora, sometimes the labia minora, sometimes all of these. The *ostensible* reasons are to promote cleanliness, to decrease passion and, therefore, more nearly insure virginity, for the promotion of greater pleasure to the man, for the promotion of vaginal, at the expense of clitoridean sensitivity, i.e., shifting of the erotogenic zone.[21]

Female circumcision (according to Bryk) could have originated only in a culture governed by maternal law. Woman, emancipating herself, could not bear to be ignored, sexually, by the man. There was also the desire to have an external token of maturity and the obvious course was a parallel to the circumcision of boys. Just as our society women imitate the men by smoking, wearing their hair short, and fencing, the shepherd woman did the same through circumcision.[22]

PUBERTY RITES

A second source of evidence as to the motives and significance of religious mutilation is to be found in the various initiatory ceremonials inflicted upon adolescents among aboriginal tribes in many parts of the world. These are known in anthropological literature as puberty rites, and may be conceived of as religious in nature. They are not usually *self*-mutilation and hence do not exactly belong here but they are cooperatively submitted to in such a way as to make it clear that while actually inflicted by a second party they gratify *some* wishes of the victim,[23] even though it be only the wish to conform with the customs. But these customs are a product of the minds of the group and hence represent crystallizations of "wishes" of the individuals composing that group.

[21] Bryk, Felix, *Voodo-Eros*, American Ethnological Press, 1933.
[22] Bryk, Felix, *Circumcision in Man and Woman*, American Ethnological Press, 1934, p. 115 ff.
[23] I should not say "victim" but "initiate" or "candidate" because heroic and sometimes horrible as these ceremonies are, they are usually the occasion of a festival and accompanied by great rejoicing.

The rites vary among different peoples. In some instances a tooth is knocked out, amid much noise and ceremony; more frequently the principal initiatory rite consists of circumcision performed with a sharp stone or piece of glass or with a knife; sometimes an incision is made in the penis and the blood is mixed with water which the boys and men drink. Following and preceding the circumcision the boys are compelled to go through various forms of torture. They are made to fast for many days, "feigned attacks are made upon them," so-called spirits appear to them in masks of animals and threaten to eat them; occasionally an actual fight takes place between the men and their sons. Sometimes the boys run the gauntlet while the men beat them violently. Among the Karesau islanders black ants are allowed to bite the novices. The Mandan Indians thrust a knife with a saw-edge through the youth's arm, forearm, thigh, knee, calves, chest and shoulder and then push pointed pieces of wood into the wounds. All of these methods seem to carry the significance of death for the candidate, followed by rebirth. This rebirth drama is also enacted by the novices after the ceremony when they appear to have forgotten all about their previous existence, do not recognize their relatives, and cannot eat or speak or even sit down without being shown how. If they do not adhere to this formality they must go through a second and much more severe ceremony which may result in actual death.

There is in these rites the purpose of detaching the youths from their mothers and of admitting them to the community of men.[24] Women are forbidden to attend the ceremony and the feast under pain of death, or if they are allowed to witness the rites they must stand at a great distance. The women mourn and wail for the boys as if an actual death had taken place and there is rejoicing when the boy is returned to his home.

Thanks to the collections of data made by Frazer, Malinowski, Byrk and other anthropologists and the psychoanalytic constructions formulated by Freud, Abraham, Rank, Theodor Reik and the combination of observations and interpretations made by Roheim, we have fairly definite ideas as to the psychological function of these rites.

Two views of the matter are held, both of which explain puberty rites as ceremonial devices for overcoming what it known in anthropology as the "incest taboo," or to put it in psychoanalytic terms, for solving the Oedipus complex.

[24] Reik, Theodor, *Ritual*, Norton, 1931.

From one standpoint the genital mutilation inflicted upon the adolescent can be seen to gratify the hostility of the parents toward him for his secession from their authority, to punish him for his incestuous wishes, and to intimidate him with respect to their (further) gratifications; that is, the suppression of the sexual and aggressive impulses of the adolescent with reference to the parents. The other aspect of the function of puberty rites is that of atonement, not in retrospect but in prospect, i.e., the circumcision and all the other mutilations used for this purpose are a price paid by the initiate for admission into the rights of adulthood.[25]

The castration fear, i.e., the boy's fear that his life or his penis would be taken from him by his elders were he to use it in the forbidden direction of sexuality would hang over him always were it not removed ceremonially by the symbolic castration represented in the puberty rites. Instead of cutting off the entire penis, a part of it is cut off, a part standing for the whole just as it does in all sacrificial offerings.[26]

There is really no conflict between these two aspects of the puberty rituals. Both are undoubtedly valid; one emphasizes intimidation, suppressive, and atonement elements and the other the permissive, propitiatory elements. I cannot agree with Reik that the former are much the more important simply because they are unconscious, whereas the latter are conscious.

Money-Kyrle[27] refers to the more complicated rituals in which the severed foreskin or the extracted tooth is hidden

[25] In regard to puberty rites as a permit for the beginning of sexual life, A. LeRoy sees in circumcision an *interdit levé;* only through the blood sacrifice of mutilation of the penis can the *permis d'user* be bought. Reik is of the opinion "that the prohibition, the partial lifting of which is bound up with the rites of puberty, was first set up within the narrow frame of the family and only later extended beyond these limits." (LeRoy, A., *La religion des primitives,* Paris, 1906, p. 236; Reik, Theodor, *Probleme der Religions-psychologie.,* Vol. I, Leipzig und Wien, 1919, p. 981.)

[26] This significance of sacrifice, i.e., a technique of giving up a part in order to preserve the whole, has been studied psychoanalytically by various writers. In addition to Rank, referred to above, Alexander (*Psychoanalysis of the Total Personality,* Nervous and Mental Disease Publishing Company, 1930) has essentially the same thing in mind in his idea of conscience-bribing and in another article ("Zur Genese des Kastrationskomplexes," *Internationale Zeitschrift für Psychoanalyse,* 1930) he describes the mechanism in terms of sacrificing anal values in order to save the genitals; Rado ("Fear of Castration in Women," *Psychoanalytic Quarterly,* July-October, 1933, pp. 425-75) has referred to it as "the choice of the lesser evil."

[27] Money-Kyrle, *The Meaning of Sacrifice,* London, Hogarth, 1929, p. 161.

in a tree. He quotes Frazer's opinion[28] that this may have originally been intended to insure the rebirth of the circumcised men and his own psychoanalytic inference that the circumcision may serve to relieve the neurotic fear of death.

If this interpretation is correct, such mutilations, even when they are consciously intended to remove the fear of death and thereby to secure the hope of rebirth, are vicarious sacrifices. They are accepted by the super-ego in place of the self-castration that it would otherwise demand. Further, since a relation of identity often seems to subsist between the external soul and the soul of the ancestor, the foreskin that is hidden in the tree may, from one point of view, be regarded as made over to the ancestral spirit, which is itself nothing more than the projection of the super-ego. Such a sacrifice might well be combined with a pantomime of return to the womb.

C. SELF-MUTILATION IN PSYCHOTIC PATIENTS

Remote as these far-flung speculations about the aborigines *et alia* may seem, it is not such a big step from the consideration of savage behavior to the consideration of insane behavior, which is our next topic. The savages and the insane have this in common, that they act without deference to demands of a civilization which often modifies primitive tendencies almost beyond recognition. In a sense, what we call insanity is simply a regression to the savage state in which one does not have to consider these restrictions.

Among the many forms of psychotic behavior, self-mutilation is not one of the most frequent but is, on the other hand, quite typical. It is typical because it is so apparently senseless or is justified by such irrational and illogical explanations. The type of injury inflicted is quite varied but

[28] In regard to castration as a purchase of life rather than as a manifestation of the death instinct: "Frazer believed that he had found the long lost key to the significance of circumcision in the fact that East African Kukuyu had formerly associated circumcision with the ceremonies of rebirth which are now celebrated separately and because in central Australia the amputated foreskins are put into the same totem trees, totem rocks, and other totem centers in which human souls spend their time between the departure from the individual and their rebirth in a child. Renz, as quoted by Zeller (Dr. Moritz, *Die Knabenweihen, in Arbeiten aus dem voelkerkundlichen,* Institut d. Universitaet Bern, I Heft, Bern, 1923, pp. 1-160) has also pointed out that the circumcision rites of savages, including as they frequently do, a hut of isolation in which the boys must spend a long time, are connected with ideas of rebirth from the belly or stomach of a spirit so that he supports this idea of Frazer's that circumcision represents a rebirth in numerous senses." (Bryk, *op. cit.*)

generally tends to be more conspicuous, bloody, and painful than serious from the standpoint of life. As we shall see, there is probably a very definite reason for this. Self-mutilation occurs in most of the major psychoses—paresis, mania, melancholia, schizophrenia, epileptic psychosis, delirium. Apparently, therefore, it bears no fixed relation to the clinical form of illness but is an expression of some more general tendencies. Let us make our discussion specific by citing an actual case.

A boy of twenty returned from the war to find that the girl to whom he had been engaged had married another man. This was the precipitating factor in the development of an acute schizophrenic illness with delusions, hallucinations, and queer posturing, which after a few relapses became chronic and necessitated continuous hospitalization. From the standpoint of care he was an exceedingly difficult patient in the hospital because of his persistent efforts to injure himself. He would, for example, tie string tightly about his toes with the evident purpose of producing gangrene. He would slip up behind the heavy doors of the hospital as they were being closed after a physician or nurse and put his fingers into the cracks so as to have them crushed. Upon several occasions he snatched pins from the front of a nurse's uniform and attempted to jab them into his eyes. He would seize and separate the fingers of one hand and by using his leg and his other hand attempt to pull them apart so violently as to tear the webs between them. With his thumb and finger nail he would pinch chunks out of his ear lobes. He frequently dived or plunged from his bed onto the floor, head first, as if attempting to crush his skull. Once he was found nearly asphyxiated as a result of having forced several large stalks of celery deep into his throat.

In such examples as this, typical psychotic self-mutilation, all the aggressive tendencies seem to have been reflected upon the aggressor himself. We can only guess for whom they were originally intended unless the patient tells us—which this one did not. Undoubtedly they were originally directed against some external object, ostensibly loved but unconsciously hated.

I have cited this case in spite of its incompleteness for several reasons. First, it represents graphically some of the variety of psychotic mutilations.[29] Secondly, it demonstrates

[29] Cf. also the following: MacKenna, R. M. B., "Extensive Self-Mutilation of Scalp, Presumably Following Trichophytic Infection," *British Jour-*

the entire absence of a real wish to die. Anyone strongly determined to kill himself could have done so with one one-hundredth the effort that this boy used to cause himself suffering. He is still alive after ten years of it. Thirdly, there is here the disguised evidence of the sexual element. His psychosis was precipitated, it will be recalled, by a frustrated love affair and many of the attacks upon himself have a sexually symbolic character.

A fourth and the determining reason lies in the fact that instead of being single and clearly specific as in the case of the man who cut off his arm, and in any of the other examples cited, his attacks upon himself were multiple and much less clearly localized. The man, for example, had a guilty hand and arm; he had killed his child with it, so it was appropriate that he should cut off the offending arm. But this boy attacked himself all over and this we find disturbing to our assumption that there is something specific about the particular organ or part of the body attacked which leads to its selection as the object or focus of the self-destructive effort. There is probably in all cases some conditioning, i.e., specific experiences involving that part of the body in either an actual or symbolic way which help to determine its selection.

For example, in the case which I cited previously in which my patient made violent attacks upon his own hair without knowing why, it will be remembered that as a child he had had beautiful hair, his only point of superiority over a brother of whom he was bitterly envious. In spite of this hair, however, his brother was preferred by his parents and by almost everyone else, so that my patient came to feel that having such beautiful hair was of no avail in the struggle for the favors of the world. He felt, so to speak, as if his hair had "let him down," for not only did it win him no friends but it was by this luxuriant hair that his father was wont to seize him when he administered beatings, usually inflicted because of my patient's mistreatment of his envied brother. For these reasons he had, on the basis of his childhood thinking, good reason to be angry at his own hair. (Personifying a part of the body in this way is quite characteristic of primitive "pre-logical" thinking.)

nal of Dermatology, July, 1930, pp. 313-19; Sharma, H. R., "Self-Mutilation: Extraordinary Case," Indian Medical Gazette, June, 1930, pp. 327-28; Urechia, C. I., "Autophagia of Fingers by Patient with General Paralysis and Cervical Pachymeningitis," Revue Neurologique, Paris, March, 1931, pp. 350-52.

Similarly we could probably show, if we had access to all the material, as is not infrequently the case, that a patient who attacks his ear, for example, does so because of certain auditory experiences of childhood of an unpleasant nature, or one who deliberately injures his eye does so because of some original visual shock which enhanced the culpability of this particular organ. It is as if he would say, "My eye was responsible for revealing to me such and such a terrible [or forbidden] scene." [30] This, for example, was the reason that the surreptitious observer of the naked Lady Godiva was supposed to have gone blind; here God did the punishing.

But we have still not answered the question provoked by the case of the boy who attacked all parts of his body without discrimination. It is scarcely likely that he could have had grudges against so many different parts of himself on the basis of experience only. From this we conclude that there must be another element which determines the selection of the part of the body. This element has to do not with the real significance of the various parts but with the symbolic significance. The apparently indiscriminate attacks upon himself by the patient were actually not so indiscriminate. They always related to organs or parts of the body which experience has taught us may symbolically represent the sexual organs. Indeed it would appear from clinical study that all attempts to cut off parts of the body represent substituted and therefore symbolic attempts to deprive oneself of his sexuality, i.e., to cut off or mutilate an organ symbolizing the genitals. The Skoptsi and others, as we have seen, actually did this directly instead of seeking a symbolic method of accomplishing it and, as we shall shortly see, the same is true of many psychotic patients.

Before we pass to these examples, however, let us discuss a little further the idea that in the unconscious various parts of the body may represent the genitals. We see this best in hysteria, which we shall take up in the next chapter, but we also see it in the condition known as "fetishism," in

[30] Cf. the case reported by Hartmann. This was a woman who gouged out both her eyes, ostensibly "as a sacrifice to Christ" because "one sins mostly with one's eyes during such fantasies." It was discovered that she had always been excited by certain visual experiences including the sight of almost any man. As a child she had slept in a room with her parents and had often observed her father's genitals; she had observed the parents having intercourse and was scolded by her father for "always watching." (Hartmann, H., "Self-Mutilation," *Jahrb. f. Psychiat. u. Neurol.*, 1925, Vol. XLIV, p. 31, abstracted by Keschner, *Arch. Neurol. & Psychiat.*, March, 1926, pp. 384-86.)

which the total personality, the body, the face, even the genital organs of the beloved are of no sexual interest to the patient but only one isolated part of the body, and this part is never the genitals. Such individuals, for example, become sexually excited and ultimately gratified by the contemplation and caressing of a foot, a toe, a finger, the ear, the hair, and sometimes even objects which are not really a part of the body, for example, a shoe or other articles of clothing, belonging to the loved one. When such patients are psychoanalyzed, i.e., when they trace completely the psychological connections between these things, connections which they themselves did not know, they reveal to themselves and to us that these parts of the body were unconsciously taken by them as substitutes for a part of the body which they were too repressed and too fearful to acknowledge frankly.

The unconscious symbolic substitution of one organ for another is by no means limited to hysterical persons or fetishists. It is only more obvious in them. But we all do it. A clear example of the substitution of hair for a more socially-tabooed appendage was recorded some years ago[31] by a psychoanalyst friend of mine, who understandingly observed a young child. The boy had suffered from a slight inflammatory tightness of the foreskin and, at two and a half years of age, was taken to a surgeon who relieved the condition by means of stretching. The little fellow had behaved very well indeed and was praised by the surgeon who gave him a piece of candy. After the child was dressed and was saying good-by, the surgeon, still quite jovial, laughingly said to the little fellow that he had been a pretty good boy this time but next time he would "cut the whole thing off for you with these," showing him a large pair of surgical scissors. The surgeon laughed in a friendly way but the child ran to his father with a cry of terror and "trembling with agitation sobbed in my arms." The parents endeavored in every way to assure the child that the surgeon had been joking and gradually he seemed to forget the episode. A year later the child had a slight inflammation of the penis which responded easily to local bathing; in connection with it he began of his own accord to speak of his experience of the previous year with the surgeon. He recounted cheerfully and with remarkable accuracy all the *unimportant* details of what had happened in the surgeon's

[31] Simmel, Ernst, "A Screen Memory in Statu Nascendi," *International Journal of Psychoanalysis*, Oct., 1925, pp. 454-57.

office, mentioning many items which the parents had forgotten. But concerning the final episode, the joke about the scissors, he did not say one word. Thinking that he might help to remove the painful impression of the experience, his father asked him if he did not remember anything else —something the doctor said. No answer. "Don't you remember the joke he made?" No answer. "Didn't he have a pair of scissors?" The child laughed. "Oh, yes, a pair of scissors. He made a joke about the scissors."

But in spite of prompting from his father he could not remember what the joke had been. Finally his father asked him if the surgeon had not talked of cutting off something. Immediately the child cried out merrily, "Oh, yes, I remember, he said he would cut my *hair* off."

This incident is most interesting because it shows so clearly how a child represses something painful and replaces the painful matter with a disguising joke. The merriment, excitement, and laughter which the child exhibited served the purpose of denying or guarding against the anxiety which is so close to the surface and which would appear if the child accepted into consciousness the memory in its original form

It is also interesting to note that the hair was selected as a symbol of the organ which the surgeon actually threatened to cut off. The child could laugh at this because it is not of such great consequence if the hair be cut off; it doesn't hurt and it will grow again.[32]

Now we can see how even in the case of the boy who mutilated his own hair because it had played him false there was probably a disguised element so that not only the unpleasant experiences with his brother but also the association with his sexual life dictated his behavior.

Let us now examine some of those psychotic cases who do not resort to symbolic means of punishing or rejecting their own genitals but mutilate themselves directly in the form of self-castration.

[32] Incidentally, as Simmel sagely remarks, the surgeon was unconsciously cruel in making the joke; he could laugh at it because he regarded it as so foreign to his real purposes. But for the little child this cruel tendency was wholly undisguised. He reacted not to the joke but to the cruelty. Later, when his unconscious disguised the memory by making it hair instead of penis, he was able to defend himself against the anxiety by a device very useful in the present-day civilization where we curb our cruelty and only allow ourselves to injure our fellow men mentally. "Nevertheless there are many adults who remain all their lives helpless children in the face of attacks of this sort. They are saddened or wounded if people jest with them because, as we say, they do not 'understand a joke' —in reality they understand it only too well."

N. D. C. Lewis[33] has reported numerous such cases in detail and many other less complete reports are available.[34] From these a few typical cases may be selected.

The following case is one reported by Dr. Lewis from the records of St. Elizabeth Hospital. Little is known about the man's earlier history. As seen in the hospital he was at first depressed, indifferent, very dirty and uncooperative, taking but little food. He would reply to no questions and mumbled to himself incoherently. He sat with his eyes closed, the lids quivering, and a silly smile on his face. All this is quite typical of schizophrenia.

A year later he was still untidy and inaccessible but in addition very destructive. He had begun to repeat profane phrases. Occasionally he would become excited, pacing up and down cursing. He began to strike at people occasionally, some of whom would retaliate. He broke out a few windows and became very noisy. During the next year or two his activity and combativeness increased. He developed the habit of throwing himself about the room, apparently in an effort to do himself harm, which sometimes happened. He threw chairs at the attendants. It finally became necessary to transfer him to a locked ward where, however, he continued to injure himself in many ways so that he had to be restrained. He bit himself on various parts of the body, chewed the lower lip till surgical repair was necessary and finally, in spite of careful watching, lacerated and incised his scrotum with his finger nails and removed the testicles.

In this case we have nothing but the stark behavior from which to draw conclusions so that while we cannot say

[33] "The Psychobiology of the Castration Complex," *The Psychoanalytic Review*, 1927, Vol. XIV, pp. 420-46, 1928, Vol. XV, pp. 53-84, 174-209, and 304-23, *Ibid.*, "Additional Observations on the Castration Reaction in Males," same Journal, 1931, Vol. XVIII, pp. 146-65.

[34] DeMassary, Leroy & Mallet, "Sexual Auto-Mutilation in a Schizophrenic Case," *Annales Medico-psychologiques*, Paris (pt. 2), July, 1929, pp. 144-50; Ferrer, C. O., "Self-Mutilation of Hypochondriac Alcoholic Patient," *Semana Médica*, Buenos Aires, Jan. 9, 1930, pp. 91-3; Galant, I. B., "Masturbation and Auto-castration in Cases of Paranoid Forms of Dementia Praecox," *J. Nevropat. i. Psikhiat.*, 1928, Vol. XXI, pp. 307-85.

For other references on self-castration see: Blondel, C., "Les Auto-mutilations la castration volontaire," *Tribune Médicale*, Paris, 1906, N. S. Vol. XXXVIII, pp. 533-36; Eckert: "Zur Frage der Selbstentmannung," *Archiv. f. Kriminal-Anthropologie und Kriminalistik*, Leipzig, 1912, Vol. XLVI, p. 287; Ingegnieros, J., "Un Caso de auto-castration en un degenerado hereditario con neurosthenia y sifilofobia, *Semana. Médica*, Buenos Aires, 1901, Vol. VIII, p. 73; Nacke, "Uber Selbstentmannung," *Archiv. f. Kriminal-Anthropologie und Kriminalistik*, Leipzig, 1903, Vol. XII, p. 263; Schmidt-Petersen, "Uber Selbst-Kastration," *Zeitschrift für Medizinal-Beamte*, Berlin, 1902, Vol. XV, p. 735; Strock, D., "Self-Castration," *Journal of the American Medical Association*, 1901, Vol. XXXVI, p. 270.

what the motives for self-castration may have been, we can see how the destructive tendencies were first externally and later internally directed, focusing them upon various organs of the body and finally upon the genitals.

Another case will bring out more of the motives. A thirty-year-old naval officer, married, was brought to the hospital with a history of having mistreated himself and of having contemplated suicide. He was quiet, neat, mildly depressed.

The history was that his father had been very religious, but very difficult to get along with and had deserted the family while the patient was yet small. The mother had been obliged to work very hard to support them. The boy himself had to go to work at an early age but in spite of this obtained a fair education intermittently. He had joined the navy and had worked himself up to petty-officer rank. A year before admission he noted that he worried about his work and asked his friends if they noticed that he was not doing so well. He became increasingly depressed.

Then he began to notice strange noises, thought he heard his shipmates talking about him and accusing him of perverted practices (i.e., of being homosexual). (Individuals with such fears and hallucinations rarely *are* homosexual overtly, but react with terror to the thought that they might be—just as "normal" persons do, but in greater degree.) Finally he went to the bathroom and with a safety razor blade amputated his penis.

When questioned about it the patient said he had been confused and hadn't known what he was doing. He seemed however, to show little concern or regret. Later he jumped overboard but climbed back aboard the ship on the anchor chain. He admitted, however, that the thought of drowning had always fascinated him.

The examination showed that he still suffered from auditory hallucinations with voices telling him to do odd things and commenting on what he did. Concerning the charge of homosexuality he was quite perplexed because he had never indulged in it but began his heterosexual life very early. Except for the mutilation his physical condition was excellent and his intelligence above average.

Later the patient announced that he was "ready for the supreme sacrifice" (suicide) and wrote a note saying, "I am a pervert and will pay the penalty." He became increasingly restless and disturbed and exhibited impulses to fight with patients and attendants.

Many more such cases could be cited but those given are

sufficient to give us a composite picture which is quite definite. These patients, sometimes very mild and pious at first, become increasingly aggressive toward the outside world, then aggressive toward themselves, all of them emphasizing their sense of guilt about sexual sins. These sexual sins are sometimes related to women, sometimes related to other men (homosexuality) and sometimes to auto-erotic indulgences (masturbation). In all instances sexuality is identified with the genitals and since these patients are psychotic, and therefore very direct and undisguised in their logic, they do the obvious thing of ridding themselves of the guilty part of their body.

There is, however, another element which we must not lose sight of. A man who feels guilty about his sex organs because of conscious or unconscious homosexual impulses, accomplishes two purposes when he cuts off his genitals. He punishes himself, but at the same time he converts himself by this deprival into a passive, penis-less individual, anatomically comparable with the female. By this anatomical identification, he comes closer to the homosexuality about which he feels guilty than he was before the act. He feels guilty about his homosexual wishes and by castrating himself appears to atone for and relinquish them, but in reality only changes himself so as to be incapable of the active role and even more predisposed to the passive role.[35]

This enables us to conclude, then, that psychotic self-mutilation corresponds to the formula for a neurotic symptom in that an erotic goal and a self-punishment are both simultaneously achieved. It is as if a bargain had been struck between the instinctive and the repressing forces, and the symptom produced as a compromise which, however, could not be acceptable to any but a very sick and powerless ego. To the extent that such a symptom, i.e., such a compromise, is effected, a relative peace has been brought about. The symptom (even a mutilation) is, therefore, an attempt at self-healing, or at least self-preservation. This gives us a clue to the paradox that local self-destruction is a form of partial suicide to avert total suicide.

[35] This phenomenon falls into the formula first mentioned by Freud in *Totem and Taboo* where, in regard to ceremonial feasts, he pointed out that "the propitiation (ceremony) repeats the crime." This was discussed at greater length by Roheim in his article, *Nach dem Tode des Urvaters*, and by Abraham in his studies on melancholia. It is the subject of an entire chapter of Theodor Reik's *The Unknown Murderer* entitled "No Expiation Without Repeating the Deed." Reik goes further and shows that the oath, torture and trial by ordeal arose as symbolic repetition of the crime as a means of expiation.

But in the psychotic self-mutilation, the attempt at self-healing is a very weak one. In this the self-mutilations of psychotic patients resemble the self-mutilations of the fanatical religious sects and differ from the self-mutilations of neurotic patients and of more familiar religious ceremonial mutilations in the following way: In the psychotic patients reality is almost completely disregarded and the ego makes a particularly bad bargain, in fact almost no bargain at all, with the conscience. It sacrifices everything and gains almost nothing except punishment[36] and the

[36] It scarcely needs demonstration that castration, both actual and symbolic, has been used throughout the ages as a punitive device. The retaliation upon Abélard by the uncle of Héloïse is, of course, classical. Such treatment of military captives was, of course, the rule with the Mohammedans and is said to be still used by the warring peoples of northern Africa.

Indeed, von Autenrieth over 100 years ago (*Abhandlung ueber den Ursprung der Beschneidung bei wilden und halbwilden Völkern mit Beziehung auf die Beschneidung der Israeliten*, mit einer Kritik von Praelat v. Flatt, Tuebingen, 1829) derived the origin of circumcision from the custom of certain peoples of bringing home the genitalia of killed or even living enemies as an invaluable trophy of victory, but who in order to avoid suspicion that these signs of victory might have been plundered from their own dead adopted this means of making certain.

"Marie Bonaparte (*"Die Symbolik der Kopftrophae,"* Imago, Vienna, Vol. XIV, 1928) has given full particulars on the diffusion of this ancient war custom, especially in East Africa. That it has existed even in Europe in recent times is attested by Kraus (Kraus, H., *Münchener Medizin Wochenschrift*, 1908, Vol. LV, No. 10, p. 517), who writes that 'Montenegrins are accustomed to castrate their prisoners during campaigns and carry their penises with them as amulets. Many a warrior has a whole string of such amulets. The bandit wars of Macedonia, which for years have been taxing Europe's diplomatic art to the utmost, would probably long have died out if the occasional victors ceased from the fatal custom of mutilating their captured enemies and thus causing innumerable campaigns of revenge. Sicilian myths also mention similar mutilations.' King Saul's command that David bring him one hundred foreskins of the Philistines which David promptly fulfilled is possibly a reference to a similar war custom among the ancient Jews.

"Castration as a punishment is still customary today among many peoples in Europe. See, for example, Czekanowski (Dr. Jan, *Forschungen im Nil-Kongo Zwischen-Gebiet*, Leipzig, 1927, Vol. V, p. 12 ff.) and Pelikan, E. (*Gerichtl.-mediz. Untersuchungen ueber das Skoppentum in Russland*, Deutsche Uebers. v. Nicolaus Iwanoff, Giessen, 1876)"; (Bryk, Felix, *Circumcision in Man and Woman*, American Ethnological Press, 1934).

In American lynching episodes a common preliminary to the burning or hanging of the victim is the amputation of his genitals. In a fictional article (*American Spectator*, March, 1933) based upon actual occurrences a female relative of the injured girl is permitted to burn off the penis of the still living Negro with a gasoline blowtorch.

The removal of other parts of the body as a punitive device is even more familiar. The blinding of the young Princes in the tower and many similar punishments are well known. The lopping off of hands and arms is also common in criminal records. Peter the Great issued an edict that all those convicted of murder should have the flesh and cartilages of the nose torn away so that only the bones remained and no one could ever be in doubt as to the murderous history of the victim. Cutting out of the tongue was until relatively recent times a part of the criminal code of many countries, including our own. The Quakers, it will be recalled, were

secondary advantages of passivity. It surrenders all active goals. The neurotic person also punishes himself by a sacrificial self-castration, but it is a symbolic castration, not a real one. Moreover, he uses it as a permit for active satisfaction of some tangible and real value. It has, therefore, an opportunistic or, one might almost say, prophylactic purpose. The psychotic person, however, mutilates himself without regard for the net reality gain; e.g., he freely offers up—or rather throws away—his genital organs or highly prized symbolic substitutes for them, e.g., the eyes.[37]

D. SELF-MUTILATION IN ORGANIC DISEASES

Acts of self-mutilation of extreme degree are occasionally reported as occurring in physically ill people who, however, show no (other) indication of mental disease. These are of great theoretical interest because they appear to represent a sequestration of the self-destructive impulse as the result of organic brain injury. As we shall see, the psychological pattern does not differ materially from that of the other forms of self-mutilation heretofore examined.

Goodhart and Savitsky[38] reported the case of a high school girl of sixteen who at the age of eight had developed what appears to have been epidemic encephalitis. Although she was well for a year after the acute attack, it gradually

frequently punished by the Puritans by ear-clipping. In the most celebrated of all executions, that of Damiens, who assassinated Louis XV of France, which was intended to be an everlasting example, after various other tortures had been inflicted the crux of the sentence was carried out in that four horses were attached to each of his four limbs and he was "pulled asunder." An interesting account described the great difficulty of the procedure: physicians suggested that the tendons should first be cut, which was done; "the horses began to draw anew and after several pulls a thigh and an arm were torn from the body. Damiens looked at his severed members and had some remains of sense after his other thigh was pulled off; nor did he expire until his other arm was likewise torn away." (Bierstadt, Edward H., *Curious Trials and Criminal Cases*, Coward-McCann, 1928, p. 161.)

Finally, one must think of actual castration as it is carried out at the present time in the form of sterilization of criminals and of the insane, and also in the fact that some surgeons still appear to believe that the proper treatment of sexual offenses and perversions is castration, apparently motivated chiefly by their moralistic and sadistic feelings rather than by scientific deductions.

[37] Bryan, D., "Blindness and Castration," *International Journal of Psychoanalysis*, March, 1921, p. 71; Harries, "Self-Inflicted Injuries of Eye by Insane Persons," *Psychiatrisch-neurologische Wochenschrift*, July 6, 1929, p. 342; Smith, J. Allen, "Voluntary Propulsion of Both Eyeballs," *Journal of the American Medical Association*, Jan. 30, 1932, p. 398.

[38] Goodhart, S. P. and Savitsky, Nathan, "Self-Mutilation in Chronic Encephalitis," *The American Journal of Medical Sciences*, May, 1933, p. 674.

showed itself unmistakably in a chronic form characterized by sleepiness and left-sided parkinsonism. In addition, she had shown at the age of thirteen some changes in personality, chiefly in the direction of aggressiveness. She would lie, exhibit temper tantrums, tear her clothing, strike her mother and sisters, once even breaking some windows in the house. After such outbursts she would be remorseful and repeat, "Why do I do it? Why do I do it? I can't help it."

It was at this time that she began to lock herself in the bathroom occasionally and appear a short while afterward bleeding from the mouth from which teeth were missing. She said she "could not help taking them out." Over and over she did this until only nine were left which were subsequently removed by the dentist because of infection.

At the age of sixteen she was admitted to a hospital because of some swelling and redness of her right eye. That night of the day of admission the nurse found her holding her right eye in her hand. The patient insisted that it had fallen out while she was sleeping. She answered all questions unhesitatingly and appeared mentally clear and intelligent. She complained of no pain. The nurse described her behavior as quite normal except for her seeming indifference regarding the eye; she did not seem in the least disturbed.

The following morning the nurse found that the *left* eye had also been removed. Again she did not complain of pain and showed no emotional disturbance. A psychiatrist, who examined her the following morning, found nothing abnormal except that she could not remember any details about her self-mutilation.

Subsequently she admitted other self-mutilations, saying that she was compelled by some peculiar force to do those "horrible things," but showed an intense reluctance to discuss them. She finally admitted that she had been untruthful in maintaining a lack of knowledge about the eyes, confessing that she had torn them out with her own fingers.

The psychological factors were more discernible in a case reported by Conn.[39] This was a young woman who at the age of twenty-one suddenly began to complain of sharp pains in the back of the neck, later down her back. They became so severe that she screamed wildly and had to be

[39] Conn, Jacob F., "A Case of Marked Self-Mutilation Presenting a Dorsal Root Syndrome," *The Journal of Nervous and Mental Diseases*, March, 1932, p. 251.

forcibly restrained. The pain continued, unabated, and two months later there were several episodes of visual and auditory hallucinosis in which the patient saw members of her family who were not present and heard voices accuse her of masturbation.

About six weeks later, apparently still suffering from the sharp pains in spite of many drugs, she arose in the night and fractured the small bones, first of her left hand and then of her right hand, using the bed springs to help accomplish this. She also fractured a phalanx of the left small toe and on the following night dislocated both thumbs. She gave as her explanation that this relieved her pains in the back. When her mother entered her room in the morning and saw her mutilated, bleeding hands which the patient exhibited in a "happy way," the mother fainted.

Six months after the mutilation episode, she was admitted to an excellent hospital where a careful examination was made. This was negative except for the mutilated hands, in spite of which she did work in occupational therapy. When shown before a clinic she "behaved admirably, delighted in the telling of her illness, giving details of how she broke her fingers, and was anxious to have her hands on display." Subsequently, however, she scratched at her ear until she lay bare the cartilage and made threats of re-breaking her fingers.

In the course of the mental examination at admission she was asked as to what went on in her mind when she was breaking her fingers. She replied, "About going out of your mind. I had to see blood. I wanted to see blood come out. I wanted to keep the blood from reaching my head so I would not go out of my mind, as I had not menstruated."

The author recites the family history as being essentially negative, the patient being the oldest daughter and the third oldest child in a large family. At the office where she had worked for four years, she was described as having been "calm, dignified" and as having "managed the most difficult situation in an efficient manner."

The home attitude toward sex was a rigid one; she claimed to have received no sex instruction nor to have heard any sex discussion at home and was badly frightened when she first menstruated. She began to masturbate at fifteen, had strong feelings of self-reproach and ideas of "going crazy." She felt that she would be disowned if discovered and she was a terrible disgrace to her family. Notwithstanding this she had continued to masturbate up until the period of her self-mutilation at the age of twenty-one.

Conn points out that the girl's guilt about masturbation, the fear of losing her mind, her anxiety over her failure to menstruate and her wish "to see blood" (as if this would reassure her that she had not been made abnormal or pregnant by the masturbation), together with the hallucinatory episode in which she had heard voices reproaching her for this masturbation, are convincing evidence that this latter was the central theme for her guilt feelings. The sense of relief after her self-mutilation, her pride in exhibiting the bleeding hand (guilty and punished) to her mother and later her scarred and deformed hands to other people confirm this interpretation.

It would certainly seem that in this case the combination of free associations, memories, compulsive acts, and the shrewd observations of an intuitive psychiatrist had combined to give us a very clear example of precisely the mechanisms we find in other cases of self-mutilation, namely, the sense of guilt arising from masturbation, the fear of punishment, the need for a propitiatory or substitute punishment which is then self-inflicted and the results "happily and proudly" exhibited to the world (and in this case, first to the mother as the presumptive representative of the super-ego).

The author points out that the dorsal root syndrome may or may not have been an infectious disease, but assuming that it was, it served only to release unconscious self-mutilation tendencies which were normally inhibited.[40]

In a study made some years ago[41] I attempted to show that a comparable phenomenon takes place when the outbreak of the mental disease picture schizophrenia is precipitated by an infectious disease. The effects of the organic disease appear to be that of releasing unconscious tendencies which had been held in control only by a maximal integrative effort which could not sustain the additional burden imposed by the physical illness. This might tempt

[40] In April, 1934, I saw, with Doctors Perry and Brian of the Topeka State Hospital, a patient who suffered from a chronic form of encephalitis and who bit his tongue so persistently and so severely that surgical measures were necessary at times to prevent dangerous hemorrhage, and the entire anterior third was severely scarred and mutilated. The patient could offer no explanation for the act except that he could not refrain from doing it. The psychological motives were not investigated.

[41] The Schizophrenic Syndrome as a Product of Acute Infectious Disease. Schizophrenia (Dementia Praecox), An Investigation by the Association for Research in Nervous and Mental Disease, Hoeber, 1928, pp. 182-204.

us to some speculations as to what the function of the physical illness may have been, but this we shall defer. We can say with definiteness that these self-mutilations which are evoked by or appear in connection with organic brain disease do not appear to differ in psychological structure from those we have studied in connection with the psychoses, neuroses and religious ceremonials.[42]

E. SELF-MUTILATION IN CUSTOMARY AND CONVENTIONAL FORMS

There are certain forms of self-mutilation which have become so well known to us in everyday "normal" social life that we find it difficult to think of them as directly related to the more radical self-mutilations observable in the savages, the psychotics, neurotics, and others. Indeed, we are no sooner conscious of an act as being definitely self-destructive than we think of such an individual as belonging to one of these categories. The fact remains, however, that all of us practice self-mutilation in the sense that we cut off parts of our body, the fingernails for example, out of deference to custom and convention, if not to deeper unconscious demands. The advantages of these conventionalized forms of self-mutilation are so obvious and so great that the original motives are difficult to trace. However, from what we have seen, on the one hand, in connection with nail-biting, and from our knowledge of the unconscious dominant law of claw and fang, on the other, we can scarcely avoid suspecting that the custom of nail-trimming has unconscious determinants related to the restraints on these tendencies demanded by civilization. One might say that the civilized practice of trimming the nails may represent not only a gesture of repudiation of those primitive tendencies which demanded their use, but also a self-protective device against yielding to the temptation of indulg-

[42] Self-mutilation and attempts at self-castration have been observed among the lower animals with direct reference to emotional conflicts. Tinklepaugh (Tinklepaugh, O. L., "The Self-Mutilation of a Male Macacus Rhesus Monkey," *Journal of Mammalogy*, 1928, Vol. IX, p. 293) at Yale describes in detail an experience with a monkey at the primate laboratory at the Institute of Psychology who showed marked antagonism toward the introduction of certain female monkeys and the substitution of one which he did not like for one he did like. He bit his feet, tore huge jagged places in his legs, tore a three-inch gash in his hip, ripped open his scrotum, lacerating and exposing one testicle and mutilating the end of his tail. For about four months following this he seemed to be in a "state comparable to the depression of some psychoses."

ing these tendencies.[43] We all know that these gestures and protective devices are sometimes ineffective.

It is in relation to the hair that conventionalized self-mutilative practices prevail most commonly among civilized peoples. The widespread practice of shaving can be seen to be a deliberate cutting off of a part of the self, i.e., a self-mutilation. Here again it is a form in which the aesthetic value for society has become much greater than the subjective value for the individual, but this need not prevent us from estimating what the unconscious subjective value really is and why the social value has become so great.

Some of the historic significances of hair-cutting make it apparent that this seemingly casual process has been associated in the past, at least, with deeper meanings.[44] Egyptain travelers, for example, did not cut their hair until the end of a journey and then shaved their heads as a thank-offering to their god. Greek youths offered their hair to the local river on reaching manhood. Achilles kept his hair uncut because his father had vowed it to the river Spercheius if his son should come home from war. Both in Arabia and Syria it was customary to cut the hair as a puberty rite. This custom was also followed at Rome where the hair was dedicated to some patron deity. Nero is said to have dedicated his first beard to Jupiter. Orestes offered hair at the tomb of his father and this seems to have been a common practice among mourners. The Roman sailors' most desperate vow was to offer their hair to the sea god. A Nazarite was commanded to let his hair grow while under a vow; afterwards he shaved his hair at the door of the tabernacle and burned the hair as a sacrifice. There was a rule prohibiting hair- and nail-cutting during a religious festival. In many of these cases it is thought the offering of hair is a substitution for the whole person.

The American Indians, like the Greeks, seemed to regard the hair as the seat of life. The scalp-lock was supposed to represent the life of the individual and it was regarded as a grave insult to touch the lock lightly. The Pawnee Indian cut the hair close except a ridge from forehead to crown which he stiffened with fat and paint and made to stand erect and curved like a horn. Other tribes decorated the

[43] There is a legend that the impurity of the serpent which caused Adam's fall was *under the nails!* (See *Hastings' Encyclopaedia of Religion and Ethics,* Scribner's, 1910.)

[44] For most of the following illustrations I am indebted to the article on hair in *Hastings' Encyclopaedia of Religion and Ethics, op. cit.*

scalp-lock with ornaments that marked achievements and honors.

Difference of rank was often shown by cutting the hair, the shorn hair being characteristic of the slave as contrasted with the long locks of the free man. Among the Franks only the kings wore their hair long.

Cutting off the hair was a punishment for adultery in India and among the ancient Teutons and for other offenses among the Assyro-Babylonians. (Compare this with the time-honored custom of cutting the hair of criminals to distinguish them from law-abiding citizens.) Peruvian women, instead of jumping into the funeral pyres of their dead husbands, cut off their hair and threw it in (a clear illustration of partial "suicide" substituted for total suicide).

That hair may represent sexual virility is apparent from the popular conception of the hairy-chested man, such themes as O'Neill's *Hairy Ape*, the story of Samson, and many others. Furthermore, the vast extent of the hairdressing business, the acknowledged importance of hair of certain color and texture to the pride of women and the satisfaction of men, with embarrassment or even shame concerning baldness, all bear witness to this.

But certain exaggerated instances with which psychiatrists are familiar have the value of bringing this out much more clearly. Tendencies which are probably inconspicuously present in all of us can be readily recognized from those unfortunate individuals in whom they become disproportionately emphasized. In what is known as *hair fetichism* for example, the most intense consciousness of pleasure is associated with this isolated part of the body. Such individuals may be content to admire or caress the hair of the beloved person, but more typically they transfer all of their desire to the hair itself and wish to possess it, which they often do by cutting it off. They get the pleasure from this act of obtaining the hair and are quite satisfied in the joy of possessing the hair detached from the person to whom one might expect the love to really belong. The police in all cities are familiar with those hairstealers or "clippers" who often surreptitiously cut hair from the heads of total strangers.[45]

A psychoanalytic colleague has reported the case of a

[45] The American Indians did essentially the same thing, of course, in scalping their conquered foes. But here the erotic element was lacking, or at least more completely disguised, in the sadistic destructive satisfactions.

man who in very early childhood had found great pleasure in braiding his mother's hair which seemed to have been one of the factors which conditioned him in an abnormal interest in hair throughout his life. Seeing a little playmate's hair cut off caused him great excitement and when he became older and began making regular trips to the barber he experienced definite sexual excitement of extreme degree each time. The average person can scarcely conceive of such a prosaic experience as having one's hair cut as affording sexual excitement or satisfaction but that is because the sexual value of hair has been so diluted and disguised by the process of civilization. Neurotics and psychotics throw aside these screens and reveal the primitive feelings to their own embarrassment but to our enlightenment.

A somewhat similar but even more striking case was studied by Dr. Robert Knight, who kindly gave me the following data. This was a young man who became sexually excited the first time he attempted to shave at about fourteen years of age and at each subsequent attempt thereafter. He would rise at 4 o'clock in the morning in order to have the bathroom to himself for two hours before his father arose at 6 o'clock and in this time he would carry out extensive rituals in connection with the removal of the beard. One of these, which was associated with severe pain, was the application of a hot depilatory substance to his face and the peeling off of the mask thus formed with the hair clinging to it. At the same time the patient began picking at the stubble with his finger nails, trying to gouge out the hairs of the beard. This led to the development of a severe acne which the patient aggravated by pinching the acne lesions to express the pus. The eruption became chronic so that at the age of twenty-one when the young man came for treatment his face was marred by an *acne indurata.*

This case is particularly interesting not only because of the sexual significance attached to shaving, but also because it shows the exploitation of a conventional form of self-mutilation in association with a definitely neurotic form (gouging out the hairs with the fingernail), both evidently carrying the same significance to this individual.

Casual reflection upon the barbershop rituals of both men and women will show us that their significance is not completely disguised even in normal people. The extreme satisfaction that many women and some men find in the varying tonsorial maneuvers, the gossipy or jovial atmosphere of the barbershop or hair-dressing parlor, the touchiness about having women in men's shops and vice versa—these and other details which will occur to the reader indicate that hair-dressing and hair-cutting still retain much of their unconscious erotic value. (This is most interesting as it pertains to cutting off the hair as opposed to merely combing it or dressing it.) Cutting off hair represents a partial renunciation of the virility and power, for example in the story of Samson and the prostitute Delilah. It is a surrender of primitive tendencies in favor of the more desexualized requirements of civilization. Someone has said that the extent of the use of the razor is an index of civilization.[46]

We know that this partial renunciation is done for the purpose of an ultimately greater fulfillment. The unshaven man may give some evidence of greater virility but he has less chance in the modern temper of winning feminine admiration. Hence for his minor sacrifices the man who shaves really makes a greater gain.

Additional confirmation is to be found in the cutting off of the Chinese men's queues when, under the influence of Sun Yat Sen, a centuries-old custom was abolished almost literally within a few months. This again would seem to indicate some wish to be accepted by civilization in return for the sacrifice of a totem or badge of virility.[47]

It was suggested to me by Dr. Leo Stone that the fact that hair and the genitals are as closely identified as these studies have shown them to be explains the reasons why the ancient and orthodox Jews required of their male members not only circumcision, on the one hand, but the abstention from barbering, on the other, i.e., the hair was retained as if to counterbalance the loss of a part of the genitals and permitted for that reason. I am not sufficiently familiar with the details of Talmudic instruction and ritual to know whether this is further supported by the external matter of the original prohibitions.

One distinguishing characteristic of those forms of self-mutilation which we have noted in normal people is that

[46] Harnik (Eugen J., "Pleasure in Disguise, the Need for Decoration and the Sense of Beauty," *Psychoanalytic Quarterly*, July, 1932, pp. 216-61) relates an Arabic Jewish traditional Biblical myth about Adam and Eve: "And when they had eaten of the tree, their hair fell off and they stood naked" (*Die Sagen der Juden*, Frankfurt, 1913, Vol. I, p. 343), which further illustrates the significance of hair as a symbol of sexuality.

[47] For a stimulating discussion of the symbolism of dress, including hair-dressing, see *The Psychology of Clothes* by J. C. Flügel, International Psychoanalytic Library, No. 18, London, Hogarth, 1930. Flügel (*op. cit.*) makes this point.

they are not usually irrevocable. Hair and nails grow again. In fact, women often use the argument when contemplating having their hair cut that if it is not becoming to them they can let it grow again. Sometimes this process of cutting and growing again is repeated over and over according to the individual's psychological pattern and the change of styles.

Conventional forms of self-mutilation also differ radically from most of the forms we have described in that they are rarely painful. The normal person is able to accept pleasure without guilt and therefore does not feel compelled to make the self-punitive personal atonements of the neurotic and psychotic persons. Finally, the very fact that these so-called "normal" self-mutilations are customary and conventional distinguishes them from other self-mutilations, most of which contain a large element of exhibitionism and usually subject the individual to derision, pity, or at least embarrassing conspicuousness.

SUMMARY

Let us now try to get together the evidence contained in these studies that points to the motivation for self-mutilation and attempt to answer some of the questions raised in the beginning.

We see that self-mutilation is to be found under widely varying circumstances and conditions, including psychosis, neurosis, religious ceremony, social convention, and occasionally as a behavior symptom in certain organic diseases. From representative examples of all of these we are able to detect certan motives in a fairly consistent pattern.

It would appear that self-mutilation represents the surrender or repudiation of the active "masculine") role, accomplished through the physical removal or injury of a part of the body. Even if there were not already abundant psychoanalytic evidence to the effect that the prototype of all self-mutilation is self-castration, there would be strong reasons for inferring this from our material, in which we frequently find self-castration to be undisguised; and in the cases in which another organ or part of the body is the object of the attack, the associations, fantasies, and comparable analogies make it clear that the substituted organ is an unconscious representative of the genital. This may be, as we have seen, either the male or female genital but has the significance of activity generally associated with the male. This sacrifice of the genital or its substitute appears to satisfy certain erotic and aggressive cravings and at the same time to gratify the need for self-punishment by a self-inflicted penalty.

The aggressive element in self-mutilation can be of both the active and passive variety. The act of self-mutilation may be directed toward an introjected object, as in the example of the man who, hating someone else, cut off his own arm, a process epitomized in the familiar expression of "cutting off one's nose to spite one's face." The passive form of aggression is even more conspicuous because it is directed toward real and present rather than fantasied or distantly removed objects; the provocative behavior of nail-biting children or of malingerers who so exasperate their friends and physicians, clearly illustrates this.

The erotic gratification achieved by the surrender of the active in favor of the passive role is partly dependent upon the innate bisexuality of everyone and the unconscious envy on the part of men of the female role. There is also a tendency, however, on the part of the erotic instinct to make the best of a bad bargain and to exploit the consequences of this rash expression of the aggressive, destructive tendency by erotization. In this sense the erotic gratification of self-mutilation is both primary and secondary.

Finally, there is the self-punishment implicit in self-mutilation, which has the curious Janus-like property of looking both forward and backward. The self-mutilation atones or propitiates by sacrifice for the aggressive acts and wishes of the past, and it also provides an anticipatory protection as if to forestall future punishment and permit further indulgences by the advance payment of a penalty. Incident to the latter, self-mutilation by the sacrifice of the aggressive organ safeguards the individual against the possibility (and therefore the consequences) of further active aggressions.

Our material does not enable us to dilate upon the nature of the aggressive fantasies from which the sense of guilt arises beyond saying that they are connected with castrating or mutilating fantasies originally directed toward the parents and siblings. We know from the work of many analysts that these are usually connected with the *Oedipus* complex and arise from the wish to kill or castrate the father and take the mother, or to kill or mutilate the mother for "faithlessly" preferring the father or a sibling.

It would appear from this summary that self-mutilation is the net result of a conflict between (1) the aggressive destructive impulses aided by the super-ego, and (2) the will to live (and love), whereby a partial or local self destruction serves the purpose of gratifying irresistible urges and at the same time averting the pre-logical but anticipated consequences thereof. The reality value of the self-mutilation varies greatly; the symbolic value is presumably much the same in all instances. To the extent that the psychological needs can be met by a symbolic self-mutilation with minimum reality consequences, as in such socialized forms as nail-trimming or hair-cutting for example, the device is a useful one; but in those individuals whose reality sense is diminished or whose conscience demands are inexorable the device is literally self-destructive.

In any circumstance, however, while apparently a form of attenuated suicide, self-mutilation is actually a compromise formation to avert total annihilation, that is to say, suicide. In this sense it represents a victory, even though sometimes a costly one, of the life-instinct over the death-instinct.

THREE / *Malingering*

Physicians use their professional energies toward the end of alleviating suffering and healing disease; they are, accordingly, utterly confounded by such paradoxical behavior as is represented by self-mutilation. Unable to detect any material advantage from the process and unacquainted with the unconscious gratifications which we have outlined in the previous chapter, they are inclined to think of such acts as *prima facie* evidence of "insanity." But where self-mutilation appears to be capitalized by the patient for obvious secondary gains, the physician's attitude changes from one of bewilderment to one of indignation. Malingering has quite evidently puzzled, irritated, and distressed clinicians for centuries.

Not all malingering is self-mutilation but if we compare self-mutilative malingering with other forms of self-mutilation we obtain some insight into its peculiar psychology. We see it as a form of self-destruction, for all the obvious and sometimes considerable secondary gains for which it is ostensibly performed.

For a long time there was not a very clear distinction in the minds of physicians between malingerers and neurotics, and perhaps there are still those who think of neurotics as deliberate fakers. To the extent that a neurotic person consciously makes use of the secondary gains of his illness, he is of course a malingerer, and to just the extent that he is conscious of this does the neurotic patient deserve to share in the opprobrium that attaches to malingering. Freud discussed this in the account of Dora, his first reported history of a case.[1] Dora made bitter reproaches against her father, charging among other things that he was malingering, in that he used tuberculosis to justify expeditions with a woman who was at the same time his nurse and his mistress. This reproach, as Freud pointed out, while true, actually rose out of her own bad conscience, and was a self-reproach not only for earlier states of ill health—aphonia, coughing, etc.—but also for more recent ones. What she hoped to gain by her immediate illness, Freud pointed out, was the detachment of her father from his mistress, something she had been able to achieve by no other method. Thus she was also malingering. "I felt quite convinced," said Freud, "that she would recover at once if only her father were to tell her that he had sacrificed Frau K for the sake of her [Dora's] health, but I added that I hoped he would not let himself be persuaded to do this, for then she would have learned what a powerful weapon she had in her hand, and she would certainly not fail on every future occasion to make use once more of her liability to ill health." (This, as is known, is precisely what neurotic families encourage certain members of the family to do.) Freud continued that those "crudest and most commonplace views" of hysterical disorders, i.e., that they could be cured by some catastrophe, are in a certain sense correct, but that they overlook psychologic distinctions between what is conscious and what is unconscious. One can say that the neurosis always contains a certain amount of malingering, i.e., a certain amount of conscious secondary gain from the illness, although in some instances this amount may be very small.

There is, however, another element in malingering which distinguishes it from every other form of self-mutilation, namely, the frank appearance of the aggressive purpose. For in exploiting or capitalizing the secondary gain of the illness the patient necessarily thwarts and deceives the

[1] Freud, *Collected Papers*, Vol. III, p. 52.

physicians and others whose interests run counter to his necessity for continuing his illness. He thus finds himself in the predicament of fighting those who seek to relieve him, and his aggressions are displaced from whatever or whoever originally provoked them onto the entirely innocent and unsuspecting physician. And because it is so unjustified and unexpected, this aggression strongly tempts or stimulates the physician to retaliate.

This becomes clear if one reads in a detached and impassive way almost any account of malingering in the medical literature. What impresses one most is the apparent irritation, hostility, even righteous indignation of the authors toward the subjects of their investigations.

In their comprehensive monograph on the subject, for example, Jones and Llewellyn[2] returned time after time to the moral obliquity of the malingerer, his knavery, his rascality, his unscrupulousness. Many pages of their book, as well as many of the articles that appear in medical literature, are devoted to the technique of distinguishing between malicious and unintentional deception in disease. The authors assume it to be self-evident that the malingerer's behavior, and therefore his intention, is morally reprehensible, and that his success in concealing its factitious origin is even more so. The moral attitudes of condemnation follow naturally from the assumption that the immediate and sole purpose of the simulation is material gain.

It would seem evident that as to the moral reprehensibility of the malingerer, the scientist has no more justification for forming an opinion than in the case of any other clinical phenomena. The medical scientist is fairly entitled to judge as to whether or not a given condition is injurious to society; he is justified, for example, in quarantining a patient with smallpox. But to decide as to the morality of the illness has never been the physician's function. He does not attempt, for example, to pass on the sinfulness of syphilis. The scientist who becomes angry with the subject of his investigations is to that extent no longer scientific.

How then can one interpret the curious attitude which may be detected in those who write on malingering, and in the way in which physicians, lawyers, and employers discuss such cases?

The first explanation lies in the widespread fallacy of assuming that conscious motives can be regarded as explana-

² Jones, A. Bassett, and Llewellyn, Llewellyn J., *Malingering*, Blakiston, 1917.

tory of human behavior. Especially is this lost sight of by medical writers who, accustomed to deal with physiologic functions over which the conscious intention has a minimum of authority, turn on rare occasion to the analysis of behavior. Behavior cannot be understood in terms of conscious intention alone; unless one considers the unconscious motives which determine an act one cannot understand the significance of the act to the actor.

Moreover, a second reason for the irritation exists. Intuitively physicians grasp one of the unconscious motives of malingering without clearly perceiving it as such; they react to it emotionally. For a man to injure himself so that he escapes responsibility or obtains money is reprehensible from the standpoint of the employer and of society at large. It is an aggression against society, although done in the form of an aggression against the self. But this is not sufficient reason for the many aroused emotions of the physician; he is only too familiar with many examples of aggression against society in the form of sickness. The shoe pinches because malingering is also an aggression against the physician himself. It is an attempt to deceive him, to perplex, perhaps to overtax and ridicule his diagnostic acumen and his therapeutic efforts. In the reported cases of malingering, one frequently perceives how the mounting concern of the ingenuous physicians, puzzled at the recurring exacerbations of the wound, gives place to suspicion, anger or a sense of triumph over having exposed the meretriciousness of the patient. Some authors even describe how the patient was reproached, sharply spoken to, summarily dismissed, or otherwise punished. It is this which clearly indicates that the physician recognizes intuitively that one of the motives of the patient was not so much the material gain as the unconscious wish to fool the physician and, coincidentally, to make a bid for punishment.[3]

One often sees the same aspect of this phenomenon clearly demonstrated in the course of psychoanalytic treatment. The patient begins to give evidence of regarding the treatment as a competitive struggle with the analyst. This may be subtle, or the patient may frankly announce it. "You have got to yield; I never will," said one of my patients,

[3] So dogged is this refusal to confess the deception that patients will go to incredible lengths in their submission to treatment. I know of the case of a man and woman who claimed to have effected a suicide pact and to be dying of self-inflicted poison. They were taken to a hospital and given heroic treatment with a powerful antidote which resulted in their deaths, and it was not until shortly before death occurred that they confessed that they had not taken poison.

clearly recognizing, even as he said it, that it was a defensive and, at the same time, aggressive gesture. Such patients are like the skeptic described by Karin Stephen[4] who, when told of the significance of slips of the tongue, declared, "One or two instances like that would never convict [convince] me."

Such a competition with the analyst takes this specific form: "You may be a wise and highly-regarded analyst, but now you have met your match. I will show you that you can't cure me." Such dreams as the following are familiar to all analysts: A baseball game is in progress. A man resembling the analyst is the pitcher, and he has achieved a remarkable record. He has struck out nearly every batter that has faced him. The dreamer goes to bat and knocks a home run (he is going to give up the analysis and go home). Or, in another and still more specific dream he steps up to the plate and knocks foul after foul so that the pitcher, in spite of his wonderful record, is unable to fan him out and is, on the other hand, worn out with the contest. In such a dream it is almost self-evident the foul balls are the unscrupulous devices for resistance used by the patient to prolong and stalemate the analysis, exhaust the patience of the analyst, and provoke his exasperation.

From this, one can hazard the assumption that the original act of malingering serves chiefly as a provocative aggression, i.e., that it is a minor self-attack designed to excite a major attack from another person. In this it corresponds to the criminality from a sense of guilt described by Freud [5] and elaborated by Alexander.[6]

CLINICAL EXAMPLES

Since malingering is usually imitative or simulated, many forms of illness or sickness can be represented, but in general there are two forms: those in which incapacity is claimed because of subjective evidence (for example, the patient insists that he feels too sick to work), and those in which the incapacity is ascribed to an evident local injury which has been self-induced. Only the latter can serve as illustration of focal self-destruction. I shall cite only a few examples.

The first is that of a woman, aged twenty-nine, whom I

[4] Stephen, K., *Psychoanalysis and Medicine: The Wish to Fall Ill*, Macmillan, 1933.
[5] Freud, S., *Collected Papers*, Vol. IV.
[6] Alexander, *The Criminal, the Judge and the Public*, Macmillan, 1930.

saw briefly, in consultation with a surgeon who was certain that she had a basal skull fracture. Her pillow was drenched with blood, and she was tossing about as if in great pain, responding to questions in a confused semi-delirious fashion. She begged constantly for morphine, which was given her. I incurred the surgeon's displeasure by recommending that he defer a craniotomy which he had considered to be immediately imperative.

After a few days' observation the nurses detected her in the act of picking the skin of the external auditory canal, which was presumably the way in which she had brought about the profuse hemorrhages which, by that time, had almost exsanguinated her. A few days later she disappeared from the hospital. A month later I was urged by a colleague in another city to come at once in consultation on a case, the description of which made it obvious that it was the same patient. Later, also, I learned from various sources that she had succeeded in persuading a competent surgeon to do a cranial decompression, and that in several cities she had collected money from insurance companies and corporations, to whom she was able to make it appear that they were in some way responsible for her self-induced injuries.

The elements of aggression, exhibitionism, and self-punishment are obvious in this case, in spite of the brief opportunity available for studying it. To say that the patient wanted money, morphine, or attention, or all three, is, to say the least, to disregard the extraordinary means which she used to obtain them. It would be accepting the face-saving rationalizations of the ego at par value, in the teeth of striking neurotic stigmas.

What was most enlightening about the case was the effect it produced on the professional men who saw her. The first effect was to create in the nurses and surgeons great interest and concern. As her shocking condition became more apparent, these emotions changed to pity and a strong wish to give her relief. When, however, the nature of her illness became known, the strongly positive feelings were exactly reversed. The surgeon was angry at the deception and was considerably put out with himself for having expended so much time and sympathy and for having been so completely taken in. Under such circumstances one may properly apply a technical device which experience has proved useful in clinical psychoanalysis. When, in spite of one's scientific training and an effort to maintain an objective attitude toward the patient's behavior symptoms, one finds oneself strongly moved emotionally in a certain direction, toward pity or anger or exasperation, it is a useful measure to ask oneself if it is not precisely this result which the patient is unconsciously attempting to produce.

A most enlightening contribution to the understanding of malingering comes from the descriptive accounts given by dermatologists of what would appear to be a rather common clinical entity: "dermatitis factitia" or "dermatitis artefacta." This is a condition in which lesions are voluntarily inflicted on the skin of the person himself, with the aid of corrosive chemicals or mechanical agents such as penknives, fire (particularly from matches), cigarettes, the finger, or some other object, perhaps most commonly with the fingernails. I exclude from consideration the cases in which there is an acknowledged compulsion to pick at the skin until the lesion has formed. This is not malingering, since it is not in any sense concealed, but rather the result of unconscious impulses which a patient cannot explain, but does not deny. What characterizes "dermatitis artefacta," as all dermatologists point out, is the persistent denial of authorship, even in the face of absolute proof.[7]

"Many of these patients," Netherton[8] writes, "are subjected to repeated and extensive surgical procedures, and may even suffer irreparable damage and mutilation. In fact many cases are on record in which an arm, finger, etc., have been unnecessarily removed with the full consent of the patient. "In three of my cases the patient submitted to repeated abdominal operations. Besides the economic loss involved in such cases, the inconvenience sustained by innocent members of the patient's family is frequently little short of tragic."

In these few words this intuitive dermatologist strikes at the psychologic factors which I regard as the most important in malingering: the wish to suffer, the wish to conceal, the wish to injure oneself and, to an even greater extent, to wish to cause other people pain, distress, and embarrassment. In other words, here are all the factors one finds in suicide: the wish to hurt oneself, the wish to be hurt, and the wish to hurt someone else.

Later we shall see how surgical operations are apparently

[7] Medical readers interested in the technical literature on this subject, which is quite large, are referred to the bibliographic references in the author's "Psychology of a Certain Type of Malingering," *Archives of Neurology and Psychiatry*, March, 1935, pp. 507-15.

[8] Netherton, E. W., "Dermatitis Artefacta, with a Report of Seven Cases," *Ohio State Medical Journal*, March, 1927, p. 215.

sought and demanded as expression of some unconscious need for self-mutilation at the hands of another person, and the observations of Netherton and others that this type of malingering was frequently associated with repeated surgical procedures foreshadows the chapter to follow. In four of the cases Netherton cited, the self-mutilation began after an uneventful appendectomy. The first case is particularly striking, since in this instance *six or more major operations were performed subsequent to the original appendectomy,* which began the self-induced ulcerations of the skin of the abdomen in the vicinity of the scar. It was as if the patient was compelled to have operations performed on her abdomen. Seven surgical incisions did not suffice; she must continue the process by making innumerable attempts to open her own abdomen by a frustrated and incomplete, but undoubtedly painful, method. Netherton's account of the case leaves little doubt as to the burden which her continued sickness caused her parents. The vicious circle established depended on the fact that by her suffering she simultaneously made the desired aggression against them, atoned for it, and justified herself in additional aggressions.

I am indebted to Dr. Joseph Klauder for the account of the following case of the same sort. The patient was a woman of thirty-five years who, for six months, had had recurrent attacks of a dermatitis. Her husband was insistent that something be done for her, and the family physician sought a consultation with a dermatologist. She presented curious band-like areas of erythema encircling her wrists like a wrist watch and below the knee like a garter. These led to the diagnosis of "dermatitis factitia." When the patient was taking a bath, her room in the hospital was searched, and a bottle of compound solution of cresol was found. Dr. Klauder accused her of producing the lesions with it, but she stoutly denied it. Later she admitted using it to wash her hands and to apply to the skin in order to prevent the skin disease, which she had been told was a streptococcic infection. This was a partial confession of the truth. Her emotional tone was normal, and she presented no neurologic abnormalities, except that her conjunctiva and hard palate were anesthetic. This and the "dermatitis artefacta" led to a diagnosis of hysteria.

Dr. Klauder discovered that her illness had become "town gossip" in the small town in which she lived. Her family physician had been obliged to issue a daily bulletin as to her progress. She was the recipient of many gifts, flowers, and cards, both at her home and after she entered the hospital. She arranged the postcards in a kind of picture-gallery exhibit about her sickroom.

It will be observed that the patient endeavored to bring about the confusion and embarrassment of the physicians, as well as to carry out the evident purpose of exciting sympathy and attention. It is particularly desirable to emphasize the absence of any monetary gain, which the industrial surgeon is apt to regard as the only motive for malingering.

The chief elements in malingering of the self-mutilative type are: the infliction of a wound on the self which results in pain and loss of tissue; exhibition of the wound to persons who react emotionally to it and give sympathy, attention and efforts to cause healing; the deception of the observer as to the origin of the wound and often distinct efforts to defeat therapeutic measures, and the obtaining of monetary or other material reward or detection, exposure, with constant humiliation, reproach and sometimes actual punishment. The cases presented show that one cannot subscribe to so naïve a view as that consciously advanced by the detected malingerer, that he was willing to gamble with his chances in the exchange of a self-inflicted wound for gain. With so much gambling spirit in the race, the infrequency of malingering would, in itself, contradict this interpretation. Again, it is well-known that the pain endured is frequently out of all proportion to the anticipated monetary gain. Furthermore, such interpretation ignores the unconscious factors which, however unfamiliar to the malingerer and the public, are now well known to medical science.

The well-known disparity between the great suffering voluntarily endured and the objective gain is to be explained on two bases: first, that the gain is only partly represented by the monetary reward, but includes also the satisfactions in exciting sympathy, attention, perplexity, and dismay, and, second, the pain is not only incident to the device used for obtaining the gains, but is psychologically demanded by the conscience as a price for indulging in them. Actions speak louder than words, and it is clear that however conscienceless the malingerer appears (or claims) to be, he unconsciously feels guilty and inflicts his own punishment. Unfortunately, there are available as yet no precise instruments with which to measure emotions, but probably there is a precise quantitative relationship, so that the externally achieved punishment is reciprocal with the amount of self-inflicted suffering. The less of one, the more there is of the other. A man who enucleates his own eye meets with less reproach and condemnation than one who burns himself with a match, even though each may do so for the same external purpose. This, to be sure, depends to a large extent on the sense of justice implicit in us, but it is precisely this in everyone and in himself that the patient takes advantage of to achieve an equilibrium of emotional forces.

SUMMARY

Malingering of the self-mutilative type may thus be described as a form of localized self-destruction which serves simultaneously as an externally directed aggression of deceit, robbery, and false appeal. The aggression is of such an inflammatory sort that it, in turn, obtains for the malingerer not only sympathy, attention, and monetary gain (at first), but, ultimately, exposure, reproach and "punishment." Both aspects of the induced treatment by the outside world are strongly tinctured with the perverted erotic satisfaction incident to masochism and exhibitionism.

From this, one may conclude that the original act of malingering of this type serves chiefly as a provocative aggression; i.e., it is a minor self-attack designed to excite a major attack (both indulgent and punitive) from other persons, the pain involved being the price demanded by the conscience for the unconscious satisfactions achieved which are both erotic and aggressive.

FOUR / *Polysurgery*

It will have occurred to the reader in reviewing the diverse forms and conditions under which self-mutilation takes place, and the regularity with which it is possible to discover aggressiveness, erotization, and self-punishment as the deeper motivation for these acts, that in some instances the practical usefulness or the social necessity of the self-mutilation must be a far more important determinant than the gratification of these unconscious trends. Regardless of the existence or non-existence of past aggressions on the part of the individual, society and material reality are so constituted that self-mutilation may sometimes be the price one pays to live, not because of his own aggressions but because of adventitious circumstances which envelop him. These may be heritage or tradition, like the savage custom of puberty rites already described. The victims of such mutilation may themselves be innocent of any aggressions whatever, the self-mutilation being performed entirely from reasons of social compliance. They may, on the other hand, be the result of empirical science. The best example of this is the surgical operation. Here is an instance in which, while we do not actually mutilate ourselves, we do submit ourselves to the surgeon and even petition him to cut something from us, *not* for unconscious reasons of aggressiveness, guiltiness, or distorted pleasure technique, but for consciously practical and justified reasons, arrived at by medical science from the experience of centuries. Indeed, to refrain from a needed surgical operation would seem more clearly to indicate self-destructive intentions than the submission to the "mutilation." This, then, would be a reductio ad absurdum; a focal self-destruction in the narrowest sense, but not self-destruction in either the psychological or in the practical sense. But, as we shall see, there are exceptions to this, exceptions which, withal, prove the rule.

When a patient submits to a surgical operation, at least two persons are concerned—the patient and the surgeon. Unconscious motives combine with conscious purposes to determine the surgeon's election to operate no less than the patient's election to submit to the operation. We generally assume that the conscious and rational motives of both are strongly predominant. For although it is obvious that surgery is a very immediate sublimation of sadistic impulses, it *is* a sublimation, and an exquisitely refined and very fruitful one which has already, in its relatively brief career, prolonged the lives and relieved the misery of millions. Of course, sublimations may break down, or they may be from the start only neurotic disguises; then the decision to operate, instead of depending upon the objective factors of infection, deformity, hemorrhage, and the like may depend upon a feeling of compulsive necessity. The ideal surgeon is neither anxious nor reluctant to operate; he is impelled only by the evaluation of reality factors. Unfortunately, careful inspection of surgical practice reveals the fact that surgeons sometimes operate for quite other reasons, such as those mentioned, i.e., a compulsion to do some cutting. Some surgeons are obsessed with the necessity for removing thyroid glands, others for removing the ovaries, still others for various surgical procedures upon the viscera. That such operations are sometimes scientifically justified there can be no doubt, but the way in which certain surgeons discover operative indications of precisely the same sort in patient after patient is so precisely comparable to repetitious neurotic behavior of other sorts that we have good reasons for suspecting that such surgeons are more neurotic than scientific.

An occasional example of frank sadism in surgeons is unfortunately not lacking. I myself have been particularly impressed with the utter inability of many surgeons, even otherwise "good" and capable surgeons, to understand or sympathize with the suffering or fear of their patients. Certainly nothing is so barbarous and so fraught with the danger of subsequent disaster to the personality as the widely prevalent custom of taking a little child into a strange white room, surrounding him with white-garbed strangers with outlandish headgears, permitting him to see queer paraphernalia, glittering knives, and often blood-splotched linen and at the height of his consternation and terror pressing an ether cone upon his face and telling him to breathe deeply and soon his tonsils will be "out." The anxiety stimulated by such horrors is probably never surpassed in the child's subsequent life and I confidently believe that in the majority of instances such terror does far more harm than the condition which the surgeon is preparing to relieve. The very indifference as to how the child must feel under such circumstances, the fact that the surgeons do not stop to think that this, which seems so familiar to them, is unfamiliar and terrifying to the child and has deleterious effects upon him—these things indicate a serious psychological obtuseness on the part of some surgeons which I relate to this neurotic impulse in the direction of sadism which partially sublimated may make a skillful technician but not necessarily a considerate surgeon.

We should not lose sight, however, of the peculiar difficulties of the surgeon's position. He is looked upon as a miracle man and is often expected to do the impossible. He must make the decision and perform the operation and at the same time take the responsibility and blame if it is unsuccessful and a good deal of reproach and complaint sometimes even when it is successful. It is no wonder that surgeons develop a certain callousness. They must have the courage to be apparently cruel when cruelty seems necessary. We cannot blame them, therefore, too much if they are occasionally, for neurotic reasons, poor judges of its necessity.

So much for the unconscious motives as they penetrate or elude their disguises and appear in the work of surgeons. It has already been mentioned, however, that it usually requires two people to enter into the performance of surgical operations, the surgeon *and* the patient; we should consider what reciprocal motives may lead some patients to co-operate with surgeons in unnecessary operations. For there is no question but that some patients are operated upon much too frequently, more frequently than the strictest medical criteria can justify. It is almost axiomatic that the more operations a patient has had the less benefit he has derived from any of them.

But are we justified in laying this at the surgeon's door? I can recall many patients with a history of having gone to one or more surgical clinics to be successively relieved of teeth, tonsils, appendix, ovaries, gall bladder, colon, prostate, and thyroid, or some combination of these. I formerly visualized them as defenseless, suffering, distracted victims, snatched at by meretricious, or at best, over-enthusiastic surgeons, who, whether for money and prestige, or from honest conviction, applied a mutilating treatment which only added a further burden to the woes of the afflicted one. This was in the days before I, at least, realized, as I think many of us have now come to do, how frequently the neurotic patient forces himself upon the surgeon, demanding the operation either verbally, or, as is more often the case, demanding it in some physiological way. We all know the facility with which the hysterical patient can produce symptoms which gratify his unconscious needs and if that need can be further gratified through a surgical manipulation, the means will not fail him to bring about a condition which even the most conscientious surgeon will be inclined to regard as indicative, if not imperative, of surgical interference.

Instances of repeated operations excite varying reactions of sympathy, suspicion, and ridicule in proportion to the transparency of the unconscious motives for the polysurgical demands. They cannot always be labeled "unnecessary" operations because such patients are very often able to make the particular operation appear to be imperative. Moreover, there is frequently no doubt about the necessity of the operations, the only question being whether the necessity is a psychological one or a physical one. Such individuals, dominated by the repetition compulsion, return again and again for more surgical mutilations. Jelliffe, for example, refers to a woman whom he saw at the age of twenty-one who had already obtained for herself twenty-eight different operations on different parts of the body. Perhaps one is therefore justified in describing this phenomenon as addiction to polysurgery.[1]

It would not be scientific to leave unrecorded the fact that however unnecessary these operations appear to be from the physiological standpoint and however much in the nature of placebos they may seem to be, they not infrequently achieve therapeutic results. Freud points out in *Beyond the Pleasure Principle* that organic disease or injury often relieves traumatic neurosis, depressions, and schizophrenia by binding the unmanageable quantities of libido stimulated by an unprepared-for stimulus.[2] He might have added that surgical operations may do so. It is the disturbing experience of every psychiatrist to have treated a psychiatric case without success only to have the patient get well promptly after an operation which the psychiatrist did not believe was necessary or even advisable; indeed, sometimes performed by a quack or an irregular surgeon because more conservative and conscientious surgeons had likewise felt it inadvisable. Jelliffe[3] reported a case in which a protracted psychoanalysis was only brought to a successful conclusion after the patient had obtained for herself a final surgical attack. It would be just as unscientific for psychoanalysts to deny the psychotherapeutic utility of surgery as for surgeons to deny the psychotherapeutic value of analysis. What we must do is to evaluate more accurately the real significance of the surgical operation which, of course, entails a consideration of the whole problem of somatic conversions.

For some time I have been particularly interested in the

[1] Of course I do not refer to or include instances of skillful two- or three-stage operations or to the frequent operations necessary in certain bone diseases and plastic surgery where the greater the skill of the surgeon, perhaps, the more attenuated and gradual the technique.

[2] See Menninger, Karl A., "The Amelioration of Mental Disease by Influenza," *Journal of the American Medical Association*, Vol. XCIV, pp. 630-34, 1930.

[3] Jelliffe, Smith Ely, "The Death Instinct in Somatic and Psychopathology," *The Psychoanalytic Review*, Vol. XX, pp. 121-32, 1933.

work of the plastic surgeons through the suggestion of one of them that his results were achieved as much psychologically as mechanically. It is very striking in studying the surgical literature that the plastic surgeons themselves recognize "a morbid neurotic craving on the part of the patient to have something done" to correct a defect which they rarely evaluate objectively. Blair and Brown,[4] for example, advise caution in the correction of slight defects to which the individual seems to attach an exaggerated importance. They mention many cases in which the operation was clinically successful but the patient remained as dissatisfied as ever, and they also mention cases in which the clinical result was not successful but it appeared to satisfy the patient surprisingly well. On the whole, one gathers from the literature that the surgical correction of facial deformities usually results in a gratifying improvement of a patient's mental condition.

The impression of clinicians, both surgeons and psychiatrists, seems to be that surgery may sometimes result in the relief of a neurosis or a psychosis but that such a result is inconstant in occurrence and apt to be transitory in its effects. All we can say at present is that we have insufficient data upon which to conclude how frequently surgical operations avert or relieve mental illness.[5]

I once had a patient with an hysterical loss of voice who had three times been temporarily cured by a major operation and who insisted that having another one was the only thing that would help her. I endeavored to dissuade her, and tried every type of psychotherapy except psychoanalysis in vain. She could find no surgeon, on this occasion, who would risk his reputation by operating for no other than a psychological reason. Since then I have had the opportunity to study several similar patients psychoanalytically. In addition, I have paid particular attention to psychiatric cases passing through our clinic in which surgical

[4] Blair, Vilray Papin, and Brown, James Barrett, "Nasal Abnormalities, Fancied and Real," *Surgery, Gynecology and Obstetrics*, 1931, Vol. LIII, pp. 797-819.

[5] Of course there are many recorded instances of mental illness being *precipitated* by surgical operations. See, for example, the following accounts: Washburne, A. C. and Carns, M. L.: "Postoperative Psychosis; Suggestions for Prevention and Treatment," *Journal of Nervous and Mental Diseases*, Nov., 1935, pp. 508-13; Lehrman, P. R., "Postoperative Neuroses," *Medical Journal and Record* (supp.), April 1, 1925, pp. 422-24; Gardner, W. E., "Postoperative Psychosis," *Kentucky Medical Journal*, Oct., 1928, pp. 537-46; Barker, P. P., "Neuropsychiatry in the Practice of Medicine," *Medical Bulletin of the Veterans' Administration*, June, 1931, pp. 571-82.

operations have entered into the previous treatment. On the basis of data obtained from these cases I have tried to formulate some conclusions as to the unconscious motives and mechanisms which lead people to the operating room, especially those who return time after time.

UNCONSCIOUS MOTIVES IN THE ELECTION OF AN OPERATION

One of the chief unconscious motives for which a surgical operation is chosen by an individual is *to avoid facing something else which he fears more* than he does surgery. Of course, this same motive of flight from the unpleasant and, on a deeper analytic basis, bribery of the conscience, also finds expression in many non-surgical illnesses. But the peculiar advantage of a surgical operation is that a second party is brought into the field and made to assume the responsibility for the evasion. As I write these lines I am reminded of the reason for this vacant hour. A patient has telephoned that she has had to have a minor operation on her ear and although she protested to him that she felt well enough to come for her analytic hour, the *surgeon* would not permit it! I knew she had dreaded the hour; the surgeon didn't know it, but she used him to escape it.

Recently a patient who had been engaged to a professional man postponed her wedding date for the fifth time. This exasperated her fiancé and he insisted that she come to us for examination. The history recited many attacks of typical anxiety hysteria with much right-sided abdominal pain. Time after time she had been examined by physicians who were in doubt as to whether or not to operate. The leucocyte count was occasionally as high as 12,000 but it must be added that the following day it would fall to normal. (Cases of pseudo-appendicitis have been reported in which even the fever was not lacking.) Finally the patient actually begged for an operation and it was performed. Her attacks of panic and pain in the lower right abdomen were relieved only, however, until the approach of the postponed wedding date. Then they all returned and again she insisted upon going to a hospital. In such a case it is quite evident that the demand for surgery is only a choice of the lesser of two evils as a way to escape a heterosexual relationship which her infantilism made it impossible for her to face. Other motives contributed but this one was conspicuous.

All psychoanalysts are familiar with the following phenomenon: A physician refers a patient for treatment of a neurosis; psychoanalysis is recommended. The patient concurs in the view that this is the most promising treatment, decides to go home, arrange his affairs, and return in sixty days to begin his analysis.

A few weeks later a letter comes from his physician stating that the patient whom he had sent us and who was planning to return for treatment had unfortunately been taken with an attack of appendicitis (or gall stones, or hyperthyroidism or hemorrhoids) and would have to have an operation. This is an almost regular prelude to the analysis of individuals of certain types. Very often after convalescing from the surgical operation they come on for analytic treatment anyway, but not always.[6]

That flight into a surgical operation is sometimes an attempted flight into health is strongly suggested by such cases as the following: A university student of twenty-three who had twice been chosen on the all-state football eleven began to feel uneasy, vaguely disturbed, incapable of grasping his lessons, and sleepless. After some months of distress he left school and demanded that his parents take him to several doctors. They could find no physical basis for his illness and told him so. Subjectively he seemed to grow worse. He demanded that his tonsils be removed. A physician thought it unnecessary. The patient insisted and it was done. Thereafter he felt distinctly better for a month or so, after which the same symptoms recurred and continued to grow worse until at his own suggestion he was brought to a psychiatric clinic; there he was found to be definitely schizophrenic.

In such a case I think it would be erroneous to assume that the operation aggravated the illness; I think we may take the patient's word for it—and that of the relatives—that it partially and temporarily relieved him. I think we may assume that it represents a frantic effort at staving off the mental dissolution by an attempted flight back to health by way of surgical sacrifices. The deeper meanings of the operation we will discuss later, but here I wish only to stress the fact that the unconscious may grasp at the surgical operation to escape mental disease as well as to escape mental treatment. I have cited this case only be-

---

[6] In one instance which I observed, the patient obtained an appendectomy in this way, just before beginning his analysis. Near the end of the analysis he developed (again) attacks of severe abdominal pain reminiscent of his old "appendicitis." They were so realistic and disabling that I feel sure it would have been regarded as a surgical problem had the appendix not been already removed.

cause it is brief. Numerous others in which not one but repeated operations were sought by the patient prior to a
complete surrender to psychotic regression have come under our observation. This is in line with the suggestions of
Dr. Harry Stack Sullivan and others that the personality
threatened with disintegration grasps frantically at various
neurotic compromises in order to avoid the catastrophe of
psychosis.

A second motive which determines the choice of surgical
operations is the *erotic* one. This is usually dependent upon
a (father) transference to a strong dynamic surgeon who
is omniscient, omnipotent, kind, and yet cruel. The in-
cisiveness, firmness, strength—one might almost say ruth-
lessness—of the surgeon, and the general mental and physical superiority common to so many surgeons cannot but be
of great influence in the unconscious choice of the neurotic
patient. To this one must add the sadistic-masochistic complex which undoubtedly strengthens the transference (positive and negative) to such surgeons for some patients. To
those who crave the love of a father and will submit even
to surgery in order to obtain it, we must add those whose
acceptance of love from the father is conditioned by masochism such that they can only accept love from a father
which is conveyed in the form of pain. It is well known that
some of the most successful surgeons have been the least
noted for the tenderness of their clinical approach.

One of my patients had a series of nasal operations
which he is now convinced were totally unnecessary except
that they enabled him to continue to be the chief object of
his father's solicitude and anxiety. "I remember to this day,"
he said, "how the blood which seeped from my nose after
the operations seemed to fill my father with loving apprehensiveness which more than paid for the pain of the
operation and was infinitely better than the beatings I had
formerly had."

In considering the motives for surgical operations, one
must distinguish, of course, between the primary or para-
nosic gain and the secondary or epinosic gain. In the latter
category we must class the amenities associated with the
hospital experiences, particularly the period of rest subsequent to and sometimes preceding the operation, the solicitousness of friends and relatives, the physical attentions of
nurses, and the reassurances of the physician. I am not sure,
however, that some of these factors may not enter deeply
into the primary motivation for the surgical operation, par-

267

ticularly in connection with the wish to receive attention, sympathy, and even pity as the only acceptable form of love and the wish to be mothered in one's suffering by solicitous father- and mother-surrogates. The repeated attention of physicians (including surgeons) is often solicited chiefly, it would appear, in order to obtain for the patient the satisfaction of being pitied for his suffering in lieu of being loved in a more normal way which a sense of guilt prohibits him from asking or accepting.

In its extreme form, this motive is closely allied to exhibitionism. In a case more fully cited below the exhibitionistic value of the operation was clearly apparent in the confessed fantasies of the patient at the time of the operation —his perineum and genitalia being exposed to the surgeon and nurses to his great satisfaction. An over-reaction to this is, of course, frequently seen during the preoperative hours in many patients in the form of shame and apprehensiveness in regard to the exposure. Convincing evidence as to the widespread existence of such hidden satisfactions is to be derived from observing the frequency with which operative experiences are discussed socially and the success of numerous capitalizations of this—for example, in Irvin Cobb's *Speaking of Operations* and in one of Eddie Cantor's pictures (and the corresponding play) *The Nervous Wreck*, in which two men vie with each other in displaying their surgical scars. Psychoanalytically we must regard this as the wish to prove that one is castrated, i.e., has submitted, endured, survived—and the price paid. "See," they unconsciously say, "I am harmless—you need not (or may not) kill me." This is the exact reverse of the conscious content of my patient's fantasy (above) and of the thought content in overt exhibitionism, namely, "See, I am not castrated, I really am a man."

That operations are sought by both men and women to fulfill an ungratified infantile *wish for a child* would also seem to be strongly indicated,[7] particularly where the

[7] Nearly thirty years ago this was recognized by Freud as indicated in his account of the treatment of "Dora." An attack of "appendicitis" had occurred shortly after the death of an aunt of whom she had been very fond; there had been high fever and pain in the abdomen. Dora had previously read about appendicitis (and perhaps also about sexual matters) in the encyclopaedia because a cousin of hers had been reported ill with it and Dora developed just the symptoms she read about. They occurred, furthermore, *just nine months* after an episode in which she received improper proposals from a man whom, it afterwards developed, she secretly hoped might marry her and for whose real children (by his real wife) Dora cared and whom she loved tenderly. It was clear, Freud pointed out, that the appendicitis was the realization of a child-birth fantasy.

Caesarian section theory of birth has been well developed in the patient as a child, and in those girls who have been reared with strong parental repression with reference to the burning question of where babies come from.[8] I once had as a patient an adolescent girl with conversion hysteria whose symptoms were that many times a day she would try in vain to move her bowels, insisting that there was something in her abdomen. Most of the time, of course, she would be unsuccessful. Then she would demand an operation. Shortly before this she had had an erotic experience with a boy, had seen a calf born and thought it came through the cow's rectum, and had known that a relative went to the hospital to have a baby. Obviously her theory was that she had a baby within her which must come out through the rectum or else through the abdomen and if she couldn't expel the fecal child she must have a Caesarian operation.

A more thoroughly studied case was that of a woman who had been operated on thirteen times in thirteen years. From the earliest recollections of her childhood she had wanted babies above all things. She had wanted to have "a dozen" children. As a girl, she too had confidently believed that babies were born through operations. Therefore, she concluded that the man most likely to give her a lot of children would be a surgeon, and she married a surgeon. And then, year after year, she developed symptoms which made it necessary to have a surgeon perform operations, most of them abdominal sections. "I see now," she said, "that I was simply trying over and over again to have a baby according to the conceptions that I had held as a child."

Another satisfaction determining the unconscious wish for the surgical operation is related to the *wish to be castrated* (more specifically, the wish to be relieved of anxiety by submitting to castration). In such a wish we recall from the first chapter of this section that we found there were at least two elements: (1) the need for punishment, and (2) the erotic capitalization of it (masochism, exhibitionism, etc.). In submitting to castration a man pays the penalty for his crimes (guilty fantasies and wishes) and at the same time he is converted into a de-masculinized or feminine person so as to be more capable of receiving love, i.e., to approach more nearly the enviable position of the female

[8] See Horney, Karen, "The Denial of the Vagina," *International Journal of Psychoanalysis*, 1933, Vol. XIV, pp. 57-70.

who is loved and sought after not for what she does, but for what she is, for her "own sake."

In psychotic cases, as we have seen (Chapter Two), self-castration is very common; for them to request that someone perform the castration upon them is even more common. In the neuroses self-castration is usually achieved only indirectly, for example, by impotence, financial failure, marital disaster, venereal disease. If actual castration is contemplated, it is usually requested in a more or less subtly disguised way, in the sense of sterilization (vasectomy) or the removal of a testicle rather than of penis amputation.[9]

How this procedure, which is surprisingly frequent, may be rationalized by the *physician* may be discovered by reference to the current medical literature; in the *Index Medicus* castration is even recently reported as a form of therapy for neuroses, perversions, sexual crimes, sexual abnormalities, mental diseases, and even tuberculosis.

How it may be rationalized by the *patient* appears clearly in the following cases, for the first one of which I am indebted to Dr. Henry Shaw of New York. A rather brilliant young scientist was determined to accomplish certain researches, in pursuit of which he felt his erotic impulses to be a most unwelcome distraction. He ascribed his inability to complete his studies to the intrusion of these carnal desires. He had concluded that if his testicles could be removed his sexual desires would abate and he could then accomplish his great purpose. Accordingly he consulted various surgeons petitioning them to perform this operation. One of them agreed to do so if it were recommended by a psychiatrist. But no psychiatrist could be found who would approve of such focal self-destruction. Finally, however, a surgeon was found who performed the operation, to the patient's great satisfaction; he recounted afterwards his great feeling of relief when he was actually shown his own severed testicles. The sequel to the story is rather astonishing; his virility was, curiously enough, not lost, in spite of the operation, but he came to regret exceedingly his emasculation when, having divorced his first wife, he desired to remarry and have children.[10]

[9] Dr. R. M. Brian, formerly of the Topeka State Hospital, told me of a patient who first persuaded surgeons to remove the epididymis on one side, later that on the other side; later still one of the testicles and finally the other testicle. This seems to me to be a clear acting out in an undisguised form of the polysurgical addiction with the wish to be castrated as a dominant motive.

[10] The literature contains several references to similar instances: this one, for example, reported in 1843 (Chowne, "Castration for Neuralgia,"

Another illustration will perhaps further illustrate this theme, the emasculation being more subtly accomplished. A young minister, who was about to get married and then go to the jungles as a missionary, went to a surgeon and requested that he be sterilized. His rationalization for this operation was that he wished to protect his wife against the danger of pregnancy in the jungle. The surgeon finally acceded to his request, explaining that he would do a vaso-ligation which would not in any way interfere with the patient's sexual desire or potency. To this assurance the patient replied that he didn't care if it did abolish his sexual urge; in fact he had hoped it would, as sex was fraught with too many dangers for him to care about it, and he would just as soon be done with it. At the same time, vaso-ligation, removal of the uvula and a submucous resection on the nose were performed (i.e., various symbolic castrations).

When the patient was under analysis for a "nervous breakdown" ten years later, the analytic material showed very clearly that not only the flight into the ministry and thence into the jungles but also the marriage itself were all undertaken in a compulsive way to defend himself against strong guilt feelings connected with masturbation and strong perverse and incestuous sexual drives. In other words, the patient preferred castration to an anticipated and feared greater punishment (death) which might be visited upon him if he were to attempt to gratify his sexual urges. This patient had for years regarded sex as "messy," "dirty," "filthy" and was, as a matter of fact, impotent most of the time. This attitude toward sex was very well brought out in a dream in which the patient saw himself standing on the edge of a cliff which was undermined in such a way as to make his position a precarious one. While standing there he realized he had something in his hand. He looked down at it and discovered it to be a rotten sausage. In disgust he flung it away into the chasm.

London Lancet, Vol. I, 131). A man of 33 ascribed "great bodily weakness and great mental depression" to "an irritable testicle." He went to various physicians for treatment, demanding operations. One testicle was removed in 1841; he improved, then developed similar symptoms in connection with the other testicle, which he finally succeeded in having removed in 1842. Again he improved for a short time, only to be oppressed again by the same pains, weaknesses, exhaustion, and depression of which he had complained in the first place.

The author remarks that it appears extremely probable that the man's symptoms prior to the operation, as well as afterwards, were the result of "a morbid state of mind." It says nothing of the state of mind of the surgeons whom he inveigled into performing the operations.

What we have to remember, then, is that the wish to be castrated is not, as one might assume, identical with self-destruction. In one sense it is precisely the antithesis of this, as we saw in the study of self-mutilation; it is the wish to *avoid* death. It is offering up the genitals as a sacrifice in place of the total personality. This is why the patient threatened with a psychosis seeks an operation and why a boy worried about masturbation goes to a urologist for circumcision. Just as the circumcision is a sacrificial offering tendered in lieu of the entire genitals which the boy fears will be taken from him because he has masturbated, so offering the penis is a sacrifice to propitiate the self-destructive tendencies. It is a substitution of local self-destruction for total self-destruction. It is a last-minute attempt at saving the whole by sacrificing a part. This explains why it can be so successfully erotized masochistically: it is actually an opportunity for the triumph of life-instincts, not of the death-instinct.[11]

Recently a psychotic patient who came in an acute anxiety state reproached his father in these terms: "My father sinned against me because he did not have me circumcised. If he had done so I would not have masturbated. If I had not masturbated then I would not have lost everything." He evidently considered his illness as a result of and a punishment for his masturbation and his reproach against his father can be interpreted to mean, I believe, "If my father had imposed upon me the smaller sacrifice [of circumcision, i.e., symbolic castration], I would not have had to pay this greater price of psychosis, confinement, disgrace, etc." It is only a more advanced degree of the same thing when the psychotic patient says, "Cut off my penis, castrate me, or I cannot live. You (or I) will kill me!" [12]

The sense of guilt seems to have a curious propensity in some cases for dissatisfaction, i.e., for demanding the sacrifice successively of one organ after another, and one frequently feels that there is a frantic effort on the part of the unconscious to find enough sacrifices to prevent the threatened destruction of the whole. All parts of the body may become genitalized, one after the other, so that some

[11] For an excellent psychoanalytic study of the service of an operation in filling the subjective needs of an individual, see Oberndorf, C. P., "Submucous Resection as a Castration Symbol," *International Journal of Psychoanalysis*, 1929, Vol. X, pp. 228-41.

[12] Another patient undergoing psychoanalysis made almost the same reproach against his father who was a doctor. Because this surgical punishment (circumcision) was denied, the patient proceeded to secure other types of punishment for himself, including several operations.

individuals literally permit themselves to be cut in pieces. It is these compulsory repetitious symbolic castrations that I think are so well represented in the phenomenon of polysurgical addiction.

Every physician sees many instances of the successive genitalizations of the different parts of the body so that the surgical necessity seems to migrate like the metastatic focus in a septicemia. But as a rule, such cases do not come to the analysts because an equilibrium is apparently established so that the unconscious punitive demands are held in abeyance or perhaps because such patients are directed toward psychotherapeutic treatment only after it is too late, if at all.

Another illustration of this seeking for punishment via surgery will bring out more clearly the reasons for the sense of guilt, and thus lead to the consideration of another, thus far ignored, motive in surgical punishment seeking.

This man[13] was a Jewish merchant who came to Dr Updegraff, a plastic surgeon, to have his nose recon-structed, not because of its Semitic character, but because it had been injured in childhood so that it gave him, as he thought, a pugilistic appearance which he believed in-timidated his business associates and was in direct antith-esis to his peaceful proclivities. The operation was suc-cessful and he was much relieved of feelings of anxiety and "isolation" from which he had previously suffered. This patient was very cooperative in an effort to analyze these factors and told me spontaneously that just preceding the operation he had had a dream that it had already been performed and had rendered his nose larger and uglier so that he was "hideously deformed." I told him that this led me to suspect that he had felt guilty about something and had been seeking punishment. This he denied. A little later, however, in retracing the events leading up to the operation he revealed the fact that he had recently broken off a love-affair with a Jewish girl to begin one with a Gen-tile girl. He was quite sure, he said, that he had no discom-fort from the fact that he was a Jew, that he had no fealty to Jewish traditions. Immediately after his affair with the Gentile girl, however (which itself may have been an effort on his part to deny or relinquish his Jewishness), he felt a great depression and it was in this depression that he

---

[13] See Menninger, K. A., and Updegraff, H. L., "Some Psychoanalytic Aspects of Plastic Surgery," *American Journal of Surgery*, Sept., 1934, pp. 554-58.

consulted the surgeon in regard to an operation. One could see how, in spite of his conscious feelings to the contrary, he had a strong conflict on the Jew-Gentile question, and felt very guilty about his behavior with respect to the two girls, realizing that he had been very *aggressive* toward both of them, and had sought and obtained punishment, whereupon he felt relieved.

This aggressiveness which is tied up closely with the need for punishment was particularly apparent in a man whose many surgical operations had not been successful in preventing the recurrence of severe depressions, for which he came for analysis. When thwarted by his mother in favor of a preferred brother this patient had developed a great hostility toward her and turned his affections entirely to a very strict father. From the dominance of this father he in turn took flight during adolescence into an orgy of rebelliousness, doing all the things that a normal boy would do, and a little more, in the way of masturbation, stealing, and heterosexual experiments. He did these things in a very aggressive spirit, directed primarily toward the parents, especially the father. The most aggressive and disturbing feature of his behavior, however, was his passive indifference to his father's wishes—he simply would not do anything useful.

After a very free life of this sort for several years he one night awoke from a terrible dream feeling that everything had gone to pieces. He feared he had contracted gonorrhea and that his penis had shriveled up; he had nervous chills, sweating, persistent palpitation, extrasystoles, and an overwhelming fear of sudden death. His parents took him immediately to leading heart specialists and internists in several of the larger cities. They were told that their son was seriously ill, that his systolic blood pressure was 240 and that he must therefore cut out alcohol, tobacco, women, work, exercise, and lead a life of simplicity and deprivation. This he did only, however, to develop a depression.

The depression disappeared with the institution of a series of surgical operations. First his appendix was taken out; the following year a goiter was to have been operated upon but x-ray treatments were substituted as a compromise; shortly thereafter his tonsils and adenoids were removed; two years later his hemorrhoids. Meanwhile his depression had been held in abeyance but it reappeared with the cessation of the surgery.

Such a case also illustrates how the punishment repeats the crime, i.e., the persistent wish to be castrated (operated upon) carries with it the erotic value of an enforced feminine submission which, in turn, is used for the more subtle purposes of passive aggression. In the case just cited the resignations and self-punishments of the patient were really more costly and more distressing to the father than the rebellion for which they were the atonement, and, moreover, they served the purpose of obtaining for the patient the love from his father which he so much craved, plus opportunities for exhibitionism and passive submission to the surgeon—all of them secondary exploitations of the punitive situation.

In pursuance of this theme (the aggressive element in polysurgery) I should like to refer again to the woman of thirteen operations in thirteen years. One of her dreams revealed clearly how the aggressions and self-punishment were fused in the surgical operations. She dreamed that a vicious cow (herself) with a knife in its mouth was charging everyone who came near; in particular it pursued one person (the analyst) over a porch upon which the person had taken refuge. Time after time it made lunges over this porch (the daily analytic sessions; my office is over a porch). Finally "it fell back on to the knife [surgical operation] and was killed."

She immediately interpreted the cow as herself and the knife as her sharp tongue. At the time of the dream she had been bitterly attacking the analyst for many days and had herself remarked that this was precisely the way in which she had brought about her marital unhappiness. Her husband, whom she often attacked in a similar fashion, she had fallen in love with immediately after the death of her brother whom she had most tenderly nursed but toward whom as a boy she had had the most intense envy. When she met her future husband, the doctor, she had the feeling that he "could see right through me." This was her conscious thought; the unconscious elaboration was—"He knows that beneath my sisterly affection for my brother was the great envy and hate and he will punish me—not too severely, not with death as I deserve, but with a painful submission, and a giving up of something."

And so, even before the wedding, she persuaded her future husband to operate upon her for a "chronic appendix." Thereafter followed a removal of her tonsils, then another abdominal operation, and then—after the birth of a child—

a gynecological repair, which was repeated three years later. So operation followed operation.

The analytic material indicated that, without a doubt, the driving motivation of her childhood had been envy directed toward her brothers, chiefly toward the one who had died. These operations performed by this kindly but inexorable impersonation of her conscience served to punish her for this envy and hate. To "fall back on the knife" is clearly a reference to her polysurgical addiction, the fate that befell her because of her own surgical (castrative) wishes toward men. Each operation was for her a forestalling of the death sentence unconsciously feared. For this reason she welcomed the operations and often commented on how little she suffered, how quickly she recovered, and how well she always felt afterwards. Actual partial self-destruction was elected in order to avoid an anticipated (but usually only fantasied) [14] total destruction.

SELF-PERFORMED OPERATIONS

We have assumed throughout this chapter that the submission to surgical operations was a form of (justified or unjustified) self-mutilation *by proxy*. Sometimes, however, both the operator and the patient are the same individual; the surgeon operates upon himself! A few years ago the newspapers were full of the account of a well-known surgeon, who at the age of fifty-nine gave himself a local anesthetic and removed his own appendix and at the age of seventy operated for an hour and three-quarters upon the repair of his own abdominal hernia. Two days after this operation this doctor walked to the operating room and assisted a colleague in a major operation. [15] Another American surgeon, Alden, also performed an appendectomy upon himself. [16]

Doctors Frost and Guy [17] of Chicago have collected a number of instances of self-performed operations, including one of their own observation. They remind us of the self-performed operations of a Rumanian surgeon (Fzaicou) and a French surgeon, Regnauld (both performed

[14] I say *usually* because *some* of this patient's operations were by any clinical standards surgically imperative.

[15] *Time,* January 18, 1932, p. 19.

[16] Gille, M., "Autosurgery," *Echo med. du Nord,* 1933, Vol. XXXVII, p. 45.

[17] Frost, John G., and Guy, Chester C., "Self-Performed Operations with the Report of a Unique Case," *Journal of the American Medical Association,* May 16, 1936, p. 1708.

herniotomies), and of the Parisian surgeon, Reclus,[18] who operated upon a lesion on a finger of his right hand, using a local anesthetic and later reported not only his own case but that of two other surgeons who had operated upon themselves. Still another surgeon removed a stone from his own bladder, using a mirror.[19] My associate, Dr. Byron Shifflet, told me of a classmate of his in the University of Pennsylvania Medical School who successfully enucleated his own tonsils in 1931.

Unfortunately none of these cases could be studied psychoanalytically but the very fact that these operations were self-performed when custom and convenience are so strongly set in the other direction—when so many good surgeons were available whose judgment and skill were almost certainly more objective than the self-operating operator—all this suggests very strongly that unconscious motives chiefly determined them.

SUMMARY

In addition to the objective scientific reasons for surgery and those adventitious motives which may occasionally influence some surgeons, there appear to be, on the patient's side, unconsciously determined purposes of focal self-destruction, obtained (usually) by proxy, i.e., at the hands of a second party. The aggressive, punitive, and erotic roots discoverable in other forms of self-destruction are again apparent here, in various combinations. The aggressive element is relatively inconspicuous; the punitive element less so. The erotization of the suffering, of the transference relation to the surgeon, of the passive feminine role, and of the fantasies of obtaining a child or a male genital by magic are apt to be strongly developed.

Thus, we may conclude that the compulsion to submit to surgical operations is a form of localized or focal self-destruction, a partial suicide, allied in its motivation to major suicide and differing from it in this respect: that the pervading dominance of the death-instinct is absent, death

[18] Reclus, P., "Local Anesthesia and Surgeons Who Operate on Themselves," *La Presse médicale*, Paris, Aug. 17, 1912.

[19] Several women because of intolerable pain have performed Caesarian section upon themselves and delivered their own children. (See Cowley, Thomas, *London Medical Journal*, 1785, Vol. VI, p. 366.) These women were, of course, not surgeons, nor was the patient whom Frost and Guy (*op. cit.*) report; he was a mentally-defective janitor who had seen many animals and human beings operated upon and felt unable to afford surgical fees so he successfully operated upon himself once, but was less successful the second time.

of the total organism thus being averted by the sacrifice of a part for the whole. It differs from both suicide and self-mutilation in that the responsibility for the act is partially shifted to a second party, and also in that opportunities for erotization and for reality advantage are utilized to a far greater extent.

FIVE / *Purposive Accidents*

Further evidence as to the motives and devices of focal self-destruction accrues from the study of certain "accidents" which upon analysis prove to have been unconsciously purposive. The paradox of a *purposive accident* is more difficult for the scientific-minded person to accept than for the layman who in everyday speech frequently refers sardonically to an act as done "accidentally on purpose."

Indeed, it is probably upon the basis of an intuitive recognition of this paradox that superstitious fears have arisen with respect to certain "accidents," e.g., spilling salt, breaking mirrors, losing wedding rings, etc. These have become conventionalized and hence no longer capable of specific interpretation although they are sometimes taken seriously. The philosopher Zeno is said to have fallen down and broken his thumb at the age of ninety-eight, and to have been so impressed by the significance of this "accident" that he committed suicide (from which we might guess the unconscious meaning of the accidental fall and injury).

We must exclude from this category any conscious deception, i.e., *pretended* accidents. But quite aside from this there exists the phenomenon of *apparent* (i.e., consciously) absent intention in acts which gratify deeper hidden purposes. I recall that I was once seated at a formal dinner by a woman for whom I had some dislike, which, however, I resolved to blanket completely so as not to spoil the conviviality of the party. I believe I succeeded quite well until an unfortunate piece of clever clumsiness on my part resulted in upsetting a glass of water over her gown into her lap. My dismay was the greater because I knew that she knew that "accidents [to quote from a recent insurance advertisement] don't happen; they are caused."

In many of these accidents the damage is inflicted not upon someone else but upon one's own self. The body then suffers damage as a result of circumstances which appear to be entirely fortuitious but which in certain illuminating instances can be shown to fulfill so specifically the unconscious tendencies of the victim that we are compelled to believe either that they represent the capitalization of some opportunity for self-destruction by the death-instinct or else were in some obscure way brought about for this very purpose.

Such cases have been reported frequently. In one of his earliest case histories, Freud [1] cites an example of this. Herr K., a former lover of the patient, Dora, and latterly the object of her accusations and hostilities, came one day face to face with her on a street where there was much traffic. Confronted with her who had caused him so much pain, mortification, and disappointment, "as though in bewilderment and in his abstraction, he . . . allowed himself to be knocked down by a car." Freud comments in this paper of thirty years ago that this is "an interesting contribution to the problem of indirect attempt at suicide." [2]

[1] Freud, *Collected Papers, op. cit.*, Vol. III, p. 145.

[2] *Ibid.* Additional illustrations Freud gives in his *Psychopathology of Everyday Life* (London, Benn, 1914, pp. 198-209 and p. 216). The following is a striking example. A young married woman gave an exhibition of dancing one evening for an intimate circle of relatives. Her jealous husband was greatly annoyed, and reproached her by saying that she had behaved like a prostitute. After the incident she spent a restless night and the next morning decided to go driving. She chose the horses herself, refusing one team and demanding another. She refused vehemently to allow her sister's baby with its nurse to accompany her. During the drive she was very nervous and warned the coachman that the horses were getting skittish and finally when the animals "really produced a momentary difficulty she jumped from the carriage in fright and broke her leg, while those remaining in the carriage were uninjured." As Freud points out, the accident prevented her from dancing for a long time.

Abraham, also, in his *Selected Papers on Psychoanalysis* (London, Hogarth, 1927, pp. 58-62) cites numerous examples. One of these describes a girl who from childhood had an exceedingly strong affection for her brother. She grew to womanhood measuring every man by the standard of her brother, and had an unhappy love affair which left her depressed. Shortly after this she twice got into serious danger through her own carelessness on a climbing party, much to the wonderment of her friends who knew her to be a good climber, not likely to fall twice in safe and easy places. It appeared later that at this time she was in a hospital where she was accustomed to go for walks about the grounds; there was a ditch being dug in the garden which she used to cross by a plank bridge, although she could quite easily have jumped over it. At that time her beloved brother was to be married and this was much on her mind. On the day before his wedding, as she was out walking she

The significant and differential thing about purposive accidents is that the ego refuses to accept the responsibility for the self-destruction.[3] In some instances it can be seen how determined the ego is to make this evasion. This is sometimes ascribed by insurance companies and their attorneys to the wish to obtain double indemnity for the beneficiaries, but there must be more than this philanthropic motive back of it, even when it is conscious, and here I repeat that it is only *unconscious* purpose that I now have in mind.

If one thinks of his own occasional hazardous blunders in street navigation, he is apt to ascribe them (if not to carelessness) to impulsiveness, absorption in other lines of thought, distraction, etc. But, after all, if one permits himself to so far relinquish interest in his own personal safety in favor of contemplating the stock market or the purchase of a new dress, one is certainly betraying self-destructive indifference to reality. And, as for impulsiveness, a volume could be written about the disastrous consequences of this symptom. It has ruined many a business, many a marriage, and many a life. The tragedy of Romeo and Juliet is, of course, a dramatic exposition of the way impulsiveness combines with hate to produce self-destruction. Romeo's impulsiveness lost him his sweetheart just before he met Juliet in the same mood. His subsequent impulsiveness first resulted in the death of his best friend (he started to intervene in the duel and did so in such a way as to allow his friend to be stabbed) and then, in the avenging of this death, his own exile. Finally, had he not been so impulsive in jumping to conclusions after he observed Juliet in the tomb and so precipitous in resolving upon suicide, neither his suicide nor Juliet's would have been necessary.

Someone might ask if such impulsiveness, granted that it be a symptom of imperfect psychological organization, is

sprang over the ditch instead of crossing by the bridge as usual, and did it so clumsily that she sprained her ankle. "Later on these self-injuries occurred so frequently that even the attendant began to suspect that there was something intentional in them. In these minor accidents her unconscious was obviously expressing the intention to commit suicide."

[3] The way in which the individual may be obliged to carry out the dictates of his super-ego through the utilization of "accident" is graphically illustrated in the following news item:

THREE WISHES

"In Detroit, Mich., Mrs. John Kulcznski said to John Kulcznski: 'I wish you'd go out and have an accident.' He was run over, lost part of a foot. Then Mrs. John Kulcznski said to John Kulcznski: 'I wish you'd lose the other foot.' He did. To stop Mrs. John Kulcznski from wishing a third wish, John Kulcznski is seeking a divorce."—*Time*, March 26, 1934.

for that reason alone necessarily self-destructive in its purpose. We can only answer this by saying that experience shows that it is frequently self-destructive in its consequences; as to its origins, we have no right to speak with too much generality or definiteness. However, in numerous individual subjects the consequences of their impulsiveness has brought them into such serious straits that they sought psychiatric treatment. We do know that the impulsiveness arises from an ill-controlled, partially disguised aggressiveness. This is almost transparently so in certain individuals who rush at their tasks or opportunities as if to sweep everything before them and, as they themselves put it, "to tear into it," only in the end to abandon the task prematurely or to make a botch of it in some way. They often appear to have the best of intentions but friends come to regard these as inconsequential bluffings. In love-relationships viewed both from the psychological and the physical standpoint such prematurity is often extremely disappointing to both parties and its unconscious aggressive intent often suspected.

To turn from these clinical observations and theories to the matter of traffic accidents which have justifiably concerned all of those interested in public welfare in recent years, we now have statistical verification for the theory that certain individuals are more likely to have accidents than the average person. In a study of the street car motormen made in Cleveland, Ohio, by the Policy Holders Service Bureau of the Metropolitan Life Insurance Company, it was found that thirty percent of the motormen on a certain division of the railway had forty-four per cent of all of the accidents. The National Safety Council has discovered this same propensity for accidents among automobile drivers. The people with four accidents were about fourteen times as numerous as they should have been on the basis of the theory that bad luck might be only pure chance, while people with seven accidents each during the time of the study were nine thousand times commoner than the laws of chance would require. Furthermore, those persons who had numerous accidents showed a pronounced tendency to repeat the same type of accident. "Chance plays but a small part in accidents" concludes this study by J. S. Baker,[4] engineer of the public safety division of the National Safety Council.

[4] Baker, J. S., "Do Traffic Accidents Happen by Chance?" *National Safety News*, Sept., 1929.

Automobile accidents often occur under circumstances which are suspiciously indicative of at least unconscious intent.[5] We sometimes say of a man who drives his car recklessly that "he must want to kill himself." Sometimes in the course of psychoanalytic treatment the evidence for a particular instance of this becomes convincingly great.

Patients frequently confess to conscious fantasies of "accidentally" driving their cars off cliffs or into trees in such a way as to make their death appear to have been accidental. Such an episode occurs, for example, in Michael Arlen's play, *The Green Hat*. One can only conjecture how frequently fatal accidents are brought about through some more or less conscious suicidal intention.

That they are sometimes determined by unconscious suicidal impulses is suggested, for example, in a press clipping[6] describing an automobile accident in which the driver did not fall asleep but a companion beside him did. This companion awoke suddenly while they were traveling between 35 and 40 miles per hour, wrenched the wheel from the driver's hands and whirled it around so that the car upset in the middle of the road killing the driver. The companion later explained that he had had a vivid dream in which he thought the automobile was heading straight for a telephone pole. In great anxiety he had seized the wheel (so he dreamed) and turned it away from the threatening pole. Psychoanalytic experience with fantasies of saving someone would lead us to believe that this dream must be taken into conjunction with the symbolic significance of the telephone pole, the car, driving, etc., suggesting a near-the-surface fear of homosexual attraction to the driver with a consequent impulse to escape from this situation and at the same time punish himself (and exterminate the driver).

What is the difference between fatal accidents of this sort and accidents in which only a part of the body is destroyed? Here again we may assume some failure of full participation of the death instinct and suspect that it has been bought off. In this it would correspond with other forms of focal suicide which we have been studying.

[5] In the following double tragedy, for example, one can well imagine how the grief and a vicarious sense of guilt for the act of their son was related to the self-destructive accident of the parents, almost at the same spot. "A life for a life."

"At S——, N.Y., near where their son, B——'s car killed two in an automobile accident, Mr. and Mrs. X. Y. Z. were killed in their own car." (*Time*, Nov. 10, 1930.)

[6] *Boston Globe*, Sept. 5, 1932.

Such speculations are supported by the more dependable evidence of psychoanalytic case material. One patient, for example, had the following experience: She had talked for several weeks about the expense of the analysis, of how stingy her husband was, and how he would not allow her to complete the analysis, of how small and mean he was about money matters, and of how mercenary the analyst was because he insisted on a definite business arrangement in regard to the fee. It became clear that she felt very guilty about her own grasping tendencies which she refused to admit, and for this reason could not bear to accept money from her husband, toward whom she was very aggressive. She preferred to take money from the analyst and contrived to do so in the following way: She came to the analytic session one day and announced that she had managed to secure a loan from a friend which would enable her to continue the analysis without being dependent on her husband's generosity, but that she would be obliged to reduce the fee she was paying by almost half, provided this was satisfactory to the analyst. As the hour was almost at an end when she made this announcement, the analyst merely said that she herself should analyze this suggestion.

After leaving, the patient drove to her home, some distance away, in her own car. On the way she ran into another car and both automobiles were badly wrecked. Her dreams, associations, and other minor accidents which she sustained at this time showed plainly that she felt very guilty for cutting down the fee paid the analyst (taking money from the analyst) and that her sharp sense of guilt and her subsequent desire for punishment led her to drive in such a way as to have brought about the wreck. She freely confessed that it had been her fault, although she was ordinarily an excellent driver. It seemed also to serve as sufficient punishment to permit her to continue the financial arrangement without any conscious pangs of conscience.

Not only automobile drivers but pedestrians as well often show by their actions that they are dominated by a strong wish to destroy themselves.[7] "PEDESTRIANS KILL SELVES WITH

[7] The following example cited by Alexander (*Psychoanalysis of the Total Personality*, p. 30) is a case in point:

"This very intelligent man suffered in middle life from a severe depression which developed out of an unsuccessful struggle for existence. He came from a well-to-do socially eminent family but married into a different social stratum. After this alliance his father and family refused to have anything more to do with him. His unsuccessful struggle for existence through many years terminated (on account of neurotically-determined inhibitions) in a total psychic collapse. I advised him to begin an analysis

CARELESSNESS," reads a newspaper advertisement of May 14, 1936, used in a campaign against traffic accidents. "Nearly 7,000 persons in the United States last year *jay-walked their way to death* [italics mine]. *They couldn't wait* until they reached the intersection and the respective safety of traffic officers or signal lights. And so, by the thousands, they jaywalked their 'last mile' to eternity. . . . They crossed in the middle of the block, crossed at the intersection against the signal, played in the streets, or walked in the roadway—all in direct contravention to common sense if not to the law."

According to the National Safety Council, the statistics are actually worse than this. "Approximately 340,000 times every year pedestrians using the streets and highways of the United States find themselves 'walking into trouble.' That is the number of injuries annually which result from motor vehicle-pedestrian collisions." Over 16,000 of these proved fatal.[8]

We are sure that *some* of these 16,000 deaths were the fault of the victim and my endeavor is to show that frequently this cannot be explained away by such a word as "carelessness." After all, to be careless with one's own life is in itself a symptom and from my point of view a symptom directly related to the self-destructive impulse. What

---

with a colleague, because I had personal relations with him and his family, and was well acquainted with his previous history. He found decision difficult. One evening when the final decison about the analysis was to have been made, he wanted to visit me, in order to talk over once more the pros and cons. But he did not arrive, because he was run over by an auto in the neighborhood of my home. He was taken to a hospital suffering from many severe injuries. It was only the following day that I heard of the accident. When I discovered him in the third-class division of the hospital he was bandaged up like a mummy. He could not move and all one could see of his face were his eyes, shining with a euphoric light. He was in good spirits, free from the oppressive melancholy of recent days. The contrast between his physical condition and his mental state was particularly striking. The first words with which he greeted me were, 'Now I have paid for everything, now I will at last tell my father what I think of him.' He wanted to dictate a determined letter to his father immediately demanding his share of his mother's estate. He was full of plans and was thinking of starting a new life.

"The economic relationships are very obvious in this case. He desired to replace the analysis by a different form of treatment, by automobile accident, in order to free himself of the pressure of his sense of guilt. Instead of recognizing these feelings of guilt, he lives them out."

[8] Sidney J. Williams, director of the Public Safety Division of the National Safety Council, from whom I obtained these statistics (see *Accident Facts*, Chicago, 1936), writes me that the statement in regard to the 7,000 people quoted above should not be attributed to the National Safety Council. He does not feel that we know enough about accidents yet to use statistics in such a way as to imply blame or responsibility and, of course, he is entirely justified in this.

else can the statistician mean by "in contravention to common sense" (see above) than that such behavior is contrary to the natural instinct to preserve one's life?

For an example of a different type of purposive accident I am indebted to Dr. G. Leonard Harrington, a psychoanalyst of Kansas City. A twenty-year-old girl suffered from fears so great that she had been unable to attend school since the age of ten. During the analysis she mentioned one day the desire to exhibit herself nude and shortly afterwards the thought occurred to her that she would like to *cut off* her pubic hair. Then she confessed that the day before this she had used her finger to masturbate. The analyst recalled that upon that same day she had reported having "accidentally" *cut her finger* with a razor blade. Here, then, were two sets of two associated events of precisely the same sort—a forbidden sexual act followed by a cutting.

In another case, a patient, who was prone to act out his aggressions and hatreds in a dramatic way on various members of the community, had given himself justifiable cause for the notion that he might have acquired gonorrhea. He had done so by a sexual attack on one whom he identified with his own brother toward whom he had homosexual feelings and also great hate. He felt very guilty on account of this episode and proceeded to punish himself in many ways (aside from the gonorrhea). He became very depressed and penalized himself severely in the matter of pleasures; he spent an unnecessarily large amount of money on doctors, restricted his diet, and with the idea that he might infect someone refrained for a time from going to see any of his friends. Besides this, he had many fantasies of self-punishment. He learned of the seriousness of gonorrheal infection of the eye and tortured himself for several days with the notion that he might get some pus in his eye and go blind. For this reason he left off all reading which he greatly enjoyed. He washed his eyes and guarded them with scrupulous care and with a constant anxiety that he could not prevent their being injured.

One evening as he sat brooding he noticed that the door of his room did not close easily. He seized a razor blade and without procuring anything to stand on attempted to scratch and shave the door in such a way that it would close more easily. In so doing he managed "accidentally" to scratch a splinter of wood or hardened paint into his upturned eye, painfully injuring it.

Of course this immediately gave him occasion for more solicitousness about his eye, more visits to the doctor, more appeals for sympathy, and more justification for aggression. He himself recognized all this and described it as a purposive accident. It is another clear example of self-mutilation equivalent to self-castration since we know that attacks upon the eyes, as well as fears concerning them, are directly related to castration anxiety.

While accidents reported in the daily press are exceedingly unsatisfactory material from which to draw scientific conclusions, one cannot avoid seeing certain implications in the following circumstance: *In one year* I was able to collect without the aid of a clipping bureau five instances of the same remarkable phenomenon. A man plans a trap for another unknown man, usually a thief or burglar. He sets the trap to protect his home property, forgets that he has done so, returns after an interval, goes into the place he has so carefully protected and is himself killed or wounded. I submit the clippings.

DIES IN HIS OWN BURGLARY TRAP
TURKEY GROWER WHO RIGGED UP SHOTGUN
IN CORRAL DOORWAY FORGETS

Compton, Calif., Dec. 8 (AP)—After repeated thefts of his turkeys by night prowlers, E. M. M., 59, rigged up a shotgun in the doorway of his corral with a string to pull the trigger so the weapon would be discharged at the opening of the door.

Sunday morning M. hastened out to feed the fowls and forgot the trap. The gun charge struck him in the stomach and he died in a hospital.

—*Topeka State Journal,* December 7, 1931.

DIES IN HIS OWN THIEF TRAP
DR. B. H. B., NATURE WRITER,
KILLED WHEN HE OPENS DOOR

Doylestown, Pa., June 1 (AP)—Dr. B. H. B., nature writer, was found dead tonight in his home in the artists' colony at Centre Bridge, near here, a victim of one of his own burglar traps.

Dr. B. evidently had been dead since Friday. A gunshot wound had blown away part of the right side of his chest. He was killed when he opened the door of a closet in which a shotgun had been rigged as a burglar trap.

—*Topeka Daily Capital,* June 2, 1931.

TRAP

At Midland Beach, Staten Island, N.Y., Capt. Peter L., 63, of the Barge *Landlive,* rigged a double barreled shotgun, pointing toward the front door of his bungalow, a string stretched from its trigger to the doorknob. Then he closed the bungalow, went a-voyaging in the *Landlive*. When he returned, he went to have a look at his bungalow. Forgetful, he went in by the front door, got his own leg blown off.

—*Time*, Jan. 1, 1931.

WALKS INTO HIS OWN THIEF TRAP

Davenport, Ia., Dec. 21 (AP)—A. F., 71 years old, was getting tired of visits from chicken thieves. He arranged a gun inside his barn with a contrivance that would discharge it if the door was opened. He forgot about it and opened the door himself. He was wounded in the leg.

—*Detroit Free Press*, Dec. 21, 1931.

The following additional instance was sent to me:

MAN IS SHOT BY OWN BURGLAR TRAP

A burglar trap that really works is kept on guard in the —— and —— tire shop here. So well does it work that C. L., a member of the firm, is in the hospital for treatment of a wound in his hip which was inflicted this morning when the trap got into action as he was opening the shop for business. Upon opening the door, Mr. L. is reported to have forgotten to turn off the switch attached to the trap, containing a .45-caliber pistol. As he turned on the light switch the pistol was discharged.

—*Owensboro Messenger*, May 14, 1933.

The following example is similar to the burglar trap cases in that the man accidentally made himself the victim of his avowed enemy:

"In Chicago, Veteran Blacksmith P. R. boasted on his 63rd birthday that automobiles would never put him out of business. Blacksmith R. shod his last horse, closed his shop, stepped from the curb, was hit by an automobile, died."

—*Time*, Nov. 9, 1931.

Such illustrations afford strong circumstantial evidence as to the unconscious intention and necessity for such individuals to kill themselves on account of their unconscious wishes toward someone else, under the guise of an accident.[9] From psychoanalytic studies we know that such an

---

[9] Theodor Reik (*The Unknown Murderer, op. cit.,* p. 74) points out that the criminal often betrays himself or actually brings about his own self-punishment by a purposive accident, a point which has also been emphasized by Alexander. From several examples given by Wulffen (*Kriminal-Psychologie*), Reik quotes the case of Franz Gal, who heard that his neighbor Varga had sold his oxen for 900 kronen. He waited till Varga and his wife had left the house, then he stole the money. Their little girl of six was alone at home and Gal determined to do away with

unknown marauder usually represents a particular person in the unconscious fantasies of the person who prepares the trap.

I recently examined a man convicted of murder in which this special meaning of an unknown man (the victim of the murder) was vividly illustrated. The murder had been committed under the following circumstances: The "patient" (prisoner) and two companions were driving across country and had left their car at a garage for some repairs. They walked down the street late at night and saw a man asleep in an automobile parked by a curb. Without any provocation, without even seeing the face of the man whom he shot, the young man raised his gun and killed the sleeper. He plead guilty and was sentenced to life imprisonment. The murder occurred several years ago, but to this day the murderer can offer no explanation whatsoever for his act. A study of his life, however, disclosed that to him (although he was quite unaware of this) the person killed represented the man who had married the patient's beloved older sister. Of course, such identifications of "an unknown man" are well known but it is rare that the neurotic compulsion can go to such criminal extent without either some rationalization, some consciousness of the identifications, or else a psychosis. In this instance, however, the stranger was unconsciously identified with the stranger who had intruded upon the young man's happy love-life with his sister.

Press reports must be relied upon, also, for evidence concerning unconsciously purposive accidental suicides for the obvious reason that such cases, if they are successful, are no longer amenable to clinical study. Sometimes they seem quite obvious. One can have little doubt, for example, from such an account as the following that the fatal accident was in part a self-inflicted consequence of terrific rage:

WHOOPEE

In the Bronx, N.Y., Rose McM., 14, was given 25¢, told that she might go to a cinema. Overjoyed, she danced about, shrilled Whoopee! Her somnolent father, Thomas McM., bade her be still. Again she crowed. Savage, wrathful, Thomas McM.

the unwelcome witness. He tied a rope to a beam in the ceiling, made a noose, and asked the child to put her head into it. She asked him to show her how to do it, so he climbed a chair and showed her. Suddenly the chair slipped from under him and he was caught in the noose. The frightened child ran out of the house. When the parents returned the man was dead. This [says Reik] is an instance of a faulty act appearing as an accident, of suicide disguised as clumsiness.

sprang up, tripped, fell headlong into a china closet, cut his throat, fractured his skull, died.

—Time, Feb. 9, 1931.

One should read in connection with such an episode a more familiar one in which the suicidal reaction to rage was intentional. For example the following:

CHILD LAUGHS: DAD OF 11 KILLS SELF

J. G., 52, of ——, near ——, shot and killed himself yesterday after a series of petty annoyances. He had a job as a stationary engineer, and earned a fair living for himself and family of eleven children. Yesterday was his day off and he was busy making minor repairs about the house. On a trip for plumbing materials he damaged his car slightly—and then found the supplies defective. One of the children laughed and this seemed to irritate him.

—Chicago Herald Examiner, Nov. 26, 1930.

It is not sufficient to indicate that these accidents serve an unconscious purpose. It is essential to know exactly what purpose and this we are able only to *infer* from the newspaper accounts, whereas in the psychoanalytically studied cases we are able to see precisely how the accident serves to punish the individual for guilty acts or wishes. In those cases which are not fatal, however, this punishment serves not only as the price of atonement but as a permission for further indulgences in the same guilty acts or fantasies. This is quite clear in one case cited above. The guilty act stimulates the conscience to demand of the ego a price. In some instances this price is a (self-inflicted) death penalty. In other instances, however, it seems to be less severe and yet, curiously enough, to be an overpayment. This can only be accounted for in terms of psychological economy if we assume that the local self-mutilation is in some way or other a ransom and protects the ego against the imposition of the death penalty. This offering of a part for the whole, not alone for past atonement but for future protection, is as well known in American politics and racketeering as in the old Jewish religious rituals of sacrifice. The proprietor of an illegitimate business pays "hush money" or "protection" to the police in his district who, in order to retain this graft, pay a portion of it to the officials higher up, and so on. Occasionally, however, this entire system breaks down; for example, if the proprietor refuses to pay the price. In such a case the external forces of law and order are invoked and the illegitimate business is snuffed out

One can see this same principle of periodic payment for the continued indulgence in forbidden erotic or aggressive tendencies in many neurotic patients, and melancholia is often forestalled or deferred by various obsessive and compulsive techniques. Particularly is this principle discernible in those patients described as "neurotic characters." (See Part II, Chapter Four.) In such individuals the aggressions, as we saw, are apt to be acts rather than fantasies and are quite well known to those intimate with the patient. One might suspect the same mechanisms in the lives of certain individuals who seem to fall victims to successive disasters with an uncanny, sometimes almost incredible, regularity.

The following example of such a case was summarized in *Time* (March 19, 1934). This man, states the report, had been struck by lightning three times; he had been buried alive in a coal mine; he had been blown through the air by a cannon, suffering the loss of an arm and an eye; and had been buried alive under two tons of clay. "Next he fell thirty feet off a cliff, still later he was thrown by a horse and dragged through a barb wire fence. Then he fell from a speeding bob sled fracturing his skull. At eighty he recovered from double pneumonia. At eighty-one he was downed by a paralytic stroke. At eighty-two he was run over by a horse and wagon. At eighty-three he was run over by an automobile." The same year he slipped on the ice and fractured his hip!

We can hardly expect to have the opportunity for the psychoanalytic investigation of an eighty-three-year-old man with such an array of accidents, but in the light of cases we have studied and of the principles we are able to derive from them we can infer something of the unconscious mental content of a personality that is forced into repeated contests with death but is able each time to emerge victorious, though at the cost of suffering.

One of our former patients had had twenty-four major disasters in his life including, for example, the accidental poisoning of his own child and three successive automobile accidents at the same spot in which each time his car was entirely demolished. He wrecked successively eleven automobiles. It was possible to discover that his guilt arose in part from terrific unconscious wishes to kill certain members of his family.

For this consistent *addiction to accidental self-destruction* no very good term exists to my knowledge but newspaper men have rather aptly christened such victims of "fate" "hard-luck champions." Everyone knows such individuals— persons who seem impelled to get themselves into trouble, not as the result of complications of their own behavior as in the case of the neurotic characters discussed above, but as the result of some conflicts with reality which seem to be fortuitous.[10] Their lives are but a series of misadventures, of blows of Fate,[11] of untoward accidents. It would be difficult to say how many of such characters unconsciously elect the stony path through life which they seem obliged to travel but the suspicion lurks in one that in some persons this is actually a case of unconscious choice.

Examples of this phenomenon are better obtainable from the daily press than from clinical practice because these persons usually do not regard themselves as in any way responsible for their misfortunes, and hence not proper psychiatric subjects. A few typical examples culled from the papers follow:

PETER AGAIN FOOLS FATE

5-YEAR-OLD HARD-LUCK CHAMPION SURVIVES ANOTHER ACCIDENT

Blackburn, Eng., Aug. 30 (AP)—P. L., 5, has survived another accident.

He was taken to a hospital tonight after being kicked in the face by a horse. Earlier in his short life he had been run over by a horse and later by a bicycle. Then he fell out of a bedroom window and dislocated his shoulder. Recently he climbed out on the roof of a mill and waved his cap to a horrified crowd until he slipped and fell. He caught on a ledge, however, and was rescued.

Last night he fell for the second time in his career into a deep canal and was almost drowned.

—*Topeka Daily Capital*, Aug. 30, 1929.

Another example:

Sioux Falls, S.D., Nov. 20.—E. P. L., Sioux Falls traveling man, has the right to claim the melancholy title of world's champion accident victim. It began when he was 11 days old. He fell from his cradle and broke his left arm.

At the age of four he fell off a horse and broke his right arm.

---

[10] The newspapers use the term "hard-luck champion" for both types.
[11] Dr. Helene Deutsch has described the "Neurosis of Fate" in the *Revue Française de Psychanalyse*, Vol. IV, No. 3 (abstracted in the *Psychoanalytic Review*, July, 1935, pp. 315-16, No. 3), but with a somewhat different emphasis.

Then, at six, while trying to drive a stake with a hatchet, he cut his left foot to the bone. A year later a bull gored him so badly he was nearly killed, one arm, four ribs, a collar bone and both legs being broken.

Then he had a few years of immunity. In his early 'teens he joined a circus. One of his tasks was to dive over three elephants into a net. Once he fell while doing this and broke his much fractured left leg again.

His prize accident came in 1906 while he was a brakeman on a freight train. Running along the top of a moving train, he stepped on a rotten footboard and fell to the track. Thirty-seven cars passed over him, but none hurt him until the caboose came along, when his clothing caught in the wheels and he was dragged for three miles. His left arm was cut off, nine toes were severed, his skull was fractured, and his left side was crushed. But he lived.

It was 1925 before another serious accident occurred. Then, riding in a passenger coach, he tripped in the aisle and broke a vertebra in his spine, getting temporary paralysis. Recovering, he went for an auto ride. The auto went over a 45-foot bank into a river and he was nearly drowned.

This year he again tripped in a Pullman aisle, wrenching his spine and spraining both ankles. Then he got scarlet fever and spent six weeks in the hospital. During his convalescence he got inflammatory rheumatism and did not walk for 19 weeks.

This was followed by the explosion of a gas stove in a tent in a tourist camp. L. was enveloped in flames, and only prompt attention by friends saved him from being burned to death.

Despite his many accidents he is cheerful.

"You have to taste the bitter part of life to enjoy the sweet," he says.

—*Topeka Daily Capital,* Nov. 21, 1927.

These occasional instances of repetitious accidents are interesting from the standpoint of our theory. Although they probably occur more frequently than we realize, such extreme instances as have been illustrated cannot but be regarded as exceptional and in a sense freakish.

But all accidents have in times past been regarded much in the same light, i.e., as "just accidents," unfortunate, occasional, freakish, but except in a few instances not very important. Such an attitude is now being vigorously combated by numerous organizations and individuals for whom the fact that 100,000 people or more are killed in the United States every year in accidents is only one of many startling testimonials as to the unjustifiability of such a casual attitude toward them. The National Safety Council computes the economic cost of accidental deaths, injuries, and motor vehicle damage to be approximately three and a half billion dollars a year. It would surprise many people to know that more men die daily in accidents than from any single disease except heart disease, and that accidents rank third among the causes of deaths to all persons in the United States. From the ages of three to twenty accidents kill more persons than any disease, and from the time he is three years old until he is forty a man is more likely to die of an accident than in any other way.

Every five minutes someone is killed in the United States in an accident and while one is being killed in an accident a hundred others are being injured. It is somewhat startling to think that while you have been reading these pages several people have been killed and several hundred others injured in our country alone.

Such statistics can only call our attention to the seriousness of the problem. Numerous plans are underway for reducing accident hazards in industry, traffic, agricultural life, and in the home. But all of these plans and the work of most of the agencies interested in the problem, it seems to me, fail to take into sufficient consideration the self-destructive element lurking unseen behind many "accidents."

SUMMARY

In conclusion, it may be said that while some of the most dramatic illustrations of purposive accidents and of habitual victimization by "fate" are to be found in news journals, accurate and definite understanding of them awaits more retailed data. From psychiatrically studied cases of this type, however, it is possible to make certain of the existence of the same motives familiar to us in other forms of self-destruction whether extreme (suicide) or partial (self-mutilations, compulsive submission to surgery, malingering). These motives include the elements of aggression, punition, and propitiation, with death as the occasional but exceptional outcome. The latter observation leads us to suspect that the principle of sacrifice is operative here so that in a sense the individual submits himself to the possibility or certainty of accidents in which he has at least a chance of escape rather than face a destruction which he fears even though it may threaten only in his conscience and imagination. In this way a partial neutralization of the destructive impulses is achieved. Meanwhile, practical interest in the very important problem of accidental death and injury is increasing, but thus far without benefit of research into this fundamental aspect of the matter.

SIX / *Impotence and Frigidity*

One of the results of the scientific exploration of the unconscious mental life was the recognition of something which no child, no savage, no animal, and no simple, honest natural man needs to be told—namely, the importance to the individual of his genital organs and his sexual life. It seems strange now that for Freud to have pointed out this obvious fact and the way in which civilization tended to obscure and deny it hypocritically, should have called forth upon him such a torrent of abuse from all quarters, abuse which only branded its authors as ignorant, hypocritical, or neurotic. Nevertheless, it is still possible to discover traces of this formerly prevalent prudery.

Take, for example, the general attitude toward the functional impairment, functional *destruction*, of genitality, i.e., sexual impotence and sexual frigidity. So widespread are these affections in some degree or other as to be regarded by some authorities as almost universal among "civilized" peoples, an inevitable sacrifice to the advance of civilization.[1] In the face of this, it is an eloquent testimony to the persistence of the Victorian (and earlier) hypocrisy that even in scientific circles this subject is still taboo. To write or speak of it is almost to label oneself a charlatan or a sensationalist. A leading standard textbook of medicine, for example, refers to impotence in only three places and to frigidity nowhere; references to the impairment of walking, on the other hand, occupy in the same book more than a *full page of the index!*

The bookstores are flooded of late with well-meant and well constructed treatises on sex and many of them are

[1] See Freud, *Collected Papers, op. cit.,* Vol. IV, *Contributions to the Psychology of Love,* pp. 192-235; and *Civilization and Its Discontents,* Cape and Smith, 1930, p. 76.

quite explicit about those serious and widespread afflictions, gonorrhea and syphilis. Impotence and frigidity are far more prevalent and, from the patient's point of view, more serious.

Impotence as a transitory symptom is an almost universal experience—although it is often denied. Habitual impotence, partial or complete, is much more frequent than is generally known or assumed, even by physicians. Some men are constantly humiliated or depressed about it, while others accept it philosophically as something inexplicable but irremediable. Some actually do not realize their own condition. Many men who believe themselves to be potent and who perform the sexual act in a mechanically correct way, often to the complete satisfaction of their wives, obtain from it only a minimum of pleasure; this absence of pleasure is an unrecognized form of impotence. Another manifestation of this same kind of psychic impotence is a feeling of regret and loss after the completion of the act. I recall one patient, for example, who, having insisted upon the intercourse would, upon its completion, reproach his wife bitterly for having permitted him to perform it, declaring that now he would be nervous and exhausted all day, might catch cold, and might be weakened mentally. Still another form of impotence, frequently not recognized as such, consists in a prematurity of orgasm.

It may not be self-evident that frigidity in women is identical, psychologically, with impotence in men. Certainly in the popular mind they are not the same; impotence is assumed to be exceptional and frigidity to be frequent but less serious. Numerous statistical investigations as to the frequency of frigidity in women have been made, but no one thinks of making such an inquiry among men. This is partly due to the more subtle forms which male impotence so often takes, but even more, I think, to the tacit approval of sexual repression in women. There are actually people of both sexes who do not know that conscious sexual feeling is ever experienced by women.

A total disinterest in genital sexuality, a tolerance of intercourse "for my husband's sake," a complete lack of feeling, either painful or pleasurable, characterize a very large number of women, if clinical experience and statistical inquiries are to be given any reliance. Women so afflicted frequently show some intellectual interest in sex, may even read books on the subject, but as a rule, like their male counterparts, do not consult physicians, do not discuss it with friends or neighbors. The whole subject is a closed book, to be mentioned as little as possible.

In sharp contrast to the preceding group in this respect are those women who have faint or inconstant feelings of pleasure connected with intercourse and even—at long intervals—an occasional orgasm. These women are, as a rule, genuinely concerned over their affliction and make energetic efforts to become normal. They read books on the subject in great numbers; they consult friends, neighbors, doctors, and quacks; they try all sorts of experiments. I recall a man and wife who had been so distressed over the wife's frigidity that they had even tried the experiment of having a friend of the husband cohabit with the wife to see if this might "make a difference." Probably many instances of marital unfaithfulness in women depend in part upon this motive.

These conditions—both in men and in women—have been interpreted in many ways. Occasionally (rarely) structural, "organic" changes have been found and causality ascribed to them; operations without number and (in my opinion) without rationale have been performed; glandular theories have been evolved and appropriate treatments devised to fit these theories, and all of these have—occasionally—had therapeutic success. But so have hypnotism and snake-oil; it is trite but necessary to add that occasional therapeutic success proves nothing.

All these theories of structural and chemical etiology are correct, but they are not true. They are *part* of the truth; but they ignore the psychological factor. Physical factors (structural changes) do contribute to the pathology; chemical factors (glandular misfunctioning) do contribute also; but psychological factors also contribute, and (in my opinion)—*in this particular affliction*— are more accessible to view, more amenable to change, and more responsive to therapy, in the average case, than the physical and chemical factors. For this reason I have selected this syndrome with which to begin an exposition of the role of the psyche in somatic afflictions to be taken up more fully in the next section.

We can consider such functional impairment as an inhibition, a negative symptom as it were, and, in a sense, a loss or *destruction* of normal activity, normal pleasure. It is the functional equivalent of actual self-castration, the motives for which were discussed heretofore, in that the genitals, while not sacrificed in substance are treated as if non-existent. And just as self-castration is the prototype of all self-mutilation, so impotence is the prototype of all functional inhibitions. In this sense it might be said to constitute the original pattern and exemplification of hysteria. The characteristic feature of hysteria is this surrendering of a function in lieu of surrender of the organ itself.

When we speak of a symptom as hysterical in its origin, what we mean is that it has arisen through modifications in form or function of an organ to satisfy certain unconscious purposes and intentions of the personality. We know that all functions of the organism strive to carry out the wishes, the instinctive cravings, of the individual in the face of a hostile or indifferent environment. The physiologists have demonstrated that when danger threatens and we wish to fight, the body automatically prepares itself. Blood rushes *from* the skin and *to* the muscles, glycogen is mobilized in large quantities, adrenalin and prothrombin are poured out to expedite physiological defense. All of this is accomplished automatically by the body to make possible the fulfillment of pugnacious wishes, wishes which may be scarcely conscious.

These defense reactions may involve more complex units. For example, a soldier in the trenches is "shell-shocked." Paralyzed with fright, his legs conveniently refuse to carry him into the field of greater danger. These extended defense reactions are not discriminatory and not so automatically self-regulating as the older and simpler ones, and so such a man's legs also refuse to carry him anywhere else, even to a place of greater safety. Thus we recognize that such defenses, although carrying out the purposes of one wish, violate other wishes of the personality—and hence we call them symptoms. Symptoms are, in a sense, always destructive and when they arise in this way they may be fairly described as products of self-destructive combinations. This is true, even though the determining "wish" or impulse leading to the conflict and the symptom is self-preservative. The soldier sacrifices (for a time) the use of his legs in order to save (as he thinks) his life. Self-preservation wins, but at the cost of a minor (at least a lesser) self-destruction.

The fact that the conflict is unconscious is intrinsic in the explanation. A *conscious* wish can be dealt with rationally—either gratified or denied and the solution accepted. But unconscious wishes (including fears from which we wish to escape) are dealt with in unconscious automatic ways, often exceedingly irrational and unpropitious for the personality, by symptoms and inhibitions. Back of these is always an unconscious wish and a conflict.

Impotence and frigidity may be regarded as strictly comparable with an hysterical paralysis of the leg from shellshock. We must ask ourselves what in the normal act of reproduction can assume for so many people the terror and danger of a battlefield, so much so as to induce the voluntary surrender ("self-destruction") of the power and pleasure of the act? What great and irrational fear can be harbored in the unconscious to make necessary this automatic defense reaction in the face of such powerful conscious wishes to the contrary? We must expect great difficulty in ascertaining this because the functions of the sexual organs excite the highest degree of pride and shame; they are, therefore, veiled most obscurely.

The practicing physician's first thought would be what some of his women patients have told him. "I want very much to let myself go," one says, "but I'm so afraid of pregnancy." Or perhaps she says because she is so afraid of being hurt by her husband. Men patients also complain that they cannot be potent with their wives for fear they may hurt them and are too much afraid of venereal disease to be potent with anyone else.

But we must not take these *conscious* fears too literally. Of course, they may be partly justified by reality, but only partly so. There are ways of circumventing pain, there are ways of avoiding venereal disease, there are ways of precluding pregnancy. We know from experience that such conscious fears are only "alibis." Beneath them are unconscious fears of great power, fears arising from various sources. We have seen evidence of them before in the analysis of martyrdom, polysurgery, and self-mutilation, but now we shall study them genetically in a special situation, a situation we regard as psychologically fundamental.

THE FEAR OF PUNISHMENT

One of the most powerful determinants of unconscious fear is the expectation of punishment. In normal adults a distinction is made between things which society really does punish and acts for which one expects punishment only because of a childhood misapprehension. For many people sex is still a kind of evil doing, hence punishable.

A man married to a woman who unconsciously represents

to him a new edition of the mother who successfully inhibited his sexual activities during boyhood, could not possibly overcome this fear sufficiently to permit his body to act out his instinctive desires. The Hindu who sits on one foot for twenty years because he believes it to be his religious duty, could not possibly leap to his feet and begin to run, even if he were threatened by a fire or coaxed by a great reward.

One is unconsciously dominated by childhood attitudes throughout life. In the normal person, the unfortunate misunderstandings of childhood are corrected by later experience but it implies no weakness of intelligence that some persons cannot overcome them. The reactions of conscience are determined in early life and change but little as a result of experience. Accordingly, with or without the presence of conscious fears and quite independent of them, there exists in the unconscious of many people a compelling fear of punishment which is excited to great activity at the very moment when the ego believes itself threatened with an alluring temptation of a nature once associated with punitive pain, and the prohibition of this pleasure is, at the same time, a punishment in itself.

All manner of devices are utilized by the unconscious to circumvent this fear and to permit the forbidden sexual indulgences to be psychologically acceptable. For example, I recall a woman who could not enjoy intercourse with her husband because during the act a picture of her father with a stern, disapproving expression on his face would always appear before her. This woman and her husband had themselves discovered that if her husband would first strike her as if in anger she could then enjoy sexual intercourse normally. It is quite clear, I think, that this woman had the feeling so many children do that punishment squares everything, and one punishment will do as well (or better) than another. Therefore she could dispel this frowning face of her father by carrying out the punishment which she felt she deserved for indulging in an act of sex which he disapproved.

Precisely the same thing holds true of men. Indeed it is this need for punishment which explains the favorable results sometimes obtained by painful treatment administered to the genital organs by urologists and gynecologists, in spite of the fact that rarely, if ever, is either impotence or frigidity dependent upon structural pathology, endocrinopathic and neurologic cases excepted.

How is this fear of punishment to be related to the wish for punishment with which we have met so frequently heretofore? I shall repeat what was said above: *hysteria,* of which impotence and frigidity are typical, indeed prototypical, is definable as a condition in which the function of an organ is surrendered or modified—the purpose being the forestalling of anticipated injury to or removal of that organ. Put into more familiar terms, the hysterical organ invites (wishes for) punishment of a lesser order to avoid punishment of a greater order.

THE AGGRESSIVE COMPONENT

Back of such expectation of punishment may lie only these childhood misconceptions and false associations. But clinical experience has shown that these are apt to be fused with less innocent elements. A common fear back of impotence and frigidity—sometimes conscious, more often unconscious —and common to both men and women, is the fear of injury to or being injured by the sexual partner. Such fears betray sadistic phantasies. We know that back of much that passes for love there is deep unconscious hatred, hatred that denies the erotic satisfaction one consciously seeks and at the same time, by means of this very self-denial, expresses the aggression—the hatred, rejection, contempt for the partner. This is particularly clear in the condition known as *ejaculatio praecox* where the man actually soils the woman, in addition to thwarting her, like an angry baby who wets his nurse.[2]

But why should a man hate a woman whom he thinks he loves? There are three common reasons for this:

One of the commonest bases for unconscious hate is the wish for revenge. This may be revenge for something that has recently happened or something that has happened long ago at the hands of an entirely different person. Many people go through life trying to take out on someone feelings that were generated within them as children. One recalls that Don Juan, the world's great cad, was deserted by his mother in early childhood; he spent his entire life treating other women in exactly the way that his mother treated him, first making them love him and then leaving them.

[2] This condition was studied and the psychological factors analyzed in a masterful article by Abraham (Abraham, Karl, *Selected Papers on Psychoanalysis,* English translation by Bryan and Strachey, London, Hogarth, 1927, pp. 280-98).

A male patient, a very successful man, was under psycho analytic treatment on account of periodic depressions. In the course of treatment it developed that he manifested a certain kind of impotence with his wife. His erotic overtures were accompanied by tenderness and love which would greatly arouse his wife, whereupon he would either lose all interest or suffer *ejaculatio praecox*. In his analysis it became quite clear that the purpose of this was to thwart his wife, and in this it was indeed very successful. Intuitively she perceived the hostile nature of this abortive treatment and would become hysterically nervous and so distressed that she would cry and strike him with her fists. This would cause him to be remorseful and depressed. As a child this man had been raised in a family presided over by a very capable, energetic mother who was much more interested in her clubs and social activities than in her children. The patient had been the first-born and was probably unplanned for because he interrupted a project which his mother had gotten under way and to which she devoted herself for a number of years after his birth, leaving him largely in the hands of a governess. During his analysis he remembered with great emotion how bitterly he had resented his mother's frequent desertion of him which even as a child he had protested against by fierce crying and what were called temper tantrums. When he was punished for these he only grew more resentful. He was thwarted by his mother and the wish to thwart her in return he had carried throughout his life.

Another reason for unconscious hate, especially on the part of women, is a wish not so much to get revenge for themselves as to avenge their mothers. They think as children that their mothers are suffering at the hands of their fathers and when they learn something of sexual intercourse they interpret it as a violent act of cruelty. Of course many women actually favor this impression on the part of their daughters, setting them against their own fathers and warning them that all men are to be feared. Such mothers think they are safeguarding their daughters, but we know they are also revenging themselves on their husbands. For these various reasons the daughter grows up determined to pay back this old grudge against the male. She masks this spirit of vengeance with love but sooner or later her husband feels the consequences.

A third reason for hate is envy. Unconsciously men envy women and women envy men to an extent far beyond

301

ordinary recognition. This we have seen and discussed repeatedly in preceding chapters. To play the normal passive feminine role seems to some women a kind of humiliation which they cannot bear. In the presence of the hate dictated by such envy a woman cannot be other than frigid. Some men, on the other hand, often begrudge women not only their protected status and their social privileges, but (more fundamentally) their ability to bear children. This unconscious rejection of their biological role by men may be compensated for by their developing some other type of creativeness, but in other instances it betrays itself in direct but disguised manifestations of hate and envy of women on this basis.

I have in mind a patient, a successful, popular and apparently very normal man who underwent a long treatment at the hands of several competent physicians on account of one symptom, namely, the development of terrific anxiety wherever additional family responsibilities devolved upon him. Chief among these was the wish of his wife for some children. Intellectually he concurred in her wish but the contemplation of such a plan threw him into such distress that he had to resign his position and seemed to some of his physicians to be on the verge of a complete mental collapse. Another similar instance was a man who was a nationally known figure in the world of finance but, in his own home, a most pitiful object; his wife had begged him to give her a child but so frightened would he become at such a prospect that in spite of intense sexual desire and great emotional conflict he would discontinue all relations with her for months on end rather than run the "risk." The situation became so acute that his wife divorced him. He married another woman who became pregnant by him but before this child was born the man died!

CONFLICTING LOVES

But fear and hate are not the only things which produce impotence and frigidity. The desire may be inhibited instead by conflicting erotic aims which decrease the available erotic energy. To put it very simply, a man may be impotent with a woman because he loves someone else and doesn't know it. The person loved may have lived long ago, may have been a childhood ideal such as in the case of the boy who is prevented from loving his wife because he is "tied to his mother's apron strings," and cannot love any other woman. Many men who marry are nevertheless so attached to their own mothers deep in their unconscious that they cannot give to their wives anything but the child-like love which a boy gives to his mother. In the sense that she is a wife, a sexual partner, such men cannot really accept her or treat her as she craves to be treated, providing, of course, that she, herself, is normal. Frequently one sees such mother-attached men falling in love with women who want to be mothers. Such unions may be fairly satisfactory; they cannot, however, be regarded as normal sexual unions, and many of them go upon the rocks.

Precisely the same sort of fixation occurs in the lives of many women. A girl may be so much in love with her own father that she cannot possibly accept a husband sexually. She may go through the motions of living with him, of loving him, and of cohabiting with him, but however well she may fool him—indeed, however well she may fool herself—she cannot enlist the services of her unconscious in this deception. The body cannot respond to a love situation which all her repressed feelings regard as disloyal to her first and real love.

There is another kind of conflicting love which is not so easily recognized as the fixation on the parents or a brother or a sister but which is almost as frequent. We know that in the process of transferring the affection which he first concentrated upon the father and mother to other persons outside the family the child goes through a stage in which he prefers persons of the same sex as himself. This *homosexual phase* in the course of the individual's development is ultimately repressed and represented only in the sublimated form in normal persons as the basis of much of the friendly intercourse of later life. In many individuals, however, either because it is excessive in quantity or because it has been favored or nurtured in some way, this homosexual element does not disappear. Such persons remain strongly but unconsciously attached to homosexual love objects, even though consciously they think they are normal heterosexual individuals. In fact it is just those unconsciously homosexual people who go about the world with Leporello[3] lists proving how heterosexually potent they are, as if to deny the secret which their unconscious whispers to them.

[3] Leporello, valet to Don Juan, in Mozart's opera of that name, enumerates in his famous aria the many women who were seduced by his master.

Finally there is a conflicting love which is more powerful than any of these and also more prevalent. This is the love of the self. We should not forget that all object love— that invested in husband or wife, friends, neighbors, brothers and sisters, and even parents—is only the overflow of self-love. We all love ourselves first and last and most. In the normal person, however, experience enables one to see the advantage of drawing upon the treasury of self-love and investing some of it in the love of others; in a vast number of individuals, however, this process is inhibited. For various reasons—sometimes a lack of self-confidence, sometimes a fear of deprecation by others, sometimes because of painful experiences, sometimes because of faulty training—this cannot be done. For such people a true and deep relationship with another person is impossible except on such a basis as feeds this self-love instead of detracting from it. Such persons may fall in love but they fall in love with people who are like themselves, with people who flatter them, who feed their vanity and build up their self-confidence by a constant process of emotional nourishment. If one is so much in love with himself, then one cannot accept the role in which he must give love; he can only accept the role in which he is always the recipient of love, like a little child whose self-love is fanned and fed by the attentions of his mother.

In the sexual act, such persons may be at times very potent, particularly if the circumstances of the act are such that their vanity is flattered, their feeling of omnipotence encouraged. This is not real sexual potency, however, and such individuals sooner or later are apt to meet with disaster. They are very proud of their sexual organs and, indeed, it is not inaccurate to say that such persons prefer masturbation to sexual intercourse. Such intercourse as they perform is frequently only a kind of intravaginal masturbation and as such is really a kind of impotency which sooner or later becomes manifest.

The prudishness in regard to sexual matters has placed the treatment of impotence and frigidity under a cloud. On the one hand there are countless sufferers from this affliction who do not know that there is *any* efficacious treatment, while others become the easy prey of quacks and charlatans. Still others are treated by well-meaning but, in my opinion, mistaken physicians who ascribe all impotence and frigidity to physical or chemical factors and use corresponding methods of treatment. It is, as Crookshank[4] has put it in another connection, as if a doctor seeing a woman weeping should label it "paroxysmal lacrimation" and recommend treating it with belladonna and astringents, local applications, restriction of fluids, a salt-free diet and the avoidance of sexual excess, tea, tobacco and alcohol with the further reservation that in the event of failure of these measures the surgical removal of the tear glands might be imperative.

Nevertheless it is true that sometimes the suggestive or punitive value of these treatments helps to produce a good result but more often I believe they are utterly futile. A rational method of therapeutic approach would enable the patient to become aware of and repudiate the unconscious influences which act as a deterrent. Those who minimize the seriousness and frustration of impotence and frigidity are unlikely to welcome so considerable and major a treatment program as psychoanalysis entails. They may be too proud to admit their disappointment or they may be reluctant to face the fact that an entire characterological revision is necessary, the impotence or frigidity being but a symptom which they would like to isolate and treat as if it were a trivial inconvenience instead of a significant index.[5]

SUMMARY

The inhibition of sexual function and pleasure would appear to be another form of functional focal suicide brought about in response to unconscious motives, i.e., to solve unconscious emotional conflicts. These conflicts arise from fear of punishment, fear of reprisal, fear of the malignancy and consequences of unconscious hate, together with deficiencies in the erotic investment of the act due to conflicting aims. There is also the tendency to repudiate or resign the appropriate biological role in favor of unconscious "perverse" erotic gratifications. But these are precisely the motives we have previously discovered in self-destruction of other sorts—aggressive, self-punitive, perversely and inadequately erotic.

We may say, then, that impotence and frigidity—the

[4] Crookshank, F. G., Organ Jargon. *British Journal of Medical Psychology*, January, 1931, pp. 295-311.
[5] Many articles in the psychoanalytic literature deal with this subject. Recent and authoritative is Bergler, Edmund, *Die Psychische Impotenz des Mannes*, Berne, Hans Huber, 1937; also, by the same author and E. Hitschman, *Frigidity in Women*, Washington, D.C., Nervous and Mental Disease Publishing Co., 1936.

repudiation of normal genital pleasure—is a focal self-destruction. In the sense that it involves organs it might be called "organic" but this is not the usual meaning of the word. Ordinarily by "organic" we refer to structural changes in an organ.

But—and here is the crux of the question—many cases of impotence do have some minor structural ("organic") changes. Are these cause or effect? In either case they are definitely related to self-destructive *motives*, and de facto represent destructions.

This leads us into the considerations of our final topic, structural *organic* lesions with discoverable self-destructive motives. This will form the material of the section to follow.

PART V **Organic Suicide**

ONE / *The Totality Concept in Medicine*

Thus far we have considered partial self-destruction in the form of general personality constriction and in the form of focal attacks upon the body brought about mediately or immediately. It would seem but a short step, logically, from these generalized and focalized self-destructions brought about through external devices, to those internally arising destructive processes, general or focal, which constitute the substance of ordinary medical practice. If deep, unconscious purposes are found to lie back of the impulse to gouge out one's eye or cut off one's ear, may it not be possible that the same deep purposes sometimes find expression through physiological mechanisms in diseases which attack the eye or the ear? If, as we have seen, there appear to be, in many persons, strong impulses to starve or beat or deny themselves and to protract a living death, may we not suspect that in pulmonary tuberculosis, for example, we have more than a tubercle bacillus to blame, a bacillus notoriously widespread, notoriously weak, notoriously apt to thrive in individuals who give other evidences of inadequate life adjustment? We have seen how some people rush to get one organ after another removed surgically and how this compulsion to sacrifice an organ has self-destructive determinants which are quite unconscious, concealed by being ostensibly self-preservative; is it not justifiable to inquire just when this focalized self-destructive impulse took form and began its work? For not all such operations are "unnecessary" even from the physical and pathological standpoint; is it not conceivable that the surgical operation, as an elected sacrifice, may represent only a sudden acceleration or final step in a progressively developing self-destructive process which had been focused upon an organ?

Such queries as these are apt to arouse staunch resistance and incredulity in both physicians and laymen. One reason for this, curiously enough, is theological. For many centuries the misbehavior of one's organs has been regarded as a medical problem independent of the "will," and hence immune from the orders of church and state. The functioning of one's limbs, however, was another matter. The "voluntary" nerve supply and the striated musculature of these parts of the body were the basis for excluding them from the immunity of science; hence the misbehavior of one's liver and heart consigned one, automatically, to the doctors, whereas the misbehavior of one's arms and legs put one at the mercy of the judges and priests (later, also the psychiatrists). It was only long afterward that the medical (scientific) attitude toward behavior wrested some of the latter cases away from their human, all too human, wardens. Indeed, this is scarcely yet a matter of common knowledge; to recognize that crime is a completely logical, causally predetermined reaction to certain stimuli and certain capacities is still beyond the emotional comprehension of the average citizen.

Nevertheless, the present trend is all in the direction of such a unity of concept. The traditional moralistic and legalistic methods of viewing behavior are being gradually replaced by the scientific methodology of psychiatry. To be sure, in the minds of many psychiatry is still limited to the treatment of the psychotic. But working with these so-called "insane," the psychiatrists found them more comprehensible and less enigmatic than the more conventionalized subjects of general medical and social study. Psychiatry has even gone so far as to apply its methods and its theories to the traditional subject matter of general medicine. We have only made a beginning but, based on a few practical results, an auspicious one.

Because of the peculiar dichotomies of mind-and-matter, spirit-and-body, that dominated human thought through the Middle Ages, and which have—or seem to have—certain practical advantages, such pathological behavior as suicide is scarcely yet clearly recognized to be a medical problem. The attitude of the state and of the church toward suicide is much better defined than is the attitude of the medical profession. In a broad discussion of the ways in which self-destruction is accomplished, we cannot limit ourselves to the arms-legs methods; we must also consider other ways in which the same motives may be given expression, and these lead us directly into psychiatric and medical fields. Each man has his own way of destroying himself; some are more expedient than others, some more consciously deliberate than others. Perhaps organic disease is one way.[1]

Such a concept does not contradict anatomical or physiological facts. For years such a theory has been held by a few discerning and courageous medical men, notably Georg Groddeck in Europe, and Smith Ely Jelliffe in this country.[2] We know that the deep insistent cravings of the personality which in neurological terms are designated "endogenous stimuli," are transmitted in various ways to organs as well as to muscles. The transmission may be chemical or physical, i.e., by hormones or by nerve fibers. Neural transmissions may be by way of voluntary or involuntary systems, both of which contain stimulating and inhibiting fibers. It is theoretically possible, therefore, that impulses arising from a trend toward or basic purpose of self-destruction might be conveyed through the autonomic nervous system and carried out through the non-striated musculature, as well as in the more familiar form of voluntary nervous system impulses sent to striated musculature. This, then, would result in the injury of an organ as postulated above.

The exact nature of the injury which may result to an organ from such endogenous causes is the crux of the question of psychogenesis in somatic disease. All doctors know and agree that paralysis, tremor, swelling, pain, atony, cramps, and other "functional" symptoms may appear in all parts of the body and be directly related to

[1] I supposed, erroneously, that the expression "organic suicide" in the sense of self-destruction via somatic disease was a creation of my own. I find that it has been used by several others; e.g., Hesnard and Laforgue (*Les Processus d'Auto-Punition*, Paris, 1931) remark, ". . . Ill people commit organic suicide," and proceed to illustrate this with cases "from all branches of medicine in which it would seem that the organic affection is utilized for purposes of self-punishment."

[2] Over twenty years ago Jelliffe first advanced this idea, reporting a case of skin disease associated with emotional conflict, and since then he has consistently adhered to this view and persisted in his scientific observations. and reports concerning it in the face of ridicule, skepticism and contradiction. Studies of the emotional factors in asthma, bronchitis, tuberculosis, hypertension, nephritis, bone and joint disease, spinal cord affections, thyroid imbalance, and eye disorders have come from his pen. It would be impossible to quote the more than four hundred titles in his bibliography, but in addition to the articles cited below, see "Psychopathology and Organic Disease," *Archives of Neurology and Psychiatry*, 1922, Vol. VIII, p. 639; "The Death Instinct in Somatic and Psycho-pathology," *The Psychoanalytic Review*, April, 1933, Vol. XC, p. 121; and "What Price Healing," *Journal of the American Medical Association*, 1930, Vol. XC, p. 1393.

psychological factors. Such symptoms are technically designated *hysterical*. But they are all regarded as reversible phenomena, i.e., they do not involve structural changes in the body. The injury of the organ, the "self-destruction," is a functional or philosophical one. For example, all doctors are familiar with hysterical blindness. The patient cannot see, although examination of his eye reveals no detectable structural pathology. In such a case the *sight* is destroyed (usually temporarily) but not the eye; in a practical sense, however, this distinction is invalid; gunpowder that is wet is destroyed even if none of its substance has been lost. Most physicians, however, think of such functional impairments as being entirely different from and unrelated to the structural pathology of "organic" disease.

Three things, however, disturb our easy satisfaction with this assumption:

1. These "hysterical" lesions sometimes become chronic and structuralized.

2. Actual, visible tissue-destructive lesions can be and have been produced by suggestion, i.e., as the result of ideas alone.[3]

3. The same motives may be demonstrated to exist in both types of illness, hysterical and organic. Study of the personality often shows that the "organic" disease is only a part of the total personality disease and fits into a pattern which seems to have the definite purpose of destroying the self. It may even happen that a functional and an organic disease may exist side by side, both serving the same need as it were, or that one may replace the other as the malignancy of the self-destructive impulse waxes or wanes.

These three facts destroy the comfortable illusion of the separation of mind from matter which prevails in popular and medical thinking, whereby a doctor feels relieved of responsibility if a symptom can be shown to have psychological roots. He likes to think that the "self-preservative instinct" would not tolerate biological mayhem; that whatever the "crazy" *mind* of the patient might do, the "sane" *body* processes can be depended upon to be corrective, constructive, and defensive against malignant environmental

[3] This has been repeatedly demonstrated, experimentally and clinically, both in the production of blisters (which required time to heal and left scars) and other lesions and in the removal of some adventitious tissue such as warts. See Dunbar (Dunbar, H. F., *Emotions and Bodily Changes,* Columbia, 1935), pp. 374, 379-80, and 401 ff. and see also a lengthy review, *Journal of the American Medical Association,* January 18, 1936, p. 235.

and psychological forces. He likes to think that the patient comes to him for help when overtaken by fate, ill-fortune, bacteria, or some other invader against which he is fighting single-heartedly in an effort to preserve his body intact. The doctor would like to shut his eyes to the fact that sometimes the foe with which the patient fights is not something out side of him but something inside, a part of himself, and that this part is willing enough to have the doctor assume the re sponsibility of the combat, and often does its best to oppose his efforts. Bacteria, bad food, and sharp corners do exist and do inflict injuries, but it is often observable that such injuries are invited.

The foregoing remarks might lead one to the inference that the author is attempting to deny external reality in its contribution to human illness. This is not the case. My purpose is rather to call attention to the facility with which one may forget or neglect the unconscious purposes of the individual in one's efforts to evaluate his disease. We know that often what *appears* to be an accident is a definite in tention of the victim; it will be recalled that even such a non-psychoanalytic body as the National Safety Council wonders if there are really any "accidents." People *elect* misfortune—they elect misery—they elect punishment— they elect disease. Not *always*, not all people, not all dis eases; but this is a *tendency* to be dealt with and one which is not ordinarily considered by medical science and which masquerades under various plausible but incorrect or in adequate explanations.

Take, for example, that well-known type of local, organic destruction known as a boil. As physicians, we have been educated to think of disease in terms of physics and chem istry; hence, if a patient presents himself to us with a boil on the neck, we think of all sorts of things that we have learned from research and experience. We think of the bacterial flora, the mechanical complications, the blood sugar concentration; we think of the participation of chem ical forces of immunity and resistance; we reflect upon the leucocytes, the antigens, the hydrogen ion concentration of the blood; we consider the distention of the skin, the fever, the pain, and the best time and method for relieving it. But I venture to say that the feelings, or wishes, or disappoint ments of the person whose neck bears the boil would never enter our minds (as physicians) as a practical considera tion. No one, I suppose, seriously believes (offhand) that there exists a "psychology of the boil," or that emotional factors contribute to its existence. A concrete instance, however, shows that this may be possible. I was once consulted by an intelligent young married woman who was distressed at her inability to be gracious to her husband's numerous relatives. She had managed by dint of great effort to conceal her feelings from them, but apparently only by a process of turning all the hostility which they aroused in her back upon herself. Three years previously when her mother-in-law had come to visit her she had developed "an outbreak of frightful boils which resisted all treatment," but which disappeared immediately after her mother-in-law went home. Precisely the same thing occurred several times thereafter—"Whenever any of the family came to stay with us I promptly had a boil!" Shortly before she consulted me, while preparing for a visit from her mother-in-law, she had developed (instead of boils?) a "nervous breakdown," accompanied by severe sciatica lasting two months and a half.

What do these phenomena mean? One can ignore them or say they do not mean anything, but that is an evasion. One can say that we do not know what they mean, which is commendable scientific agnosticism, but does not preclude an attempt to see what they might mean. They could, of course, be explained as coincidences or as malingering, but these explanations appear the less probable in view of the relative frequency of the phenomenon. (I do not mean, of course, that boils are frequently evoked by mothers-in-law. What I do mean is that both in the medical literature and in our everyday experience we often see physical disease significantly connected with emotionally-charged events and situations: the stenographer whose facial eruption disappears when her detested employer leaves on his vacation, the college student whose headache begins always in the classroom of a certain severe teacher, the lawyer who develops insufferable pains in his right arm whenever he sits at the left of his senior partner, the concert pianist who is prevented from a career by an attack of profuse sweating of the hands just before every projected concert and at no other time. This list could be indefinitely extended from the experience of any observing physician. But boils can be seen, as well as felt, and hence this example serves us well.)

Could it be hysteria? This means, to translate from traditional nomenclature, that these were not "real" boils, that they were in some vague way unconsciously (not deliberately) produced and their size and painfulness exaggerated. The point is that they were still "boils," still hurt, still served their purpose. What is gained by calling them "hysterical"?

In the study of self-mutilation (Part III) and other self-imposed injuries (bear in mind that these also are often inflicted upon the skin), we discovered that quite regularly the unconscious motives for such attacks upon the self depend upon (1) impulses relating to the expression of (otherwise) inexpressible resentment or hostility toward someone or something in the environment, (2) impulses relating to the punishing of the self in response to the sense of guilt which such hostility engenders, and (3) the erotic capitalization of the suffering in a masochistic way. In addition, of course, there are the obvious conscious motives of secondary gain.

Now it is entirely possible to carry over this explanation, hypothetically, to the case of boils just cited. It would seem entirely plausible to suspect that this woman's hostile emotions, the origin of which was quite understandable, could not be expressed to the point of complete satisfaction by deed or word of mouth so that they must be held back and reflected upon herself, only to appear via some unknown physiological mechanisms in an organic expression. As in other cases studied, this served the triple purpose mentioned. It expressed her hatred, vividly; it punished this very conscientious woman for exhibiting the hostility of which she was so ashamed, and it supplied a justification for a self-concern not otherwise permitted to her. Finally, it appears to have served the external and secondary purpose of discouraging the coming of the people she so dreaded to see, and thus served her usefully in spite of its disagreeableness.

This, it seems to me, is a more complete and therefore more "truthful" interpretation of the boils—causally and therapeutically—than the analysis of the varieties of staphylococci involved in the infection, although the one need not exclude the other. I am not proposing psychogenesis. Indeed, except for practical purposes of convenience, it is—according to this conception—incorrect to speak of psychogenesis, just as incorrect as to limit "genesis" to physics or chemistry. The self-destructive and self-preservative tendencies—psychological, physical, chemical—appear to carry on a continuous battle in the organism, and this battle is reflected in the psychological experiences and sensations as

315

well as in the structural and physiological processes which we know somewhat more about. I do not assert that there is any constant *primacy* of the psychological processes; I only propose that they afford us opportunity to discover and interpret in words a certain unity of purpose in the physical, chemical, emotional, and behavior manifestations of the personality—perhaps, indeed, as Freud suggested, in all biological phenomena.

It would appear that these unconscious self-destructive tendencies at one time are manifested through conscious volitional expression and at other times through unconscious attacks on the internal organs or some part of the body. Sometimes there is a joint expression of both. It is only occasionally and with difficulty that we are able to show the relationship between these. *Practically,* in the majority of cases, it probably does not matter, but *theoretically* this remains the task and the opportunity of psychoanalysis, viz., *to identify and relate specifically the emotional factors contributing to somatic disease.* It may be that the future textbook of medicine will consist of a systematic inquiry into the relative importance of the external, environmental factors and the internal, emotional factors responsible for the incidence of every physical disease.[4] This will only be possible as a result of continued cooperative researches by internists and psychiatrists which are becoming increasingly numerous.[5] Whether or not they will verify the hypothesis of so-called organic disease representing in motive as well as in fact a form of self-destruction, such studies cannot fail to promote a more comprehensive conception of the human being as a product of physical, chemical, psychological, and social forces.

For the present it is better to confine ourselves to the exposition of our main thesis, making the assumption that the self-destructiveness implicit in organic disease has some

[4] As far as the nervous system is concerned, this has already been done by Jelliffe and White (*Diseases of the Nervous System*), Philadelphia, Lea & Febiger, sixth ed., 1935). In the preface the authors state:

"Taking as our fundamental proposition that the human organism is an open energy system engaged in the capture, transformation and delivery of energy, we have undertaken to follow this concept through on the basis of the general principles of energy distribution as they have been disclosed in other departments of knowledge."

My suggestion, however, had in mind not only the nervous system but all departments of medicine, diseases of the heart, of the lungs, the digestive organs, the skin, etc. Jelliffe, himself, as stated above has contributed much to the now rapidly accumulating literature on this subject.

[5] Especially in the Institute for Psychoanalysis, Chicago, the Presbyterian Hospital, N.Y. and at the Menninger Clinic, Topeka, Kan.

psychological representation, sometimes discoverable. We can return to the formula of other self-destructions, already studied, and examine some instances of organic disease with an eye to the presence (or absence) of those same component elements—aggression, guilt, eroticism.

TWO / The Psychological Factor in Organic Disease

A. THE SELF-PUNITIVE COMPONENT

The belief that sickness is a punishment decreed by the gods for sins of the people is centuries old. Perhaps we have gone too far in our scientific rejection of it as superstition. For we know that every man creates and obeys his own god or gods, and that every man decrees and executes judgments of punishment upon himself. To say that any organic disease may represent such a self-punishment will probably incur no contradiction, but the general assumption would be that this is only a use to which the suffering is put, i.e., an epinosic evaluation. That such a purpose might have entered into the etiology, the election, or the formation of the illness, would be less likely to obtain credence.

Nevertheless, in studying some organic illnesses one is impressed with the strength and dominance of such a need for punishment in the individual, sometimes apparent even before the outbreak of the illness. One observes how necessary it is for some persons to have their daily stint of punishment and pain, and how—if an accustomed form is taken from them—they seem obliged to replace it promptly. Sometimes an external cross is replaced with an internal one, an organic disease, and sometimes one organic disease is replaced by another.

In Dickens' *Little Dorrit* there is a good illustration of the novelist's intuitive perception of this principle. Mrs. Clennam, who by the misdeeds of her past life had brought about Mr. Dorrit's long confinement in the debtor's prison, is now herself a helpless invalid unable to stir from her room. "A swift thought shot into his [Mr. Dorrit's] mind. In that long imprisonment here, and in her own long confinement to her room, did his mother find a balance to be struck? 'I admit that I was accessory to this man's captivity. I have suffered for it in kind. He has decayed in his prison; I in mine. I have paid the penalty.'"

Such observations lead us to suspect—even though they do not prove—that this need for punishment and this compulsion to punish one's self is unconsciously one of the determining factors back of the appearance of the symptom and even of the organic disease. Let us examine a few clinical examples.

A man of fifty-five had been known by his physician to have had an essential hypertension (high blood pressure) for at least ten years. During the year prior to this report he had become increasingly less communicative, anxious, and mildly depressed; with this, in spite of excellent medical treatment, his blood pressure slowly rose and stood at 230 mm. of mercury (a high point) most of the time. He one day confided to his physician that he had been remiss in numerous petty financial matters and that he regretted that his life had not been "a little more moral." (As a matter of fact, he had always been scrupulously moral and, as the doctor well put it, "abnormally honest." It was his custom, for example, carefully to place two cents in his own cash drawer when he removed a stamp therefrom.) The increasing depression culminated in an attempt at suicide, a singularly violent and bloody attempt, in which death was averted only by the skill and alacrity of his nurses. He made numerous subsequent attempts at suicide.

Here we have evidences of an unendurable or implacable self-destructive urge dictated chiefly by a tyrannical conscience. On the psychological side this appears as over-conscientiousness, merging into guilt-feelings and self-reproach, then into depression, and finally into overt self-destructive behavior. On the physiological side we see a fear response shown in a rise in blood pressure with presumptive damage of the heart and kidneys. In other words, this man attempted suicide in two ways at once, in a mechanical way and in a physiological way. Both of these techniques of self-destruction probably emanated from the same source, namely, the hypertrophied, one might almost say the cancerous, conscience. Since we know so few of the details in this particular case, we can only offer a hypothetical explanation, but one which we know to have been applicable to similar conditions. Unendurable thwartings lead to unendurable resentment which, lacking the opportunity of a justification or the proper psychological set-up for external expression, is repressed, directed inward, absorbed for a time by the administration of the ego but with the ultimate result of an overtaxing of its powers of assimilation. This is an elaborate way of saying that unmastered self-destructive impulses insufficiently directed to the outside world or insufficiently gratified by external opportunities are reflected upon the self, in some instances appearing in this form of constantly maintained anxiety which, in the end, produces the very result which had been anticipated and feared, namely, annihilation.

A case which well portrays the strength of the self-punitive element was reported by my brother and myself.[1] This patient was a man of sixty-one with an organic heart affection which seemed to us to bear a definite relation to his psychopathology. He had been subject for more than four years to attacks of severe chest pain which radiated down both arms to his wrists and was accompanied by profuse sweating. He had been to many doctors, all of whom agreed as to the seriousness of his illness and counseled rest. He began to have violent headaches. He was living very quietly; for a year and a half before consulting us he had given up work and followed a careful regime of breakfast in bed, rest in bed until noon, then dressing for lunch, resting several hours after lunch, going for a drive of a few miles in his car driven by a chauffeur, and then returning home to bed once more. In spite of all this he complained of never feeling or sleeping well.

Examination showed him to have a generalized arteriosclerosis (hardening of the arteries) with involvement of the vessels of the brain and heart.

Coincident with or even antedating the onset of this patient's heart attacks, he had begun to feel vaguely nervous, uneasy in the company of other people, and troubled at night by dreams of the past (especially of old business associates). For many years he had been troubled by severe constipation and a variety of other "colonic" complaints. By the time the patient came to us, his nervous complaints were preponderant and had attained the magnitude of an incipient paranoid psychosis. He confided to the doctor that he had masturbated and that he believed that all of

[1] Menninger, Karl and William, "Psychoanalytic Observations in Cardiac Disorders," *American Heart Journal*, Jan., 1936, p. 10.

the townspeople knew of his habit and were talking about him. He was greatly troubled also by erotic dreams in which a male bedfellow would usually become the object of his advances while he slept, and then reprimand him for the advances.

In life, the patient had been a small-town business man. He was a bachelor in the pre-senium. His entire past history (including a predilection for prostitutes, a love for male company in hotels, and an absence of sustained mature interest in any woman) pointed to strong unconscious homosexual propensities, against which he had waged a successful struggle until recently. He had latterly shown a tendency to become excessively fond of young male employees in his home and although there had never been any history of overt homosexual practices, the approach of these inclinations to consciousness was undoubtedly responsible for some of the fear represented by the symptoms of the illness. He showed a remarkable improvement in all of his symptoms as soon as he was admitted to the sanitarium where, of course, he was protected against any such temptations. His paranoid trends resolved entirely. While there was considerable evidence of anatomic coronary artery disease, he showed a functional improvement in his heart condition that was truly surprising. Whenever he contemplated returning to his home his symptoms increased in severity. It was evident that, aside from the routine sanitarium therapy, the patient had derived considerable benefit from separation from the influences which had been stimulating his homosexuality excessively. He was able to make an acceptable transference to a doctor and thus relinquish much of his need for punishment and his paranoid and hypochondriacal defenses against homosexuality.

The fact of the patient's improvement was unquestionable, although it is difficult to estimate the exact proportions of the psychologic factors in his illness. It is, of course, entirely possible that the somatic and visceral disturbances incident to the pre-senium served as the initial traumata which broke down a well-sealed psychologic system and then assumed definite roles and were elaborated within that system. The powerful effect of the guilt feelings associated with the disordered sexual life is, however, quite apparent.[2]

[2] While it offers only circumstantial evidence unsupported by medical testimony, the bare facts of the following instance are strongly suggestive of the way in which the heart can respond to the need for punishment by death when other means fail:

"In Mexico City, Z. Y., who had tried to commit suicide by: throwing

The sense of guilt is particularly liable to become evident in connection with violations of sexual conventions, and it is not surprising that organic lesions of the genito-urinary organs should arise in direct relation to such episodes. I have observed several instances of this, and reported them in technical detail.[3] Indeed, I am convinced from my observations that even venereal disease is sometimes acquired partly because the victim invites the infection, not only by his behavior (e.g., carelessness) but by some unknown subtle modification of tissue resistance.

Affections of the eye are frequently traceable to powerful unconscious guilt feelings and this is the more understandable when we remember that the eye is perhaps more closely connected and identified with the sexual life than any other organ except the genitals themselves. Seeing something forbidden in early childhood is almost as serious (in the mind of the child) as actually doing something forbidden. Indeed, a definite form of sexual perversion exists (voyeurism) in which the gratification sought is merely to see some forbidden thing, usually naked women or a cohabiting couple. This is interpreted by the psychoanalysts as the persistence of unsatisfied cravings of the curious but thwarted child. If this is true, and there is good evidence for it, the *tendency* is universal[4] and we should not be surprised to find frequent "punishments" of the eye for fantasy offenses of this kind.

Ophthalmologists, as a rule, do not pry into the emotional factors back of the cases of eye disease which come to them, and while many of the patients who consult the psychiatrist have eye symptoms it is sometimes difficult to isolate them sufficiently for particular study. A British ophthalmologist[5] has expressed a very frank opinion as to the essential nature of much eye "disease."

himself under a train (but was prevented); shooting himself in the head (but the pistol failed); asphyxiation (but relatives broke in); drowning (but he was hauled out of the river); hanging (but he was cut down); made one more attempt. He climbed to the roof of his house, jumped off, died (not of the fall), but *of heart failure.*" (*Time,* July 27, 1931.)

Compare this with the instance cited in Part II of patients who made numerous such attempts but seemed to lack the will to die.

[3] Menninger, Karl A., "Psychological Factors in Urological Disease," *Psychoanalytic Quarterly,* Oct., 1936, pp. 488-512.

[4] The nearness of this impulse to the surface can be judged from the popularity of burlesque shows, fan dancers, and abbreviated bathing costumes.

[5] (Inman, W. S., "Emotion and Eye-symptoms," *British Journal of Psychology,* 1921, Vol. II, pp. 47-67.) "During the past fifty or sixty years, it has been customary to regard errors of refraction as the cause of many symptoms of ill-health. Headache, tics, insomnia, inability to concentrate attention, photophobia, flushing and watering of the eyes,

". . . I have found again and again that headache, eye ache, inability to focus upon reading or sewing or fine work have begun at some period of emotional stress. Strangely enough the patient is never aware of this fact and is always astonished when it is revealed."

I was very much impressed by a girl I saw once, however, then twenty-four years old, who for the previous twelve years had done almost nothing else but go from eye specialist to eye specialist in cities all over the United States. All schooling, social life, and other activities had been discontinued either because prohibited by the condition of her eyes or because she was busy going to the doctors. She had symptoms of pain and aching and whenever she attempted to use her eyes she had a sensation that they were about to fall out of their sockets. Many of the specialists she had consulted had prescribed exercises, drops, and other treatments but some had told her that the condition was primarily psychological.

This it proved to be. The illness had broken out acutely following the news of the death of her brother in the World War, a brother toward whom she had been very envious as a child, so envious in fact that she had entertained many fantasies of killing or castrating him. His death evoked into consciousness her earlier guilt feelings for such ideas.

In her case genital envy seems to have arisen in connection with some forbidden peeping which she did; she wanted to see if her brother was different from herself and had ascertained this by surreptitiously going to his bed and looking at him while he was asleep. The guilt, therefore, was associated not only with the envy of the brother but with the peeping.

Since then I have seen numerous cases of eye trouble with much the same general character, namely, an anxiety connected with the eyes which leads to varying degrees of inability to use them and secondary physical changes such

neuralgia, anorexia, constipation, anemia, mental dullness, sleepiness and languor, squint, migraine, hysteria in many of its forms, are but a few of the troubles attributed directly or indirectly in modern English textbooks to eyestrain. Some American ophthalmologists have been even more extravagant in their views and claim to have cured scores of other ills by means of glasses. The mental and emotional state of the patient has not been considered, and the possibility of this state determining the eye symptoms instead of the eye condition causing the general manifestations appears to have eluded both oculist and physician. It is the object of this paper to show that the eye rarely produces other than ocular symptoms, unless the patient is emotionally unstable, and that he frequently is relieved, not by glasses but by suggestion or else by some adjustment of the inner life usually unknown to the oculist."

as congestion, edema, pain, and muscle weakness. The unconscious symbolic identification of the eye with the genitals lends strength to the utilization of this organ in a substituted way for self-punishment connected with sexual guilt feelings.

That functional eye disease may proceed to more serious organic lesions is, in my opinion, fairly certain but clinical proof is not abundant. However, the self-punitive element in an undoubtedly organic disease of the eye was vividly brought out in a case reported by Groddeck.[6]

He (the patient) had grown up in a mountain village far from civilization, and had never been to school, but had spent his childhood as a shepherd boy. Only when he left home in later years did he learn to read and write. At fourteen he was taught shoemaking by the village shoemaker, and from morning till night he had to sit silent at his work, his only distraction being the conversation his master had with passers-by. Among those who came to the shop was a certain blind man whom all the village people called a blasphemer of God. They were ignorant enough to believe absolutely that he had been made blind by God as a punishment for not going to church.

This man had made an unforgettable impression on the boy. After some time he gave up his shoemaking and took to wandering, for he was suffering from retinal hemorrhage, and the doctor warned him he must find some other work less trying to his eyes. Years later he came to consult me, for his eyes had gradually gotten worse and the oculist had told him nothing more could be done for him. The retinal hemorrhage was continually starting anew. The very day he came to me his oculist had discovered fresh bleeding. He told me the autumn was the worst time for the hemorrhage, and also he suffered from great depression in autumn as now—in October. When I asked him how he explained the outbreak of bleeding in October, he said it might be connected with the dying of Nature. The fall of the leaves made him sad, and it might well be that his eyes grew weaker on this account. Moreover, on this occasion he knew of another reason for the hemorrhage: his little daughter had struck him in the eyes while playing. At that time I was still a little bold in my associations, and I told him that while there must be some connection between autumn and his retinal hemorrhage, it was obvious that it was nothing to do with the dying of Nature, since Baden Baden in October gives no impression of death, but rather of glowing, fiery life. I asked the patient whether anything serious had ever happened to him in October, but he said there was nothing. As I was not convinced, I asked him to name any number, and he gave me "eight." To

[6] Groddeck, Georg, *The Unknown Self,* London, Daniel, pp. 113-17, 1929.

my further question whether anything had happened to him when he was eight years old, he again replied in the negative. At that moment it occurred to me that he had told me how the blind man was called a blasphemer of God, so I asked him whether he had ever blasphemed God. He laughed and said he had been very pious as a child, but for many years now he had ceased to trouble himself about these things, God and the Church; they were only bogies used to deceive the common people. Suddenly he stammered, grew pale, and fell back in his chair unconscious.

When he came to himself again he fell weeping on my neck, saying: "Doctor, you are right. I am a blasphemer of God, just as the blind man was, of whom I told you. I have never told a single soul about it, not even in confession, and now when I think of it, I find it almost unbearable. And you are right too about the autumn, and about my being eight years old. It all happened in autumn in the year I was eight. In my home district, which is strictly Catholic, there are wooden crucifixes on the borders between one village and another. At one such crucifix we, my brothers and I and a few other boys, were throwing stones, when I was so unfortunate as to knock the figure of the Christ from the crucifix so that it fell and broke in pieces. That is the most terrible experience in the whole of my life."

When he had calmed down a little I told him that I could not associate today's hemorrhage with the blow in his eye he had had from his little daughter. There must be some other connection, and he must think about the preceding day and name any hour to me. He said, "five o'clock," and to the question whether he remembered where he was at that time, he replied that he knew exactly, for he had got into the tram at a particular spot at five o'clock. I asked him to go again to that spot, and when he came back, he told me with some excitement that immediately opposite the place where he had mounted the tram there stood a crucifix.

I explained to him that it is possible to look upon every illness as a measure of protection against a worse fate, so one cannot escape the idea that retinal hemorrhages arise in order to prevent the sufferer from seeing something—in this particular case, so that the patient might not be reminded of his blasphemy by the sight of the Cross.

It is a matter of indifference whether this suggestion has any justification or not, and I know full well that it is not a complete explanation of the problem of disease, but it does not matter to therapy whether the doctor's action is correct or not. All that matters is that the patient should make use of this action in order to get himself well. I must conclude that this patient did so use my observations, for he had no further hemorrhages for a couple of years, although he gave up his outdoor occupations and settled down to sedentary work which required a great deal of writing. Two years later he had a fresh attack, which proved to be associated with the sight of an iron cross worn by an ex-soldier. This cleared up, and from that time, thirteen years ago, no hemorrhages have occurred. Yet he is now a bookkeeper and must use his eyes more than most people.

To seek examples in still another medical field, some of the most dramatic illustrations of the influence of the self-punishment motive in illness are to be found in some of the case reports of thyroid disease or goiter. It is an accepted medical fact that the thyroid gland is a part of the physiological machinery of "emotion" and that some forms of goiter are usually, if not invariably, *precipitated* by unusual emotional stimulation and stress. The specific nature of the emotions provoked by these stresses are usually ignored in the course of the more urgent and practical matter of surgical treatment for the goiter, but in our present study they are of great interest.

As I have said, the fear of (and wish for) punishment seems to be very prominent in many of them. Doctors Newburgh and Camp[7] of Ann Arbor reported the case of a thirty-two-year-old woman with severe goiter (hyperthyroidism) and other glandular symptoms. Study of the patient disclosed the fact that it had developed while she had been nursing her sick mother. She had become obsessed with the idea that she had done something which might contribute to her mother's death, and when, after several months, during which her sense of guilt was mounting, the mother did die, the patient was for a time overwhelmed with anxiety. This (and the goiter) subsided under treatment but arose again in connection with another incident involving ethical questions. Under psychotherapeutic treatment she recovered and a personal communication from the doctor states that a year later she was still in good health.

Emerson[8] has reported several cases of goiter studied by him from the psychological side with certain striking findings pertinent to our topical theme. One woman, for example, after a rather profligate youth had married a highly moral man who, as a rebuke to her on account of some confessed or discovered delinquencies, *shot and killed himself*

[7] Newburgh, L. H., and Camp, C. D., "The Influence of Anxiety States on the Thyroid Gland," *Annals of Clinical Medicine*, June, 1926, pp. 1006-11.

[8] Emerson, Chas. P., "The Emotional Life and Its Importance in the Production of Pathological Conditions," *Journal of the Indiana Medical Association*, Dec. 15, 1926, p. 475.

in her presence. The symptoms typical of her thyroidism including the swelling of the gland began promptly and were in full bloom four weeks after this event!

Another case, a man of twenty-two, developed typical hyperthyroidism immediately after being appointed foreman of a gang assigned to an important construction job. The fear of failing on this first chance to make good seems to have precipitated a goiter which followed within a few weeks of the appointment. In addition, the patient confessed that while in the South on this assignment he had become engaged to a girl and then immediately quarreled with her, whereupon she *pretended to commit suicide, swallowing some pills, and falling to the floor in front of him screaming.* The patient took immediate and sudden leave from that part of the country and did not learn until later that the girl had been pretending.

In a third case, an American woman of twenty-two with a huge goiter, exophthalmos, extreme restlessness, tremor, rapid speech, and emaciation, turned out to have recently married a man much older than herself with whom all had gone well so far as anyone knew until one day shortly before her admission to the hospital when she heard screams and *rushed out of the house just in time to see her husband shoot and kill his two brothers.* She was the only witness and so was held by the authorities. On a plea of self-defense, her husband was given life-imprisonment instead of the death sentence but he reproached his wife claiming that if she had made her testimony strong enough he would have been freed. The goiter was said by the patient and her mother to have developed over a period of seven days following this event.[9]

Recently I was consulted by a woman of forty-five who had a goiter of twenty years' duration during which time she had care from the very best of medical advisers. She had had several operations and various kinds of treatment without permanent relief. Most interesting to me, however, was the nature of its onset, and her remarkable insight into this. I asked her why she now consulted a psychiatrist.

"Because of my nervousness," she said. "The doctors treat my goiter but they don't treat my nervousness. The nervousness comes from the goiter."

[9] The sequel to this case is even more convincing than the extraordinary circumstances of its precipitation. Dissatisfied with the surgeons' decision not to operate upon the huge goiter, the patient went to another hospital and found a surgeon who was willing to operate, but the patient died on the day of the operation.

"Do you think it is possible that the opposite might be true," I asked her, "that the goiter in some way or other comes from the nervousness?"

"Yes, Doctor, I have always thought so. Just from the way it began. You know," she went on without stopping, "we had a tragedy in our family." (Here she burst into tears.) *My brother shot and killed my stepmother.* I think that had something to do with my goiter. It began immediately afterward . . . they took him to the penitentiary . . . and later they found him in a well up there, drowned. . . . Maybe he did it himself."

It was very striking that this case of mine should have been so similar to those three reported by Emerson, in that murder seems to have been associated with the initiation of the goiter. I made some further inquiries which I think explain more specifically the probable mechanisms operative in this case.

The patient's brother was two years younger than she; there were no other siblings. The mother had died at thirty-five, when the patient was seven. Thereafter the patient lived with her grandparents who were exceedingly indulgent to this brother but gave the patient almost no attention. The children later returned home to live with the father who, in the meantime, had married an irritable, exacting domineering woman. It was a number of years later, apparently without any immediate provocation, that the brother killed the stepmother.

There is no proof, of course, that the goiter was caused by the emotional shock of the murder but the chronological association is striking. One psychological reconstruction in line with our experience in other cases studied (see, especially, the discussion of suicide in pairs) would be that this girl hated both the stepmother and the brother, and when one of them killed the other one she felt as guilty as if she had done it herself. She had always been discriminated against by the victim and held responsible for the misbehavior of the assassin. In other words, since she had been punished for his misdeeds before, she now unconsciously expected to be punished again.

The fact that in the four cases just mentioned the hyperthyroidism appeared to have been precipitated by the witnessing of a violent death may represent only a coincidence. I must confess that I was very much surprised to discover it. This surprise was even greater when in Therese Benedek's recent study[10] I noted that of the two cases of hyperthyroidism discussed, one lived in a house with a woman who committed suicide, and the thyroid disorder developed immediately afterwards, while the second, although not a witness of any violent death scene was obsessively worried over the thought that she might be to blame for the murder of a young girl whose body had been found, and could not free herself from the self-accusation, "You are the murderess! You killed that young girl." Both of Dr. Benedek's patients thus felt themselves to be murderers.

These cases are few in number, infinitely so in comparison with the thousands of similar afflictions which are being studied and treated by physicians daily, *without* any psychological study.[11] But my purpose was not to show what is—or may be—*always* present, but what has been, in a few illustrations, *sometimes* present. In these examples one thing, I think, does stand out, namely, the terrific sense of guilt and the corresponding fear of punishment and compelling need for punishment. We can't disprove, of course, that these patients only capitalized a "punishment" which "happened along" which would have come anyway (e.g., the goiter). But no better explanation for the onset is forthcoming, nothing in the facts contradicts our hypothesis, and the picture conforms to what we have seen in those more accessible forms of self-destruction in which the voluntary nervous system participates.

B. THE AGGRESSIVE COMPONENT

It is not difficult to believe, as the common people always have, that sickness represents punishment, and we have seen that scientific evidence supports this idea to the extent of ascribing to an unconscious sense of guilt some of the motivation in some organic disease. But it is not so obvious that back of such pain, misery, and incapacitation

[10] Benedek, Therese, "Mental Process in Thyrotoxic State," *Psychoanalytic Quarterly*, April, 1934, p. 153.

[11] It is only fair to say that numerous forward-looking internists have recognized the importance of the psychological factor in goiter, heart affections, gastrointestinal disorders, various kinds of skin disease and other conditions. Not only have they recognized this but some of them make careful psychological studies of their patients. Dunbar (*vide infra*) has collected thousands of published reports of such studies. My purpose here is not to present a summary of all the scientific work bearing on this theme but to indicate by these few illustrations the nature of the psychological factors operative.

there lie aggressive motives. Yet such strong demands for punishment must have a cause, a provocation. "Where there is so much smoke, there must be some fire."

Our next inquiry, therefore, should be directed to the crime—real or fancied—which is related to this form of self-punishment. In other words, what are the evidences that aggressive impulses also are implicated in the production of organic illness.

The existence of fierce but repressed hate is strikingly apparent in several forms of somatic disease, instances of which have been psychologically studied. In the study of heart disease previously mentioned, for example, my brother and I found evidence for concluding that heart symptoms and presumably heart disease were sometimes a reflection of—or an expression of—strongly aggressive tendencies which had been *totally* repressed. Heart disease is very apt to occur, as is well known, in externally mild, gentle people and, in our series, in men who had been strongly attached emotionally to their fathers and often more or less definitely hostile to their mothers. The conscious affection for the father usually completely obliterates the deeply buried hostilities for him. If, then, the father has heart disease or symptoms of heart disease it is very typical for certain sons to include these symptoms in their identification of themselves with the father and to carry out the inexpressible patricidal impulses reflexly by unconscious focal (organic) suicide. (It has been suggested by some of the analysts who have studied these cases that this identification is not with the father so much as with the father's preferred love-object, i.e., his wife, the patient's mother, and that in this sense the heart disease is at the same time symbolic of the "broken*heart*edness" of disappointment, and of the womb, i.e., the female sex organ.)

That the aggressive tendencies seem to be most important in the development of heart affliction is supported by the fact that coronary sclerosis is so enormously more prevalent among men than among women.[12]

By way of illustration a few cases might be cited. One

[12] Our data were entirely insufficient to prove anything; they did suggest, however, that these psychological factors are sometimes of importance in the development of cardiac pathology. Whether they act by way of bringing about a disordered function which in turn becomes established as organic pathology or in some more direct way, we have no evidence or opinion. The therapeutic effect on the patient of the psychological investigation is also to be regarded thus far as a secondary, though fortunate, corollary of the investigational process.

reported by Stekel,[13] for example, was a man fifty-one years old, of herculean proportions, who had never known a day's illness until one night he awoke with a feeling of being strangled. He fought for his breath, feeling that he was dying. The attack soon passed off and he thought it was due to a heavy supper the evening before. A few nights later, however, he had another attack and from then on they occurred frequently in the day as well as at night. He consulted a physician friend who diagnosed his illness as arteriosclerosis and told him that with care he might live two years longer. On the advice of his friend the patient entered a sanitarium. He became more and more dejected and felt that his death was approaching. Eventually he came to Stekel for treatment, in the course of which he discovered that the heart attacks originated in a severe emotional conflict. He had lost the woman he loved and with whom he had had a *liaison* for five years to his best friend. Terrific resentment was thus stimulated against a man toward whom friendship prevented its expression. For many weeks prior to the onset of his symptoms he struggled secretly with the wish to strangle his friend for this betrayal. The analytic treatment was successful and the attacks entirely ceased. Ten years later the patient was still "perfectly well, happily married, and at the height of his creative powers."

A recent report has been made by an American research worker[14] who has been studying the psychological side of various somatic diseases at the Presbyterian Hospital in New York in conjunction with several colleagues. He cites one case of an unmarried girl of twenty-six with severe precordial pain of about seven years' duration. She had suffered what was diagnosed as sunstroke at the age of eight years, at which time she had fainting spells and choreiform movements. These symptoms, however, never occurred at home and it was necessary for someone, usually her mother, to accompany her whenever she went out. When this illness left her the heart condition developed and at the same time she became constipated. She had taken cathartics regularly for years and for the previous two years had used enemas daily. In the first six months of psychotherapy her constipation disappeared but the anginal attacks proved more ob-

[13] Stekel, W., *Conditions of Nervous Anxiety and Their Treatment,* London, Kegan Paul, Trench, Trubner, 1923, pp. 172-81.
[14] Wolfe, T. P., "Dynamic Aspects of Cardio-vascular Symptomatology," *American Journal of Psychiatry,* Nov., 1934, pp. 563-74.

stinate to therapy. Beneath a polite exterior there was considerable repressed resentment against her parents and her younger brother of whom she was intensely jealous. Severe attacks ceased and minor attacks became infrequent following the psychotherapy.

These cases show clearly enough, I believe, the intensity of the repressed aggressiveness. Sometimes this aggressive purpose can be secondarily gratified by the illness, as in Wolfe's instance of the girl whose cardiac illness necessitated the labors and attendance of others. This does not prove the original strength of hostile impulses in the production of the illness, but it does indicate the strength and persistence of these powerful tendencies in such patients.

That this conflict with unendurably great hate may be expressed by increased blood pressure is almost common knowledge. Plethoric, irascible old men are constantly expected (desired?) by their relatives to die in an attack of rage. They themselves use this as a weapon against other people. Was it not Clarence Day's father who used to fend off invitations by reminding his long-suffering family to "look out for my blood pressure"?

Of course, to explain a sustained elevation of blood pressure, it must be assumed that there is a continuous series of such stimuli, and indeed, the early clinicians often mentioned the frequency of hypertension in those obliged to undergo long-continued nervous strains, such as railroad engineers. On the other hand it is also well known that many, if not most, persons subjected to such strains fail to develop hypertension and furthermore many, if not most, sufferers from essential hypertension are neither exposed to nor conscious of any such long-continued "nervous strain," fear, anxiety, or rage, beyond those incidental experiences of life to which we are all exposed.

It is just here that psychoanalysis can offer help from its explorations of the unconscious. We know that many who have no superficial awareness of inner hidden feelings of anxiety, fear, anger, and hate, give other evidences of having such emotions, and can be helped to an envisagement, or recognition and confession of them. An illustration occurs to me which is particularly vivid. A woman came to us because she had suddenly lost the ability to write, by which she made her living. This was the only symptom of which she complained although she was discovered to have a blood pressure of over 200. She had not written anything for two years and was desperately discouraged about this.

In my office, however, she suddenly began to write—automatically, as it were, in a handwriting not her own, and signed by a strange name. Pages and pages, hundreds of them, she dashed off in this way. She realized what she wrote only *after* she had written it. What she wrote told her—and me—how terrified she was, and had been, how greatly she hated certain people whom she had at first told us she loved fondly, how she had wanted to kill them, and finally how close she herself was to suicide or "insanity." When she had written this down, with all of the details of the origins of these terrific feelings, she recognized it as altogether true, and was utterly amazed, now, to discover that she hadn't (previously) realized it! Incidentally, her blood pressure fell concomitantly.

It would be going far beyond the facts to postulate that all or even most cases of hypertension are similar instances of constantly maintained inner tensions dependent upon *unconscious* repressed emotions (especially fear), but it is a fair presumption that some of them are.[15]

A psychoanalytic colleague[16] has reported a case in which an extraordinary therapeutic result was achieved by psychoanalysis in a case of high blood pressure of long standing, the symptom disappearing suddenly and permanently. This was a man of thirty-two whose hypertension had been discovered fourteen years previously and in whose family history there were many instances of cardiovascular disease and hypertension. His own blood pressure was very high as early as the age of eighteen. Complete medical study was negative except for the "essential" hypertension and this diagnosis had been made in two recognized cardiac clinics.

He came to psychoanalysis ostensibly for other reasons than the hypertension but following a particular treatment hour one day, the details of which are about to be recited, his blood pressure fell to normal and remained so. No other

[15] MacWilliam (MacWilliam, J. A., "Blood-pressure and Heart Action in Sleep and Dreams: Their Relation to Hemorrhages, Angina and Sudden Death," *British Medical Journal*, 1923, Vol. II, pp. 1196-1200) showed that in persons without organic disease of the circulatory system the blood pressure may rise to a point far beyond the limits ordinarily reached in moderate muscular exertion as the result of disturbances of sleep, particularly by dreams. For example, he reports a rise from 130 mm. to 200 mm. during one dream. One can speculate what the effect of such sudden blood pressure rise may be, both in the way of bringing about organic changes and in the way of furthering lesions already in existence.

[16] Hill, Lewis B., "A Psychoanalytic Observation on Essential Hypertension," *Psychoanalytic Review*, Jan., 1935, Nc 1, 60.

treatment was administered and there was no change in habits of living.

Naturally, one would like to know exactly what happened in this extraordinarily effective treatment hour. The patient was relating a scene of his childhood. He began to dramatize it and became furiously angry, seized a heavy ash tray and made as if to attack Dr. Hill, although addressing his remarks as if to his mother. His rage increased to a very high point, his face was red, his neck vessels distended. He then relapsed into a state of pallor and sweating and was amnesic for the episode.

Gradually, not only the episode but details of its original setting returned to him. He had said something about a buggy whip during the attack and by association he recalled that as a child he had been teased by his sister until he had struck her, whereupon their mother took up a pony whip, which happened to be at hand, with the evident intention of striking him in punishment. In his fear he seized it from his mother and ran and was brought to bay standing upon a bed, intending to defend himself by hitting her with it. He lost his courage and meekly surrendered the whip with the hope of avoiding punishment, but his mother whipped him angrily. Subsequently he had forgotten the experience completely.

That the recalling of such a relatively simple episode should make such a profound change in a condition of long standing seems remarkable. It is presumable, however, that the episode represented the crystallization of a situation which had existed between the mother, sister, and child for a long time at a critical period in his childhood. Dr. Hill believes the whipping was more painful to his self-esteem and self-confidence as a child than could be borne. Unable to defend himself or to attack someone or even to *feel* his rage effectively because of his fear and weakness, he had no recourse but to repress it and dissociate it from the rest of his personality so that it became productive of the symptomatology representing inhibited rage.

Whatever constitutional tendency toward hypertension may have been present in this case (as suggested by the peculiar liability of this patient's family to this affliction) one may see that his reactions to a dominating mother, against whom he could not defend himself nor adequately express his rage, were a contributing factor. The treatment enabled him to assimilate the original episode into the totality of his experience so that it could undergo corrective modification in the light of his intelligence and in this way save his vasomotor system from the excessive burden of a constant reaction to a tremendous unconscious and otherwise unexpressed emotion.

One is most apt to be impressed by his own observations even when they are less convincing in some details. I recall in particular a man sixty years of age whom I was called to see in the hospital where he had been for the greater part of a year. He had been refused life insurance ten years before on account of high blood pressure. He had had very competent medical treatment but his blood pressure had not receded, and, indeed, he had suffered a slight "stroke," a cerebral thrombosis (blood-clot) partially paralyzing his right arm.

On account of his age and other circumstances, formal psychoanalytic treatment was out of the question but a modified type of psychotherapy based upon the psychoanalytic method was instituted with most extraordinary results. The man, who had closed his business affairs, resigned his position in business, and given up expectations of further activity in life, after six months' psychiatric treatment left the hospital, resumed his work, entered into it diligently, did more business and made more money than he had ever done before. His systolic blood pressure, in the meantime, receded from 250 (January 1, 1931) to 185 (August 31, 1931), near where it remained for the subsequent two years that he remained under observation. At the end of that time he considered himself entirely well and did not return any more for treatment. He still lives actively and, I understand, in good health in spite of external disasters and distresses.

In this case what I found to be of definite effect upon the hypertension was the existence of a terrific battle with social and economic factors over which, although *apparently* successful beyond the dreams of the average man, the patient really never won a victory. Poverty of great degree surrounded his childhood. His father deserted the family, he himself went to work at twelve and supported the family by dint of self-sacrifice and prodigious labor. A kind of genial friendliness combined with hard work and a sharp trading instinct enabled him ultimately to arrive at great wealth. But then new foes assailed him, all of whom he could master except one—his own son, whose rebellion against his father was crafty and powerful. My patient transferred his hostility for his own father to this son, and, though they worked together, the warfare between them was almost murderous. His resignation from the business was a partial surrender and the paralysis of his right arm was undoubtedly related to an unconscious inhibition of his wish to strike the son down, the recoil of the wish almost striking the other down. He was never happy with his wife, but maintained the most tender love for his mother to the day of her death.

I felt that his high blood pressure represented the constant stimulation of his aggressive tendencies, a constant preparation for fighting, associated with constant pervading fear. His improvement can be understood as a physical and psychological response to the relief from some of this fear afforded by the feeling of security furnished by the physician, and also (more significantly) by the quantitative diminution in his aggressiveness resulting from the conversion of some of it into verbal expression.[17]

Intense aggressiveness is observable in the background of other affections than cardiac and vascular. Joints, for example, become stiff and swollen with what we call arthritis or rheumatism, for which all sorts of etiologies and pathologies have been described. Some types are apparently produced *chiefly* by infection (although we do not know why the infection sometimes selects certain joints). Others apparently result from some internal changes—chemical, metabolic, mechanical. Into all of these, we may fairly speculate, emotional factors enter, although usually without detection. Of late, however, numerous physicians have been reporting their observations relative to the psychology of arthritis,[18] and here again the aggressive component is conspicuous.

[17] Many persons might assume that the psychiatrist has a peculiar bias in the selection of such cases. Because he finds high blood pressure in some of his patients, he has no right to assume that similar mechanisms determine the high blood pressure of patients who do not come to psychiatrists. To eliminate this possible source of error, I solicited the cooperation of some of my medical friends, who kindly permitted me to make a psychological study of a number of their private patients who, except for this research, would not have gone to a psychiatrist or considered psychiatric patients. In nearly every instance significant psychological tensions were discovered which I felt had a very definite relation to the high blood pressure; in general, they corresponded to the general formula outlined above.

[18] See, for example, Nissen, H. A., and Spencer, K. A., "The Psychogenic Problem in Chronic Arthritis," *New England Journal of Medicine,* March 19, 1936, pp. 576-81; Thomas, Giles W., "Psychic Factors in Rheumatoid Arthritis," *American Journal of Psychiatry,* November, 1936, pp. 693-710, and Jelliffe, S. E., "Bodily Organs and Psychopathology," *American Journal of Psychiatry,* March, 1936, p. 1051.

Take, for example, a case described in a letter which I recently received from a woman I have never seen. She was the mother, she said, of two boys. The younger brother was the victim of a "non-infectious polyarthritis," which seems to include all of his joints, including those of the spine. Apparently thorough medical treatment was instituted, a tooth was extracted and temporary improvement followed, with a characteristic recurrence, subsequently complicated also by bladder infection. It is of some significance that the patient was described as a strong, handsome young man who never had any children's disease except a "few blisters of chicken pox." He had always "been very strong, fine, and clean, and very popular with everyone." His brother, on the other hand, twenty months older, while talented, appears to have taken advantage of his younger brother's amiability throughout their childhood, presuming upon him in every way, jeering at him, cheating him out of his privileges and his property. He left home apparently about the time the younger brother developed the arthritis although this is not specifically stated, drifted from pillar to post, drank increasingly, and sank lower and lower, "humiliating us in every way by his behavior and associates." He cashed bad checks which the younger brother made good. He justified himself by accusing his mother of favoritism for his younger brother, came to his grandmother's funeral drunk, and in the meantime continued his financial dependence upon the mother and sick brother who conducted a small store.

The mother appeared to be a very intuitive person. She recognized that the younger brother even as a youngster "just couldn't express deep hurts" and that "his love for his elder brother was crushed and thrown aside and its possessor ridiculed. He is now disillusioned, bitter, and frantic."

The mother seemed almost to sense that the younger brother with his courteous, restrained, refined make-up, incited as he was to the utmost hatred by a brother whom he had at first served and loved, had turned that hostility back upon himself in the form of disease, disease of a type which, had it been visited upon the guilty brother, would have prevented most of the derelictions which so seriously disturbed the family.

Jelliffe (*op. cit.*) has reported a similar case of a more gifted, more inhibited younger brother with a widespread arthritis, the bony changes confirmed by x-ray. In this case another object of hatred was a son-in-law with whom there had been long drawn-out legal contests. Insight into this greatly improved the arthritis.

Dr. John Murray of Boston told me of the following case which came under his observation. A young man who suffered acutely by self-comparison with his very successful father, and who had more internal than external justification for his hostility, exhibited his aggressions indirectly by defeating his father's purposes with evasion, idleness, extravagance. These methods were gradually superseded by excessively severe migraine which he used as a justification for an increasing alcoholism, so that between the two he was at times completely incapacitated.

The next step in the process was his marriage which had the extraordinary consequence that both his alcoholism and his migraine disappeared only to be replaced with a progressive and painful arthritis. The arthritis became completely incapacitating and no treatment gave improvement of any permanence. Two years before seeing Doctor Murray he had made up his mind that he would never walk again, and, although since that time there had been decided improvement, he had not yet succeeded in regaining his ability to get around alone. It is also interesting to note that he teased his child, his oldest son, of whom he was very fond, in a brutal and sadistic manner concealed under a veneer of the "all-in-fun" spirit. This may be regarded as another indirect and unacknowledged emergence of his hostilities, originally directed toward his father, and now directed toward his own son, that is, toward a symbolic part of himself.

Coughing is a symptom which may or may not indicate organic pathology of the respiratory tract, but which does frequently indicate strong aggressive tendencies. Everyone must have reflected upon this at times when a concert or a speaker is repeatedly interrupted or competed with by an incessant cougher.

That most intuitive and discerning clinician, Georg Groddeck, wrote at length about the psychology of the cough, using himself as a case illustration.[19] He happened to be suffering acutely from a cold at the moment of writing but also "chronically all of my life. All my family had the same habit as I have of responding to disagreeable impressions by a fit of coughing."

He began his observations by remarking how much his

[19] Groddeck, *The Unknown Self*, *op. cit.*, p. 131.

coughing delighted his nine-month-old baby, who seemed to be much impressed by these vigorous noisy expulsive activities on the part of the father. "It is only by the aid of this gift of scrutiny that the child is able to perfect those activities, imitative or independent, which must astonish anyone who once takes the trouble to consider the amazing amount of mental work a child gets through in his first three years." Groddeck thought the child realized from the facial expression of the cougher, as well as from the act itself, something of the purpose of the cough; to express either "the wish to blow off something which is regarded as unpleasant or to get rid of something already felt to be within the organism, whether as a part of himself or as a foreign body, and whether of a mental or of a physical nature." He confirmed this by pointing out that his stepson, no blood relation to him at all, shared his habit of responding to what was disagreeable by coughing, and once in the course of a conversation which had nothing at all to do with medical matters had told his stepfather what a terrifying effect Groddeck's violent coughing had had upon him when he was a little boy. Groddeck himself recalled with a lively recollection how as a child he both recognized and made use of the alarming effects of a cough. "One evening, for some reason or other, my mother took my sister and myself to her weekly meeting. Since we very soon wearied of the gossip of the grown-ups, we were taken to the next room and told to go to sleep. I don't know how the notion came into my head that the greater the number of witnesses, the more impressive an illness would be, but anyhow, I suddenly had the idea of setting up a coughing duet with my sister, in the hope of ensuring a day's holiday from school for both of us. The plan succeeded beyond all expectation. We not only stayed away from school, but we brought our mother home earlier than she had intended. It is true we had to stop in bed all the next day, but that did not trouble us, for we were still sleeping in the same room and sharing all our joys and sorrows with each other."

In a patient whom I studied over a period of several years, my observations confirmed with astonishing correspondence these of Groddeck's. This patient was a lawyer of thirty whose analysis was begun and pursued not on account of physical complaints at all but on account of well-recognized emotional disorders which led to serious conflicts with the family, with business associates and others, to the extent of making it necessary for him to withdraw temporarily from his practice. Very early in the treatment of the case, however, the persistent cough from which he suffered became the subject of much of his discussion. At times this cough would become so violent as to interrupt his conversation for a matter of several minutes or even longer; it had become so severe that according to his own statement he would sleep less than half the night on account of being awakened by it. His family declared they could recognize him in the theater when they sat in different parts of the show by the loud, ringing cough with which they were so familiar. In one apartment building other tenants complained about this family, partly, it was presumed, on account of the incessant, noisy coughing of my patient.

In the psychoanalytic hours he would complain at times most bitterly about the cough, declaring that I ignored it or at least offered no remedy for it, that during these two years of treatment it had gotten no better but that I had still clung to the idea that it must be psychological in origin. My observations about the cough were that it would be absent for as long as two or three months, only to recur when the patient's resistance began to manifest itself again rather strongly. I also noticed that in spite of its loud, spasmodic nature, and the fact that the patient's face and body were contorted and jerked by the coughing, he rarely raised any sputum. But the most pertinent observation was that he would frequently have a period when he would not cough at all until I started to speak, in the course of some interpretations or explanations. Then the cough would immediately appear. In scores of instances my interpretations seemed to be met by a cough in such a way as to leave no doubt that unconsciously the cough was a protest against the explanation, a disguised invective hurled at me so loudly that I could not continue speaking.

The further utility of this cough was made clear by a dream which the patient had, which, though he was exceedingly opposed to recognizing the psychological factors in the cough, he himself acknowledged and interpreted. The dream was that he was in a Kiwanis Club meeting and the members had threatened to drop him from the club. He coughed violently, "a death rattle" as he described it, as if to say to them, "You see, you did this—you caused it," just as he used to do when he wanted to make his mother and father feel sorry by saying to them, "I wish I were dead." The patient himself pointed out that in the psychoanalysis, as in his childhood, he threatened revenge by dying, thus reproaching the physician for his unfeeling attitude. The cough represented to him a demand for attention, a defense against unwelcome interpretations, and a threat of punishment, cloaked by a bid for sympathy.

The patient had gone to no less than twenty doctors seeking explanation and treatment for this cough. Most of them would assure him that they could find nothing, although a few of them so alarmed him by vague or ambiguous comments that he would use these as justifications for going to more and more doctors to get a confirmation or refutation or a more positive diagnosis. Some of the physicians in our clinic examined him upon several occasions and were unable to find evidences of structural disease. One must always think in these chronic, undoubtedly psychogenic, coughs of the probability that ultimately certain structural changes result. As Groddeck (*op. cit.*) put it, "How far the habitual practice of coughing at first intended for defense ultimately leads to anatomic and physiological modifications and disturbances is very early hidden from view and not easily discernible later on. So far no attempt has been made to inquire into such a problem."

One final case to illustrate the aggressive factor in the picture of organic self-destruction. There is a condition known as scleroderma which consists of a hardening of the skin such as one sees occasionally in the "ossified man" of the museum. This disease is of unknown etiology and is ordinarily considered hopeless. Groddeck[20] has described a case of scleroderma accompanied by dermatitis (inflammation of the skin) over the greater part of the body. The skin over the elbow joints was so contracted that the arms could not be fully outstretched. Of his many details I shall mention only the final determinants of the symptoms.

As a boy, his patient had kept tame rabbits at a time when he was struggling with bitterly hostile feelings toward his father and brother. He used to watch these rabbits in their sexual and other activities; one large white buck, however, he would not allow to mate with the females. When the rabbit would occasionally succeed in doing so the patient would seize him by the ears, truss him up, hang him from a beam and beat him with a riding whip till his arm was tired. It was the right arm, the arm that first became affected. The memory came out during treatment with the

[20] Groddeck, *The Book of the It, op. cit.*, p. 86

340

very greatest resistance. Over and over again the patient evaded it and brought on a variety of severe organic symptoms. One of these was particularly significant; the sclerodermic patches on the right elbow grew worse. From the day on which this memory came out completely from the unconscious these got well again and healed so completely that the patient was able from then on to bend and stretch his elbow joint to its fullest extent, a thing he had not been able to do for twenty years in spite of much treatment. And he did it without pain.

Groddeck goes on to make clear that the white rabbit, which the patient kept from sexual pleasure and punished so cruelly for sexual "sins," represented the patient's father toward whom he had precisely comparable feelings of jealousy with reference to sexual privileges, and hate because of his own thwarting (for which he thus took revenge on the substituted rabbit). The main point I wish to emphasize here is the evidence of terrific hate and aggressiveness concealed in the organic lesion.

These few case illustrations cannot be expected to do more than demonstrate the definiteness with which the aggressive impulses familiar to us as a regular constituent of self-destruction in other forms can be recognized in some instances of organic disease.

The question arises as to whether repressed aggressiveness may not be equally strong in many persons who have not been examined and who have not fallen ill and hence cannot be considered a determinant of illness. This we must concede may be true. The fact that in some cases the illness can be definitely and directly connected with a psychological conflict—for example, in Groddeck's case, just cited, or in Hill's case—is also not conclusive proof of the pathogenicity of the aggressiveness, for it may still be possible that the illness was brought about by something else entirely and only offered itself as a convenient vehicle for expressing the psychological disturbances in symbolic form. Again, the fact that therapeutic benefit results from psychological understanding cannot be used as positive evidence that the causative factor has been demonstrated because, unfortunately for purposes of clarification, it is well known (although not always taken into account by enthusiastic observers) that some of the conditions I have mentioned, notably high blood pressure, respond favorably to a great many different kinds of treatment providing these are accompanied by a reassuring, protective attitude on the part of the physician.

The correspondence of the somatic disease with the demonstrated psychological needs of the same individual may, of course, be only a coincidence. Indeed, the bugbear of coincidence hangs over our head constantly in psychoanalytic observations because our material is, after all, so scanty in comparison to the millions of cases seen and treated by general practitioners. We cannot *prove* that the events have a causal connection; we can only indicate that they *appear* to have, and that this apparent relationship occurs in repeated—albeit numerically few—instances.

The most conclusive evidence that aggressiveness actually contributes to making people sick is to be found, I believe, in the study of the entire personality of the sufferer. When we see a person struggling with tensions and emotional conflicts which are too great for him to handle; when we observe signs that his repressions are breaking down as shown by such symptoms as sleeplessness, irritability and aggressive, provocative and self-punitive behavior of all kinds; when we find physical illness as a part of such a pattern taking its place as a substitute for or as an accompaniment to recognized mechanisms for dealing with strong aggressive tendencies, there is presumptive evidence that the illness has arisen from the same source as the other symptoms.

Furthermore, one may frequently observe in himself in the little illnesses of everyday life how one is overwhelmed by anger, oftentimes masked as depression, until he actually makes himself ill, expressing his rage in a headache, stomach symptoms, or a cold in the head. It is not difficult to conceive of greater pathology resulting from greater and more constant emotionalism of the same sort.

The expression that something or someone "gives me a headache" is part of everyday thinking and speaking. In this sense the public is psychologically-minded in contrast to those physicians who are strictly physically minded, and who would say, for example, that the irritability and disagreeableness preceding an illness is a symptom of it, a result of the disordered physiological condition rather than a cause of it.

I should like to repeat here, then, that it has not been my purpose to show that the psychological symptoms *cause* the physical symptoms; to say so, is, I believe, just as incorrect as to say that the physical symptoms cause the psychological symptoms. The point I would make in this section is that self-destructive trends have both psychological *and physical* expression. *Trends* themselves are no more (and no less) psychological than they are physical, but psychological expressions of them are sometimes easier to understand than physical expressions, and therefore a case in which there is some psychological representation of a trend which is also expressed physically affords us an opportunity for a clearer understanding of the latter than if it were merely seen as an isolated tissue lesion. Among these expressions are, as we have seen in this section, that of uncontrollable and, at the same time, inadmissible hate.

C. THE EROTIC COMPONENT

That an organic disease may, in addition to its other functions, express a kind of self-love is an inference one might draw from the observations of previous chapters. The diseased organ becomes the chief object of the patient's attention, concern, and, it is not inaccurate to say, affection. This is a *local* narcissism in contrast to narcissism in the more general sense in which it is usually envisaged. Focusing narcissistic affection upon an organ does not necessarily result in a lesion; some people are notoriously "in love with" their noses, hands, faces, or figures. But if we examine any case of illness closely we find what Freud, Ferenczi, and others have described, namely, an increase in the normal investment of "love" in that organ at the expense of the ordinary investments in outside world objects.

According to our theory, such a narcissistic investment of love is a consequence of the selection of the organ for the self-destructive and self-punitive attack. The erotic "flow" is transferred there primarily to neutralize or hold in check the other elements, and to reduce to a minimum the damage inflicted. We should expect, therefore, to find evidences that this element enters into the fundamental psychologic structure of all organic disease.

Unfortunately we cannot examine "all" organic disease, nor have we any practical devices for definitely detecting and measuring the "organ libido," i.e., the amount of love bestowed upon a particular organ, and its quantitative variation from the normal. In certain accessible cases, however, we can get definite evidence as to trends and we can infer something as to the quantitative variations, as I did, for example, in some of the cases cited in the course of describing the aggressive and self-punitive trends apparent in certain cases. To these I shall add only a few illustrations of somatic illness in which the erotic element was clearly visible.

We should not expect to find this only in those long-drawn-out chronic afflictions which render their victim something of a martyr. Probably even the most brief, transitory illness is a representation of this concatenation of self-destructive impulses, neutralized and "healed" by the influx of the erotic element—an element present, perhaps, from the start but only latterly effective. One may say that to the extent to which it is psychotherapeutically necessary in a given case, one expends love upon his injured organ. This can be made more clear by some simple examples. A dog that licks his injured paw tenderly hours on end probably does not do it so much for the rational reasons ordinarily assigned, but because the injury has directed an increased amount of libido to the paw so that the dog regards it with a tenderness ordinarily reserved only for a more highly cathecticized part of his body. The same mechanism is clearly seen in human beings. The man with a carbuncle on his neck cannot possibly have the proper interest in his sweetheart. His painful neck attracts and receives his entire attention.

The curious thing is that this erotic investment, which seems to serve the useful purpose of mitigating the destructive consequences of the aggressive and self-punitive investment in the organ, may itself enter into the self-destructive process in a positive way. We recall in our study of self-mutilation, martyrdom, and other forms of self-destruction that the erotic component played this role very definitely, and we saw that it was usually due to a distortion or perversion of the instinct which then attempts to make up in quantity what it lacks in quality.[21] The same thing occurs in organic disease. For example, I remember an adolescent girl who was brought to us from a long distance because of her extreme agitation over a pimple on her nose. The pimple was actually no longer visible but she had pinched, patted, rubbed and steam-packed her nose so incessantly that it was red and swollen.

[21] "A strong egoism is a protection against disease, but in the last resort we must begin to love in order that we may not fall ill, and must fall ill if, in consequence of frustration, we cannot love." (Freud, *Collected Papers, op. cit.*, Vol. IV, p. 42.)

This, of course, was "voluntarily" inflicted, narcissistic self-destruction; one sees the same thing, however, in the over-reaction of some organs to injury. The simplest example I can think of is the tremendous swelling that occurs in some individuals as the result of an insect bite; the pain and itching is due more to the healing process than to the original injury. The excessive formation of new tissue in the healing of a cut or ulcer, so-called "proud flesh," is another example of this. It may not be apparent that there is anything erotic about this although the increased attention to a wound which swelling and itching stimulates is a matter of common knowledge.

I once had the opportunity of observing the development of a severe cold in a woman of unusual intuitive penetration who was, at the time, undergoing psychoanalysis. It occurred when there was no epidemic, in a woman who was not ordinarily subject to colds. Indeed, she was proud of her immunity to them and had had but few in her entire life.

I have reported the details of this case in the psychoanalytic literature[22] and my findings have been confirmed by other psychoanalysts in other cases. It is unnecessary to cite all the material; the substance of the matter was that this "cold" marked a turning point in the woman's psychological reconstruction; she had begun just at that time to admit how much she wanted to be loved. She apparently gratified this wish in an autoplastic way by centering the restructive-erotic conflict first on one organ and then another; her eyes, her nose, her throat, and finally her chest were successively involved in the infection. In a sense, each one of these organs represented her whole personality which wanted love but felt too guilty to receive it without paying for it in suffering. That the illness had a psychological import for her was shown by her own comment, in which she referred to an interpretation I had made some time before concerning her repressed aggressiveness.

"Perhaps," she said, "you were right after all, that I do want to take things, want to so intensely that I lean over backward and try to persuade myself that I don't want to accept anything from anybody. But now this cold comes along and I speak of 'taking' a cold and my use of that expression catches my own attention which makes me think

[22] Menninger, Karl A., "Some Unconscious Psychological Factors Associated with the Common Cold," *Psychoanalytic Review*, April, 1934, Vol. XXI, pp. 201-07.

that perhaps I have decided I *would* take things from now on. Perhaps this had something to do with my better relations with my husband over the week-end."

There was much more to it, as I have said—and perhaps the reader will feel dissatisfied with the explanation that a woman who has always fought off the love she really wanted, developed or "accepted" a naso-respiratory tract infection just when she decided to let down the bars of her defensiveness. But so I believe it was.

And the same motive is discernible, I believe, in many cases of tuberculosis. This, as a matter of fact, has been observed by intuitive laymen. M. deTraz,[23] for example, in speaking of the tuberculous patients of Leysin, wrote: "We see that tuberculosis often depends upon the spiritual life and that it develops under the influences of sorrow, moral shock, and worry." He described a psychology common to these patients:

> The world on whose threshold they stand—even if they do not know it, even if they are never to know it—is readily invented. They have fewer memories than plans. Saved from small failures by one general failure, overwhelmingly disillusioned rather than robbed of illusion bit by bit, they are wonderfully prepared for dreaming. Stretched out on their *chaises longues* for days without end, they create their own illusory joys and fictitious ambitions. Their possibilities are unlimited because they need never be carried into effect. No other patient is more of a dreamer. Thus tuberculosis is not so much a disintegration of the flesh as an exhaustion, a fervor, and a state of spiritual seething. The tenderest visions, the purest exaltations that have been proffered to miserable humanity have come to us as the gift of those who were ill with tuberculosis.
>
> They are so in need of love. "Just like everyone else," you will reply. No, more than anyone else. First, because they are alone, and sad, and often forgotten. The cowards among them want to be pitied; the disillusioned, to be understood. And then, unable to live by acting in the present, they vacillate between the past and the future, between memory and expectation. They live by their hearts. And the heart—much used and over-refined —becomes more and more hungry.

Tuberculosis is, after all, a graceful way to destroy one-self—slowly, tragically, often with relative comfort, good food, rest, peace, and the sympathetic tears of all. It is prone to occur, too, in individuals whose need of love is

[23] deTraz, Robert, *Les Heures de Silence*, Grasset, Paris, 1934. Reviewed by Edmond Jaloux in *Nouvelles Litteraires*, Paris, and in *The Living Age*, June, 1934, pp. 357-58.

obvious—notoriously in young women of a certain wistful, ethereal beauty. A friend of mine who recovered from this disease expressed the opinion that the vivacity and optimism of tuberculous patients, the *spes phthisica,* is often only a screen to hide the real depression from which they suffer. It is a mood assumed with the purpose of obtaining the much-needed love to which deTraz refers. When all the doctors and visitors leave the ward, a perceptible pall of depression settles down again.[24]

A few cases of tuberculosis have been psychoanalytically studied and this need for love, this substitution of the disease for an affaire d'amour, is quite striking in some of the reports. A man forty-three years of age was studied by Jelliffe and Evans.[25] He was the youngest of six children and had been considered a delicate child by his mother who told him he had been left so when he had whooping cough at the age of two. He did not remember being particularly delicate but he did remember that it was pleasant to have his mother protect him from the hard work of the farm. When he was about ten he had a severe cold which enabled him to avoid weeding the garden and which brought him special attention and privileges. He used to cough violently whenever he knew his father could hear him. His cough served to keep him out of the fields, although his father opposed his going away from the farm to school as the boy longed to do. At the age of twenty-six, however, he entered college where, freed from the restraint of the home, he found new life and health. His money was gone after three years and he was obliged to return home where he became ill and his cough became incessant. After two years he again entered college and finally went abroad on a scholarship. During the years of study abroad his

[24] Psychological factors in tuberculosis as intuitively perceived by a great artist have been recorded in detail by Thomas Mann in his masterpiece *The Magic Mountain* (English translation by H. T. Lowe-Porter, Knopf, 1930). "Then there was . . . Natalie . . . with the black eyes and the gold rings in her ears; coquettish, fond of dress, but a perfect Lazarus and Job in female form, whom God had been pleased to afflict with every kind of infirmity. Her entire organism seemed infected. . . . The woman's state was truly pitiable, and she was alone in the world; for she had left home and children for the sake of a lover, a mere youth, only to be forsaken in her turn. . . . But his family had taken him away from her, by guile and force commingled—and perhaps he too had been revolted by her illness, which had suddenly and violently broken out. 'Perhaps the gentlemen were revolted, too?' she asked coquettishly, and her inborn femininity triumphed even over the eczema that covered half her face." (Pp. 395-96.)

[25] Jelliffe, Smith Ely, and Evans, Elida, "Psychotherapy and Tuberculosis," *American Review of Tuberculosis*, Sept., 1919, pp. 417-32.

cough ceased and he felt well although he often longed for someone to love and care for him as his mother had done. He was anxious to find a wife and became engaged while abroad but broke off the engagement a few months later, after which the old depressions returned and his cough became constant. He had two slight hemorrhages. Frequent examinations of sputum showed no tubercle bacilli but his longing to be cared for increased until he found a home in the family of a trained nurse where he went to bed with frequent attacks of indigestion and high fever. Tubercle bacilli were discovered in the sputum a year later.

The psychoanalysis of this patient showed clearly his infantile oral dependence upon his mother. As the authors put it, "He has been coughing to attract her all his years of manhood." Insight gained through treatment enabled him to face and repudiate this infantile attitude and to cease running from everything disagreeable as his mother had encouraged him to do through over-protection.

Most convincing of all, because most explicit, is the evidence afforded by the cases of stomach and intestinal disease. It is common knowledge that psychological as well as physiological purposes are fulfilled by our digestive organs. But it may not be so familiar to the non-medical reader that a large number of patients consult physicians with all sorts of complaints referable to their digestive system. The symptoms range from acute pain to mild discomfort or nausea and are associated with all phases of the digestive process. Many patients present themselves to the physician with a self-made diagnosis, usually a very vague and inaccurate one—stomach trouble, heartburn, bowel trouble, nervous indigestion, biliousness, etc. Others come (or go) with long lists of articles of food which they must avoid in order to enjoy life, because these foods "don't agree with" them, "poison" them, make them ill, cause them to have pain, diarrhea or constipation. The number and variety of these digestive afflictions are legion and the patients suffering from them, even though they may be intelligent and tractable people in other respects, are often illogical, superstitious and eccentric in a high degree with reference to these symptoms. The possibility that the pain, indigestion or constipation might be related to psychological or emotional factors never occurs to them and is apt to be rejected summarily if suggested.

Nevertheless, it has been known to a few discerning

medical men[26] for some time that some of these patients can be relieved of their symptoms by engaging them in a discussion of their *other* "troubles"—business anxieties, family problems, personal difficulties of all kinds. But it is one thing to know that symptoms of this sort can be relieved by a discussion of the emotional problems of the patient who has the symptoms and another thing to know why this relief occurs and how the symptoms were produced in the first place. A group of research workers[27] at the Chicago Institute for Psychoanalysis undertook to investigate this problem, hoping to discover what the deeper psychology of patients suffering from gastro-intestinal disease really was. They were not endeavoring (primarily) to cure these particular patients, but to find out why they were sick, and why, as with Freud's original cases, the very investigatory process seemed to carry along with it a therapeutic value. Not all of these Institute cases were cured, nor were the workers able in all cases to discover exactly what the psychological factors were or how they were related to one another. On the other hand, they did discover rather definitely that certain psychological tendencies were present in their cases which might almost be said to resolve themselves into certain formulae.

It was discovered that those cases in which the symptoms were primarily gastric were in nearly every instance persons who seemed to have an inordinately strong desire to be loved, and that this wish to be loved seemed to follow an infantile pattern of acquisition. There was, however, in these cases a reaction against these strong oral cravings in the direction of a defiant, compensatory independence, as if to say, "I am an efficient, active, productive person; I give to everybody, support many people, help many people, assume responsibilities, and enjoy having people depend upon me; I am an entirely self-sufficient leader, active, aggressive, fearless." This attitude was likely to be expressed

[26] See, for example, the reports of Hartman, Alvarez, Alkan, Draper, Touraine, Oppenheimer, Underwood, Sullivan, Chandler, Deutsch, Dreyfus, Heyer, Schindler, and Bergman. There are probably many others who have known this principle and applied it but who have not appeared in the medical literature and many others who have published reports which I have not the space to mention. A very complete list of these is to be found in Dunbar's excellent compilation (*op. cit.*). She quotes one (Stiller) who over fifty years ago wrote: "That people develop gastric disturbances after financial losses and suffer from them until their financial conditions turn to the better, is an everyday experience."

[27] Alexander, Bacon, Wilson, Levey, and Levine, "The Influence of Psychologic Factors upon Gastro-Intestinal Disturbances: A Symposium," *Psychoanalytic Quarterly*, 1934, Vol. III, pp. 501-88.

verbally and in behavior. But it was found that underneath it was a strong tendency in precisely the opposite direction, i.e., an extreme, often violent, craving to be taken care of, nursed, fed, protected, loved, mothered, ministered to, and this craving was expressed by the stomach. Of course many people have such tendencies quite consciously but these individuals had them only unconsciously and repressed them very strongly, replacing them by this camouflage of denial and pseudo-independence and self-sufficiency. But the price they pay in denying their underlying wishes is too high and against this unconscious duplicity of the personality there arises a protest in the form of intense gastric suffering (and —as I believe—gastric erotization).

I shall quote one case summary practically verbatim:

In one of our peptic ulcer cases (a forty-six-year-old man who was subjected to an anamnestic study of three weeks) . . . it was much more the external life situation than a deeply situated internal rejection of his passive wishes that had deprived the patient of the satisfaction of his oral receptive tendencies. During his childhood and adolescence he profusely indulged in receptive gratification, was not at all the leader-type but on the contrary his attitude entirely lacked the usual ambition so frequent in peptic ulcer cases. He married an extremely able, intelligent, intellectually superior, active woman of the leader-type; his marriage, however, soon disappointed all his expectations of finding in his wife a superior person who would serve as a substitute for a generously giving mother. Not that she changed after their marriage, but from the beginning she devoted her life entirely to the promotion of her career, to learning, working, and producing. Moreover, their sexual life was most incomplete. The wife was frigid and the patient suffered from premature ejaculation. The husband received nothing from his wife and being thwarted in his receptive tendencies, he soon was driven into a competitive attitude toward his wife who even financially was the chief supporter of the household. Instead of being mothered by his wife, her superiority drove him toward ambition and effort which he deeply detested and rejected. He never succeeded in any active efforts and remained always mediocre in his profession. At the peak of this conflict situation, after twenty years of marriage, he developed a severe hemorrhage as a result of a peptic ulcer. But during all these years he suffered from gastric symptoms, chiefly from pain a few hours after eating, which was relieved by food, and from chronic hyperacidity. The ulcer was the end result of the gastric disorder of eighteen years' duration.

Shortly after this hemorrhage he started a sexual relationship with another woman of a motherly type, the exact opposite of his wife. His wife, he complained, never would cook for him, but this woman did. She was a nice, soft, everyday type of woman who did not drive him into unattainable ambitions. He could live with her the modest life of the petty bourgeois, which, as he openly admitted, was his only ideal. Since establishing a sexual relation with this woman, all the symptoms have disappeared. Life supplied a cure in allowing him the gratification of his receptive tendencies.

Alexander comments:

In the light of psychoanalytic theory it is not difficult to understand why the functions of nutrition are especially adapted to express the repressed receptive tendencies which we find predominant in all of our cases. The infantile wish to receive, to be taken care of, to be loved, to depend upon someone else is most ideally gratified in the parasitic situation of the suckling infant. Thus these emotional qualities of receptivity, the wish to be loved and taken care of, become closely associated in an early period of life with the physiologic functions of nutrition and consequently if they are excluded later from normal expression due to repressions, they will appear in the original pattern as the infantile wish to be fed. Such repressed receptive tendencies can be considered as chronic psychic stimuli of the stomach which lead to its dysfunction. This stimulation of the stomach is independent of the physiologic state of digestion. It has its origin in emotional conflicts entirely independent of the physiologic state of hunger.

My present notion is that the stomach under this permanent chronic stimulation behaves constantly as it does during digestion. A chronic hyper-motility and hyper-secretion may be the consequence. The empty stomach is thus constantly exposed to the same physiological stimuli to which, under normal conditions, it is exposed only periodically when it contains or is about to receive food. The symptoms of the nervous stomach, epigastric distress, heartburn, and belching probably are the manifestations of this chronic stimulation which sometimes may even lead to ulcer formation. . . .

Detailed case histories are supplied by these workers to support their conclusions. They are much too lengthy for full inclusion here but one will be cited in abstract to convey some idea of the abundant clinical evidence obtained.

Bacon, for example, describes a woman who came because of epigastric distress of seven years' duration which was at times so agonizing as to require opiates; there were also severe attacks of belching, flatus, and occasional attacks of diarrhea or constipation. She also had attacks of bulimia (compulsive over-eating) lasting from ten to fifteen days, during which she would put on ten to twenty pounds of weight.

She was married, thirty-five years old, very feminine in appearance, nicely dressed, and very attractive to men. She made many friends but usually kept them for only a short time. Born in Europe, the youngest of three girls, she came to this country at the age of eight, after her father's death. Her parents had formerly been wealthy but had lost everything. Her father was well educated and respected by his townspeople, but she remembers little of him. Her mother, on the other hand, was ignorant and coarse but made the patient her favorite. At the same time, however, the mother was cruel to her and neglected her. A typical example of this which the patient recalled was that at the age of six a man tried to attack her and when she screamed for help her mother came out and beat her without trying to find out why the child had cried out. Throughout her childhood she had to work very hard, helping her mother. She was jealous of her next older sister whom she felt to be a selfish and demanding girl, most successful in getting what she wanted.

The patient was married at twenty to a man fifteen years her senior and for the first time in her life received a great deal of care and attention. Her husband was successful and intellectually superior which corresponded with the position occupied by her own father. She traveled about with him a great deal. For two years he sent her to a boarding school. She was always frigid in her sexual relations with him but quite happy in the dependent, childlike position she occupied.

This state of bliss was disturbed, first, by the birth or their child seven years after the marriage which required that she give it the attention of which she had formerly been the recipient; second, by the increased necessity for her husband to be away from home on business; and third, by her discovery made nine years after her marriage that her husband was supporting a previous wife and child. To this discovery she reacted with great rage and resentment and it was at this time that her gastro-intestinal symptoms began, continuing for the next seven years, until the beginning of her analysis.

Matters became complicated through difficulties encountered by the husband; he lost his job and also his sexual potency, to both of which she reacted with enormous anger (and gastro-intestinal symptoms). In spite of this anger, however, she worked hard to keep up her home, take care ot her child and prepare elaborate, well-cooked meals for her husband, even when she was so sick that she could not eat them herself.

Her conscious attitude toward herself was one of approval. She felt that she was superior to her associates, praiseworthy in her efforts, always doing things for other people, even to the point of "stuffing my kindness down their throats." Underneath this attitude, however, could be seen strong tendencies to demand love and attention from people, especially men, and to seize it if it wasn't forthcoming. Denial of these demands seemed to provoke in her the destructive anger of thwarting which is so characteristic of the personality type called by the psychoanalysts the oral type. Her bitter resentment at her husband's inability to support her in the latter days, his loyalty to an obligation to a former wife, his failure to satisfy her sexually, and his necessary absence from home have already been mentioned. She carried this rage to the point of seeking to avenge herself by deliberate infidelity, pursuing several love affairs, none of which seemed to be motivated by any deep attachment to the lovers so much as by a wish to hurt her husband. An apparently curious but actually very characteristic feature of these extra-marital love affairs was that she became bitter and enraged at her lovers for precisely the same reasons that she was angry at her husband; she complained that they did not satisfy her, took delight in thwarting her, broke dates with her, and gave her nothing.

As an indication of the way in which oral activities were, for her, a mode of sexual satisfaction, her attacks of overeating were observed to appear at periods when she was conscious of unfulfilled sexual desire, e.g., when one of her lovers was breaking off with her. Conversely, during the brief periods of happiness in her love affairs she lost all interest in food.

What has been cited is sufficient to show how this patient loved, as it were, with her mouth, instead of with her sexual organs, the mature, normal, biological method of female expression. She was vaginally frigid but she could eat and kiss and beg and, in a manner of speaking, suck; she could, moreover, reproach, denounce, and bite. This use of the gastro-intestinal system to carry out functions which should be carried out by the genital system overloads it, so to speak, to the point of breakdown. From the psychoanalytic standpoint, the symptoms may be regarded as a regressive mode (oral) of obtaining "love" and self-inflicted punishment, on account of the guilt associated with the oral aggressiveness.[28]

One can see in such microscopic analyses that it is as though such persons were obliged (as we all are) to love and be loved in order to live, but were unable to do this in a normal manner. Instead, they regress, upon the occasion of some degree of thwarting, to primitive, infantile (therefore "perverse") modes which entail a mixture of this substituted erotic quality, and of the rage and resentment (i.e., aggressiveness) which the thwarting and disappointment engender. This aggressiveness, in turn, comes under the disapproval of the conscience and a punishment is demanded. All of these things—the oral craving (and the mediate and immediate "love" it obtains), the aggressiveness (both the original impulse and the aggressive uses of the illness) and the self-punishment are neatly gratified—"solved"—by the development of the stomach ulcer.[29]

In the foregoing pages we have adduced some material to indicate the presence of the erotic component in organic disease, a component which apparently enters into all self-destructiveness in a dual capacity. Its normal function would seem to be to neutralize or diminish the destructiveness of the aggressive and self-punitive elements but sometimes, perhaps always to some extent, it defeats its own purposes and serves to augment the destructive result. The erotic component may thus turn the tide of an illness by mobilizing the healing forces or may seek in illness its extravagant fulfillment, feeding itself at the expense of the personality. At present we can only conjecture what determines the optimum proportion or quality of this component, what throws the balance in some instances to the

[28] The treatment of this patient lasted a year and a half and the symptoms were entirely relieved.

[29] But is this, someone may ask, any evidence of the organic investment of love? Granted that such persons crave love, can it be logically deduced that these organic consequences of obtaining it involve any eroticism? This is a hard question and I cannot give the neat answer that may be expected. In those who feel starved for love (let us put it that way for simplicity) there is apt to be a return to greater-than-normal narcissistic self-comfort. (This much we would all agree to.) It is my idea that in these organic involvements the individual identifies himself, so to speak, with the affected organ, in the way described in the first paragraphs of this chapter, and this local narcissistic investment of the organ compensates for the deficiency of love received from (or given to) the outside world. The organs are a part of the personality and must share the love-lessness with all other parts. But this is still a tenuous hypothesis, and I realize upon what uncertain evidence it hangs.

aggressive and self-punitive forces, leaving the erotic component to make the best of a bad bargain and console itself with the intense immature "organ love" we have described, and, in other instances, to the side of the more normal function of the erotic instinct of neutralizing the destructive forces so that they subside in the process of healing.

SUMMARY

Organic disease is the resultant of many cooperative factors, not only extraneous elements such as bacteria, but numerous internal elements including the psychological components. When the responses to emotional stimuli overwhelm the customary or available devices of manifest expression, they fall back upon the more primitive "spillways" of the autonomic system to "say it with symptoms." But when these symptomatic expressions become habitual or chronic we are apt to forget all we know about their psychological meaning. The same doctor who would immediately understand how a man could have an involuntary bowel movement in a moment of great fear is utterly amazed and incredulous at the proposal that *chronic* diarrhea may express *chronic* and continuous fear. Yet one need only postulate a continuous stimulation to expect a continuous symptomatology, which in turn leads to adaptive (but destructive) organic changes.

The subdivisions of this chapter are to be regarded as having been made only for convenience of exposition and do not imply that in some conditions only one element of the triad is present. Sometimes, as we have seen, one is more conspicuous than the other—but this may be only an artefact. What we are safe in concluding is that the psychology of some organic disease runs parallel with that of some behavior which we regard as self-destructive, manifests the same mechanisms, contains the same elements. That there are structural differences is certain, and in the next chapter we shall try to indicate what these probably are.

THREE / *The Choice of the Lesser Evil*

The concentrated consideration of the usually neglected psychological factors in disease is apt to convey a false impression, one which is immediately dispelled by a glance at the long lines of sufferers at the doors of the clinics, or at the elaborate research studies of medical scientists investigating pathogenic bacteria, traumata, toxins, neoplasms, and the dire consequences of their ravages in the bodies of man and beast. No sensible person would deny that flesh is vulnerable or that the individual may be attacked without any provocation on his part, by agents capable of inflicting injury which can in no sense be interpreted as self-destruction. On the other hand, these things are so obvious and so well known that the tendency is to forget that even in the matter of bacterial infection it takes two to make a bargain, i.e., that there are questions of diminished immunity and resistance, as well as of inoculation and virulence. This is the more plausible in the case of such bacteria as the tubercle bacillus and the pneumococcus which we know to be around us at all times and to which most of us succeed in maintaining our immunity successfully. Everyone has had the experience of "catching a bad cold" at just such a critical moment in his life as to leave a strong presumption that it was some way or other influenced by his emotional state.

It is reasonable, therefore, that we should divide diseases into at least three groups: those in which the environment unexpectedly attacks the individual and in which his self-destructive tendencies do not in any way participate, those in which there is some degree of participation in or exploitation by the self-destructive tendencies of an occasion perhaps largely or primarily furnished by the environment, and finally, those diseases in which the environment is merely a passive contributor.

So far as the latter two groups are concerned, those in which the element of self-destructiveness is to some degree discernible, it is immediately apparent upon inspection of the various forms which have been considered that they can be arranged in a progressive series from suicide, as the most complete and irreversible form, through organic disease and hysterical disease to those attenuated forms of self-destruc-

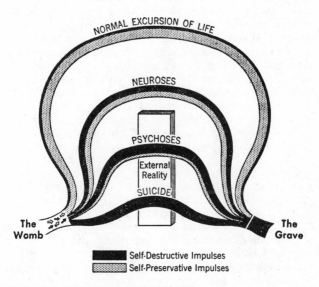

DIAGRAM I. PSYCHIATRIC CATEGORIES

tion which are so widespread and innocuous as to be fairly described as "normal," e.g., smoking.

This serial arrangement can be represented in the form of a diagram (see Diagram I) in which the destructive impulses (black) are diverted by the opposing factors of reality (white) and, more especially, by internal tendencies toward self-preservation and love for other people (gray). The normal result is a wide excursion around such obstacles.

The general concepts of normal behavior, neurotic behavior, psychotic behavior, and suicide are arranged as a progressive series. The neuroses will be seen to avoid serious conflict with external realities but to lack sufficient of the erotic neutralization (gray) to allow of full expansion to the limits of normal living. The psychoses, on the other

357

hand, show sharp conflict with reality, a feature which both determines and defines them. Only suicide is more restrictive, more self-destructive than a psychosis.

A similar series could probably be constructed for each special form of modified self-destruction representing varying degrees of neutralization. For example, it will be recalled that self-mutilations may be of a relatively normal, socially acceptable form, hair-cutting and nail-trimming for example. Then there are other forms which, while they do not bring the individual into serious conflict with reality, do show the effects of an insufficient quantity of erotic neutralization. These represent the neurotic self-mutilations. Next, there are those which seem to overcome both the opposition of the erotic (self-preservative) factors and the restraining forces of reality and represent the psychotic and religious forms of self-mutilation. Then, of course, there are those severe self-mutilations which are almost equivalent to suicide.

Finally, pertinent to the type of modified self-destruction now under consideration, one could construct such a diagram to show the relation of hysterical illness to structural illness of organs. (See Diagram II.)

In this diagram, health is represented as the circumvention of the impulse toward self-destruction, the ultimate accomplishment of which is thus postponed so indefinitely as to be indistinguishable from the so-called normal processes of senile decay. Less severe are those functional or "hysterical" lesions which involve serious demands upon the internal erotic reserves but adjust themselves in a practical way to external reality factors. Organic disease, on the other hand, to some extent overwhelms both and would seem, therefore, to be a short-circuiting of the self-destructive tendency comparable to that represented in the voluntary nervous system series by the psychoses. The ultimate and extreme short-circuiting is, of course, represented by death itself. (Cf. SUICIDE in Diagram I.)

Such analogies are valuable because the serial relationship which thus becomes apparent implies a dynamic or economic interpretation. This interpretation, which answers the question as to the choice of illness, revolves about the principle of sacrifice as follows:

The self-preservative tendencies or life instincts battle to the limits of their power against the self-destructive tendencies and while it is true they ultimately lose, they do man-

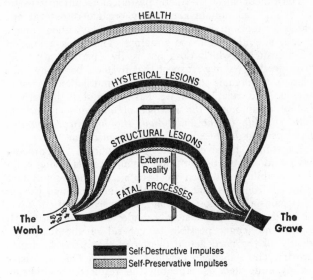

HEALTH

HYSTERICAL LESIONS

STRUCTURAL LESIONS

External Reality

FATAL PROCESSES

The Womb

The Grave

■ Self-Destructive Impulses
▨ Self-Preservative Impulses

DIAGRAM II. MEDICAL CATEGORIES

age to permit each of us, on the average, some seventy years of more or less comfortable existence. Now it would appear that they do so only by dint of offering at certain critical points, in response to the demands of the self-destructive urge, certain sacrifices—greater or lesser. An illness of any kind is such a sacrifice or compromise and the choice of illness might, therefore, be considered to represent a choice of the lesser evil.

The ego strives to make the best possible bargain with the conflicting forces of reality, instincts, and conscience. Sometimes it is necessary to pay such a high price to the demands of reality that the instinctual gratifications in outside investments are definitely restricted; then an internal problem develops and the tension may become so great as to force aggressions denied other outlets to break through the self-protective defenses, whereupon the responsibility of the ego is to restrict this self-destruction to the least serious, least costly, sacrifice. For this task, the capacity and wisdom of the ego vary greatly in different individuals.

359

The functional or so-called "hysterical" solution is useful because it can imitate almost any organic disease at any site but differs in being usually reversible without much, if any, alteration in tissue structure. Thus it is a kind of self-destruction which does not really (permanently) destroy, so that we may suspect that hysteria bears the same relation to organic disease that self-mutilation bears to suicide. This relation, as we have suggested, is perhaps that of compromise; *the sacrifice of an organ is made to spare the life of the individual, the hysterical symptom develops in order to spare the life of an organ.*

Sometimes, however, as suggested above, this process, this pseudo-destruction of some organ, loses its saving grace of reversibility, and then we have an organic lesion.[1] One supposes from this that the death-instinct in some way or other gains a little more foothold, like weeds that gain upon the gardener in a momentarily neglected flower garden. It is then no longer possible to get rid of the temporary "death" of the part; actual death (of that part) begins to threaten, and sometimes definitely to ensue. This, as I have already suggested, is probably the result of overwhelmingly powerful impulses in the direction of self-destruction. These, however, we know to be actuated by overwhelmingly powerful impulses toward the destruction of someone else, which, however, are turned back upon the self either through the threatening aspect of reality or (and probably most powerfully) at the instigation of the conscience.

It would seem incumbent on us at this point to substantiate the theory of sacrifice with the evidence of clinical material. Every physician is familiar with case histories in which one illness replaces another and sometimes it seems quite fairly presumptive that an illness of one kind seems to be elected by a patient in lieu of an illness of another kind which either was or seemed to the patient to be a more serious one. It is, however, difficult to prove that the patient himself had anything to do with this selection. One of our patients, for example, alternated between severe depressions with complete physical health and severe physical illnesses without depression. One infers that these were

[1] Jelliffe has repeatedly made this point. "In the neurotic stage of maladjustment (organ neuroses) the processes are still reversible . . . but after a certain number of years of such faulty adaptations . . . the processes become irreversible. The leaning tower of Pisa has leaned too far and organic disease has begun." (Jelliffe, S. E., "Psychoanalysis and Internal Medicine" in *Psychoanalysis Today,* edited by S. Lorand, Covici, Friede, 1933, p. 300.)

substitutions and re-substitutions but it can scarcely be proved. Alcoholism frequently appears to be accepted by a patient as the inevitable alternative to a frank psychosis and in our study of polysurgery (Part IV) I cited several examples in which an individual elected or actually demanded a surgical operation to escape, as he thought, a more serious fate, either from anxiety stimulated from his own conscience or from some external agency.

Patients admitted to a clinic for nervous or psychotic conditions often give the history of having suffered from physical illnesses which cleared up as the mental illness developed. Furthermore, as a general thing, the physical health of psychiatric patients is far above the average. For example, during a mild influenza epidemic eight of our nurses and several doctors were seriously ill, in bed, at one time, and several others acquired it later. During the entire period, however, not a single one of the patients with whom they had been associated daily had even so much as a bad cold. The most careful physical, neurological, and laboratory examinations of most psychiatric patients generally yield essentially normal results. This would suggest that the psychosis satisfies the demands of the destructive impulse without the necessity of physical sacrifice.

This has been borne out by a statistical study[2] which showed that many physical diseases occur far more frequently in the community at large than in hospitalized psychiatric cases. For example, coronary sclerosis and angina pectoris occurred thirteen to fifteen times more frequently as the cause of death in cases outside of state hospitals than among state hospital patients; diabetes five and a half times as frequently, goiter nine times as frequently, peptic ulcer over three times as frequently, nephritis three times as frequently, cancer four times as frequently. (Arteriosclerosis and tuberculosis, on the other hand, occurred only about one-fourth as frequently.) Even suicide is about twice as frequent in the community at large as among state hospital cases!

Many times patients are admitted to the sanitarium on account of more or less acute mental symptoms, for example, depression; a few days later all signs of the depression have disappeared, the patient will be in the best of humor, cheerful, sociable, cooperative, delighted with everything but, unfortunately, confined to bed or to his room

---

[2] Gregg, Donald, "The Lethal Power of the Emotions," *Mental Hygiene*, January, 1936, p. 30.

with some physical affliction, such as a bad cold, pains in the joints, a headache, sciatica. This happens so often that we can no longer regard it as a coincidence.[3]

Another recent statistical study[4] confirms the same impression. Careful investigation of a group of Illinois school children showed in general that well-adjusted children had more physical illnesses than the maladjusted—more frequent, more serious, and more prolonged illnesses. For example, a history of having had few diseases was twice as common in pupils classified as poorly adjusted as it was in those classified as well adjusted with the same age status and from similar types of home environment, and three

[3] Dr. George Wilson of Chicago very kindly reported to me the main outlines of a case later to be published in detail in which there was a clearly discernible therapeutic progress step by step from the "inner-circle" (cf. Diagram II) of organic self-destruction through the intermediate or less severe stage of hysterical conversion to an increasingly normal life adjustment. Something of this sort happens regularly in psychoanalytic therapy but not always with such diagrammatic clearness as in this case.

It was a young woman, a dentist, who, desperate to the point of suicide because of various frustrations, had finally substituted homosexual and autoerotic gratifications for a more normal sex life. These ultimately proved unsatisfactory; indeed, they were potentially fatal to her social and professional standing and had to be given up. This was done rather suddenly and was immediately superseded by an acute duodenal ulcer, demonstrated by x-ray. This affliction was treated medically and was of short duration (about one month). It then disappeared completely and a severe arthralgia began which became so serious as to lead three separately consulted orthopedists to recommend plaster cast fixation. Nevertheless, the subsequent developments showed that this was almost certainly an hysterical conversion. Its particular meaning I shall pass over here. Sufficient to say that it, too, disappeared completely and rather suddenly when the patient—finally overcoming all of her inhibitions with respect to a normal sexual life—became engaged and married with a complete disappearance of the back pain. Sexual frigidity remained as the last remnant of her self-destructiveness, but finally this, too, disappeared and no other symptoms or disease took its place.

Diagrammatically, the series developed as follows:

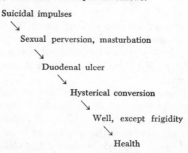

Suicidal impulses

Sexual perversion, masturbation

Duodenal ulcer

Hysterical conversion

Well, except frigidity

Health

[4] Hardy, Martha C., "Some Evidence of an Inverse Relation between Health History and Behavior Adjustments during Childhood," *Journal of Abnormal and Social Psychology*, January-March, 1937, p. 406.

times as many serious illnesses such as scarlet fever, pneumonia, meningitis, and appendicitis occurred among the well adjusted as among the poorly adjusted. Among the children described by the teachers as having very happy, cheerful dispositions, less than ten per cent had been relatively free from illness as compared with twenty-three per cent of the children who appeared to be unhappy and morose.[5]

Psychoanalysts are very familiar with the following phenomenon: A patient who has suffered from a neurotic illness for many years will upon advice begin psychoanalytic treatment only to develop severe physical symptoms temporarily exempting him from the dreaded analysis. One of my patients developed appendicitis, another a peri-rectal abscess, another influenza, etc. Or again, a patient will begin analysis and within a few months appear to be completely free from long-standing symptoms. In the earlier days of psychoanalysis, this so-called transference cure was unfortunately misinterpreted in spite of Freud's warning. Now we know such a patient has merely substituted psychoanalysis itself for the neurosis and in that sense is reacting toward the treatment as if it were an affliction which is cheerfully but bravely endured and which makes it no longer necessary to sustain the neurotic illness. Such a phenomenon is most frequently seen in masochistic individuals who like to interpret any treatment given them by physicians as a form of heroically-borne torture. Physicians other than analysts are also familiar with such individuals; they go from one doctor to another telling what terrible sufferings the previous doctor inflicted upon them. In this way, they excite the sympathy and pity of the second doctor, who then tries earnestly to give them some appropriate treatment to which the patient submits bravely for a time, shows marked improvement, then relapses and goes to still another doctor to whom he describes again the abuses to which he has been subjected by physicians.

[5] We do not know the cause of brain tumor. Some medical men and many laymen have been of the opinion that severe injuries to the head might be at least a pre-disposing cause. However, a statistical study by Parker and Kernohan of the Mayo Clinic ("The Relation of Injury and Glioma of the Brain," *Journal of the American Medical Association*, Aug. 22, 1931, p. 535) showed that not only was there no evidence of this but actually the incidence of brain tumor and head trauma show an inverse correlation. One could scarcely say that blows on the head prevent brain tumor but it is true according to these carefully controlled observations that the history of head trauma is less frequent in patients who develop brain tumor than among patients with other diseases or among the general population.

These illustrations but serve to show that as a matter of clinical observation one disease or syndrome often appears to be substituted for another. That this occurs because of some unconscious wish to economize, as it were, in the matter of suffering and danger, is a theory which is probably not susceptible of proof, but which satisfies the necessities of an explanation for the observed facts and develops logically from our general theory of disease as a form of self-destruction.

SUMMARY

My thesis, then, it that some forms of organic disease represent structuralization of perverted functions forced upon these organs to solve unconscious conflicts, the nature of these conflicts being related to the opposition and interaction of aggressive, self-punitive, and erotic components of the self-destructive tendency. The hypothesis is that organic lesions, so frequently requiring as they do direct agents from the environment such as bacteria or trauma for their initiation, differ not only in this respect but also in certain psychological respects from so-called functional disorders, mainly in that the sacrifice demanded by the destructive tendencies is a greater one and that the conflict is more strongly and deeply repressed, i.e., less accessible to consciousness.[6]

[6] These conflicts, in order to be related to organic affections, must be assumed to express themselves via complicated physiological mechanisms concerning which psychoanalysis and physiology are only recently attempting to establish a cooperative understanding. The physiological mechanisms would seem to lean heavily upon the laws of conditioned reflex action which have been so elaborately studied experimentally by Pavlov. The application of these principles to psychoanalytic data and theory has been attempted with great promise by Dr. Thomas M. French of Chicago ("Interrelations between Psychoanalysis and the Experimental Work of Pavlov," *American Journal of Psychiatry*, May, 1933, pp. 1165-1203). It seems not unlikely that we shall be able in the not distant future to define more precisely the physiological details of the expression of unconscious wishes.

In the meantime, progress has also been made in this direction by the neurologists, physiologists, anatomists and endocrinologists. The work of Cannon with respect to the chemical elements in the personality, specifically the mechanisms of endocrine gland activity, has enabled us to speak with some definiteness as to some of the relationships between wish and the symptom, including some of the anatomical pathways. My colleague and former associate, Dr. Leo Stone, has presented a considered analysis of these possibilities as far as they are known to us at present. (Stone, Leo, "Concerning the Psychogenesis of Somatic Disease, Physiological and Neurological Correlations with the Psychological Theory," *International Journal of Psychoanalysis*.)

PART VI **Reconstruction**

ONE / *Clinical Techniques in the Service of Reconstruction*

We have completed a survey of the various ways in which human beings destroy themselves, beginning with suicide and carrying through the various chronic and indirect forms to the postulate that some somatic disease may be conceived of as indirect organic self-destruction. Concomitantly, we have seen that both internal and external forces operate in opposition to the self-destructive tendencies so that the actual outcome is a compromise between the will-to-live and the will-to-die, the life-instinct and the death-instinct. To this extent there is always a degree of spontaneous self-*reconstruction*[1] along with the self-destruc-

---

[1] Von Hartmann reminded us in his great "Philosophy of the Unconscious" (Von Hartmann, Eduard, *Philosophy of the Unconscious*, Harcourt, Brace, 1931) that many of the lower forms of life are able to effect reconstruction or regeneration of injuries to parts of the body, and even points out that a spontaneous or voluntary rejection or detachment of an injured or threatened limb may be the first act of the reconstruction process. He called attention to the curious adaptability of the *Holothuriae*, organisms of the Philippine Islands region which eat large quantities of coral sand. If they are taken from their native haunts and transferred to clear sea water, they spontaneously eject from the anus *their entire intestinal canals with all of the organs attached thereto* in order to form new viscera more in harmony with the altered medium.

Von Hartmann also called attention to the unfortunate circumstance that the higher the ascent in the animal scale the less potent, as a rule, is the unconscious power of self-healing. His explanation, in part, was that the organizing force (regenerative energy) turns always more and more away from the machinery of the body, so to speak, and bends its whole energy toward the final goal of all organization, the organ of consciousness, in order to raise that to the highest perfection. Also, he thought the organs of the higher animal classes were, in consequence of their mode of life, less liable to fracture mutilation; for the majority of the wounds and injuries they receive the available healing power of nature is sufficient. Von Hartmann recalled and elaborated the theories of J. Mueller and Virchow (Chapter 6, p. 143 ff.) to the effect that the first condition of reconstruction is inflammation.

tion, and the details of this interaction I have commented upon in the various instances. From the standpoint of an arm-chair philosopher who gazes upon the behavior of human beings with detached curiosity, the analysis submitted might seem to be the end of the task.

But in this concentrated attention upon the *wish-to-die* which has absorbed us in the previous chapters, we must not forget that there is also a *will-to-live*. In spite of the death-instinct, we see life all about us. If we become aware of destructive tendencies which threaten the disintegration of a human being or of the human race, we cannot look impassively and disinterestedly upon it, or accept an inactive role with reference to it, even if we are told that it is the nature of man, or that it is the will of God or the decision of a dictator that we do so. Indeed, the recognition of self-destructiveness has as its object the combating of such self-destruction and the encouragement and support of the life-instincts in their battle against it. This is the professional task of the physician to whom the masses of the people, from peasant to president, look for salvation, salvation from their own self-destructiveness. To it the physician brings an optimistic hopefulness which he shares with innumerable workers in science who, though they be daily reminded by the very content and discoveries of their own researches that all of our petty human activity and knowledge amounts to but little in the immensity of the universe, nevertheless plod steadfastly and hopefully forward in the direction of increasing our defenses against death.

And although it would be difficult to be certain about this, it would appear that we already have something to show for our work and some basis for our optimism. That actual suicide and murder are slowly decreasing is I think of less importance than that in a few moments of cosmic time we should have apparently happened upon and discovered a few devices for postponing death so that the average life span is now considerably greater than formerly.[2] And this is in spite of the mortality of young men in war, which reminds us that the militarists and others seem as determined to bring about the destruction of lives

[2] In 1850 the expectation of life at birth in Massachusetts, for example, was about 40 years (38.3 for males, 40.5 for females); in 1935 it was about 60 years (59.3 for males, 62.6 for females). It is generally believed that this is a result of decreased mortality from infectious and contagious disease which has resulted from the application of the principles of preventive medicine. These figures were kindly furnished by the Statistical Bureau of the Metropolitan Life Insurance Company.

as the scientists are to salvage them. But *de gustibus non est disputandum.* As physicians, we enjoy trying to save things; the destroyers will continue to do as *they* like. And perhaps, in spite of this, the will-to-live can be assisted to greater victory.

Accordingly, let us direct our attention to the problem of whether or not it is possible to apply the resources of intelligence and ingenuity deliberately to combat the self-destructive trends which our analysis has uncovered. Is it possible that we can by taking thought add a cubit to our stature? Can we abet or encourage the life-instinct in its battle against the death-instinct and in this way achieve an almost divine detachment from ourselves and become in a larger measure, or in a more nearly complete measure, the masters of our own destinies? In short, can we still further postpone death, and how?

We have seen that in the practical accomplishment of self-destruction there appear to be activities and functions derived from three elements of motivation, the aggressive, the self-punitive, and the erotic. It would be logical to examine the possible methods of dealing with each of these components; let us begin with the first.

A. THE DIMINUTION OF THE AGGRESSIVE ELEMENT

If we consider the available means for combating the aggressive element in human behavior we think first of all of such direct opposition as must be offered when such aggressions become overtly expressed, and dangerous. Under such circumstances it would seem obvious that force must be brought to meet force. A man impelled to kill somebody must be prevented from doing so, if necessary by physical restraint. A man who is impelled to kill himself must similarly be restrained. If the method of self-destruction he has elected is so simple and manifest as suicide by drowning, for example, we can remove him from all available bodies of water. We know, however, that devices for self-destruction are quickly interchangeable and we should expect that a suicidally impelled individual thwarted in this direction might turn quickly to the use of a knife or a gun. For this reason our program for the blocking of such overt aggressiveness as this must be more generic, and it is a commonplace of psychiatric experience that such individuals are best confined and kept under close surveillance. Innumerable preventable suicides occur each year because friends, relatives, and physicians neglect to take seriously the warnings of impending self-destruction. Psychiatrists are all familiar with a phenomenon for which it is difficult to gain popular credulity; namely, that many patients ask to be admitted to psychiatric hospitals, to be confined behind locked doors and even to be restrained in more secure ways than this because of the fear they have of their own destructiveness. Such a high degree of insight may far surpass the intuition of the relatives and of the physician himself; there may not seem to them to be much reason for the hospitalization or protection of such a person.[3]

It must not be assumed, however, that the only method of combating direct evidences of aggressiveness is through restraint. As a matter of fact, it is obviously the most primitive method of all. Furthermore, it deals only with such direct destructive tendencies as appear in behavior and leaves entirely out of account those destructive modes which express themselves by inhibitions, and in organs through the invitation to infections and by other such somatic devices as were discussed in the previous section. For these we must use a chemical counterattack, and under such a categorical head one thinks first of quinine for malaria and antitoxin for meningitis and arsphenamine for syphilis. Surgery, too, in its direct assault upon the destructive process and the encouragement thereby of the healing powers implicit in healthy tissues also belongs in this category.

But not all destructive manifestations can be met in such a frontal manner. To use another illustration from psychiatric practice, a man may exhibit innumerable examples of petty irrationality including aggressive attacks upon himself and others without putting himself in such a position as to necessitate his confinement in a hospital or jail. There are many devices for justifying aggressiveness and destructiveness which completely hide it from view or at least make it difficult to combat in any immediate manner. Perhaps this is always the case in the earliest instance of the development of destructive tendencies.

At any rate, we know that such aggressions must be

[3] I recall many instances of this, but one with an amusingly paradoxical character was a patient who had originally been placed in the hospital by his relatives but who kept up a consistent bombardment of criticism against the physicians for detaining him; after a period of some months he was temporarily released but got into such serious trouble that he was brought back. He threatened suit against the hospital, engaged his attorneys, but before the suit came to trial escaped. Six weeks later he reappeared at the hospital, unaccompanied by relatives, and petitioned to be readmitted for further treatment!

dealt with quite differently. First of all, they must be recognized—recognized by their perpetrator who is, of course, ultimately their chief victim. This is sometimes hard, sometimes easy, to accomplish. Once the self-destructiveness implicit in such aggressiveness is recognized, the next step is to redirect it away from the self or the inoffensive object and to substitute proper for improper targets by displacement. This happens spontaneously before our eyes in much psychiatric treatment: we see a patient who has belabored and berated himself for months, insisting that he is too unworthy to live and begging to be permitted to kill himself, gradually turn his vituperations onto the hospital or its doctors and nurses, or perhaps onto his anxiously waiting relatives. Such an outpouring of hate is unpleasant but it is vastly encouraging; it only remains for the recovery of such an individual that these belligerencies be displaced to still more appropriate objectives.[4] Usually there are plenty to be found—it requires some vigorous fighting (the physical expression of hating) to maintain one's place and peace in the world. To aspire to the elimination of all direct aggressiveness after the patterns of Amenhotep IV, Jesus of Nazareth, and Mahatma Gandhi is an ideal which still leaves room in a practical world for self-defensive aggression. As William James has well said, pacifists often make the mistake of disparaging the commendable element in the martial spirit. For all that it so often leads to disastrous misapplications, through exploitation by the greedy and unscrupulous, the aggressive spirit properly directed has its uses.

And if appropriate human goals or targets are not directly forthcoming for the investment of this hostile energy, immaterial objects can often be substituted in which the primary satisfaction of destruction is supplemented with secondary values accruing indirectly. It is certainly more desirable for a man to pound a punching-bag or walk miles in pursuit of a golf ball than to exert the same energy in attacking the reputation of his neighbor, the peace of mind of his wife, or the functioning of his own heart. Still better, of course, so far as secondary and material benefits are concerned, would be the application of this aggressive energy to the problems of the field, the forum, and the factory.

[4] One way in which to visualize psychoanalytic treatment is as of such a guided transfer of aggression—first onto the analyst himself, who can better bear it than the patient (self-directed hostility) or his relatives. After it has been there encouraged in its full expression, it is allowed through the dispersing effect of the intelligence to seek more appropriate and controlled outlets.

Indeed, probably all work represents in large measure this 'sublimation" of aggressions, aggressions directed against what Ernest Southard called "The Kingdom of Evils": ignorance, crime, vice, disease, poverty—and let us add ugliness, and even aggressiveness itself.

For these reasons, then, we must regard with high favor all of those human activities, some deriving from play and some from work, which give an outlet to these impulses to fight and destroy: sports, games, politics, business, and the aggressive sides of many hobbies; for example, the weeding and cultivating features of gardening,[5] the very features which, by the way, many devotees neglect or relegate to others. Alexander[6] has pointed out how great mass demonstrations in the realm of sport, so familiar to Americans in baseball and football, afford a vicarious release of aggressive energy and hence bring greater peace to the individual. He recalls the words of Juvenal, as to the needs of the people—*"Panem et circenses"* (bread and circuses).

This is what William James had in mind in his celebrated essay on "The Moral Equivalent of War." [7]

There is nothing to make one indignant in the mere fact that life is hard, that men should toil and suffer pain. The planetary conditions once for all are such, and we can stand it. But that so many men, by mere accidents of birth and opportunity,

[5] I saw a very convincing illustration of this quite by accident. Some friends of mine were disturbed because of the aggressive and provocative behavior of their adolescent son. They came to visit us one Sunday and the young son offered to assist me in cutting down a patch of rather tall weeds in the corner of our place. I welcomed his assistance and he became intensely intrigued by the activity of cutting these weeds which he did with an energy and violence which could leave no doubt as to the fact that he was taking out some kind of hatred upon them. He obviously enjoyed it, however, the more so, perhaps, because it was an activity whereby he gained some approval from me; but he carried it beyond all expectations. He not only cut down all of the weeds in that particular patch but walked over many acres hunting for more such weeds to destroy and worked energetically upon these until obliged to leave with his parents. He was highly satisfied with himself as he left, and in a very good humor in spite of three large blisters upon his hands.

The general public has a way of speaking of this phenomenon which implies a partial insight. One often hears, "Let the boys work off some of their energy." The real significance of this is lost, however, if it is not clearly recognized that such energy is destructive energy and the extension of "civilization" has meant a decrease in the opportunities for some kinds of destruction which find its reflection not only in the ready accessibility to a suggestion of war which amazes us in our fellowmen, but also such wanton and lamentable expression of these impulses in the butchery of the wild life of this continent.

[6] Alexander, Franz, "Mental Hygiene and Criminology," *Mental Hygiene*, October, 1930, p. 4, No. 14, p. 880. *Ibid.*, with Staub, Hugo, *The Criminal, the Judge and the Public*, Macmillan, 1931, pp. 34-35, 222-23.
[7] James, William, "The Moral Equivalent of War" in *Memories and Studies*, Longmans, Green, 1912, p. 276.

should have a life of *nothing else* but toil and pain and hardness and inferiority imposed upon them, should have *no* vacation, while others, natively no more deserving, never get any taste of this campaigning life at all—*this* is capable of arousing indignation in reflective minds. It may end by seeming shameful to all of us that some of us have nothing but campaigning, and others nothing but unmanly ease. If now—and this is my idea—there were, instead of military conscription a conscription of the whole youthful population to form for a certain number of years a part of the army enlisted against Nature, the injustice would tend to be evened out, and numerous other goods to the commonwealth would follow. The military ideals of hardihood and discipline would be wrought into the growing fiber of the people, no one would remain blind as the luxurious classes now are blind, to man's relations to the globe he lives on, and to the permanently sour and hard foundations of his higher life. To coal and iron mines, to freight trains, to fishing fleets in December, to dish-washing, clothes-washing, and window-washing, to road-building and tunnel-making, to foundries and stoke-holes, and to the frames of skyscrapers, would our gilded youths be drafted off, according to their choice, to get the childishness knocked out of them, and to come back into society with healthier sympathies and soberer ideas. They would have paid their blood-tax, done their own part in the immemorial human warfare against Nature; they would tread the earth more proudly, the women would value them more highly, they would be better fathers and teachers of the following generation.

Such a conscription, with the state of public opinion that would have required it, and the many moral fruits it would bear, would preserve in the midst of a pacific civilization the manly virtues which the military party is so afraid of seeing disappear in peace. . . .

To what extent this direction of the aggressive tendency away from the self to these more socially acceptable goals can be accomplished through the design and intention of the physician or even by order of the state, as James had in mind, rather than spontaneously, is of course the problem of psychiatric therapeutics. We psychiatrists think it can be done. We think we have demonstrated it to some extent. It is precisely to this end that the modern psychiatric hospital employs a carefully directed recreational therapy, and not, as even the relatives sometimes assume, merely to give patients something to do to fill their idle hours.[8] Properly

[8] See Menninger, William C., "Therapeutic Methods in a Psychiatric Hospital," *Journal of the American Medical Association*, Aug. 13, 1932 pp. 538-42, and (*Ibid.*) "Individualization in the Prescriptions for Nursing Care of the Psychiatric Patient," same journal, March 7, 1936, pp

conceived and administered, recreational therapy is carefully planned to afford each individual the best type of outlet for the aggressions which he is most strongly impelled to make and yet too strongly inhibited to bring out, spontaneously, in some harmless way. Games represent battles in disguise, as everyone knows. For a patient sick from an excess of his own repressed hatred, it is even more necessary than for the average business man to have a game of something in which he can conquer an opponent. Many devices can be (and are) used to expedite this, such as naming the golf balls after hated relatives or painting ears and a face on a punching-bag. If these seem childish it must not be forgotten that all of our deepest hostilities arise in childhood and that the most effective devices known for unburdening ourselves of aggression are essentially childish. Indeed, this is one of the chief functions of play.

Even play that has been advanced to the seriousness of a professional art may still be used to serve this function, as can be readily inferred in the biographies of many painters. The artist Van Gogh certainly deferred his suicide a long time by means of his passionate devotion to the art of hurling his passions upon canvas. One of the most impressive clinical experiences in my life was to see a woman who in the depths of her illness smeared her excreta upon the wall in the form of obscene jingles and slanderous descriptions of her physicians and nurses, gradually, in the course of recovery, begin writing—first with pencil, later pen and ink—beautiful poetry. One was able to observe here in its nascent state the substitution of a socially acceptable and useful form of activity for a primitively aggressive one. Such a process every child must go through as he emerges from the mud-pie stage.

Observing a child who had broken a bottle of iodine smearing the spilled contents on the porcelain washbowl, Ruth Faison Shaw[9] reflected upon the principle that children enjoy pushing bright-colored substances about on glossy surfaces. Seeking more applicable materials she derived fingerpainting, the sheer fun of which is the least of its fruitful values in the scientific study and management of children. It bridges the gap between aggressive and creative

756-61, and (Ibid.) "Psychoanalytic Principles Applied to the Treatment of Hospitalized Patients," Bulletin of the Menninger Clinic, Nov., 1936, pp. 35-43.
9 Shaw, Ruth Faison, Fingerpainting, Little, Brown, 1934.

smearing with a play technique.[10] The child himself derives pleasure from it; he releases unconscious affects which have been blocked by the lack of so flexible and so appropriate a medium, and finally, the emotions stimulated facilitate transference relationships and the ideas expressed enable the initiated adults about him to understand his deeper intentions and restrictions. Skillful use of play is being increasingly made in a scientific way by psychiatrists, psychoanalysts, psychologists, and teachers[11] for purposes of what we should call reconstruction through a release of aggressions.

Still another technique of dealing with the aggressive element is yet to be considered. This is the enforced or deliberate renunciation of certain love-objects which are in reality hate-objects. The attachment of one individual for another (implying as it always does both love and hate) sometimes consists of too large a proportion of hate or too small a proportion of love—whichever way it pleases the reader to think of it. The actual amount of love may be great but if the amount of hate is relatively greater, the retention of such objects in the cathexes of the individual only makes for trouble because the aggressions keep bursting the protecting covering of the erotic bond. And because it is impossible for such aggressions to be directed against the object of their stimulation they are usually displaced to other objects and, most frequently of all, displaced back

[10] See Lyle, Jeanetta, and Shaw, Ruth Faison, "Encouraging Fantasy Expression in Children," *Bulletin of Menninger Clinic*, January, 1937, pp. 78-86.

[11] Levy, David, "Use of Play Technique as Experimental Procedure," *American Journal of Orthopsychiatry*, July, 1933, pp. 266-277; and *Ibid.*, "Hostility Patterns in Sibling Rivalry Experiments," *American Journal of Orthopsychiatry*, April, 1936, pp. 183-257; Ackerman, N. W., "Constructive and Destructive Tendencies in Children" (*American Journal of Orthopsychiatry*, July, 1937, pp. 301-19; Homburger, Eric, "Psychoanalysis and the Future of Education," *Psychoanalytic Quarterly*, Jan., 1935, pp. 50-68; Hemphill, Robert, "The Aims and Practices of Recreational Therapy," *Bulletin of Menninger Clinic*, March, 1937, pp. 117-22; Chidester, Leona, and Menninger, Karl A., "Application of Psychoanalytic Methods to Mental Retardation," *American Journal of Orthopsychiatry*, October, 1936, pp. 616-25; Liss, Edward, "Play Techniques in Child Analysis," *American Journal of Orthopsychiatry*, Jan., 1936, pp. 17-22; Davis, J. E., *Principles and Practice of Recreational Therapy for the Mentally Ill*, Barnes, 1936; Spring, W. J., "Words and Masses; A Pictorial Contribution to the Psychology of Stammering," *Psychoanalytic Quarterly*, 1935, Vol. IV, pp. 244-58; Klein, M., "Personification in the Play of Children," *International Journal of Psychoanalysis*, 1929, Vol. X, pp. 193-204; Wälder, R., "The Psychoanalytic Theory of Play," *Psychoanalytic Quarterly*, 1933, Vol. II, pp. 208-24; Searl, M. N., "Play, Reality, and Aggression," *International Journal of Psychoanalysis*, 1933, Vol. XIV, pp. 310-20.

onto the self. In other words, a person toward whom we have marked ambivalence, i.e., strong feelings of hate as well as of love, is very apt to be a factor in the increase of our own self-destruction in the same way that a bullet fired against a stout brick wall may ricochet and hurt us. Frequently love-objects (or hate-objects) are selected because of their narcissistic value, which always implies ambivalence, and Freud has pointed out how the violent quarrels between some lovers are due to precisely this mechanism, i.e., each party serves as the target for the self-destructive energies of the other.

Such love-objects are better renounced. Similarly, those hated objects toward whom the hostility seems to thrive upon illogical bases had better be completely removed somehow from the emotional focus of such a person. This is much more easily said than done. We know from psychoanalytic observation that such loved- hated-objects are usually representatives of earlier characters in the drama of the individual's life from whom there was ample provocation (in the child's mind) for hating and hating vigorously. The contemporary objects are, therefore, targets for aggressions of long-standing and often of such illogical but violent intensity as to be difficult of displacement or renunciation. That such individuals then become sick because they hate so much is, therefore, quite possible and had it not been bungled, "Christian Science" might have made great headway with this very sensible and truthful observation (one which was not, of course, in any sense discovered by Mrs. Eddy, who was one of the world's most energetic but pointless haters).[12]

And finally, before leaving the topic of mitigating aggressions, a word should be said for the saving grace of wit and humor, which are so bountiful a release for hostile impulses in some people. That they are sometimes employed cruelly does not lessen their great utility for those fortunate enough to have found this way out. As Freud has shown in his study of the psychology of wit and humor,[13] the pleasurable feeling for all concerned depends upon a release of repressed emotion, emotion fundamentally unpleasant. Usually this displeasure arises from the hostile element in the repressed material, but released in disguise, as humor, it

[12] Bates, E. S., and Dittemore, J. V., *Mary Baker Eddy*, Knopf, 1932. See also Haushalter, W. M., *Mrs. Eddy Purloins from Hegel*, Beauchamp, 1936.
[13] Freud, S., *Wit and Its Relation to the Unconscious*, trans. by Brill, Moffat, Yard, 1917.

makes all who share such emotions feel better. It is no accident that one of the world's greatest humorists, whose shafts reached the highest and the lowest, died a national idol and was able to say, no doubt truthfully, "I never met a man I didn't like."

B. THE DIMINUTION OF THE SELF-PUNITIVE ELEMENT

We can expect to see the punitive element in self-destruction diminished through anything which decreases the unconscious sense of guilt upon which it is dependent. This can, to be sure, take place as the result of innumerable pathological devices, devices such as projection, i.e., "It is not I who did these things or who wished to do these things to him, but it is he who did them to me or wished to do them to me." This method of relieving the sense of guilt is, however, like proud flesh in the healing of a wound; it is the evidence of a struggle toward recovery but an effort almost as pathological as the original disease. Sometimes it becomes the outstanding evidence of disease. For a long time this confused psychiatrists so that numerous illnesses, such as paranoia, were named not on the basis of their fundamental psychopathology but on the basis of the spontaneous efforts at self-cure represented by the delusional system formed. Paranoia is, in fact, a rather less serious disease than some forms of mental illness in which no paranoid ideas appear because the patient is so overwhelmed with his destructive tendencies and his guilt-feelings that he can make no spontaneous defense against them. On the other hand, the paranoid method of solution is usually a vain and unprofitable one.

Chemical methods of reducing the sense of guilt are best known to us in the form of alcohol, whose function in this direction requires no exposition from the phenomenological standpoint. Perhaps, however, one of the benefits from all sedative therapy depends upon this same principle. Indeed, it may be this very principle which renders alcohol and other habit-forming drugs so dangerous from the standpoint of addiction, because any device to decrease the guilt so easily, quickly, and completely, with so little difficulty in the way of obtaining it, makes the possibility of abuse perilously great. The exploitation of this possibility has been already considered under chronic forms of self-destruction.

The whole question of just how different drugs affect the different instinctual strivings and the different structural and functional faculties of the psyche is almost entirely unexplored. In this connection, one of my colleagues,[14] was particularly struck some years ago by the modification of the super-ego effected by sodium amytal in a case of general paresis. It is an impressive thing when the administration of a drug suddenly makes a man responsive to the demands of civilization who, only a few hours before that time, was acting like a wild beast or an imbecile, the more startling because the response is lost as the effects of the drug wear off. Precisely the opposite effect from precisely the same drug was described to me as having been observed by an attorney friend of mine. An acquaintance of his, thinking to overcome a tendency to sleeplessness, had taken some of the same drug and shortly thereafter was discovered by his friends sitting amusedly beside his bed, to which he had set fire, watching the flames roar up to the ceiling and spread to the curtains and window-shade.[15]

In a more healthy and effective direction, it would be logical to expect that the sense of guilt would be diminished if and when the aggressions which stimulate that sense of guilt have been diminished. A reduction in the latter then leads to a further reduction in the former, i.e., the "reducing" is reciprocal inasmuch as there is often a tendency on the part of one suffering from a sense of guilt to be provocative. The sense of guilt on account of past aggressions is apt to stimulate further aggressions in the hope, so to speak, of exciting retaliation and punishment.

By far the most prevalent method of relieving the unconscious sense of guilt is by atonement. As we have already seen, this is sometimes accomplished by sacrifice. Such sacrifices may be organic or they may be expressed in behavior. They may take the form of material sacrifices or of ritualistic substitutes; they may also take the form of neurotic symptoms or neurotic behavior. I am using neurotic now in the sense of being expensive, unsatisfactory and, by the standards of the reality world, illogical. A man, for

[14] Fellows, Ralph M., "Sodium Amytal in the Treatment of Paresis," *Journal of the Missouri State Medical Association,* May, 1932, pp. 194-96.

[15] Some recent investigations suggest that amytal affects certain hypothalamic functions, and these observations thus confirm a suggestion made by Dr. Leo Stone as to the possibility that the "id" is functionally ascribable to this area. Dr. Lionel Blitzsten has observed, he informs me, that analytic patients who are using sodium amytal are subject to particularly aggressive dreams, indicating that the amytal favors sleep through enhancing and facilitating such fantasy relief.

example, may beat his head against the wall to atone for the feelings of having been responsible for his brother's death but this does not revive his brother, nor does it help any living being. A woman may develop an intense headache to such an extent as to be obliged to forego pleasures and duties, and one of the chief motives thereof may be the feelings of guilt for hatred against her mother. But neither the mother nor the woman herself is benefited by the headache atonement. In that sense it is neurotic.

To substitute for such atonement something useful and socially valuable might be said to be a normal mode of behavior, although some would say that the feeling of necessity for making atonement is in any form neurotic.[16] From a practical standpoint, we can regard the process as pathological only when the atonement becomes self-destructive in its net result. If a man, for example, inherits a considerable amount of money at the death of his father and gives a part of this inheritance to further scientific research or to support the starving people in his community, he may be atoning for the unconscious sense of guilt implicit in the receiving of money from the father against whom he had unconscious, if not conscious, hostilities. But such an atonement benefits many people and affords the man who makes it a genuine satisfaction which he can well afford. If, however, driven by this sense of guilt, he atones in an extravagant degree and gives so much of his money away that he and his family are actually in want or suffer from feelings of financial insecurity, one would have to regard such an atonement as being neurotic, because of the net self-destructive result achieved.

Reconstruction is furthered, then, by the utilization of atonements ministering to or annulling the sense of guilt the net consequences of which do not involve too costly a price judged by reality standards. The greater the social or personal utility of such atonement, the greater, of course, the net gain for society; but after all this is a secondary function of atonement, its primary purpose being to placate the conscience. To this end the ritual and the ceremonial are, for some people, sufficient.

For this reason, and because it is always before our eyes, we must recognize the very definite therapeutic effect of the atonement element in religion. As we shall see later,

[16] With this I differ on the basis of definition. I see no advantage in designating unconsciously determined behavior "neurotic" unless it is self-destructive.

religion helps people in other ways than this. But the confessional and the symbolism, the ritual, the opportunities for service, penitence and acknowledged forgiveness—these and other features of nearly all religions, the Judaic-Christian no more than many of the Oriental forms, undoubtedly serve this very valuable function for many people.

Finally, the sense of guilt and the need for punishment may be diminished by the logical process of diminishing the power of the super-ego which dictates them. But this is more easily said than done. For while it is true that education and exposure to a wider range of experience with reality (testing) have some effect in lessening the power of the conscience, for the most part it is only the conscious portion of it, "the ego-ideal," that is affected. The unconscious conscience, the super-ego formed in childhood, is completely out of touch with contemporary reality; it exercises its dominion on the basis of childhood concepts and the authority of ancient standards. To put this vividly, one might say that although the conscious ego and ego-ideal live in a changing world and adapt themselves to that world, the super-ego remains fixed in its original form determined by the rules in effect at the time of its formation. The average person succeeds in mastering the irrational demands of his super-ego, of replacing conscience to a workable extent with intelligence. Not so the neurotic, however, whose weaker ego struggles beneath the tyranny of an enormously powerful but unseen, unreasonable, unyielding authority within himself. For the elimination of a pathological degree of conscience, which always implies a correspondingly weakened ego, only technical means avail. It is useless to try to educate the conscience, but it can be dethroned in favor of an expanded ego if the searchlight of the intelligence can be directed upon it. Emotional rather than intellectual re-education is necessary. This is the object of psychoanalytic treatment which is to be taken up in greater detail shortly.

C. THE ENHANCEMENT OF THE EROTIC ELEMENT

Along with ways to diminish or socialize the aggressive and self-punitive elements, we should consider the coordinate possibilities of encouraging and strengthening the erotic element, the element which we have already seen to be the saving and neutralizing force operating in opposition to the destructive tendencies to accomplish (to whatever degree it may be accomplished) the salvation of the part or the whole.

It is a great temptation to become philosophical again at this point and speak in general terms of the need for more love in the world, the desirability of encouraging frank expressions of emotional life in children, the improvement of parental patterns of affection. To do so, however valid, is only to join in the chorus of religious and inspirational exhortation to "love one another." We all recognize it to be good advice, supported now by scientific as well as by aesthetic and moral reasoning. The questions are how to accomplish it and what the specific nature of more abundant loving really is. Franz Alexander has often quoted a remark made to him by the late Sandor Ferenczi, the great Hungarian psychoanalyst: "They *want* to love one another," he said, "but they don't know how!"

It would carry us too far afield for the present to discuss all of the interferences in the development of the erotic instinct which keep us from loving, from "knowing how to love." In a sense, this has been the object of all psychoanalytic research, a problem which occupied Freud in the very beginning. How civilization has imposed greater restrictions upon us and how this, in turn, has been reflected in a higher degree of civilization without a corresponding personal gain to the individual is a philosophical corollary of the problem recently discussed by Freud in his *Civilization and Its Discontents*. But we must for present purposes refrain from such far-flung generalizations and keep to the problem of the individual.

First and foremost among the inhibitions of the erotic development are the stultifying and deadening effects of narcissism. Nothing inhibits love so much as self-love and from no source can we expect greater ameliorative results than from the deflection of this love from a self-investment (comparable to the self-investment of hate already discussed) to its proper investment in outside objects. In other words, just as self-directed aggressions are harmful because of their *immediate* consequences, so the self-direction of love is harmful through its *secondary* consequences, the consequences of the emotional starvation resulting. Narcissism chokes and smothers the ego it aims to protect—just as winter protection applied to a rosebed, if left on too late in the spring, prevents the roses from developing properly, or even from growing at all. Thus again psychoanalytic science comes to the support of an intuitive observation of a great religious leader who said, "He who seeketh his own life shall lose it but whosoever loseth his life for my sake shall find it." We need only read in place of "for my sake" an expression meaning the investment of love in others, which is presumably what Jesus meant.

For when love is largely self-invested the gradual flow of the softening, fructifying essence of the erotic impulse over the stark arms of aggression, extended in all directions, is stayed. Instead of infiltrating and ameliorating these contacts with the outside world, the libido entirely devoted to the nurture and protection of the ego remains inert, a coagulated lump of narcissism.

It is as if the personality were like a growing tree over whose dark bare branches as we see them in winter there creeps the soft verdure of spring and summer, clothing the skeleton with living beauty. But were such a tree to be so injured near the base that the sap flowed out in large quantities to promote the healing and the protection of this stem injury, an insufficient supply would be left for the development of the foliage of the branches. These, then, would remain bare, stark, aggressive—and dying, while the sap fed and overfed the basal wound.

An attack upon the narcissistic love itself sometimes has the effect of forcing its redistribution, i.e., so that some of it is converted into object love; at other times this has only the negative therapeutic response of causing a greater outpouring of narcissism or a further retreat from reality. This is what happens often in the treatment of mental illness. Some patients, properly nurtured in a new transplanting, i.e., in the tender, skillful management of one whom they trust, take root and grow. The narcissism gradually recedes in favor of greater leafing-out. In other cases, however, any and all attempts to treat the narcissistic disease—no matter how skillful—only make matters worse. The wound is incurably deep; the fear of further hurt is too great.

How narcissism rejects help, and thus defeats efforts to do more skillfully what it tries in vain to accomplish—like panic-stricken victims of fire or water who fight off their rescuers—this we see even so close at hand as in ourselves. Few indeed escape some of the cloying handicap of narcissism which hangs like a tenacious patch of plaster, applied to a wound long since healed. Every parent knows what it is to try to remove such an outworn encumbrance from the finger of a reluctant child.

It is the same narcissism in us which, as false pride or

purposive ignorance, prevents some self-destroying individuals from asking the help they need—psychiatric treatment, surgical treatment, dental treatment. It is literally true, I assure you, that some patients are too proud—too vain—too accustomed to self-ministrations and satisfactions to get well. They cannot accept help that does not merely (and of course futilely) feed their vanity. Narcissism is a thirst that is never slaked, and blocks the real enjoyment of anything.[17] In the smugness of provincialism, in the stupidity of race prejudice and discrimination, in the vanity which exalts such gods as nationalism, social prestige, and financial aristocracy and surrenders everything to them, we see this same deadening toxemia of narcissism.

In addition to the direct attack on the narcissism itself, the reconstruction of the personality can be furthered, I believe, through a deliberate, intelligent cultivation of satisfactory love-objects. There is a curious propaganda abroad in the land, prevalent among those of lesser intellectual aspirations no less than among those of the higher strata, which opposes, with a kind of cynical agnosticism, the cultivation of meaningful friendships. Many feel that the innate human tendency toward ambivalence in such relationships is too great, that as between the restrictions placed upon the instinctual life, on the one hand, and the hazards of inducing reactions to thwarting, on the other, one dare not love very much or very far. With Balzac (in *La Peau du Chagrin*) they hold that "to kill the emotions and so live

[17]   Elizabeth Bates has been to Rome
And looked at the statues there;
Elizabeth Bates has scaled the Alps
And sniffed at the mountain air.

Elizabeth Bates has winced at Nice
And quibbled at gay Paree,
And lifted her delicate eyebrows at
Indelicate Barbary.

Elizabeth Bates has "done" the globe
From Panama back to the States,
But all she saw on the way around
Was Miss Elizabeth Bates.

Elizabeth Bates has been to Spain
And sampled her ego there,
And viewed the face of the thoughtful Sphinx
And paused to arrange her hair.

Elizabeth Bates can be no place
She hasn't been there before,
But never has yet been out of herself,
So I have traveled more!

—Milo Ray Phelps,
New Yorker, December 21, 1929.

to old age, or to accept the martyrdom of our passions and die young, is our fate."

With such a faint-hearted and restrictive view I cannot agree. I grant that there are hazards in love and that reality is such that no one can escape frustrations and disappointments but I do not feel that this needs to inhibit our purpose of "loving and letting love." Moral, religious, and superstitious factors have combined to place heavy restrictions upon satisfactory sexual expression. These are now, to some extent, disappearing, so that intelligent discrimination, without an excess of irrational factors, can be expected to guide the more enlightened and emancipated, but even for them there will remain barriers of economics and physiology and psychology which are not irrational or unreal—and not inconsiderable. It is not likely, therefore, that the need for sublimation and for friendships will decrease.

Whatever we may hope or achieve in the direction of a more biologically and psychologically sound sexual morality, we shall always need the gratification afforded by the love of our friends and communion with them. But friendliness in general is subject to the anemia which is likely to blight all sublimations as they become more and more widely dissociated from direct instinct gratifications. Much that passes for friendship, for example, is motivated entirely by opportunism and the wish to be amused. Too, external barriers oppose the cultivation of friendships in a way which one of our ancestors might find very uncomfortable were he to be transplanted from his simpler but friendlier life into modern mechanistic living with its emphasis on speed, efficiency, and novelty. It is a considerable question if all the mechanical inventions for increasing the speed of communication and transportation have added anything to human happiness; it is certain that these very inventions have decreased our opportunities for friendship and friendly intercourse.

The greatest barrier, however, is internal. The capacity for friendship depends upon a kind of inner vitality which permits a strong erotic component to be injected into all human relationships. When we say that a person with this capacity has a "robust nature" we have perceived that he has achieved a vigorous development of his erotic instincts. Theoretically, friendship is possible in its finest flower only when there has been mature sexual development.

The creation of rich and meaningful friendships requires that at least one of the parties must bring to the relationship a nurturing attitude as a protection against the ambivalence and narcissistic demands that arise in every human contact. This is best represented in the attitude of the mother who takes a supporting and sustaining role in her relation with the child, without striving to satisfy her own narcissism by keeping him dependent upon her or reacting to all of his aggressions defensively.

Most people are unable to support many friendships upon these terms. The erotic component may be too weak, their fears too great, or opportunity lacking for cultivating human relationships. For many individuals, notably those of a sensitive, seclusive, artistic temperament, the inhibiting influences of civilization in general and their own particular upbringing in particular, make *all* close human contacts too strong meat, involving too many conflicts, too much danger of being thwarted and wounded, too much responsibility for another's welfare and happiness, too great opportunity, perhaps, for aggressiveness. To a certain extent all persons are affected by these considerations; for every individual there is a limit to the number of friendships which he can support.

The erotic instinct, however, may be further extended and developed through creative sublimations such as are afforded by art, music, crafts, and many hobbies. To many people these seem far more precious than any human friendships could ever be. This in itself indicates the tendency toward a reunion of the spirit with the immaterial world from which these things come. But there need be no essential conflict here; there is rather a tendency toward an inductive or reciprocal encouragement. Many will begin by loving art and end by loving one another. And in either case, whichever the device for increasing the erotic capacities and giving them satisfactory opportunities for expression and expansion, the result will be to detract from the narcissistic choking and to supply additional neutralization of the destructive tendencies.

How art fulfills this function (as well as that of releasing aggressions, as discussed heretofore) has been studied by artists, philosophers, and psychoanalysts. Of these studies I am, of course, most familiar with those of the latter. Ella Sharpe,[18] for example, writes of its function in the direction

[18] Sharpe, Ella Freeman, "Similar and Divergent Unconscious Determinants Underlying the Sublimations of Pure Art and Pure Science," *International Journal of Psychoanalysis*, April, 1935, pp. 186-202.

that I have suggested. She quotes Van Gogh as having said that his whole work was a race for life.

This race for life that art can represent in extreme pathological cases is a desperate avoidance of destruction not only of the good object but also of the self. [!] When the power to put together and create rhythmically falls too far behind, or is not equal to dealing with aggression, the sublimation breaks down.

The immense powers of the body-ego, the subtlety of accomplishment of sight, hearing, touch, allied with fine muscle manipulation must themselves proceed from self-preservation impulses, heightened by the threat of bodily destruction. Again this is a repetition; that bodily preservation itself is only possible when coordination of rhythmic movement is preserved.

In the case of Van Gogh himself all efforts to stave off the self-destructive process failed: his pictures became increasingly wild and chaotic, he attacked the artist Gauguin, he cut off his own ear, developed convulsions, and finally, as we know, killed himself. In this we can see progressively the victory of the destructive tendencies—first the failure of sublimation, then the externally directed aggressiveness, then self-mutilation, finally suicide. Another, lesser known, artist, Alfred Kubin, won a victory over self-destructiveness by means of his art. From the time of his childhood on the shores of a lake in the Austrian forest he drew pictures. At ten years of age came his first glimpse of death, his father walking wildly about the house with the dead body of his wife in his arms. Then followed two step-mothers, a boarding school, an apprenticeship to a photographer, lonely and unsupervised evenings, and finally an attempt at suicide followed by several months in the hospital with what he called delirium. As he improved he became engrossed by the sick, the dying, and the would-be suicides about him. He managed to get to Munich to study art and for the first time saw real pictures. He soon began to draw the strange macabre pictures which have made him famous.[19]

It will be seen from this that I regard the vast extension of music, art, and drama to the homes of the common people made possible by the radio, the victrola, and the moving pictures as more than a mere addition to the opportunities for passing pleasure. I regard it as supplying very definitely an additional bulwark against self-destruction. No one can hear the *Fifth Symphony*, the "Hallelujah Chorus," or the preludes to *Lohengrin* and *Parsifal* (and

[19] From the *Survey Graphic*, May, 1930. (See *Demons and Night Visions*, Dresden, Carl Reissner Verlag.)

there are comparable visual experiences) and remain quite the same personality as before. I do not refer to any specific healing qualities of music[20] or art—I simply mean that self-destruction is combated by anything which draws from us some further flow of the love that is implicit in joy.

I have already spoken of the part that work plays in utilizing the aggressions and diverting them from the self. It may also serve as a creative sublimation, even if it lies outside the province of the arts. Social work, teaching, the ministry, medicine, and many other professions may represent a sublimated expression of the erotic instinct, an expression of love that reaches out beyond the self and the immediate personal love-objects to the "neighbor" that Jesus referred to so often—the neighbor whom our most primitive instinct arrays us against, but whom our self-preservation demands that we cherish.

TECHNIQUES OF THERAPY

So much for a general survey of how, in theory, aggressions should be deflected to harmless targets, the sense of guilt relieved by some socially useful atonement, and the neutralizing flow of erotism stimulated through a sacrifice of narcissism in favor of the cultivation of proper love-objects. Such is a general outline of the program of reconstruction. But such things are far more easily said than done. And the physician waits, with his hat in his hand, asking, "And now what can I do for my patient?"

I do not intend to evade this question, but the subject of reconstruction—properly dealt with—reserves a book, not a chapter. For the present I can only outline the general principles.

Often, to be sure, the reconstruction of the personality takes place spontaneously. Sometimes medical men get the credit for it; sometimes amulets, sometimes prayers, sometimes the stars. But one must be fatalistic indeed to believe that all reconstruction may as well be left to spontaneity or amulets or the stars. No one knows better than we physicians ourselves that some of our patients get well in spite of us rather than because of us. Sometimes, also, we overrate our powers and ourselves take the credit for recoveries, the exact nature of which we misunderstand. This type of

[20] There may be some; see, for example, "The Use of Music in a Case of Psychoneurosis" (Van de Wall, Willem, and Bond, Earl D., *The American Journal of Psychiatry*, Sept., 1934, pp. 287-302). Music is used therapeutically in some modern psychiatric hospitals. See Van de Wall, Willem, *Music in Institutions*, Russell Sage Foundation, 1936.

error is bequeathed to us, in part, by our optimism without which we could not be physicians at all. It boots nothing that both optimism and pessimism are philosophically fallacious attitudes; it would seem inevitable that human beings fall into one or the other fallacy, and certainly the fallacy of optimism has more to its credit in the way of accomplishment than has the fallacy of pessimism.

But it is not a mere assumption that physicians can do something to expedite the reconstruction of a personality which would otherwise succumb to its own self-destructive impulses.

However firmly we may be able to grasp the conception of the unity of body and mind, there remains for the present a very important and practical distinction, especially when it comes to the techniques of treatment. This I have tried to make clear in the discussion of the organic affections in Part V. Let me repeat: *The etiology of an affection,* let us say of a self-destruction, *does not determine its most expedient treatment;* and *psychological therapy does not preclude physical or chemical therapy.*

A man may be excited by his neighbor to such wrath that he strikes him and in so doing breaks his own arm. Whatever initiated the chain of events which ended in the fractured bone, the treatment is based upon the concrete result and not upon the etiology. The proper investigation of the psychology of the situation may prevent another broken arm but it does not mend the arm already broken.

Such an elementary example as this might seem to be out of place but it is a point constantly misunderstood by many who seem otherwise to grasp the meaning of the psychic factor in disease. It is a confusion for which we have in part the bacteriological school to blame. The bacteriologists showed us the futility of treating some diseases purely symptomatically and quite properly insisted that we direct our attack upon the etiological agent (or, rather, on *one* of the agents). This is sometimes the proper procedure, but not always.

In medicine we must be pragmatists; sometimes the apparent or conspicuous etiological agent is the proper place to begin treatment, sometimes it is the last thing we may attack. The choice of the proper point of focusing the therapeutic endeavor is a part of the *art* of medicine; perhaps it is not possible to reduce it to a science but we are gradually acquiring more and more information about it, so that perhaps some day it may be.

At any rate, the proper treatment of many forms of suicide, the direct forms, the indirect forms, the chronic forms, the organic forms, all forms—must frequently be a chemical, a physical, or a mechanical method. To rely solely upon psychological methods would be just as absurd and unreasonable as to omit them entirely. This is not the place for a detailed consideration of the various therapies of medicine, surgery, and psychiatry. Physical, chemical, and mechanical agencies can be brought to bear which oppose the destructive tendencies and encourage the erotic tendencies but *psychological methods may also be brought into the arena, and these, too, deserve to be used for they have an efficacy which is unfortunately little realized.*

For the very reason that it is so much less well known than are the physical, chemical, and mechanical devices of medicine I propose to devote a few paragraphs to a cursory outline of the principles of psychotherapy, particularly in view of the emphasis of this book upon the psychic aspect of the instinctual forces. I shall not dismiss the whole matter as perhaps some cynical readers expect me to do, by saying that psychoanalysis could cure all of these things, because that is just as absurd as to say that surgery would cure everything. Both surgery and psychoanalysis have taught us much, but I shall leave surgery to the surgeons, and point out some of the things which psychoanalysis has taught us about the application of psychology as a therapeutic agent against the many forms of self-destruction.

We shall have to assume that the self-destructive individual for whom we are contemplating a treatment has some degree of insight, i.e., has some idea that he is sick and that he is a potential menace to himself. If he does not, psychological treatment will have to be administered quite indirectly, so indirectly in fact that probably the social or chemical treatment methods will appear to be predominant.

But if he knows that he is sick and that he is a danger to himself, if not to others, and if, in the next place, he has some remnant of a wish to get well (a wish which unfortunately succumbs in many instances to the destructive process, so that there is actually no genuine wish to get well, but only a wish to exploit the sickness and even the suffering) he is a fair subject for the administration of some psychological treatment, with or without physical, chemical, and mechanical treatment adjuvants.

All psychotherapy depends upon the principle that the conscious intelligence, that part of the personality which is called the ego, is capable under ordinary circumstances of handling the instinctual forces with a proper regard for opportunities afforded and for the prohibitions imposed by the world of reality. In the person needing psychotherapy, the ego has to some extent been overwhelmed, either through its own weakness or through the disproportionate strength of the instinctual drives or of the conscience or super-ego. Psychotherapy, therefore, is directed toward strengthening or expanding the ego and restricting or mollifying the harshness of the super-ego.[21]

The first step in psychotherapy is the establishing of some degree of rapport between the therapist and the patient. To some extent this principle applies to any form of treatment, e.g., a surgeon must have gained the patient's confidence in some measure before he can operate upon him. But in psychotherapy it is necessary to have more than the confidence of the patient in the therapist's skill and integrity. There must be some positive emotional reaction created—one might say that the patient must be won over to the point of bestowing a little love on the therapist, and expecting some from him. Usually this follows automatically if the physician is patient even with long-windedness, sympathetic even in the face of blatant self-pity, and understanding to the point of being able to identify himself with the patient sufficiently to comprehend the nature if not the degree of his sufferings.

For all psychotherapy depends for its effectiveness on the extent to which the physician is able to give the patient something he needs and cannot get or cannot accept— love. To be sure he (the patient) uses a wrong technique to obtain it, but one can alter this technique only *after* one has afforded the sufferer some degree of relief—not before. Then and then only is it possible to re-educate him, emotionally and ideationally. Hence the proper management of

[21] This does not in any way conflict with what I have already said about decreasing aggressive and self-punitive tendencies and encouraging the erotic elements. The ego can be helped to perform its functions by the proper intelligent support of an objective outsider who, as a result of his intuition or his experience, knows what to do. He is more likely to know what to do, to see what to do, and to be able to help the ego in that direction because the particular problems do not bear upon him, or at least not in the same way. (So we assume at least; sometimes, however, the psychotherapist is most interested in the very cases which suffer from problems similar to his own and for this reason he sometimes proves to be a poor guide. It is because of this consideration that all psychoanalysts now themselves undergo psychoanalysis as an essential part of their training before undertaking the treatment of patients.)

this dependence upon the physician is the key to success-ful psychotherapy.

What is at first a reasonable and understandable attitude of hope and trust and faith in the doctor tends to become, as we all know, something far more intense, variable, and unreasonable. Indeed, I think Karen Horney's definition of transference has not been improved upon—the irrational elements in the emotional attitude toward the physician. They are irrational, i.e., do not correspond to reality, be-cause they spring from the unconscious, released by virtue of the unconscious identification or equation of the phy-sician with earlier dramatis personae in the patient's life. Accordingly he may be as petulant as he was with his mother, as rebellious as he felt toward his father, as erotic as he would like to have been toward his sister or cousin. He can be this way, feel this way, and even *speak* it out because it is understood, not censored but interpreted to him.

Thus, by means of this guided relationship, an intel-lectual and emotional re-orientation of the patient is made possible, so that the ego—strengthened, expanded, made more elastic and less fragile—is enabled to handle the otherwise unmanageable components of the personality more efficiently, reduce the self-destructive trend, and in-crease the capacity for living and loving. One virtue of the psychoanalytic method of therapy is that this transference is manipulated deliberately according to scientific principles which have been accumulated by observant experience. The same thing is frequently accomplished in non-analytic psychotherapy on the basis of intuition and experience; in this type of therapy the physician does most of the talking, or at least plays the active role in the treatment—which is exactly opposite from what obtains in psychoanalysis. In either case the object is the emotional re-orientation of the patient; the intellectual re-orientation may both precede and follow. In non-analytic psychotherapy it must precede.

It will be helpful, perhaps, to examine somewhat care-fully some of the practical devices for accomplishing this intellectual re-orientation. Just what are the available tech-nical devices of psychotherapy? I do not propose to give a complete list by any means but some of the more conspicu-ous are as follows:

(1) Usually the first step, once the transference has been established, lies in the direction of giving the patient

greater insight into the reality of and then the precise nature of his self-destructiveness. There are innumerable ways to do this but in essence they consist in a comparison of the objective and subjective conceptions of the patient's behavior, situations, attitudes, or moral standards, in such a manner as to show him in just what way he is really different from others and in what ways he is *not* different. This is not done with the idea of making the patient conform to a hypothetical normality but to allay some anxiety about himself which has arisen on a neurotic basis and to substitute for it a more objective concern which arises when he considers the extent and seriousness of his problem, his self-destructiveness. The excess of the latter is, of course, largely dependent upon the former. Later, depending on the nature of the case, the responsibility for accounting for the differences may be thrown upon the patient or may be assumed by the psychotherapist, or may, for practical reasons, be disregarded.

(2) Along with this, sometimes implicitly, sometimes explicitly, comes a clarification of the purpose and motives involved in particularly troublesome situations or conflicts. Usually this leads to contrasting the conscious intention and the unconscious intention implied by the outcome. An opportunity to talk the situation out is sometimes sufficient to accomplish this automatically; often, however, it requires considerably more "catharsis" and more investigation of the personality background, sometimes also of the social (environmental) background.

(3) Next comes the recollection of, signalization of, or emphasis upon neglected considerations. These may be either reality factors which the patient does not take into consideration, consequences which he has failed to anticipate, aggressions which he does not recognize, memories which he has repressed. A few hours or a few years may be required to bring this material (i.e., enough of it) into proper focus.

(4) When these various elements are seen as a whole, a new self-estimate of the personality is possible, a new strength is given to the ego because of the possibility of relinquishing defensive aggressions no longer necessary, and the development of previously inhibited erotic investments is made possible.

(5) All of this, then, leads to constructive planning for the future in a more expeditious way. At this point also, a substitution of various active gratifications may be made

either by deliberate prescription (as in psychotherapy) or by spontaneous election (as in psychoanalysis). The result is a greater or lesser reconditioning of intentions, i.e., the development of "good" habits for "bad" habits, an exercise which we all indulge in occasionally upon necessity.

Any and all of these particular elements in psychotherapy may be used in any particular case and by any particular therapist. What I have described applies to the intellectual change; the patient begins to see himself in a new light and see the world in a new light and take a new kind of advantage of it. But an emotional re-orientation takes place (or should do so) at the same time, based on the transference already mentioned. For an individual overwhelmed by his own hostility and other emotional conflicts, even the tacit assurance that somebody loves him enough to listen to him and prescribe for him or advise him is, of itself, a tremendous reassurance. It is no wonder, therefore, that people get well as a result of the conscious or unconscious psychotherapeutic influence of all kinds of quacks, faith healers and fakirs as well as reputable physicians, psychiatrists, psychoanalysts, and others. These transference cures, however, are well known to be illusory since insecure individuals are very apt to develop these feelings again and seek for renewed assurances of affection and love. No human being is great enough, constant enough, omnipotent or ubiquitous enough to supply all the love that such individuals need and it is for this reason that religion in its positive faith-and-love aspects furnishes such people an incalculable, immeasurable therapeutic benefit. It is doubtless true that religion has been the world's psychiatrist throughout the centuries. That religion may have caused much suffering as well as cured much is also not to be gainsaid, and that something better calculated to fill the requirements may yet be conceived of is also possible. Unfortunately, too, many people cannot accept either the gratifications or the restrictions of religion because their intelligence or emotional conflicts forbid it. For these it is of little help but for the millions of others it is and will continue to be an indispensable mode of "salvation," i.e., reconstruction.

PSYCHOANALYSIS AS A TREATMENT METHOD

I find it incomparably difficult to set forth just that commentary on or description of psychoanalysis as a treatment method which will be appropriate in this final chapter.

393

Something needs to be said here because, although the entire book is based upon psychoanalytic theories and psychoanalytic data, we have not considered psychoanalytic therapy as such. The fact is that we do not yet know exactly why psychoanalysis cures people. (It is not always successful, by any means, even in cases that seem properly selected and adapted to it. But then, neither is any other method of treatment, from surgery to salvarsan.) Discussions of the dynamics of treatment still appear from time to time in our current psychoanalytic journals with no final agreement.[22]

We do know empirically that psychoanalysis as a treatment method has an efficacy in certain conditions unparalleled by any other method. Psychoneuroses which have persisted for years and have resisted all manner of treatment often yield in a spectacularly successful manner to psychoanalytic treatment. Various neuroses, some mild and incipient psychoses, conditions of inhibition such as impotence and stammering, some characterological deformities, and a few other categories of psychiatric affliction are among the acknowledged fields for promising psychoanalytic therapy. Many other conditions are still "on trial"—alcohol addiction, some of the somatic ills discussed in Part V, perversions, schizophrenia.

This is not the place to evaluate these trials, or to elaborate the successes of psychoanalysis in therapy. I shall assume the reader knows in general of these, and can learn more specifically of them in any of the recent books on the subject.[23]

I think, however, I should like to submit a schema of my own design which will perhaps be helpful to some in visualizing the essential nature of the psychoanalytic treatment process. The idea is not original but is the concept

[22] See, for example, the "Symposium on the Theory of the Therapeutic Results of Psycho-Analysis" by Glover, Fenichel, Strachey, Bergler, Nunberg, and Bibring, *International Journal of Psychoanalysis*, 1937, Vol. XVIII, pp. 125-89, and also Alexander, Franz, The Problem of Psychoanalytic Technique, *Psychoanalytic Quarterly*, Vol. IV, pp. 588-611, 1935; Laforgue, Rene, The Curative Factor in Analytical Treatment, *Internationale Zeitschrift für Psychoanalyse*, 1937, Vol. XXIII, pp. 50-59; and Searl, M. N., Some Queries on Principles of Technique, *International Journal of Psychoanalysis*, 1936, Vol. XVII, pp. 471-93.

[23] Stephen Karin, *Psychoanalysis and Medicine: A Study of the Wish to Fall Ill*, Macmillan, 1933; Cambridge (University), 1933; Hendricks, Ives, *Facts and Theories of Psychoanalysis*, Knopf, 1934; Fenichel, Otto, *Outlines of Clinical Psychoanalysis*, Psychoanalytic Quarterly Press, 1934; Norton, 1934; Peck, Martin W., *The Meaning of Psychoanalysis*, Knopf, 1931; Blitzsten, Dorothy R., *Psychoanalysis Explained*, Coward-McCann, 1936; and Menninger, Karl A., *The Human Mind*, Knopf, rev. ed., 1937.

taught by Alexander as "total interpretation." The diagrams were suggested to me by a reading of the stimulating works in topological psychology by Lewin[24] and by Brown[25] (but I do not mean to imply their approval of my diagrams).

If we let the course of psychic development be represented by an arrow (A) and any accepted adult goal in the reality situation by (G), the course of a normal life from birth (B) might be represented thus:

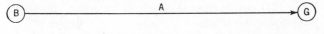

B = BIRTH   A = LIFE COURSE   G = NORMAL GOAL

If now some traumatic experiences (T) occur during the developmental period, the course of subsequent development is modified, even though the experiences themselves be forgotten (repressed, R). This results in a deflection from the goal of adult living to a displaced and sometimes less desirable goal (G'). If this substitute goal is in fact an undesirable one, as is implied—e.g., accompanied by neurotic dissatisfactions and self-destructive behavior—then the desirability of a realignment follows.

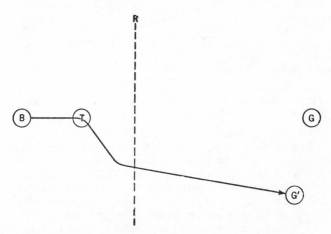

T = TRAUMATIC EXPERIENCES   R = REPRESSION
G' = FALSE GOAL

[24] Lewin, Kurt, A Dynamic Theory of the Personality, McGraw-Hill, 1935.
[25] Brown, J. F. Psychology and the Social Order, McGraw-Hill, 1936.

The above diagram, then, represents a man in need of treatment—one whose goal is disastrously displaced. Let us assume that he comes for psychoanalysis, i.e., a treatment in which the material back of the line of repression can be explored from a new artificial vantage point (P). (See next diagram.)

Now what becomes apparent to the psychoanalyst and to his patient is that the pattern of events which he (the patient) found so disastrous in his daily life, his attempts at living (G'), are duplicated exactly in his interrelations with the psychoanalyst (P), and—what is more to the point—

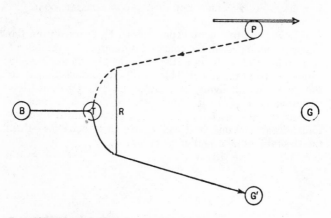

P = PSYCHOANALYSIS

(The dash line represents reminiscence.)
(The double line arrow represents the life and personality of the second person, the therapist.)

both of these repeat precisely the unsuccessful pattern incident to the traumatic period (T) back of the repression. In other words, the patient treats the analyst as he treats certain significant people in his outside life—and he finds that this unsuccessful pattern which he has kept repeating all his life began at (T), when a situation developed which exceeded his *then* powers of adaptation or solution.

The therapeutic effect of psychoanalysis seems to depend upon the alignment of these three topical areas; this is what we mean by insight. This seems to have the effect, for reasons partly known and discussed, and partly unknown, of reducing the *breadth* of the repression in such a way that the deflection of aim can be corrected, as shown in the next diagram.

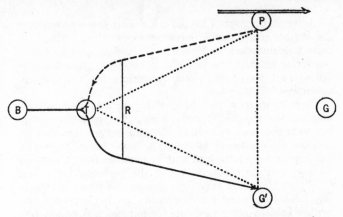

(The dotted lines represent the intellectual correlation of G′, P, and T, that is, the correlation of the patient's reality situation, the transference relationship, and the childhood situation.)

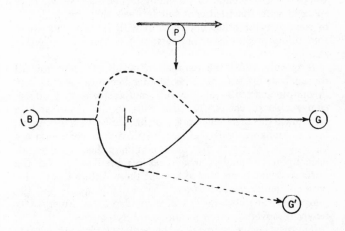

And then *both* the analytic situation (the dependence on the analyst and use of this relation as a "field" in the topological sense) and the false goal (G′) can be given up in favor of reality (G).

To cite a brief example very schematically (but based on an actual case), suppose a child born into a good home and with average prospects is subjected at the age of seven to the traumatic experience of discovering evidence of

397

infidelity on the part of his mother.[26] This shock completely distorts his conception of womankind. He does not realize, then, how distorted his view is; as he grows older he learns *intellectually* and *consciously* that not all women are perfidious and may even forget completely the early disappointment in his mother.

Then he marries, and while living an ostensibly normal married life, is actually very unhappy because of a growing suspicion and distrust of his wife on grounds that he believes to be rational. He wants a happy home, he thinks, but is prevented from having it by constant fears about her fidelity, in spite of the fact that she performs her duties loyally and is really very fond of him. He treats her shabbily, and recognizes this remissness on his part but can neither explain nor remedy it; his unhappiness impels him to make frantic efforts at self-amusement in activities which he does not enjoy. Finally, he undertakes treatment, and in the course of the psychoanalysis the same situation develops with reference to the analyst. The patient wants to succeed with the treatment but he feels that the analyst is in some way or other not truthful with him, is concealing something, prefers other patients, or is carrying on a "secret sex life."

It is only when the parallelism of his attitudes toward the analyst, his wife, and his mother becomes clear to him in minute particular and in full envisagement that he becomes able to correct the distortion in his vision and to relinquish the false conception of his wife which has made him so unhappy with her and so driven to compensatory maneuvers. At the same time he relinquishes his dependence upon the analyst which has persisted chiefly for the purpose of enabling him to act out these distorted attitudes without reality consequences. The old "false goal" and the temporary analytic goal are surrendered in favor of a newly discovered, more propitious objective.

The psychoanalysts have technical terms for some aspects of this. "Recollection" of the traumatic situations of childhood is correlated with "acting out" and "symptom" (or "reaction") "formation" in the attempts at adjustment in the outside world, and these are mirrored or repeated in

---

[26] It is not necessary that the mother actually be guilty of adultery; the prudish attitude of society toward sex makes every child hypersensitive to evidences of anything sexual, so that he often misinterprets legitimate and proper behavior. A child who has been punished for some minor sex play, for example, may regard himself as betrayed by a hypocritical mother if he soon afterwards surreptitiously observes her in intimacies with his father.

the "transference situation" with the psychoanalyst; the correlation is accompanied with "abreaction" to gain "insight."

Whatever the terms one uses, the principle is this: through the aid of a guide who encourages the patient to look at himself and who takes advantage of the patient's emotional dependence upon him to point out what the patient does not want to see, the victim of a blighted psychic development is able to see and remove the effects of the blight in its first instance and in its last—and finally to relinquish his grasp on the therapist because of his improved capacity for dealing with the environment. This improvement comes about, in terms familiar to the readers of this book, in the way of decreased aggressiveness, consequent and subsequent diminution in the power of the super-ego to demand dereistic and irrational ransoms and forfeits, and an increase in the range and intensity of erotic investments, including the further insulation of the outwardly directed aggressions.

To what extent it will be possible to apply psychoanalysis to the treatment of some of the organic forms of self-destruction it is certainly far too early to predict. We have much quicker, surer methods of treatment for some of them and for others we do not yet know if psychoanalysis can achieve anything better than our present unsatisfactory methods. Many, many patient hours of research and reflection must precede any conclusions in this field. As yet we must think of psychoanalytic therapy in organic disease as a research problem upon which we have only embarked. In its established range, however, psychoanalysis remains the queen of therapies.

Even more important, perhaps, than the direct therapeutic hope offered by the newer techniques in psychiatry is the change in popular attitude toward mental sickness and sickness in general which these discoveries and correlations tend to bring about. When it comes to be generally recognized that pains in the stomach, disturbances of the heart, blotches on the skin or "weakness" of the eyes are symptoms capable of psychiatric interpretation (and relief) no less than depression or drinking or quarreling with one's wife, some of the stigma which has been so long attached, in the public mind, to the functions of the psychiatrist will disappear. A very intelligent patient put it thus: "When I look back upon the many months I pondered as to how I might get here without anyone knowing, and the devious routes I considered and actually took to accomplish this, only to realize that some of the symptoms from which I suffer are respectable enough to be acknowledged anywhere and valid enough to explain my coming here, it all seems so utterly ridiculous. I looked furtively out of the corner of my eye at the people I met here, expecting them to betray their shame or their queerness, only to discover that I often could not distinguish the patients from the physicians, or from other visitors. I suppose it is such a commonplace experience to you that you cannot realize how startling that is to a naive layman like myself, even one who thinks he has read a little and laid aside some of the provincialism and prejudice which to some extent blind us all. I see how there is something emotional in it; if the patient feels only depressed or guilty or confused, then one looks upon his consulting the psychiatrist as a disgraceful recourse; but if some of these symptoms take form in one of the bodily organs, all the shame vanishes. There is no sense to it, but that's how it is. I have written a dozen letters to tell people where I am, the very people from whom in the past six months I have tried to conceal my need of this."

TWO / Social Techniques in the Service of Reconstruction

The discussion thus far has proceeded upon the assumption that self-reconstruction, or the prevention of self-destructiveness, is a responsibility devolving wholly upon the individual. However, no individual lives in a vacuum; self-destruction comes about as a result of (apparently) insuperable difficulties in adjusting one's self to the complexities of the environment. We all know that living, in spite of all the multiplying mechanical aids, grows daily more difficult, complicated, and restrictive.

It is therefore appropriate that we give some consideration to another point of view, namely, that some change in the organization or structure of society might accomplish something of benefit to the individuals who compose it, in the direction of lessening the necessity for self-destruction. This is the assumption of religion (in its social aspects); it is also the assumption of certain political programs which aim to decrease economic insecurity and other fears so that aggressions, external and internal, would be correspondingly decreased. Likewise, it is the assumption of various sociological programs, a few of which have recently become objects of political controversy. Psychiatry has been most interested in a special form of such social applications, centering mainly about the individual, and the sick individual in particular, but with broad social implications and extensions; this aspect of reconstruction in various forms constitutes the program of the mental hygiene movement.

As to the non-technical social changes represented by the ideals of religions, or socialism, and what in America we have come to call social security, it would seem at first blush that we should defer to the sociologists, economists, and political scientists in whose special sphere of interest such mass phenomena belong. With such obviously close relationship in the material studied, the cooperation of these scientists with medical scientists, particularly psychiatrists, would seem to be most logical. It is to the credit of neither group, however, that such cooperation does not exist to any considerable degree either in theory or in practice. The situation is somewhat comparable to the conflict between the public health program and the private practice of medicine; both have the same ideals but neither side seems to fully understand the other. The social scientists feel that psychiatrists (including psychoanalysts and psychologists) cannot see the woods for the trees. On the other hand, they are themselves accused by the mental scientists of being imbued with ethereal, pre-fabricated, Utopian principles which may have philosophical validity applied to great masses of people but which are too far divorced from the actual data of the individual unit of the mass to have practical utility.

Now and then one sees efforts at liaison. Harold Lasswell,[1] for example, has demonstrated how politics and politicians depend to a large extent upon the psychopathological impulses of certain individuals. The late Frankwood E. Williams was profoundly impressed with the reconstructive effect upon the individual of the politico-social experi-

[1] Lasswell, Harold D., *Psychopathology and Politics*, University of Chicago Press, 1930.

ment in Russia and has recorded these impressions.[2] Recently J. F. Brown has essayed an interpretation of the social order in terms of modern psychological theory.[3] And, of course, the profession of the psychiatric social worker is an effective and a working example of the possibility of a practical affiliation. It is one of the prides of American medicine that the suggestions of Richard Cabot (in regard to medical social work) and Ernest Southard (in regard to psychiatric social work) were developed into the efficient utilization of social techniques in personal rehabilitation.

The mental hygiene clinic, the child guidance clinic, and similar group forms of American psychiatric practice all imply this: that the individual can be helped to a certain extent in the direction of reconstruction by the personal ministrations of the psychiatrists, the physicians, the psychologists, and the social workers operating as a unit. Often, however, it is necessary to effect certain changes in the environment, changes which are not always so impossible to make as is tacitly assumed by some or so easy to make as is tacitly assumed by others. In a conflict between the individual and the environment, if there is too great inflexibility one or the other must yield, i.e., either the personality breaks down or the environment has injury wreaked upon it. It is the psychiatrist's task to study the individual, detect his points of great sensitiveness and rigidity and attempt with the aid of the psychiatric social worker to alter those features of the environment to which the individual finds it impossible to adjust himself. He may caution an over-zealous mother, restrain an over-severe father, enlist the help of a careless or thoughtless teacher, enlighten a prejudiced or perfunctory judge. The environment is made up in large part of individuals, some of whom possess a greater flexibility than the patient; by proper effort they may be influenced so as to effect a decrease of friction and thus decrease the defensiveness and aggressiveness of the patient to the greater happiness and comfort of everyone. In other words, the vicious circle can some-

[2] Williams, Frankwood E., "Can Russia Change Human Nature?" *Survey Graphic*, March, 1933, pp. 137-42; "The Challenge of Red Medicine," *Survey*, March, 1934, pp. 78-80; and *Russia, Youth and the Present Day World*, Farrar and Rinehart, 1934.

[3] Brown, J. F., *Psychology and the Social Order*, McGraw-Hill, 1936. See also Reuben Osborn's *Freud and Marx*, Equinox Cooperative Press, 1937, and the symposium in the *American Journal of Sociology* for May, 1937.

times be broken up where the direct approach to the patient himself would never have achieved such a result.

Such things the psychiatrist can sometimes accomplish without the aid of the social worker but experience has shown that many physicians who are skillful in their work with a patient who comes to them for treatment are very clumsy in their technique with those who are conscious of no need for help and who must be appealed to as adjuvants in the help of one who is afflicted. I would not imply that this is the only function of the psychiatric social worker but I do wish to give her credit for skill in the accomplishment of a task, the particular difficulties of which are often entirely ignored by the physician. The prejudice of some medical men against psychiatric social workers derives, in part, from lack of understanding of their work and sometimes from occasional instances of presumptuousness on the part of certain individual social workers. None of us is perfect, however, and such overassuming technicians are to be found in every field and do not represent the ideal.

The mental hygiene clinic has developed largely upon this idea and has depended for its success in great measure upon these skillful and highly trained women, who, because of their knowledge of "the good points" of both the psychiatrists and sociologists, have been able to apply psychiatric principles socially. The cooperation of experts in medical, psychological, and social fields of science is thus practically accomplished. And, since "by their fruits ye shall know them," it is unnecessary to expand upon the accomplishments of such cooperative groups. None the less, it may still be that we psychiatrists neglect at times to give sufficient consideration to the social and economic factors as such.

It has been pointed out, for example, that however interesting and satisfactory the results of psychiatric consultations and mental hygiene clinic activities may have been to a few individuals, these efforts remain so limited in scope, so handicapped by the muddled and disparate social and economic conditions that the net result is inconsiderable. "What good is it," asks the sociologist, "for you to help a handful of individuals at an enormous expense to the community when infinitely larger groups continue to suffer irremediably as a result of conditions which no mental hygiene clinic, no psychiatric consultation, no psychiatric insight will ever change? With all you have said about the desirability of socially valuable substitutes for aggression and atonement, with which we fully concur, the fact remains that our present socio-economic structure does not permit John Doe or Jane Roe to make such substitutions. It does permit a physician or a social worker to effect such a solution for a particular individual; Mr. Rockefeller, Mr. Mellon, and Mr. Morgan, and others less affluent than they may be able to accomplish it. But the ordinary man is not. You psychiatrists admit that such help as you can offer is expensive, too expensive. Yet a collective society in which the majority of people would be permitted and enabled to have such advantages is as yet regarded by large numbers of people as a threat against their economic or political existence. 'Red scares' are still endemic, and epidemic. This would appear to bear out your theme that a self-destructive impulse dominates all people, even to the preventing of their acceptance of that which would enable them to live more fully and normally. It should not, however, blind the psychiatrists to the fact that under our present system there can be no such thing as mental hygiene but only some kind of therapeutic help for a few of the more fortunate." [4]

I do not dispute the truth of all this. Perhaps I have seemed to neglect these considerations in the development of the ideas set forth in this book. But it is because my scientific training has conditioned me to study the individual, to attempt an understanding of the world macrocosmos from an analysis of the human microcosmos.

It is no excuse to say, in reply to the charges of the social scientists, that they, for their own part, have too much ignored the psychology of the individual. But I think the odds are a little in our favor, not only because of the practical exceptions cited above, and because some psychiatrists have announced definite convictions and aspirations in the direction of effecting radical social changes, but because some of us have made definite proposals as to how psychiatric principles might be applied to the effecting of changes in social situations in a direction more favorable for the comfortable and productive life of the individual.

[4] The late Dr. Frankwood E. Williams, formerly director of the National Committee for Mental Hygiene, in his article "Is There a Mental Hygiene?" (*Psychoanalytic Quarterly*, 1932, Vol. I, p. 113) supported this conclusion, but upon an empirical basis. Granting the therapeutic and social value of mental hygiene clinics and the like, he pointed out that this is not preventive work; in the main not "hygiene" but medicine.

Edward Glover,[5] for example, Director of Scientific Research at the London Institute for Psychoanalysis, has outlined in a thoughtful way a program of research on the problem of war. If poverty and unemployment seem less remote than war (and this is questionable), I am sure it would require little more than an invitation for psychologically (psychiatrically) trained medical men to cooperate with the national or local government or with universities or foundations in the direction of a more adequate understanding of what conscious and unconscious psychological factors enter into such an evil, for example, as unemployment. It is a somewhat sardonic commentary upon the blindness of somebody that the general public is at the present time more awake to the existence of such psychological factors than are those who so earnestly propose and execute various schemes for public relief. Even the medical profession itself may not have noticed what one with the slightest taint of psychological conviction must have noticed, namely, that no medical man, no psychiatrist, no psychoanalyst, no psychologist has ever been summoned to the councils of those who attempt to solve the national sociological problems of our country.[6] (This is not the case in Mexico, and perhaps some other countries.)

A convincing substantiation of the relative isolation of psychiatry is to be seen in the prevalent methods of dealing with crime. Not only does the general public still believe that crime is chiefly a social problem, but such an opinion likewise possesses most criminologists, sociologists, lawyers, judges, and legislatures. In spite of some increasing popular discussion of the matter, it is still radical if not actually heretical to consider that the study of criminals is more important than the study of crime. All programs for the elimination or decrease of crime are based upon the conception that society is itself also an individual and that the crime is a form of self-directed injury which in the terms of this book would be called focal self-destruction. By some it is treated in the philosophical way as a necessary evil which can be held to a minimum by certain gen-

[5] Glover, Edward, *War, Sadism and Pacifism*, London, Allen and Unwin, 1933.

[6] Here and there, in the administering to the unemployed and other public dependents, psychiatric inspiration if not advice has guided the hands of the leaders in such admirable exemplifications of reconstructive technique as the C.C.C. camps, the programs of reforestation and conservation, and (in the case of the Indians) self-government.

eral principles of rigidity, severity, intimidation, and by promises. The vast majority of people believes in the traditional myth that punishment is the chief deterrent of further crime, in spite of all of the evidence to the contrary, not the least obvious of which is the fact that the bulk of the prison population of the United States is recidivant. To be sure, some gestures have been made in recent years in the direction of the psychiatric, that is to say, the *medical* point of view. The American Bar Association and the American Medical Association have concurred with the American Psychiatric Association, and joint resolutions have been adopted by all of these bodies to the effect that a medical man with special training in the psychology of the individual should be attached to every court, presumably to have an advisory function in the disposition of every criminal on the basis of an examination of his motives, his capacities, and his individual circumstances. These brave resolutions have now been in effect some years without, however, anyone taking serious notice of them. There are, indeed, a few such psychiatrically equipped courts and, of course, a few outstandingly intelligent judges who have proclaimed the advantages and successes of such a revised attitude toward the criminal but these individuals are heard by few and the effect of their example is minimal, opposed as they are by the rigidity of the law, on the one hand, the stupidity of legislators, on the other, and in the background the lethargy, indifference, and suspicion of the public.

Finally, to return to the main point, it should be pointed out that the sociologists themselves cannot give more than lip service to any such plan for the reason that they are committed to principles of mass reorganization and cannot become interested in the psychological study of the individual. And because they ignore this more penetrating psychological examination of the individual they fail to understand certain aspects of mass action.

I do not know whether or not it is true that society as a whole re-enacts the ontogeny of the units of its composition; in other words, whether or not society can be thought of as an individual with any degree of logical validity. If it be true, then perhaps the social scientists will be able to discover for themselves from the study of society as a whole all that we psychiatrists discover from a study of the individual, so that after the passage of many years, we may arrive at the same conclusions and the same objectives. In the meantime, while we medical men must not recant our confession that we have too much ignored sociological factors, it continues to be the task for which we are best equipped to examine in as careful and complete a way as possible the details of the instinctual expressions and repressions of the individual. This is what I have undertaken in the expositions of this book.

And for all its social and economic phases, the phenomenon of war impresses one as the most dramatic exemplification of my main thesis.

It surely is no longer doubted by any thinking person that there is no such thing as victory in war, that the conqueror like the conquered suffers irreparable loss. In this sense war, contrary to appearances, is virtually self-destruction. This suicidal bent of nations is coldly exploited by elements within each country whose international organization constitutes a grimly anomalous cancer thriving under the official patronage of the people whom it exists to destroy. It has been pointed out that in the World War Germans were butchered with hand grenades fired by German-made fuses, that British battleships were sunk with British mines which had been sold to the Turks. In the battle of Jutland the German sailors hurled their missiles against defensive armor-plate which had been manufactured in their own country, by the same company that manufactured the guns which they were firing. Throughout the war, men of all countries were slaughtered by weapons invented, developed, and distributed to the foe by their own countrymen.[7]

No better example could be found of partial suicide on a grand scale than that of Germany who, excited to unendurable but helpless rage, by the cruelty of the Versailles Treaty, has turned a part of its destructive hostility into focal self-destruction through the elimination and persecution of several of its most interesting and intelligent elements. It is as if the German nation were acting the part of one of those individuals described in an earlier chapter of this book who changed the biblical adage from "If thy right hand offend thee, cut it off" to the following program: "If thy neighbor offend thee, cut off thine own right hand." But it would be fallacious indeed to assume that

[7] See Engelbrecht, H. C., and Finighen, F. C., *Merchants of Death, A Study of the International Traffic in Arms*, Dodd, Mead 1934; Seldes, George, *Iron, Blood and Profits, An Exposure of the World-Wide Munitions Racket*, Harper, 1934; and "Arms and the Men," *Fortune*, March, 1934.

Germany, because she is the most conspicuous in doing so, is the only nation whose politicians are directing some form of focal self-destruction, or arranging some program for more complete disaster.

Indeed, the shadow of universal war looms before us as I write, threatening to substitute for all petty individualistic and nationalistic self-destruction another convulsive effort at world suicide more violent even than that represented by the war of 1914 to 1918. The spectacle of such almost joyous preparation for mass suicide as is even now in progress cannot but fill the reflective observer with awe, and cost the stoutest heart some qualms. The brave pronunciamento of the psychiatrists of The Netherlands[8] pointing out the antithesis of medical science to such destructiveness is so sensible and so obvious that it would seem to answer all arguments, yet we realize how utterly futile and vague such feeble protests are against the unreasoning mass of hatred so easily aroused and released in mob action. For the solution of such world difficulties it would indeed seem an absurd presumption for the scientist to make suggestions, were it not for the conviction that in the deeper study of the psychology of the individual, the analysis of the origins and manipulations of the destructive tendencies, one may expect to find the key to the salvation of mankind.

We are aware, even at this crisis, of weak but insistent opposition to war on the part of single voices and intelligent minorities. To such intelligent minorities should belong all physicians, since their daily lives consist in a participation in innumerable miniature wars between life and death, and their constant striving is to increase their power in the opposing of self-destruction. Unfortunately, however, not all physicians fully perceive this struggle, either in the patient or in the world at large.

Every physician and every layman should read the following declaration of The Netherlands psychiatrists:

"We psychiatrists, whose duty it is to investigate the normal and diseased mind, and to serve mankind with our knowledge, feel impelled to address a serious word to you in our quality of physicians. It seems to us that there is in the world a mentality which entails grave dangers to mankind, leading as it may, to an evident war-psychosis. War means that all destructive forces are set loose by man-

---

[8] Issued in 1935 under the auspices of The Netherlands Medical Society, which formed a Committee on War Prophylaxis, signed by 339 psychiatrists of 30 countries and later by many others.

kind against itself. War means the annihilation of mankind by technical science. As in all things human, psychological factors play a very important part in the complicated problem of war. If war is to be prevented the nations and their leaders must understand their own attitude toward war By self-knowledge a world calamity may be prevented.

"Therefore we draw your attention to the following:

"1. There is a seeming contradiction between the conscious individual aversion to war and the collective preparedness to wage war. This is explained by the fact that the behavior, the feelings, the thoughts of an independent individual are quite different from those of a man who forms part of a collective whole. Civilized twentieth century man still possesses strong, fierce and destructive instincts, which have not been sublimated, or only partly so, and which break loose as soon as the community to which he belongs feels itself threatened by danger. The unconscious desire to give rein to the primitive instinct not only without punishment but even with reward, furthers in a great measure the preparedness of war. It should be realized that the fighting-instinct, if well directed, gives energy for much that is good and beautiful. But the same instinct may create chaos if it breaks loose from all restraint, making use of the greatest discoveries of the human intellect.

"2. It is appalling to see how little the peoples are alive to reality. Popular ideas of war as they find expression in full dress uniforms, military display, etc., are no longer in keeping with the realities of war itself. The apathy, with regard to the actions and intrigues of the international traffic in arms, is surprising to anyone who realizes the dangers into which this traffic threatens to lead them. It should be realized that it is foolish to suffer certain groups of persons to derive personal profit from the death of millions of men. We come to you with the urgent advice to arouse the nations to the realization of fact and the sense of collective self-preservation, these powerful instincts being the strongest allies for the elimination of war. The heightening of the moral and religious sense in your people tends to the same end.

"3. From the utterances of well-known statesmen it has repeatedly been evident that many of them have conceptions of war that are identical with those of the average man. Arguments such as 'War is the supreme Court of Appeal' and 'War is the necessary outcome of Darwin's theory' are erroneous and dangerous, in view of the realities of modern warfare. They camouflage a primitive craving for power and are meant to stimulate the preparedness for war among the speaker's countrymen. The suggestive force of speeches made by leading statesmen is enormous and may be dangerous. The warlike spirit, so easily aroused by the cry that the country is in danger, is not to be bridled, as was evident in 1914. Peoples, as well as individuals, under the influence of suggestions like these, may become neurotic. They may be carried away by hallucinations and delusions, thus involving themselves in adventures perilous to their own and other nations' safety.

"We psychiatrists declare that our science is sufficiently advanced for us to distinguish between real, pretended, and unconscious motives, even in statesmen. The desire to disguise national militarism by continual talk about peace will not protect political leaders from the judgment of history. The secret promoters of militarism are responsible for the boundless misery which a new war is sure to bring . . ." [9]

It is entirely compatible with his genius that it should have occurred to Albert Einstein to address a formal inquiry to Sigmund Freud [10] regarding the psychological principles involved in war.

"How is it possible," he asked, "for the ruling minority to force the masses to observe a purpose which rewards them only with suffering and loss? Why do the masses permit themselves to be inflamed to the point of madness and self-sacrifice by these means? Do hatred and destruction satisfy an innate human drive which ordinarily remains latent but which can easily be aroused and intensified to the point of mass psychosis? And is it possible to modify human psychic development in such a way as to produce an increasing resistance to these psychoses of hatred and destruction?"

And to this Freud replied with a recapitulation of the conclusions drawn from long years of clinical observation, principles which have been elaborated in the present book. It is an error in judgment, he pointed out, to overlook the fact that right was originally might and cannot even now survive without the support of power. As to whether there

---

[9] This document has now been signed by psychiatrists from thirty nations. It was sent to government officials, newspapers, and private individuals all over the world. Official replies were received from nineteen nations and it is rather significant that among the few who did not reply were Germany, Italy and Japan.

[10] Einstein, A., and Freud, S., *Why War?* Paris, Internat. Inst. of Intellectual Cooperation, 1933.

is an instinct to hate and destroy, Freud replied, of course, in the affirmative. "The willingness to fight may depend upon a variety of motives which may be lofty, frankly outspoken, or unmentionable. The pleasure in aggression and destruction is certainly one of them. The satisfaction derived from these destructive tendencies is, of course, modified by others which are erotic and ideational in nature. At times we are under the impression that idealistic motives have simply been a screen for the atrocities of nature; at other times, that they were more prominent and that the destructive drives came to their assistance for unconscious reasons, as in the cruelties perpetrated during the Holy Inquisition."

"The death-instinct," he goes on to say, "would destroy the individual were it not turned upon objects other than the self so that the individual saves his own life by destroying something external to himself. Let this be the biological excuse for all the ugly and dangerous strivings against which we struggle. They are more natural than the resistance we offer them.

"For our present purposes then it is useless to try to eliminate the aggressive tendencies in man."

This has been—but should not be—interpreted pessimistically. Such a view conforms neither with Freud's theory nor with his practice. He has not *lived* as if he believed it "useless to try to eliminate the aggressive tendencies in man," or at least to redirect them. And the same perspicacity that recognized the death-instinct, examined and demonstrated some of the devices for combating it. It is on the basis of Freud's work that others (e.g., Glover, *op. cit.*) have proposed applications of our psychological knowledge to the elimination of war and the scientific study of crime.

But most significant of all, the therapeutic efficacy of psychoanalysis itself disputes such pessimistic interpretations.[11] For if it be possible to change one individual, no

[11] This point is strongly urged by representatives of the Field Theory School of Psychology, a modernistic concept which is in agreement with psychoanalytic views with the exception of the allocation of the instinctual urges. If these are within the individual, innate and geno-typical, then such pessimism as Freud records in his later writings is justified, say the Field theorists. If, on the other hand, as the Field theorists believe, the urges are not innate, not a part of human nature but rather a part of all nature, socially, biologically, and psychologically determined, **something** which each individual makes use of so to speak, rather than merely springing from some *fons et origo* within the self, then a very much more optimistic conclusion might be drawn as to future possibilities because external manipulations are much more readily accomplished. The right economic changes, for example, might put psychiatry in a position where it could

matter how laboriously—if one person can be helped, by any of the methods which I have described, to be less destructive—there is hope for the human race. The special encouragement of the psychoanalytic method is that the individual's own intelligence can be utilized to direct his better adaptation, a diminution in his self-destructiveness. Granted that it may be a slow process, such a transformation of self-destructive energy into constructive channels can gradually spread over the entire human world. "A little leaven leaveneth the whole lump."

The sum of the whole matter is that our intelligence and our affections are our most dependable bulwarks against self-destruction. To recognize the existence of such a force within us is the first step toward its control. To "know thyself" must mean to know the malignancy of one's own instincts and to know as well one's own power to deflect it. Blindness or indifference to the existence of self-destructiveness are the devices it constructs for its continuance.

To the support of our intelligence we must bring the conscious and purposive direction and encouragement of love. In the function of friendship, that conventional term for the controlled investment of love, we must place the highest hopes. Both for those who would save themselves and for those who would save others, it remains our most powerful tool. The private citizen no less than the psychiatrist or the social worker may, by dint of the simple expedients of an encouraging smile, a sympathetic inquiry, a patient audience to an outpouring of troubles, lift burdens of depression, diminish the woes of voluntary or involuntary martyrdom and frustrate the urge toward self-destruction of many a sufferer.

And so our final conclusion must be that a consideration of war and crime, no less than of sickness and suicide, leads us back to a reiteration and reaffirmation of the hypothesis of Freud that man is a creature dominated by an instinct in the direction of death, but blessed with an opposing instinct which battles heroically with varying success

function in a preventive as well as in a therapeutic fashion. In other words, a genuine mental hygiene might theoretically be developed. It is said that $200,000 a year would permanently eradicate tuberculosis from the city of Detroit, for example; this is about 1/175 the cost of a new battleship, yet the socio-economic organization is such that the battleship is built and the tuberculosis continues. (DeKruif, Paul, *Why Keep Them Alive?* New York, 1936, p. 121 ff.) This cannot be ascribed in the opinion of the Field theorists to destructive impulses in the personnel of the war department or in the administration of Detroit but rather to the consequence of the social system. See J. F. Brown's *Psychology and the Social Order.*

against its ultimate conqueror. This magnificent tragedy ot life sets our highest ideal—spiritual nobility in the face of certain defeat. But there is a lesser victory in the mere prolonging of the game with a zest not born of illusion, and in this game within a game some win, some lose; the relentlessness of self-destruction never ceases. And it is here that Science has replaced magic as the serpent held high in the wilderness for the saving of what there is of life for us. Toward the temporary staying of the malignancy of the self-destructive impulse, toward the averting of a premature capitulation to Death, we may sometimes, by prodigious labors, lend an effective hand.

INDEX

Byron, Lord, 66n.

Cabot, Richard, 402
Calvin, John, 37
Camp, C. D., 325
Campbell, Charles M., 123n.
Cannibalism, unconscious, 37, 108
Cannibalistic fantasies, infantile, 108
Cannon, Walter B., 364n.
Cantor, Eddie, 268
Cardigan, Countess of, 53
Carns, M. L., 264n.
Castrati. See Skoptsi
Castration: as punitive device, 238n.; as "treatment" method, 239n.; fear of, case, 225; fear, solved by circumcision, 228; in American lynchings, 238n.; in mythology, 218-19; of enemy in war, 238n.; prohibited by Romans, 226; see also Self-castration
Cather, Willa, 100
Catullus, 219n.
Cavan, Ruth S., 15, 67n.
Chabanel, Noel, 101-2
Chandler, 349n.
Chidester, Leona, 19n., 375n.
Child guidance clinic, in reconstruction, 402-4
Chinese, 44, 221
Chlists, 103
Chowne, 270n.
Christ. See Jesus
Christians, 116-18; see also Jesus; Asceticism; Martyrdom; Religion
Christian Science, 376
Chuvashes, suicide among, 44
Cicero, 104
Circumcelliones, 79n.
Circumcision, 223-26, 272; as permit for beginning sexual life, 228; meaning of, 224-25; of females, 226; purposes of, 224n., 227-28; theories of origin of, 224-26

Civilization, ascetic trend in, 126
Cobb, Irvin, 268
Cocteau, Jean, 18
Cold, psychological factors in, case, 345-46
Conn, Jacob F., 240n.
Conquistadors, 110
Conscience: bargaining with, 206-7; characteristics of, 46-47; defined, 46; destruction of, cases of, 193-97; laws governing activity of, 47-49; of manic and psychoanalyzed patient compared, 196-98; power of, 47
Corneille, Pierre, 122-23
Coughing, psychological factors in, 337-40; case, 338-40
Cowley, Thomas, 277n.
Cowper, William, many attempts at suicide of, 65-6
Crawford, Nelson Antrim, ix
Crawley, 224n.
Crime, elimination of: as means to reconstruction, 405; lack of progress in, 405-6
Criminal methods in handling criminals, 176
Criminality, 175-81; as form of self-destruction, 162-63, 176-81; case, 179-81; scientific study of, 175
Crookshank, F. G., 305
Cybele, 219; cult of, 219n.
Cyprian, 119
Czekanowski, Jan, 238n.

Damiens, 239n.
Darwin, Charles, 409
David, King, 238n.
David, H., 213n.
Davidson, Henry A., 15n.
Davis, J. E., 375n.
Day, Clarence, 111, x
Death instinct, 5-7, 24, 412; in automobile racers, 68n.; in building scalers, 68n.; in mountain climbers, 68n.;

theory of, 5-6, 358-59; *see also* Wish to die

Death, postponement of, 6-7

Defense reactions, automatic, 297-98

De Groot, 220

De Kruif, Paul, 412n.

Delirium tremens, 140

Delusions, Messianic, 91

De Massary, 235n.

Dembo, T., 24n.

Depersonalization, 187; cases of, 187-90

Depression, pleasure principle in, 186n.

Dereism, 186

Dermatitis factitia: as form of malingering, 256-57; case, 257

Destructive instinct, 24; erotized, 26-27; neutralized, 25-26

de Traz, Robert, 346-47

Deutsch, Felix, 349n.

Deutsch, Helene, 291n.

Diarrhea, and fear, 355

Dickens, Charles, 60, 79, 317

Dittemore, J. V., 376n.

Don Juan, 300-1

Domitian, 225

"Dora," 250-51, 268n., 279

Dos Passos, John, 145

Dostoievski, Feodor, 49

Douglas, Lord, 182-83

Doyle, Father William, 123-24

Draper, 349n.

Dreyfus, 349n.

Dublin, L. I., 15

Dunbar, H. F., 312n., 328n., 349n.

Eating, danger connected with, 108

Eckert, 235n.

Eddy, Mary Baker, 376

Eder, M. D., 108n.

Ehrlich, Leonard, 112n.

Einstein, Albert, 410

Ejaculatio praecox, 300; case

of, 300-1; psychological factors in, 301

Emerson, C. P., 325

Encyclopaedia Britannica, 15

Engelbrecht, H. C., 407n.

Engle, Bernice, 219n.

Environmental factors, utilized in organic self-destruction, 356

Envy, unconscious, in impotence and frigidity, 301-2

Erotic element: in asceticism, 118-25; in impotence and frigidity, 302-4; in martyrdom, 118-25; in organic disease, 343-405; in self-mutilation, 249; in suicide, 59-63; in surgical operations, 267-68

Erotic element, enhancement of, 380-93; by art, 385-86; by combatting narcissism, 381-83; by crafts, 385; by cultivation of friendships, 383-85; by cultivation of satisfactory love, 383-84; by encouraging frank expressions of emotional life in children, 381; by hobbies, 385; by music, 385, 386; by other sublimations, 387

Eshmun, 218

Essenes, 99n.

Examination, fear of, 65

Exhibitionism: as motive in surgical operation, 268, 275; disguised by asceticism and martyrdom, 119-20; in suicide, 60-61

Evans, Elida, 347

Eye disorders, psychological factors in, 321-25; cases, 322-25

Fairbank, Ruth, 16n.

Farrow, E. P., 205n.

Fasting, 107-8

Fear: devices to circumvent, 299-300; of castration, 225, 228; of examination, 63; of

423